Harry Goulbourne's theme is how post-imperial Britain has come to define the national community in terms of ethnic affinity, instead of a traditional multi-ethnic/multi-racial understanding of the nation. He argues that the continuing 'reception-experience' of non-white groups in post-war Britain not only arose out of an ethnic perception of the British nation by the indigenous population, as expressed through state action, but has also, in turn, encouraged an equally ethnic awakening or mobilization among non-white minorities. The result is a failure to construct a common national ground or sense of community by all those claiming a formal British identity.

Goulbourne draws upon a diverse literature, including race relations, politics, and history. His two case studies of the Khalistan question in the Punjab and democracy in Guyana are examples of how exilic politics may affect Britain's ethnic minorities, partly or as a result of the experience of exclusion from British society.

Comparative ethnic and race relations series

Ethnicity and nationalism in post-imperial Britain

Comparative ethnic and race relations

Published for the Centre of Research in Ethnic Relations at the University of Warwick

Senior Editor
Professor John Rex *Associate Director & Research Professor of Ethnic Relations, University of Warwick*

Editors
Professor Robin Cohen *Professor of Sociology, University of Warwick*
Mr Malcolm Cross *Principal Research Fellow, University of Warwick*
Dr Muhammad Anwar *Executive Director, Centre for Research in Ethnic Relations*

This series has been formed to publish works of original theory, empirical research, and texts on the problems of racially mixed societies. It is based on the work of the Centre for Research in Ethnic Relations, a Designated Research Centre of the Economic and Social Research Council, and the main centre for the study of race relations in Britain.

The series will continue to draw on the work produced at the Centre, though the editors encourage manuscripts from scholars whose work has been associated with the Centre, or whose research lies in similar fields. Future titles will concentrate on anti-racist issues in education, on the organization and political demands of ethnic minorities, on migration patterns, changes in immigration policies in relation to migrants and refugees, and on questions relating to employment, welfare and urban restructuring as these affect minority communities.

The books will appeal to an international readership of scholars, students and professionals concerned with racial issues, across a wide range of disciplines (such as sociology, anthropology, social policy, politics, economics, education and law), as well as among professional social administrators, teachers, government officials, health service workers and others.

Other books in this series
Michael Banton: *Racial and ethnic competition*
Thomas Hammar (ed.): *European immigration policy*
Frank Reeves: *British racial discourse*
Robin Ward and Richard Jenkins (eds): *Ethnic communities in business*
Richard Jenkins: *Racism and recruitment: managers, organisations and equal opportunity in the labour market*
Roger Hewitt: *White talk black talk: inter-racial friendships and communication amongst adolescents*
Paul B. Rich: *Race and Empire in British politics*
Richard Jenkins and John Solomos (eds): *Racism and equal opportunity policies in the 1980s*
John Rex and David Mason (eds): *Theory of race and ethnic relations*
John Solomos: *Black youth, racism and the state: the politics of ideology and policy*
Colin Clarke, Ceri Peach and Steven Vertovec (eds): *South Asians overseas: migration and ethnicity*

Ethnicity and nationalism in post-imperial Britain

HARRY GOULBOURNE

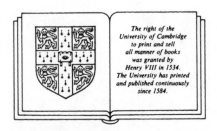

The right of the
University of Cambridge
to print and sell
all manner of books
was granted by
Henry VIII in 1534.
The University has printed
and published continuously
since 1584.

CAMBRIDGE UNIVERSITY PRESS
Cambridge
New York   Port Chester   Melbourne   Sydney

Published by the Press Syndicate of the University of Cambridge
The Pitt Building, Trumpington Street, Cambridge CB2 1RP
40 West 20th Street, New York, NY 10011, USA
10 Stamford Road, Oakleigh, Melbourne 3166, Australia

First published 1991

Printed in Great Britain at the University Press, Cambridge

British Library cataloguing in publication data

Goulbourne, Harry
Ethnicity and nationalism in post-imperial Britain. –
(Comparative ethnic and race relations series)
1. Great Britain. Race
I. Title II. Series
305.800941

Library of Congress cataloguing in publication data

Goulbourne, Harry.
Ethnicity and nationalism in post-imperial Britain / Harry
Goulbourne.
    p.   cm. – (Comparative ethnic and race relations)
Includes bibliographical references and index.
ISBN 0-521-40084-8
1. Great Britain – Ethnic relations – History – 20th century.
2. Nationalism – Great Britain – History – 20th century. 3. Great
Britain – Politics and government – 1979– I. Title. II. Series:
Comparative ethnic and race relations series.
DA125.A1G6 1991
305.8'00941 – dc20   90–20422 CIP

ISBN 0 521 40084 8 hardback

WD

For Hugh and Neil in hope

The Earthians

I had a dream last night
it was a beautiful dream
unlike the American dream
mine was a simple earthian one.

I travelled from land to land
without a passport,
I worked in fields and factories
without a work-permit
I was never called a nigger
a wop, wog, spick or a greasy Greek
I was never put in jail
kicked out or deported
for being an African or an Asian
an Arab or Jew
a Greek or a Turk
a Chinese or Vietnamese
Russian or American.

There were no frontiers in my dream
no barriers or nationalism.

Instead only one land
one country, one nation
one continent, one planet,
the planet earth,
no chosen race,
the Earthians instead.

I woke up and heard the sad news
about Ireland and Vietnam
Cyprus and Ethiopia
Africa and the Middle East
Brixton and Tottenham . . .

Alas, my dream seemed impossible
so naive and childish.

Childish?

George Eugeniou

Contents

Figures

Acknowledgements

Many people and groups have helped me to understand better the questions discussed in this book. My debt to them is all the greater, because although I did not share their views, they were always willing to give of their time and knowledge and welcomed me in their midst. I can only mention some, however, of the many individuals whom I interviewed, or who pointed me in particular directions and to whom I am, therefore, indebted. These include Mohammad Bashir, Steve Batchelor, Ann Brathwaite, Emil Chang, Dr Jagjit Chohan, Luke Daniels, B. S. Dhesi, Mohindar Palsingh Dhillon, George Eugeniou, Dr Homer S. Habibis, Richard Hart, Sonia Joseph, Harbhajan Singh Khalsa, Babusingh Mangat, S. Mypurrey, Davinder Singh Parmar, Michael Pasea, Swaran Singh Sahota, Pyare Shivpuri, Mohan Singh, John Swinney, Billy Trant, Nazir Ul-Haq and Dorann Vanhees-Wyk. I am grateful to the secretaries and members of the gurdwaras in the Midlands who patiently explained to me the tenets of the Sikh faith and their understandings of its history.

I am grateful to Robin Cohen for his characteristically gentle suggestion to me to focus on nationalism, ethnicity and some common questions in the field of 'race relations' and for his constant intellectual and (as Director of CRER during the period of my research) material encouragement to complete the book.

Thanks are due to my former CRER colleague Dr Sasha Josephides, Dr Narinder Basi and my research student Darshan Singh Tatla as well as to all who contribute in making the Centre for Research in Ethnic Relations the congenial place in which we are privileged to work. Particular thanks to our Librarian Heather Lynn, and to Rose Goodwin, senior secretary. Heather ensured that I had more newspapers, journals and books to read than I could cope with, and Rose reformatted my discs and thereby limited my time before the machine to which, increasingly, every academic's knee shall bow, even if their tongues do not confess. Such are the powers of modern means of communication that although we have never met, my thanks must also go to Dr Jessica Kuper of Cambridge University Press for her patience and encouragement. George Eugeniou was very kind to allow me to use his poem, which is published for the first time here, 'The Earthians', to make a point.

More than thanks are due to my family: to my wife Selina, not only for her general intellectual companionship, but also specifically for reading, correcting and constructively criticizing my ideas and expressions of them; and to Hugh and Neil, our sons – who, along with others of their generation may sadly have to face the consequences of what I call the *communal option* – who helped more than they presently know to shape my thinking on the questions raised in this discussion.

Expectedly, after all the assistance and encouragement generously given, I remain entirely responsible for all the shortcomings as well as the views expressed.

1

Introduction

The general problem with which this book is concerned is the classical question of the nature of the most sovereign and legitimate socio-political community modern men and women wish to live in, and to contribute to, for their own as well as their children's security and well-being. The classical answer has been that it is both desirable and worthy of emulation so to rearrange society and political authority that they can be easily recognized by all to be the community we call the *nation-state*.

The question itself has been central to political discourse since it was first asked by intellectuals during the Enlightenment and the answer guided men of rude action towards the end of the eighteenth century. The reaction in the following century to the 'age of reason', which is generally described as the Romantic Movement, rephrased but did not abandon the question. The discourse became less speculative and rationalistic, and became more a commitment to feelings, traditions and the construction of widely shared myths. The changes wrought were consistent with the nationalists' discovery of the potentially revolutionary force of the common people, which could be harnessed in the nationalists' gigantic project of reorganizing power and society. But, alongside the activities of practical men and women, who have ensured that nationalism has found expression in all areas of human endeavour, the political discourse concerning the desirable socio-political unit has continued down to our own time.

The analysis of nationalism and ethnicity offered here is located within this on-going concern over the nature of that community which would be sufficiently broad and all-embracing properly to be designated *national*. In particular, the legitimacy of membership of the national community in Britain forms the central concern of this study. The main contention is that the most powerful and influential of the attempts to redefine the post-imperial British national community is such that membership excludes non-white minorities who have settled on these shores since the Second World War. It is argued that whilst the membership of people with backgrounds in Africa, Asia and the Caribbean are accorded formal recognition, this recognition is constructed in such a manner that their legitimate presence and participation in Britain are nearly always questioned.

The study avoids the rather simplistic notion that this exclusion is only a matter of racism on the part of the majority white population. The view is advanced that this exclusion is the result of a combination of a number of powerful factors. Undoubtedly, racism is the most widespread and powerful of these factors. There are, however, others which are perhaps more deep-seated, and more easily defended, but which have been generally seen to be nothing more than manifestations of racism. These include, for example, ethnic awareness, and cultural and territorial identities, on the part of the majority population as well as on the part of minorities. It is not enough, however, simply to label questions of religious beliefs and practices, or conflict over cultural values or customs, as racism. This is to overload a concept to the point which it is no longer useful. The combination of these factors, which act to exclude legitimate membership of Britain's non-white population in the national community, not only complicates the situation but also demands a framework of analysis which goes beyond racism as an explanatory factor. Just as it was necessary to see class as an important – but only one – factor in understanding 'race relations', so it is now necessary to appreciate the combination of the multiple factors of class, racism, culture, ethnicity, religion, territoriality, and so on, as so many inputs in a continuous debate in the negotiation over how the post-imperial, national, British community is to be fashioned.

From early in the discussion which follows, a distinction is made between historical, or traditional, and ethnic nationalism. The latter characterizes the contemporary, post-imperial phase of the nationalist project to effect sociopolitical communities in which the 'people'/'community' (the nation) is in perfect congruence with authority (the state). The study then suggests that whilst Britain escaped much of the militant, and therefore disruptive, manifestations of historical nationalism, she is now one of the countries at the very forefront of those which are articulating the new, ethnic nationalism. This kind of nationalism is a phenomenon which most societies are presently experiencing. It is a mistake, therefore, to treat the British situation as unique, as indeed much of the 'race relations' literature unwittingly tends to assume it is. This admission in no way detracts from the necessity to combat racism. Rather, it calls for the need to recognize what it is that we must confront in any well-meaning, progressive effort to construct a just and non-racialist society in Britain. From this perspective of looking at the overall problem, it is further suggested that the terms of discussion proffered by the ascendent liberal/ radical fraternity and the Right establishment in Britain are far from being unproblematic and may lead us into a social and political cul-de-sac.

The question of the nature of the national community, and a number of the problems related to some of the practical answers, are treated here more in their political than in their sociological forms. This statement relates to how I have carried out the task of examining nationalism and ethnicity; it is not intended as an apology. After all, the posing of the question pre-dates Auguste Comte, Karl Marx and Emile Durkheim, some of the founding fathers of what Comte himself called a 'science of society' – the discipline of sociology. This essay is not, however, concerned exclusively with the unit we know as the nation-state and its attendant ideology, nationalism. The analysis also attempts to bring into focus a number of social questions from the developing multi-disciplinary area of what is generally called, for lack of a better term, 'race relations'. This focus would seem to suggest that the discussion might be more sociologically, or at least empirically, rooted because the field of 'race relations' has generally been dominated by sociologists in Britain, where a rich empirical literature has developed. It is my view, however, that although several aspects of 'race relations' matters await, perhaps too patiently, scholarly attention, there is an ample body of literature in the field to justify the general analysis offered here. It is offered as a contribution to how we may approach the increasingly complex problem of membership of the national community which assimilationist, integrationist and exclusivist perspectives have done little to elucidate.

The study examines the question of the national community only partly, therefore, from the perspective of discussions over 'race relations', because in spite of much talk about improved or worsened 'race relations' in Britain,[1] a thorn in the flesh of the nation remains. This 'thorn' is the question of the legitimate membership of the British nation by minorities who are physically not white.[2] A number of pressing questions, which arise from this problem, are discussed here. For example, how and why do minorities from the Indian sub-continent and the Commonwealth Caribbean continue to relate to the politics of their past homelands; how do these politics compare; what are the political backgrounds from which these minorities have come to Britain; in general terms, how do the *diasporic* politics in which some non-white minority groups participate, relate to broader questions of nationalism and a new national community in Britain.

Whilst the manner of posing these questions is new, the questions themselves are not. For example, Rex and Tomlinson raised some of them in a similar manner to this work (Rex and Tomlinson, 1979, chs. 1, 2), but these questions were tangential to their main purpose and were left undeveloped and unexplored. In general, however, British studies of 'race relations' tend to treat nationalism almost exclusively as an adjunct of extreme right-wing groups. Thus, the redefinition of the national British community has been left almost entirely to the political and intellectual right. Individuals and groups who stand on this side of the social and political spectrum have, therefore, been able to determine the content, contours and pace of the discussion, such as it is. Crucial questions relating to the membership of the national community are hardly ever set alongside the more immediate questions emanating from analyses of race relations.

The linking of questions of nationalism and race relations in Britain have, therefore, been assumed to be illegitimate for progressive individuals and groups to address.[3] One exception is Gilroy's work, which raises the question of nationhood with respect to groups from the Caribbean (Gilroy, 1987). His concerns differ, however, in important ways from mine. For example, his work focuses predominantly on culture. But, important as culture is in any discussion of nationalism, the latter cannot, as we shall see, be explained by reference to this single factor alone; culture is but one of several aspects of nationalism. Moreover, ever an elusive phenomenon, nationalism has always been wont to play shy in its British garb. In Britain nationalism assumes many guises and hardly ever adopts a loud and demonstrative pose. It is not enough, therefore, to look simply at any one minority group and its relationship to the majority population in order to understand nationalism.

Nor do most race relations studies give any serious consideration to the differential social and political backgrounds of non-white minorities. The differential *colonial* and *reception* experiences of these groups who have settled in Britain are usually underplayed in most analyses of their social and political behaviour. This study seeks to contribute to a correction of this, because it is becoming increasingly important to specify the varied contributions different groups bring to the project of constructing a new national community in a post-imperial Britain.

It would be foolhardy to attempt to tackle all the questions involved with the issues mentioned here. What is offered is a perspective on some of those I consider to be most important in trying to understand the general problem of membership of the British national community by all groups who claim this country as their home.

One starting point in an analysis of this kind is to raise problematically the question of nationhood. The end of empire forced the question of membership of the nation not only on the post-colonial states of Africa, Asia, the Caribbean and the Pacific islands once ruled by Britain, but also on Britain herself.[4] In the immediate post-colonial period most new states had to cope with the social and political problems of nationhood and the problems of social and economic development. A large body of literature that attempts to explain these problems exists in the area of development/underdevelopment studies. Less attention has been paid, however, to the reverse side of the same coin. Like post-colonial societies, Britain too has had to make serious adjustments, particularly to her demoted position in a competitive and more equal world order. One of the questions she has still not come to terms with, let alone satisfactorily resolved, is the question of the *legitimate*, as distinct from the merely formal and legal, membership of the *British nation*. Enoch Powell's view of the problem from the perspective of one white Briton was clearly expressed when he argued that a person of either West Indian or Asian background born in England cannot become an English person (Foot, 1969, p. 137).[5]

The strong emphasis being placed on ethnic *differences* amongst minorities would suggest that for them too it is not simply a question of being accepted as English, or even as British. It would appear that for some it is a question of being Asians and *perhaps* English/British, or West Indians and *perhaps* English/British, whilst for others it is enough to be Asians and West Indians living in England/Britain. But these largely negative responses by native and settler Britishers alike to the problems of a redefined, post-imperial British national identity, are grossly inadequate bases for the construction of a community large enough to embrace all groups, irrespective of their colour, domestic values and preferences.

This study of nationalism and ethnicity is, therefore, concerned with a number of closely related questions which arise from two broad sets of issues. In the first place, it looks at how the classical answer to the classical question of membership of the national community has proved to be highly unsatisfactory. This has been repeatedly demonstrated by the frequency with which subjugated nations or people have demanded national independence from imperial rulers as well as from so-called nation-states during the last two hundred years. At no time has this been more clearly the case than in our own, when the demand for new forms of socio-political arrangements make contradictory demands on the nation-state so that the result may be to undermine this kind of association. In the past, such demands were made in the name of one or other aggrieved 'nation'. Increasingly, however, much the same demands are being made in the name of a more clearly defined, more sharply delimited, ethnic group. Whether the demands such groups make in this regard on the nation-state are intended simply to create *more* nation-states as part of a broad democratic movement, or whether such demands are intended to *transcend* the nation-state construct, remains highly problematic. Perhaps only time will tell whether the nation-state is drifting, ultimately, towards dissociation and atrophy, or is being undermined as part of a more dynamic process towards larger associations, such as that intimated by European integration.

A second set of questions that this study addresses relates to the kinds of politics taking place in homelands *outside* Britain. But a word is necessary here about the utility of studying these kinds of politics. It is to be expected that Britain's non-white minorities are likely to continue for some time to have close relations with their former homelands. These relations are likely to be particularly strong during the lifetime of the first generation of recent settlers. And, contrary to the outburst of Norman Tebbit in April 1990 regarding the attachment of recent settlers to the lands of their birth, it is perfectly natural for men and women to develop a new love for the new land of settlement without abandoning the first love for their original homeland. Whilst these loyalties may create undue tensions for some groups, there is also the possibility that individuals and even groups may turn this necessary tension to good use through acts of political, social and artistic creativity. The main point is that the patriotic feelings expressed by 'seven eloquent citizens in a symposium on the nation's destiny as the loom of Europe overhangs us and doubts solidify about 1992' in a 'Fanfare On Being British' (*The Field*, May 1990, pp. 76–85), are not necessarily minimized by the capacity to hold such feelings for more than one country. Indeed, such a capacity has promise of a greater hope for a war-free, if not an entirely peaceful, world.

Two major factors, however, are most likely to determine the *nature* of, if not the prolonged interests in, the politics of 'back home'. The first of these is the attitude of the white majority towards non-whites. As long as a significant number of the majority white population continues to see the presence of people with a different hue of colour as temporary and illegitimate, then, naturally, minorities will need to maintain an interest in the political life of their original homelands, if only as an insurance against a possible rainy day. Given the Nazi experience of only half a century ago, this possibility can never be far from the consciousness of minorities in a rapidly changing Britain and Europe of the late twentieth century. Exclusion of minorities is likely to be a very important determinant in the maintenance of close attachments to distant homelands, however impractical this myth of return (Anwar, 1979) may be.

Of course, the ball is not entirely in the British court. The second determinant set of factors in the situation is the kinds of politics taking place in the homelands. These are likely to determine the intensity with which people in Britain may feel committed to supporting their former countrymen and women. Here a dynamic political situation exists. If, for example, political life 'back home' is highly unstable and the welfare of close relations and family – many of whom Britain refuses to allow to enter this country – is involved, then naturally groups of people resident here may be directly affected. This is particularly so with respect to people from the Indian sub-continent, where questions of national entities and boundaries are far from settled. There are, therefore, sound reasons to believe that it is in the best interests of 'good race relations' in Britain to examine aspects of these diasporic politics.

Chapters two, three and four of this book set out the problems of the national community, the nation-state and the relationships between white majority and non-white minorities. As indicated earlier, the analysis draws primarily upon the literature on nationalism. This is a vast and distinguished literature, which race relations studies often invoke but generally tend to under-emphasize or ignore. The attempt here, therefore, is to place the emphasis on aspects of this older and critical literature and to try to show its abiding relevance to current discussions of race relations matters in Britain.

The aspects of nationalism focused upon (such as territorial, ethnic, racial or linguistic affinities) are analysed from both a theoretical and an empirical perspective. Chapter five concentrates on the transition from *empire* to *nation* in the post-World War Two experience of Britain. The analysis here draws attention to the changes in immigration and nationality laws between 1948 and 1981, as well as the changes in the attitudes of the two major political parties over these issues.[6] This is a well-ploughed field, but I found it necessary to look for myself at the discussions in Cabinet (particularly in the late 1940s) and within the Conservative and Labour parties in order to gain a closer understanding of how decision-makers at crucial points over the past four decades conceived of the national community as reflected in our laws. Additionally, I have made a careful examination of the parties' manifestoes, pamphlets, conference reports and proceedings, and speeches by leaders. Fortunately, the abundance of available, published material on the issues with which I am concerned here made it unnecessary to conduct interviews of party leaders.

Chapters six and seven explore two examples of what I call *diasporic politics*, that is, the commitment of migrants and their offspring to the politics of their original homelands. These politics are conducted across national boundaries and with greatly improved means of travel and communication these politics are becoming more commonplace. In the past, cross-national politics involved relations between sovereign states or the politics of the exiled. This is no longer exclusively so. Migration, easy travel and the availability of telephones, videos and televisions combine to make it possible for groups of people to overcome the barriers of distance and physical isolation. Groups and individuals separated by thousands of miles of ocean and land mass can now establish close links with fellow-religionists, fellow-ethnics, fellow-adherents to a particular ideology and so forth. Such factors as personal literacy or wealth are no longer prerequisites for involvement in global activities. It would appear, therefore, that just as print (books and later newspapers) helped to extend the boundaries of the franchise, so today a series of factors are enfranchising (some would say empowering) or creating new sources of power across national or traditional boundaries of established authority.

The two examples of diasporic politics analysed in this study are those of Sikhs in Britain who support the call of fellow-Sikhs in India for an independent state of Khalistan, and the support given to groups in Guyana that are actively demanding the introduction of democracy in that troubled country once thought to be the much sought after El Dorado. Here these superficial similarities stop. What is important about the Guyanese and the Sikh situations, from the perspective of my analysis of settlers and the emerging new national community in Britain, is the fact that these groups stand in sharp contrast with each other. But the purpose is not so much to compare like with like here; the purpose is simply to illustrate my general point that, to one degree or another, the politics of 'back home', or diasporic politics, are becoming widespread and, with the Rushdie Affair still a very real issue, are obviously an important aspect of the British situation. With respect to groups from the Indian sub-continent this is of course more true than in the case of groups from the Commonwealth Caribbean, as the discussion in chapters six and seven makes clear. The decision to concentrate on the Khalistan issue was determined largely by the fact that this case combined a number of important nationalist questions such as religion, territory and language. The relative neglect of the Khalistan issue amongst researchers in Britain was also an important consideration when I commenced this work in 1986. Whilst the Guyana situation is atypical of the Commonwealth Caribbean, of all groups from the region it comes closest to the experience of groups that have settled in Britain and whose homelands are troubled by some of the vexed questions of nationalism.

It was intended that the analyses of the Sikhs and Guyanese should be complemented by a discussion of the Cypriots who settled in Britain from the 1940s, in much the same period as other British colonial immigrants, but, unfortunately, there was not enough time to complete the necessary research. I had hoped, by the inclusion of such comparative material, to overcome the prevailing (British) practice of comparing the Asian and the West Indian. I have failed. But I hope that I have been successful in avoiding the usually negative comparisons to be found in the literature on these two main non-white minorities in Britain which have nearly always been placed in a *competitive* framework, both in colonial encounters and especially in the literature on 'race relations'.

Material for the empirical chapters involved a good number of interviews with spokespersons and leaders of particular groups in Britain. I conducted over thirty in-depth interviews with individuals in the West Indian/Guyanese and Sikh communities and several more with members of the Scottish National Party (SNP) and the Cypriot community in London. Additionally, many individuals (particularly in the Sikh community) preferred to be interviewed in groups and this resulted in very useful discussions of their views on the matters which concerned them. It was also necessary to attend, as an observer, meetings and gurdwaras (temples, places of worship) in different parts of the country. I circulated a largely open-ended questionnaire to individuals and groups, around which interviews and discussions were conducted. These questionnaires were constructed with the view of gathering comparable material from different groups. This involved framing broad questions which would be relevant to the specific experiences of different groups. Moreover, I gathered as much printed material as was available in Britain about the Guyanese and

Khalistan situations. Where possible I also drew upon material published in India and the Caribbean, because it is necessary to have a clear understanding of these groups' backgrounds.

Finally, in looking at these groups the aim is not to present a profile of their communities in Britain or in their homelands. There is an abundance of material which treats adequately with these groups in India and the Caribbean. Clearer and up-to-date profiles of the Sikh and Guyanese communities in Britain would, or course, be useful. But this was not the purpose of the work. The purpose of drawing upon the experiences of members of these communities was chiefly to illustrate my overall argument regarding nationalism as articulated in contemporary Britain. In particular, my analysis focuses upon the nature of the demands for an independent Khalistan and for democracy in Guyana. After all, like other occupations, academic work operates within the context of a division of labour, and the task of describing these communities in Britain must be left largely to the sociologist and/or the social anthropologist.

It is now necessary to set out in more detail the central problem of the national community, and to relate this to the specific instances of post-imperial Britain.

2

The general problem

Introduction

However we may wish to describe or define, praise, glorify or condemn nationalism, we cannot but be impressed by its ability to continue to be the single most widespread and most powerful force propelling social and political change in the modern world. Just when we assume that it has spent its enormous store of energy, is being bypassed or transformed, nationalist sentiments or aspirations may emerge or re-awaken, heralding new departures, reasserting past or reaffirming present modes of social and political behaviour. Sometimes progressive, sometimes reactionary in its teachings and actions, nearly always disruptive, nationalism is today constantly throwing up problems which contain new opportunities and challenges. This is true for all kinds of societies, irrespective of the polarities which may distinguish them. In the industrial and affluent North as well as in the underdeveloped and poverty-stricken South, in both the Eastern and Western blocs, in open market capitalist as well as closed communist systems, nationalist upheavals are becoming once again commonplace.

For example, in the newer and less settled states of the post-colonial world in Africa and Asia, new groups constantly emerge to make demands which sound very much like those made forty, thirty or even as recently as twenty or ten years ago by nationalist leaders fighting for freedom from alien imperial powers. In Africa the decade of independence (the 1960s) was hardly over before new wars of independence commenced. Sometimes these new wars of independence were more aggressively pursued than were some of the wars against the European colonialists. The agreement between the Founding Fathers of the Organization of African Unity in 1963 to respect the frontiers drawn, in the main, by the imperialists almost a century earlier at the Congress of Berlin (1884) has not been universally respected. The Congo and Nigeria were examples of this kind of disaffection with the national arrangements reached at the point of independence from Belgium and Britain, respectively, in the 1960s. In the 1970s and 1980s there have been similar situations in Ethiopia and Sudan, whilst Angola, Mozambique, Uganda and Chad have been torn along ideological, but more often ethnic, lines. Similarly, on the Indian sub-continent, the 1970s witnessed the break-up of the Islamic state of Pakistan and the emergence of Bangladesh, following a bitter war of independence involving India. And in the case of India herself, hardly a year has passed since independence from Britain in 1947 without the union government in Delhi having to negotiate some semblance of peace with one state or another, or with one aggrieved group or the other in the country. Many of these, like the Sikhs in the Punjab, would prefer to sever their links with the union. The first half century of independence seems destined to come to an end before the ethnic problems which plague the union are resolved.

In its short but dynamic career spanning the last two centuries or so, nationalism has demonstrated an indifference to space and time. Frequently this indifference has allowed nationalism to make its sudden and unannounced appearance in quite unexpected places. In the 1970s it appeared in some of the long-established and seemingly settled states of the older bourgeois orders of West Europe and North America, where it was once believed that the national question was settled and buried. Some of the oldest peoples in Europe, such as the Basques in Northern Spain, and the Scots and the Welsh on the periphery of Britain, have evoked the spirit of nationalism; so too have the Quebecois in Canada, who were among the first European settlers on the North American continent. Given the emphases placed on internationalism and proletarian and peasant solidarity, it may have been expected that nationalism would be more easily managed by socialist regimes such as those in East Europe, the USSR and China. But from the late 1980s these regimes have been shaken by national or ethnic groups demanding the same rights as nationalists in capitalist countries. Mikhail Gorbachev's enlightened policies of *glasnost* and *perestroika* in the multi-national, multi-ethnic and multi-religious USSR have provided the occasion for the long hushed, if not entirely silent, voices of Armenians and Azerbaijanis in the south of the union, where the Christian and Moslem religions and cultures clash and confront each other, to be heard. In the Baltic states of Latvia, Lithuania and Estonia from around 1987 nationalist voices were transformed from comparatively mild cultural assertions to the resounding demand for political independence. The 1990s opens with the prospect that the USSR will inevitably experience major political restructuring, including possible changes in her membership. In 1988 China too was forced to listen to the voices of Buddhists in Tibet because they cried out to a world more attentive than hitherto to nationalist calls.

In both the developed and underdeveloped worlds, then, one major factor behind widespread, diverse and sometimes quite puzzling political disaffection is the growing awareness of groups of people that their interests may best be served outside whatever socio-political system has laid claim to their loyalties. An essential aspect of this perception of the social and political order is the view that whatever differentiates one group of people from another should be highlighted and glorified. The *assertion of difference* between collectivities of people has become the hallmark of many social and political demands. Whilst in the past *similarities* between groups of people formed the basis for unity or collective existence, the growing demand, or emphasis, today, is for communities to be bound together by the factors which establish *difference* from others.

The new nationalism presently sweeping and agitating the world is qualitatively different from earlier forms of nationalist expression which gave rise to the nation-states we now assume, more or less, to be a constant in human society. The difference between the 'new' and the 'old' nationalism lies in the ready and seemingly spontaneous chord that the appeal of the 'new' nationalism strikes in people almost everywhere. The vibrant and urgent claim made by this 'new' nationalism is that the nation ought not any longer to be so generously or loosely defined that it automatically includes a plurality of *ethnic* or *national* groups. This new nationalism demands ethnic *singularity* and seeks to make a decisive break with the *plurally* defined national community. Of course, as will become clear, the plurality I am speaking of here is not to be confused with the concepts of political pluralism, nor with M. G. Smith's theory of social and cultural pluralism.

Of course, historically the notion or concept of the nation-state has been a profound misnomer because it is the *exception* rather than the *rule* for there to be nation-states. Historically, what has in fact emerged during the course of nationalist development has been, properly speaking, the nation*s*-state rather than the nation-state. The qualitative change in definition which is taking place is, however, generally hidden from sight. This has been due, partly, to the fact that whilst the new nationalism often exhibits unnecessary intolerance and an insistence on securing particularistic rights, its righteousness and demands are generally couched in terms of strengthening democracy.

Typically, the new nationalism calls for greater political participation, accountability and responsibility, the freedom to worship, and the right to preserve small ethnic groups which may otherwise be absorbed or swallowed by larger, more dynamic communities most of which have been constructed during the rise of the nation*s*-state. In other words, the demands of the 'new' nationalism are expressed in a vocabulary familiar to all fair-minded people, particularly democrats. Moreover, movements espousing such demands on behalf of one or another threatened group fit easily into existing liberal or social-democratic moulds. But whilst the demands made by the new nationalism may be eventually reconcilable with democracy, the *utility* of its readily recognizable vocabulary, rather than the *realization* of the democratic project, may be the intention of many such movements. This does not simplify but complicates matters. Contemporary anti-democratic emphases in some forms of nationalist expressions and demands are, for example, rendered less noticeable by the very familiarity of the adopted mode of articulation.

One conclusion which may be drawn from this situation is that the emerging many-sided, versatile and complex nature of nationalism continues to impose a responsibility on all disciplines within the social sciences and humanities to uphold certain notions of the good or desirable society. After all, nationalism and ethnicity are large and amorphous social movements which demand continuous critical attention, if not by adherents of the articles of faith, then certainly by the historian and the social analyst.[1] This responsibility is, of course, a manifold one. It includes taking the lead in making sense of the diversity of forms that nationalism takes and explaining why these forms of social consciousness, the causes championed and the actions committed in their names, occur at all. Concerned intellectuals and academics cannot afford to see these responsibilities either side-stepped or taken lightly in a Britain concerned with the problem of redefining her identity and place in an uncertain post-colonial/post-imperial world.

These remarks are not uncontentious. It is as well, therefore, that I say something at this point about my overall purpose in raising some general questions which I believe are often submerged, and subsequently, do not receive the full or the close attention they deserve in discussions over 'race relations' in post-imperial Britain. The main propositions I want to explore in this essay are, therefore, the following. First, although we in Britain – both white and non-white groups and individuals – like to think that ours is a unique experience and that whatever may be happening in the rest of the world is, and can be kept, outside our physical and social shores, we are very much part of the vanguard in the general development of the new nationalism. This nationalism is being ethnically defined and it leads to what I want to call *the communal option*.

By this provocative term I mean the generalized encouragement, and the increasing desire, of many individuals to be part of an identifiable group, and for each such group not only to exist almost entirely within its own confines but also to ensure that individuals conform to the supposed norms of the group. This is rapidly becoming the British experience. Within the majority white population it is, of course, possible for the behaviour of the individual to be perceived and accepted as such, and for the specific ethnic group to which he or she belongs to remain relatively hidden from public scrutiny. The experience of a non-white individual is different; he or she is required, and increasingly wishes to, wear his or her real or supposed ethnic label. This communal perception of contemporary Britain has been welcomed by many concerned academics (see, for example, Dench, 1986; Parekh, 1989, p. 72) and informs much race relations discussion today.

Second, there are at least three disturbing major trends which have emerged in Britain in the post-imperial period, which combine to create the *communal option*, or preference, for the development of civil, though not political, society. These trends are the appeal to the apparently unquestioned rightness of the numerical majority both by the state and by some politicians who purport to be spokespersons for the white majority in Britain; attachment to the *home-land* through diasporic politics by specific groups; and the attempt to create a new sense of ethnic solidarity. Third, in order to explore these developments and indicate what they may possibly mean for the future of Britain, I propose to make a general distinction between *traditional* and *ethnic* forms of nationalism.

The questions which arise from these propositions are situated within a general discussion of nationalist and ethnic consciousness. In turn, these are located within the post-World War Two era. More specifically, the discussion focuses on the condition of post-imperial Britain's search for a new identity. My principal contention is that the *communal option* is a highly dangerous one for the future welfare of the country as a whole. It may be suicidal for the nation to pursue this present course along the cul-de-sac to which both the native white majority and the state – which in a very real sense *belongs* to the majority although it formally claims the loyalty of all – as well as the emerging forms of defensive minority communalism, all point or signal. Before turning in the following chapters to the specific problems involved in the transitions from *empire* (for the white majority and the state) and from *colony* (for the non-white minorities) to some of the problems around the inti-mations of a *new national* community in Britain, let me first clarify some basic points. I will do this by explaining some of the concepts that are employed throughout the discussion, such as nationalism, ethnicity and the notion of *post-imperial Britain*. The concept of power is also included because I would suggest that it is not possible adequately to understand either ethnicity or nationalism without an understanding of power.

Some general definitions

With its capacity to be all things to all men, nationalism has revealed many faces, and its broad outlines, as well as its specific features, are therefore manifold. Like the possessed man among the Gadarene pigs, nationalists can say with conviction that nationalism is legion. It is undoubtedly for this reason that Snyder commences the discussion in his book, *The Meaning of National-ism*, with a candid confession that he would not attempt to give 'a definite explanation of the meaning of nationalism' (Snyder, 1954, p. xi). Similarly,

Gellner ended his chapter on definitions of nationalism in *Nations and Nationalism* with an admission that it is best to proceed in an analysis of nationalism 'without attempting too much in the way of a formal definition . . . ' (Gellner, 1983, p. 7). After all, it is generally easier for the writer to assume that he or she shares a common understanding of nationalism with the reader than to have to grope for what is likely to be an inadequate definition of a slippery subject, and then spend much valuable time defending or explaining it, in the process losing sight of the substantial manifestation of the subject. One political ideologue and activist who has taken full advantage of this procedure is Enoch Powell, who argues, not incorrectly, that:

> Every society has a definition to identify those who belong to it – I shall resolutely refuse to define the word 'belong' itself, regarding it as sufficiently understood for my purpose without definition – and to distinguish them from the rest of mankind who do not belong to it.
>
> (Powell, 1988a, p. 40)

This may be called the *common assumption* approach to the analysis of nationalism. Situated at the core of the Romantic reaction to rationalism, nationalism has the merit that the manifestations of the variety of social movements and doctrines which are subsumed under its label may be more easily described than tortuously and abstractly defined. To struggle to find the essential qualities which mark off nationalism from other social phenomena, or to strive towards abstract definitions capable of commanding universal respect, are ambitious undertakings. And they are not immediately or particularly rewarding. This may become painfully apparent whether the purpose of such efforts is to convince large groups of people that a particular course of action is correct, or to promote understanding of what dissimilar groups of people in vastly different situations espouse and/or defend as nationalist aspirations.

Two notes of caution may, however, help to modify this seemingly harsh agnosticism. First, even if no definition of nationalism is likely to be universally accepted, much can still be understood about the social forces that analysts and protagonists alike claim are of a nationalist character. Nationalism's differential manifestations in dissimilar places and in different sociohistorical circumstances means that this problem of a universally acceptable definition will continue to evade us. Its chameleon-like character is naturally subject to change, but there are moments when definite colours or features are clearly evident and can be observed.

Second, it goes without saying that it is desirable to have at least a bald definition of nationalism in order to conduct a systematic discussion of the subject. It is, moreover, possible to proceed to the construction of concepts about a phenomenon before attaining a clear understanding of the thing itself as Joseph Agassi argues with respect to nationalism and zionism (Agassi, 1984, pp. 312–13). There is, therefore, no need for pangs of guilt or loss of face for not establishing an elegant and abstract definition of nationalism from the outset. But until there is at least a working definition or understanding of the subject, discussion of the forces that go into the making of nationalism is likely to be a little vacuous. Indeed, such an exercise may be even less rewarding than an inadequate definition would be. What, in these circumstances, is of crucial importance is the willingness to perceive definitions as being open-ended and useful insofar as they point to the main characteristics of the phenomena which describe themselves as nationalism.

Bearing these qualifications in mind, for the purpose of this discussion nationalism may be understood in the following manner: it is a set of broad social phenomena involving a variety of often conflicting movements and inconsistent doctrines. In the normal course of development, most of these may be expected to have an implicit or even an explicit terminus in the realization of what Max Weber described as an essential element in the construction of the modern state – territoriality. Arguably, on this point, both Weber and Snyder are undoubtedly correct: Snyder contends that nationalism 'is superimposed upon the natural order and is interpreted as the final cause and the final goal of the community' (Snyder, 1954, p. 75). I am far from happy, however, with Snyder's phrase, 'the natural order', for two reasons. First, we cannot assume that any social order is 'natural'. Second, the rise of what I shall later define as *ethnic nationalism* qualifies his definition, because there is less agreement over what legitimately constitutes the final *cause* or *goal* of any collectivity which may call itself a community.

Perceived in these terms, nationalism affects all areas of social life in its attempts to assemble – as we shall see in chapter four – not only *social* but also *natural* justifications for its existence. In the main, however, there can be little, if any, quarrel with Kohn when he argued that nationalism 'is a political creed that underlies the cohesion of modern societies and legitimizes their claim to authority' (Kohn, 1968, p. 63). Kedourie's scepticism of such claims on the part of nationalists does not detract from the elegance of his definition nor the precision of his language. For him nationalism 'pretends to supply a criterion for the determination of the unit of population proper to enjoy a government exclusively its own, for the legitimate exercise of power in the state and for the right organization of a society of states' (Kedourie, 1985, p. 1). This understanding of nationalism attempts to bring into focus both its domestic and its international dimensions, or, as we say in Britain, 'home' and 'foreign' affairs. In its actions and claims the nation-state must, after all, relate to both citizens and foreigners.

Nationalism may be said, therefore, to establish sometimes subtle, sometimes quite crude, lines of communication with groups and individuals who *feel* that they 'belong' to an ostensibly common fold. An integral part of this process of communication is for nationalism to establish clear boundaries for those who do not 'belong'. And whilst these lines of communication are essentially established within the laws of nationality, they are not at all restricted to these formal relationships. For example, the fact of being a British citizen does not of itself convey to Britain's non-white minorities a sense of 'belongingness' with respect to an entity or community called the British nation. In short, important as it obviously is to possess formal citizenship, this does not necessarily denote a sense of belonging to the community defined as the nation-state. In the case of Britain, the collective experience of racial discussion is such that the traditional understanding, or rights and obligations, of *the citizen* do not provide an adequate basis for distinguishing between those who 'belong' and those who do not; *belongingness* and *non-belongingness* in Britain are states of group consciousness which are not easily reconciled with the formal, legal notion of citizenship. In other words, whilst the development of formal legal procedures and rights over the past few centuries must be defended as real human societal gains, their limitations must not be overlooked. Specifically, in the British context this formalism has been defeated by the deeper *feelings* of elements of the majority native population, and this is often reflected by state action. Overall, then, nationalism is crucially concerned with the most sovereign unit of organized *political* power, and its *social* basis of legitimation. Before turning our attention, however, to these aspects of the discussion, I will say something here about ethnicity and its relation to nationalism.

For much the same reasons as with nationalism, ethnicity is more often *described* than *defined*. If we were to accept the dictionary or the etymological understandings of ethnicity, we could spend much valuable time and energy trying to pin down essential meanings and relate them to current usage. This course of action would lead us back to some of the earliest human groupings, where people became aware of themselves as being *different* from others as an early part of the process of the development of human society. This is also the story of the development of the awareness of the 'I' and the 'thou'; of the 'us' and the 'them'. We would also see how this difference came to be related to such matters as physical differences in colour, features, cultures, mental or physical disposition and performance, and so forth. In some cases we would have to consider how divine providence was sometimes invoked to support an evolving distinctiveness (such as the divine rights of kings of bastard feudalism)[2] or to maintain a fairly developed one as in the cases of the ancient Jews and ancient Greeks. As interesting as this kind of discourse may be, and although it would no doubt enrich our understanding of the nuances and history of ethnic consciousness, we would still not necessarily capture the meanings that people today have of the word. I shall return to this point, from a different perspective, in a later chapter, in connection with the work of A. D. Smith.

Like nationalism, ethnicity has a multiplicity of meanings. In some contexts 'ethnicity' has replaced 'race' because of the distasteful connections of the latter with such forces as Italian fascism and German nazism which based their more than usually obnoxious form of discrimination on a presumed *biologically* defined notion of race.[3] As with nationalism, there is usually a confusion between the ethnic group and ethnicity: in other words, it is difficult to distinguish between 'nation' and 'nationalism' just as it is difficult to distinguish between 'ethnic group' and 'ethnicity', partly because these theoretical and practical constructs are erected together. But quite clearly, the concepts of 'nationalism' and 'ethnicity' would have been unlikely socio-political currencies without the prior existence of some kind (or kinds) of social group which individuals, and in many cases collectivities, either feel they belong to or aspire to create. Again, as with nationalism, the variety of ethnic expressions has given rise to a plethora of explanations of these important aspects of contemporary societies.[4]

One result of the ensuing and continuous contention over the meaning of ethnicity is that it is generally so intertwined with other concepts, or so loosely used by both analysts and activists, that the general reading public may be forgiven for sometimes confusing the forms of community or social awareness, to which ethnicity points, with other forms of communal existence.

For the purposes of this discussion I would suggest that ethnicity may be taken to refer to the awareness of groups of people and/or individuals who believe that they are bound together by one or more factors such as colour, 'race', common culture or destiny, and who are living with, or surrounded by, one or more numerically and/or culturally dominant groups which are themselves marked off from others by a similar set of factors.[5] Ethnic solidarity becomes more apparent where the numerically small group feels that it must hold fast to, and cherishes, whatever it believes marks it off from the other, larger groups. This can occur for several reasons. One of these may be that the group feels that its religion is under threat from a larger secular society. The Jewish community is perhaps the best known example of this, but there are plenty of others, such as Moslems in Europe or Sikhs away from the Punjab. The defining factor need not, however, be transcendentally religious – it may very well be the kind of affinity that comes from a deep-rooted concern over material wealth and physical well-being.

There are, however, occasions when the status of being a distinctive, ethnic group is largely thrust upon others by the numerically dominant group or groups; or, alternatively or in addition, the ethnic group may wish to define itself largely in terms of those factors identified by the dominant majority population as that group's main characteristics. This may be particularly true where a loosely defined minority is subordinated on the basis of what the majority population regards as 'racial' characteristics. People of Afro-Caribbean background in Britain provide a good example of this situation. This is so because the society at large, and/or the state, demands that a group of people whose traditions are generally non-communalistic should use their ethnicity as the most important basis for a wide range of social and political action.

Members of an ethnic minority may live in specific locations together or may be scattered throughout the majority population. This is not determined by the choice or preference of individuals from the minority, but more importantly by the class, colour and religious discrimination practiced by the majority group (Dench, 1986). The point is well demonstrated by detailed studies on race and housing in Britain's cities (Rex and Tomlinson, 1979; Sarre, Phillips and Skellington, 1990). Time, location and relative size sometimes help the ethnic group to emerge as a distinct 'nation', and such a group may go on to establish corresponding territorial states. In such conditions the ethnic group is transformed into a 'national' group. This is sometimes the beginning of more intractable and prolonged problems. And this may be particularly so in highly complex situations where no new state is created or is even being demanded. The 'national' problem of Afro-Americans in the USA is an illustration of this situation of keen 'national' awareness unaccompanied by any serious demand for political separation and statehood. The same may be true for the African and East Indian populations of Guyana and Trinidad, despite the divide between these groups (particularly in Guyana, which I discuss in a later chapter). In general, however, the political loyalty of the ethnic group may be divided within national boundaries, or aspects of political loyalty may cross national frontiers. Chapter six examines this with respect to the Sikh demand for a state of Khalistan, using this as an example of ethnic nationalism and how this fits into an emerging communal framework in British national politics.

From these general remarks the close relationship between ethnic awareness, or ethnicity, and nationalism must seem obvious. The danger, however, is that sometimes this relationship is so compressed, that both ethnicity and national-ism lose their separate identities. This is true not only in loose, day to day, discussions but also in some recent scholarly works, as we will see in the next chapter.

I would suggest at this point, however, that the relationship between ethnicity and nationalism should be seen in such a way that nationalism is generally regarded as the wider, larger but perhaps paradoxically also the more compactly organized entity. As we have seen, while nationalism is difficult to pin down exactly and exclusively, its manifestations are nonetheless easy enough to identify, if only because its agenda is more specific as well as more closely related to known physical (territorial, for example) entities. National-ism, therefore, presents an option to an ethnic group to overcome some of its difficulties. After all, small nations are often in a position to negotiate a degree of respect and sovereignty as well as to increase their gains, out of all proportion to their relative sizes, in the international political arena. Once the ethnic group does this, however, it tends to lose what constituted its strength – the natural, human empathy of other groups. At this stage it becomes necessary for the transformed ethnic group to transcend the earlier boundaries which served it well.

But in specific historical contexts the falling back onto ethnicity by larger and dominant groups is not unknown: indeed, the process of development or retreat from a multi-ethnic empire to the nations-state usually represents precisely such a crisis point in the consciousness of a people who consider themselves to be essentially *different* from others around them. The emergence of Turkey out of the Ottoman empire after World War One is an example of this kind of dramatic transformation or retreat. The warnings and lamentations of woe of J. Enoch Powell amount to the cry that comes from the pain of being about to understand more clearly than many others an inevitable historical rupture and a necessary transition from the certainty of empire to the less assured placement within a world which is formally or ostensibly less unequal.[6]

The close relationship between nationalism and ethnicity is illustrated by Figure 2.1. This is a simple representation of a situation in which the national

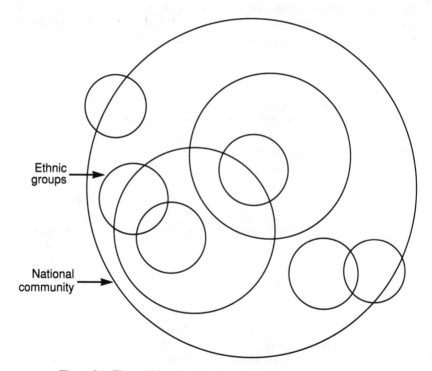

Figure 2.1 The traditional national community

community is composed of one large and/or fairly homogeneous community or group as well as any number of smaller ethnic groups; the nation in this sense is larger than the sum of its individual ethnic parts or communities. Some groups may overlap whilst others may be quite distinct. These parts or groups may or may not be equal to each other. Switzerland and Belgium are perhaps the best examples of national communities which may be said to be composed of discrete groups distinguished by such factors as language and culture (French, German, and Italian, and French and Flemish, respectively), which tend to be more or less equal in the essential areas of society, economy and political life, and which keep each other in some kind of generally acceptable and, therefore, peaceful balance. Britain may be regarded, on the other hand, as one instance in which the national community – the British nation – is more than the sum of its parts: England, Scotland, Wales and Northern Ireland, as well as groups of people from Europe who came not as conquerors but as asylum seekers, refugees and immigrants from the sixteenth century onwards. These non-conquerors have been steadily baptized or, as M. G. Smith would say, incorporated – as Figure 2.2 suggests – into the dominant culture and community of the British nation. In much the same way, the Jutes, Celts, Romans,

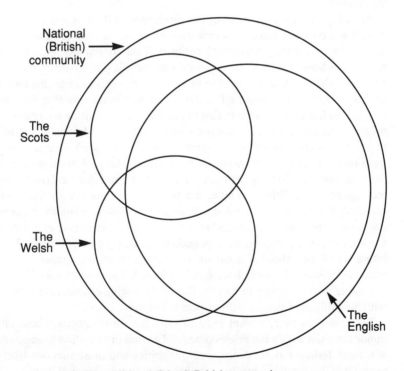

Figure 2.2 The traditional (Island) British community

Anglo-Saxons, Danes and Normans before them had also been absorbed, and these groups have all come to create what may be regarded, not as the homogeneous society the New Right speaks of, but certainly a comparatively uniform if complex national entity which we visualize as and call the British nation. Within this conglomeration of peoples, languages and folkways, the Anglo-Saxon language and tenor of society from feudal times have nominally survived, if only through the names of the country (England) and the language (English). Of course, the simple representation of this, ostensibly homogeneous community by Figure 2.2 is misleading because the native British population was never quite so straightforwardly homogenized. Nonetheless, over several centuries a fairly unified British community did emerge within these islands. Whilst this is sometimes denied, such denials cannot be taken too seriously. What is not so easily recognized, however, is that the United Kingdom today stands at a junction from which it could move to enrich further the national culture and society or to try to preserve itself as a kind of quaint historical museum. The variety of peoples and cultures which have come into contact with this island either directly through migration or indirectly through conquest and emigration *from* Britain could become an enormous resource for the country.

Arguably, largely as a result of this development there is a potential ideological and political space for a new national consciousness to be encouraged within the community designated national. This community should not be regarded as being the construction of any one specific group – this is an important point which will be returned to in different contexts in later chapters. The loss for some of the manifold inheritors of this culture is that they blind themselves from the possibility that the strength of the culture today lies in its *proximity* to, and not its *distance* from, other cultures. Additionally, the ability of what we loosely describe as culture in Britain to *absorb* what is desirable from other cultures, is of enormous importance. Many of those who seek to deny the close relationship between Island British (see Figure 2.2) and a wider, more generalized British culture, are wittingly or unwittingly involved in arresting the nation's cultural development through a complex process of *exclusion*. And this is an exclusion with no basis in morality, ethics or aesthetics, but based partly on blind prejudice and partly on a fear of the kind of future which lies ahead if a *human* as opposed to an intolerant, exclusivist ethnic or *communal* approach were to be adopted. The problems involved here are not, of course, unique to Britain. But the following chapters are concerned with their different aspects with respect to Britain.

For now, however, I want only to note that in situations where ethnic minorities exist within larger groupings and are not in a position to negotiate or win their desired independence, both majorities and minorities are likely to retreat into *imagined* laagers. In situations, such as post-imperial Britain, where majoritarian ethnic nationalism is generally on the *offensive*, minority ethnicity would appear to adopt a *defensive* posture against larger, stronger forces. The point may be expressed in another way: in a situation such as contemporary Britain, ethnicity becomes a mode or form within which those who perceive themselves to be oppressed, dispossessed, deprived and alienated – or whatever adjective is used to describe the condition of those who are subordinated even before the elaborate game over access to power and scarce resources commences – can authenticate themselves and have their voices heard.

Due largely to the development of something sufficiently widely recognized as an international opinion, and the ease of communication which together have resulted in what has been called the 'global village', small groups can now make their voices heard in a manner undreamt of in the not so distant past. Consequently, the world community has become much more sympathetic to the cause of weak minorities pitched against stronger majorities. A powerful factor that features in the relationship between such groups is the increasing tendency for the world population to be composed of minorities, as larger groups are disaggregated. Both ethnicity and nationalism, therefore, now have ample opportunity effectively to manipulate the characteristics believed to mark off one group of human beings from another, in order to achieve quite specific socio-cultural and politico-economic ends. In these situations the majority populations are also likely to reassert their predominance and thereby create situations of mutual exclusivity. In the case of Britain, however, the process commenced first with leaders of the majority population and only secondarily with the communal response of minorities, because, as migrants, these groups came to Britain with a degree of *willingness* to undergo some change. In both situations the likely destination is the cul-de-sac called communalism. Practical examples of this are to be seen in societies as diverse as India, parts of Africa, the USSR and, indeed, here at home in Northern Ireland where the general crisis of community is euphemistically called the 'troubles'.

Nationalism, ethnicity and power

The following chapter develops this aspect of the discussion, that is, the communal response to the crisis of national community, by considering alternative ways of looking at the complex relationships between ethnicity and nationalism. This may, however, be a convenient point at which to return briefly to the question of the relationship between nationalism and ethnicity on the one hand, and power on the other, because, as we saw earlier, nationalism is concerned primarily with the organization of political power. Nationalism, of course, embraces other aspects of human societal existence but from its very inception, both as doctrine and as movement (and as I have been insisting, the two must be taken together to make sense), nationalism has been concerned with the single largest organized community through which humanity has striven to arrange socio-political affairs and economic activity in modern times, namely the modern state. And, to be concerned about the state is to have an interest in the distribution of political power both within the state itself and within civil society as a whole.

Nationalism's first bid for power was a call for a radical realignment of political forces and a redrawing of political and juridical boundaries. Like its contemporary and helpmate capitalism, nationalism – depending on what it found on the ground – effected, not unexpectedly, different developments in dissimilar parts of the world. For example, the break away of the North American colonies from England in the eighteenth century occurred over the political dispute as to whether, as Englishmen physically removed from these shores but no less Englishmen for that, the colonists could be taxed without proper representation in parliament at Westminster. Less than two decades later, the far more significant and influential French Revolution dramatically posed the questions of how state power should be re-organized and which of the *estates* of the new force called 'the people' should have the upper hand in the re-shaped community called the nation of France. Since 1789 these questions concerning the distribution and exercise of power have been at the very heart of nationalist revolutions.

For example, in the colonial world of Africa, Asia, the Caribbean and the Pacific islands after World War Two, nationalists challenged their rulers and brought them low by posing the crucial question of political legitimacy. Many of the regimes established in some of these post-colonial states are at least as anti-democratic and aggressively repressive as the colonial systems people correctly rejected. Indeed, some may be more repressive and dismissive of democratic institutions and practice than were some of the colonial regimes. But this is hardly the point. Nationalism confronted colonialism on its weakest ground – namely, its legitimacy of rule over a social collectivity distinguished from their rulers by such factors as language, colour, 'race' and religion. The victories nationalists scored resulted in the construction of new relations and institutions of political power – even if the new orders were, as Franz Fanon lamented with respect to Africa, caricatures of European institutions (Fanon, 1963). In these varied historical and social situations, nationalist movements were certainly progressive forces posing challenges to established political orders.

But there is also reactionary nationalism. The rise of national socialism in Germany in the 1930s and the fascist dream of restructuring post-World War One, or Wilson's Europe after Versailles, and the nationalism of the neo-fascists in the Republic of South Africa, are perhaps the most well-known examples of reactionary nationalism, where the main mission is to maintain or revert to a state system which is not only essentially unjust but is, by any human standard, unacceptable. Through such manifestations as fascism, nazism or apartheid, reactionary nationalism denies the presence or the existence of a larger entity called humanity. It recognizes only that loyalty which is demanded of those who come within the fold of the nation, however this is defined or understood by those who are undisputedly members.

In post-imperial Britain the overwhelming impact of much state action – irrespective of which major party is in office – has been to create a new Britain in which discrete communities, defined in terms of colour/race/culture, have little in common with each other. This result is almost certainly not the *intention* of state policy and it is therefore all the more depressing that this exclusionary practice is nearly always the *effect* of such action. It may be argued that this is so because there is little by way of a vision, on the part of any national leader or party, of the kind of good society Britain could aim to construct for all her people. More often than not, one kind of bias is pitched against another kind and each finds its justification, not primarily in any moral, ethical or logical system but principally in its *oppositional* posture to the other, whatever this may be. For example, the exclusion of minorities from mainstream majority society in Britain helps to create a counter exclusivity by ethnic minorities as a kind of protection. The result is that members of both 'communities' lock themselves in mutually exclusive social zones.

Whilst the broad view of power to which I allude here relates to only some kinds of ethnicity, it relates to most kinds of expressions of nationalism. Not all forms of ethnic expression seek to effect a discrete community congruent with territorial boundaries. Nor does the broad view of power to which I am pointing here conform to the more specific perspective which seeks to account for the detailed exercise of power in specific instances. For example, Dahl's analysis of power in specific New England communities (Dahl, 1961) focused on what Harold Lasswell had earlier defined to be the essence of politics – namely, who gets what, when and how (Lasswell, 1958). This approach to the study of the exercise of power, advanced in Dahl's work and by many pressure-group theorists in the optimistic pre-1968 days, has the merit of bringing to light some of the forces involved in the decision-making process. The celebrated critique of power by Bachrach and Baratz in the early 1960s (Bachrach and Baratz, 1962; 1963) presented a major problem for the behavioural perspective of power (see, for example, Crenson, 1971; Lukes, 1974).

But it is hardly necessary to become involved in the debate over power in a broad discussion of the kind which I pursue here. I enter into these general remarks only insofar as they help to highlight the relationship I see between power, nationalism and ethnicity. My main point is that questions of nationalism and ethnicity have to do with relations of power. It is therefore necessary only to have a nodding acquaintance with the definition, or to have a working notion of power. This, for me, is derived from the Marxist view that in the relationship between dominated and subordinated groups of people – whether they are divided according to class or gender, or in accordance with the 'racial'/ ethnic group – the relationship of power is necessarily involved. Power relationships are therefore enmeshed in the socialization process whereby we come to accept certain practices as 'normal' (see, for example, Marx, 1969; Althusser, 1971). Indeed, we might even come to believe that our acceptance is one of free will rather than fate. Like ethnicity, some kinds of nationalism may have to do with forms of social control (as may be the case in Britain, where there seems to be a desire on the part of some state institutions to encourage the development of ethnic awareness in the non-white minority communities) as well as with means of maintaining or defending positions of power; or, on the other hand, with means of attacking such positions of power and privilege.

This may be a convenient point at which to explain what I mean by the term 'post-imperial' as applied to Britain. Colonialism, as a political and social force, may have come to an end with political independence for the vast majority of Third World countries – making the world as a whole almost entirely divided into nations as Rustow implied (Rustow, 1967) – but dependence and underdevelopment persist, as the haunting title (*Persistent Poverty*) of George Beckford's book reminds us (Beckford, 1972). The impact of imperialism in the Third World continues to demand the attention of statesmen in both the developed and underdeveloped parts of the contemporary world (Manley and Brandt, 1985).

In short, imperialism is still a very real factor in the lives of people in the vast majority of Third World countries. Political independence has not been followed by economic independence as in the case of the USA. Nkrumah's promise – seek ye first the political kingdom and all things shall be added unto you – unfortunately rarely materializes in the post-colonial world. It is, of course, true that political independence significantly changed the nature of the dependence but it is also true that the relationship itself remains – indeed, some would argue that this dependent relationship has deepened and taken new structural forms. The new dependence is no longer of the colony on the imperial political centre, but on multi-national industrial firms and financial houses, which are themselves undermining the integrity of the nation-state. Debates over the nature of the new dependency which were largely dominated by academics and statesmen in the 1970s, have been enjoined by ordinary men and women[7] as the problem becomes more glaringly obvious and is highlighted by drought and famine in Africa, disasters in South Asia and Central America and the debt of Third World countries.

Radical Third World critiques of imperialism that seek to highlight the nature of dependence have been built on liberal and Marxist analyses of imperialism. The critical tradition that has grown up from these approaches to the phenomenon of imperialism was contributed to by Marx and Engels, Lenin, Luxembourg, Bukharin and others, as well as by the liberal economist J. A. Hobson (Owen and Sutcliffe, 1972; also, Rhodes, 1970 and Kemp, 1967). But of the various theses propounded by these writers Lenin's is by far the most well known. In brief, he argued that imperialism was the last stage of capitalism and that the best political strategy to destroy it was to attack it at its weakest link in its chain of control. Essentially, however, Lenin's thesis was that imperialism was the export of capital from the capitalist West to the rest of the world. This was determined by the capitalist urge to overcome the problem of the law of the tendency of the rate of profit to fall as the constant capital increases over variable capital in Marx's formulation of the theory of surplus-value (Marx, 1974; Kay, 1975). This contentious thesis has generated much debate since the First World War and goes far beyond the scope of this discussion. What is of immediate relevance, however, is the strong implication from this definition of imperialism that the end of colonialism did not mean that imperialism was also at an end. Forms of political control changed, but the economic relationship of dependency remained. And if this is so, then it may be expected that relationships do not remain exclusively economic but have social and political implications, although these are now different from, and less humiliating than, those which obtained under direct colonialism.

It must now be obvious that the term *post-imperial* as applied to Britain cannot mean that Britain is no longer an imperialist country in the generally accepted sense derived from the Hobson–Lenin analysis of imperialism. For, although the overwhelming bulk of Britain's trade in the 1980s is with her partners in the EEC, some of the major firms exporting capital to the Third World remain British. Nor does the multi-national nature of most large firms entirely lessen, in this as in other respects, the importance of the firm's home in one nation-state or the other. Indeed, it is generally estimated that Britain's export of capital outside the national boundary, or foreign investment, is relatively larger than those of other developed capitalist countries (see, for example, Kidron and Segal, 1987). Of course, not all of this export is to Third World countries but these parts of the world remain important for British capital and goods, despite Britain's closer integration with Europe. In any event, Britain is now part of the unifying European Community, which is rapidly being transformed into a political as well as an economic group, and which Third World countries have to face (mainly through the Lome Conventions) as a bloc in their attempts to adjust to the inequitable terms of trade on the world market.

The term *post-imperial* is being used, therefore, in the sense that Britain has steadily relinquished, or has had wrenched from her, what was once the world's

largest colonial empire spreading over more than a quarter of the earth's
surface. The term 'post-colonial' could be used to convey the sense of change
which Britain has undergone during the post-World War Two years, but this
term would also be ambiguous. Despite several waves of conquerors from
Germany, Scandinavia and France, Britain has not been a colony since the
Roman occupation, and 'post-colonial' is usually reserved for the period
immediately after a colony's independence. The *post-imperial* experience
under discussion must therefore be taken to be the opposite side of the *post-
colonial* coin which, in the literature on underdevelopment, has received a far
more sophisticated attention than has post-imperial Britain. In these circumstances, it may be expected that Britain's adjustment to the changed conditions
of the last four decades must be different from that of the ex-colonies.

In the first instance, the ex-colonies achieved *formal* equality in a world of
ostensibly free and equal nations; in the second instance the former masters
must learn to live in a world no longer entirely of their own making. They have
withdrawn but their legacies remain in modified forms in the ex-colonies; so
too have remnants of the colonialists become parts of the former empire, the
new nation-states. The excitement of the *post-colonial* experience has generated a great deal of comment by social scientists but comparatively less has
been said about the *post-imperial* adjustment to a new experience, a new
reality. Yet, both sets of countries must face the question of how to redefine
themselves in a world in which the basic political unit is universally accepted
as the 'nation-state'. It is part of the common wisdom of our times to think
that the ex-colony inherits and has to cope with all the problems of the post-
imperial age; but whilst this is not completely untrue, nor is it wholly true,
because the ex-imperial power must also adjust to a new world not entirely of
its own making. In many respects some of the *continuing* implications of this
for a former super-power such as Britain has not yet been sufficiently recognized; far less is there a recognition of the need to embark upon a determined
search for possible solutions.

A new national British identity?

The general problem I am raising here, therefore, has to do with the question
of the kind of Britain we wish to construct as we approach the twenty-first
century. Essentially, it is a problem of how the redefinition of *the British nation*
in the post-imperial age is to be achieved so that the presence of peoples of non-
European backgrounds is not regarded as illegitimate. The problem is compounded by the fact that the settlement of non-white groups occurred at the
very point when the country was making its historic transition from *empire* to
nation. This transition may prove to be as important in its own way as any in

the past, such as the extension of the franchise in the last, and the first half of the present, centuries, or the Union with Scotland at the beginning of the seventeenth century.

Discussion of the questions and issues surrounding the main problem of the definition of a new national community in Britain is not, of course, new. In particular, a strong *cultural-conservative* position has received both academic and political circulation. It seeks, essentially, to establish a narrow sense of Britishness. Its understanding of the membership of the British national community is largely restricted to the native white majority and to those who, by virtue of their colour, can quietly 'fit in'. Norman Tebbit expressed the perspective of the cultural-conservative perfectly clearly when he complains:

> Sadly what has been almost an age of innocence is ending. Our gentle nationalism, more a sense of nationality, was never built on any sense of racial purity. After all, the early history of these islands was of successive waves of immigrants mixing Celts, Britons, Angles, Saxons, Romans, Norse and Norman French. Later Flemish, Huguenot and Jewish immigrants *were integrated to such an extent that only the Jewish community remained identifiable and that only by a religion on which the culture of the whole nation is largely based. But in recent years our sense of insularity and nationality has been bruised by large waves of immigrants resistant to absorption, some defiantly claiming a right to superimpose their culture, even their law, upon the host community.*
>
> (emphases added) (Tebbit, 1990, p. 78)

But what I am referring to here as the cultural-conservative perspective found expression, long before Tebbit's outbursts of early 1990, in the writings of those who contribute to the Conservative journal *The Salisbury Review*. These writers' attitude to post-imperial Britain and the need for a new definition of the national community is perhaps best summed up by E. J. Mishan in a rambling two-part paper entitled 'What future for a multi-racial Britain', in the June and September 1988 issues of the journal. Whilst, like Tebbit, Mishan is able to recognize contributions made to British society by white migrants from Europe, he is deeply distressed by what he described as

> . . . the increasing attention and coverage given to racial issues by government and the media. In consequence, the problems arising from race come to engage a quite disproportionate share of the nation's political energies – diverting its passions and its scarce resources from the main prevailing problems of the post-industrial era.
>
> (Mishan, 1988, p. 26)

There is, of course, a sense in which this statement is true: one result of racism in Britain has indeed been that much valuable time and resources and many lives – mostly of the victims of racism – are wasted on coping with its effects. I doubt, however, whether Mishan intended to convey this meaning. According to the view he represents, the whole experience of non-white settlement in Britain has been a national mistake and a disaster. At best, there appears to be a wish on the part of such cultural-conservatives to make the best of this unfortunate blot on the pristine (white) British landscape. As the title of Ray Honeyford's book (Honeyford, 1988) suggests, the important question facing Britain in the general view of cultural-conservatives is that of integration or disintegration. To one degree or another the positions of many national politicians of the Conservative party in the post-imperial period, as we shall see in a later chapter, reflect this view. It would be a mistake, however, to assume that the cultural-conservative position on this most important question of the composition of the British nation is shared only by members of the Conservative party, or by its politicians, or by both groups.

Many share, with liberals and radicals, a general perception of the new British national community as a multi-cultural society. Multi-culturalism recognizes the social mosaic that contemporary Britain has become in the post-imperial age. This is, of course, a matter of fact. Unlike the cultural-conservatives, multi-culturalists appear to wish to present as a desirable social good the image of Britain as a society characterized by a wide range of peoples and cultures. They wish to persuade the nation that the plurality of cultures is a resource. There is no other public document that expresses what I would call the *new pluralism* more forthrightly than *Education for All*. This was the report of the Swann Committee of Inquiry into education, commonly referred to as the *Swann Report*, after its chairman (Swann, 1985). The importance of this document has been reflected in the frequency of attacks upon it by the contributors to *The Salisbury Review*, the nation-wide debates it stimulated, and its glorification by adherents of multi-culturalism. With respect to the last point, for example, the educationalist G. K. Verma, himself a member of the Committee, entitles his recent book *Education for All: A Landmark in Pluralism*, and dedicates it to Lord Swann ' . . . whose understanding, sensitivity and skills made it possible to lay the foundation of cultural pluralism in Britain' (Verma, 1989, p. i). Whether we agree with the *Swann Report* or not, it cannot be denied that it focused the nation's attention on a pressing national question, namely, the kind of society we wish to build for the future.

The *Swann Report*'s expression of the new pluralism is at once an optimistic and a pessimistic view of British society. It is optimistic insofar as it proffers the view that social peace between the different peoples of contemporary Britain is obtainable through the recognition of what it calls a plural society. The report asserts that

> . . . a multi-racial society such as ours would in fact function most effectively and harmoniously on the basis of pluralism which enables, expects and encourages members of all ethnic groups, both minority and majority, to participate fully in shaping the society as a whole within a framework of commonly accepted values, practices and procedures, whilst also allowing and, where necessary, assisting the ethnic minority communities in maintaining their distinct ethnic identities within this common framework.
>
> (Swann, 1985, p. 5)

These very positive characteristics of the new pluralism will help Britain to create the ideal society which is ' . . . both socially cohesive and culturally diverse' (*Swann Report*). The new pluralism will build a national social order and unity based on 'common aims, attributes and values' (*Swann Report*, p. 7). Unlike the cultural-conservatives, the report recognized that *Britishness* is not a fixed, definite and inflexible entity; rather, Britishness is perceived as evolving and changing. The *Swann Report* amounts to a call for Britain to develop and extend its tradition of embracing the newcomer. Like Tebbit, it recognizes the obvious: the post-War immigrants are different from all other groups of the past. Whilst, however, Tebbit saw this as a bruising experience, the *Swann Report* welcomed the new multi-ethnic, multi-cultural dimension as a resource for the country as a whole. One sees only the danger, the other sees only the benefits.

The true situation must lie somewhere between these two positions. One major effect, therefore, of both the cultural-conservative and the extreme multi-culturalist approaches is to close-off discussion over the problem of how to define or construct a new national British community in the post-imperial age. Where the one wishes to maintain a pre-imperial, almost nativist, notion of the British community, the other would arrest the present imperfect, still emerging, moment and make this the ideal, preferred, social condition. The cultural-conservative's position suggests that Britain's non-white population have made no contribution to the community to which they, in any event, ought not to belong. Multi-culturalism holds out the prospect that the cultural differences between groups in Britain should not be respected only by social institutions; these differences should be publicly supported and maintained. Its pessimism lies in its underlying assumption that present differences between groups of people in Britain is a desirable, long-term good for the nation. There is, however, the danger here that this present situation could degenerate into becoming little more than what M. G. Smith, in the colonial context, described as socially and culturally pluralist societies held together merely by a political authority. We will examine this later. In other words, there is a need to go beyond the new pluralism which multi-culturalism represents and create a Britain in which the common ground we all occupy is steadily expanded.

Naturally, with the end of empire, economic, political and military decline, and the settlement of former colonial peoples on British shores, it would be expected that the immediate post-imperial age would be one characterized by uncertainty. But it must be admitted that to hope either to return to a pre-imperial Britain or to freeze the present moment and present it as the ideal condition for a national community is shortsighted and dangerous for all who consider Britain to be their home. To create a new post-imperial national identity which takes into account what is desirable and good from both the majority and the various minority cultures, demands that our vision of a new national community reaches beyond the narrow socio-historical horizons of both the cultural-conservatives and multi-culturalism.

Conclusion

The open discussions, which must accompany any intimation of a wide and generous sense of national community, suggest that Sked is quite incorrect when he contends that 'the disappearance of the Pax Britannica is so obvious that it cannot in itself sustain a debate' (Sked, 1987, p. 1). This proposition, as we shall see in the following chapters, is not sustainable in view of the very crucial choice confronting British society, largely as a result of the demise of empire. Increasingly, the choice would seem to lie between the communal option to which both cultural-conservatism and the politics of difference defended by the new pluralism variously promise to lead, and the building of a truly all-embracing national community. This requires abandoning much of the harping nostalgia and exclusivism of cultural-conservatism as well as the simplistic optimism and naivete of the new pluralism. This is the appropriate place at which to turn, therefore, to the question of the communal option.

3

The communal option

Introduction

In the last chapter I argued that nationalism and ethnicity are forms of social consciousness with corresponding movements which, ultimately, are concerned with the organization and exercise of power in human affairs. The relationship between nationalism, ethnicity and power is not, of course, always obvious. After all, one of the central concerns of both nationalism and ethnicity is the sense of *community* to which people feel that they belong. Nationalism and ethnicity are both vitally concerned with perhaps the most fundamental question bequeathed to us by the French Revolution, namely the kind of community men and women will construct for themselves, their children and those with whom they feel they have much of importance in common. Nationalism involves, in this respect, clearly demarcated physical boundaries, denoting inclusion and exclusion, and rights and obligations which are expressed in the notion of citizenship. In the case of ethnicity, the community need not be one confined to geographical national boundaries or even proximity of residence. Citizenship rights and obligations are rarely involved in the membership of the ethnic group but entry into, and exit from, such groups or collectivities are usually more tightly controlled than in the case of the national community – where community means the nation*s*-state. Both nationalism and ethnicity may, therefore, be seen as symptoms of a *continuous*[1] or prolonged crisis of community and they are parts of the more general attempt either to maintain or to reconstruct new forms of social and political associations.

This chapter is concerned with what I call the communal option. I want, however, to approach it by looking at two aspects of the crisis of community of which nationalism and ethnicity are fundamental expressions. The first aspect is the broader question of the relationship between ethnicity and nationalism. The second is the relationship between national majorities and minorities in situations such as that which exists in Britain. Although these aspects are very closely related, it is preferable to treat them separately.

Nationalism and ethnicity

It is necessary to look a little more closely at the relationship between ethnicity and nationalism because, as I noted in the last chapter, these phenomena are sometimes so compressed that their individual identities are lost. One way of re-establishing their separate identities is to cast a critical glance at some recent contributions to the literature on the close relationship which undoubtedly exists between the two phenomena. Perhaps the two most exciting and relevant statements worth looking at in this context are the contributions by Orlando Patterson and by A. D. Smith in their respective books *Ethnic Chauvinism* (1977) and *The Ethnic Revival* (1981).[2]

In brief, for both Patterson and Smith nationalism is the modern day expression of a very old form of community based on ethnic consciousness and loyalty. Whilst, however, for Patterson, ethnic awareness is an unacceptable 'reactionary impulse', Smith argues a strong case for ethnicity. Although these authors offer radically different interpretations of the historical development of nationalism and the persistence of ethnicity, Smith and Patterson appear to agree on one fundamental point. For both writers these forms of social consciousness, and the movements associated with them, are essentially the same. Perhaps there is no other point in their respective discussions where Smith and Patterson come closer together than at the angle from which they perceive the forms of ethnic and national awareness as being identical. This is not, of course, unusual. For example, in his definition of nationalism Gellner assumes that ethnicity and nationalism are basically one and the same thing when he states that nationalism 'requires that ethnic boundaries should not cut across political ones' (Gellner, 1983, p. 1). To one degree or another many students of these phenomena make much the same assumption. The difference in the work of Patterson and Smith is that they both tend to see these forces as interchangeable; the expression of one is the essence of the other. For Patterson this identity condemns modern nationalism as a 'reactionary impulse'; for Smith such identity validates his claim that nationalism is not of recent vintage and can therefore, presumably, enjoy the supposed authenticity of longevity.

For both Smith and Patterson the intellectual is at the very centre of the discussion concerning ethnicity and nationalism. But these authors offer quite different analyses of the intellectual's contribution to the origins and development of nationalism. Smith's intellectual appears to be a social parasite who seeks to take from, rather than to contribute to society; he conspires with the bureaucrats of what Smith calls the 'scientific truth' to hinder the full development of the ethnic community. Smith's intellectual is alienated because he is rejected by the social order of which he once wanted to be part. To this extent, Smith's intellectual is, like Patterson's, a rebel.

Patterson, however, places greater stress on the intellectual's experience of exile, his existence on the rim of society. Because of this, the intellectual is able to transcend the limitations of his community, as his exile is one of choice. For Patterson the modern intellectual is the descendant of the sorcerer, the outcast, the man who, so to speak, works out his salvation in the fear and trembling with which St Paul admonishes us to redemption. Thus, Patterson's sorcerer/exile/ intellectual is the true individualist who strives to distance himself or herself from the constraints of the group and is able, therefore, to be a net-contributor to the human enterprise of progress. Smith's intellectual, on the other hand, is at best of the gregarious spirit that you would expect in the man or woman seeking his or her place in the close-knit community, at worst a parasite incapable of making a contribution to the greater whole, and is therefore hardly an intellectual at all. In the main, Smith's nationalist hero appears to be nothing more than a poor lost soul who demands our pity.

These differences, of themselves, may not matter much in the end. The important point is that this emphasis on the intellectual is, of course, consistent with a long-standing tradition of writings on nationalism. Seen as a social and political movement, nationalism has its origins in the activities of practical men of action, but the intellectual has been deeply involved in fashioning its ideological or doctrinal framework. Indeed, in some accounts of its origins writers concentrate almost exclusively on the contributions of intellectuals such as Herder and Fichte, and pay less attention to events, such as the French Revolution which was the first major manifestation of the new spirit of nationalism (Kedourie, 1985; Anderson, 1983).

Nationalism did not, however, attract outstanding rationalist theoreticians in the way that socialism or liberalism did and therefore ' . . . it has hardly ever had any interesting ideas on which to base itself' (Agassi, 1984, p. 314). Perhaps, however, as Gellner points out, the presence or absence of major rationalist thinkers in the cause of nationalism has been irrelevant to its almost inevitable course (Gellner, 1983, p. 124). The two central points in the work of both Patterson and Smith that are of relevance here, however, are the relationship between nationalism and ethnicity, and the problem of humanism and historicism. I want to comment briefly here on the first of these, and in the following section to make some remarks about the second.

In his account, Patterson is cautious and careful at least to imply some kind of theoretical distinction between nationalism and ethnicity. Smith seems to think that no such distinction is necessary. For Patterson nationalism is a definite, a new and specific, type of ethnic expression in the modern age. Nationalism may be the most powerful expression of ethnicity but it is, nonetheless, only one aspect of what Patterson sees as a much more generalized force. Indeed, one of the worrying aspects of Patterson's work is whether he is not including too much under the rubric of ethnicity. His work runs a closer risk than Smith's of incorporating almost every human organizational expression into ethnicity. This is rather like Omi and Winant's notion of 'racial formation', which sees racial phenomena as a determinant in all areas of human endeavour (Omi and Winant, 1986). And it is, of course, difficult for people to refuse to embrace this view, given the general encouragement to do so by state institutions, academics, activists and others.

In Smith's account, ethnicity and nationalism are treated as one and the same thing. It is not that the one arises out of the other or, as with Patterson, that the one is larger than the other. For Smith there is a totality of identity. Throughout his discussion there is a bland unawareness of any difference between nationalism and ethnicity either as doctrine or as historical process. It is as if these movements, the doctrines they sustain and which in turn provide ideological justifications for specific actions, have always been assumed to be one and the same thing. What is striking in this respect in Smith's account, is how he manages to use the concepts, doctrines and movements of ethnicity and nationalism interchangeably so that any sense the reader may have of separate identities recede into the background.

Thus, by quite different routes, Smith and Patterson both arrive at the same destination. This is illustrated by Figure 3.1, which expresses the compression of both ethnic and national communities. By using such a compression, Smith is able to dismiss completely the question of the recent origins of nationalism. Patterson, concerned to show the early, almost primordial, origins of ethnicity, underplays the importance of the fact that nationalism is of recent origin. To be fair to both writers, their stated briefs are accounts of ethnicity. Their accounts, however, too readily subsume nationalism under ethnicity. In other words, much of what they both, but particularly Smith, call ethnicity, is what is usually described as nationalism.

But there are some sound reasons for stressing the recency of the historical origins of nationalism. The first of these is the confidence that we have had since the revolution in the natural, particularly biological, sciences in the nineteenth century, that if we know the origins of a phenomenon we are not only likely to understand it better but also to discover or invent ways of controlling it. One persistent problem with nationalism, however, is that it has so very many and varied sources. This in turn raises two problems. One is the difficulty involved in locating the historical genesis of nationalism. The second is the difficulty of isolating or selecting the significant aspects of major historical events which may be included in a general definition. The problem of definition was dealt with in chapter two, and in the next chapter I discuss specific aspects of what we mean when we speak of the 'nation'. An attempt at defining nationalism or nation will not, therefore, be made at this point.

With respect, however, to the problem of origins itself, writers, expectedly, differ. For example, in his highly provocative and stimulating book, *Imagined Communities*, Benedict Anderson argues that national struggles started in the

Anglo and Hispanic American colonies where settlers asserted their rights against arrogant rulers from Europe (Anderson, 1983). These governors considered themselves superior to the settlers by virtue of the accident of the location of their birth. Anderson argues that their attitudes towards the settlers helped to create a new form of community consciousness – nationalism.[3]

Contrary to the views of Smith and Patterson, an earlier generation of writers sought to make a clear distinction between these forms of social consciousness and movements. Hans Kohn, Louis Hartz and others sought to show that nationalism as a social and political doctrine is a relatively recent historical phenomenon with its roots in the Romantic Movement and the French Revolution of the late eighteenth century. They did not, of course, deny that before this time there were groups of people who had developed a deep sense of their identities and could be properly regarded as 'nations'. The ancient Jews and Greeks are the groups most often spoken of in these terms. But these writers also insisted, correctly, that the desire to achieve the congruence of 'the people' and 'the state' (the so-called nation-state/nationalism) is entirely different from these early developments. It is important to maintain this distinction if we are to understand the nature of the revolution wrought by national-

Figure 3.1 The ethno-national community

ism in different parts of the world over the last two hundred years. The distinction is also important if we are to recognize the new dimension into which nationalism is entering in the post-imperial/post-colonial, contemporary world.

There is a second reason for wanting to separate nationalism and ethnicity: in the process we should be able to isolate or dislodge some factors which have come to be regarded as aspects of nationalism. These include the sharing of a common culture and historical experiences, the sharing of a common territory, religion, language and the physical fact of colour and/or racial features. I will comment on just one of these factors here because the others will be discussed extensively in the next chapter.

The patriotic man or woman loves the land of his or her birth, upbringing or adoption. As an adult he or she may write songs or poems about the immediate surroundings, the mountains, rivers, the contours which mark off creeks and valleys, the temperature and the climate, the smells and colours of the land he or she cherishes. A person may be said to have his or her roots in such a place. But this love of the homeland – the patriotic fervour – must be distinguished from nationalism. Whether nomadic pastoralist or primitive settler-farmer, simple country folk, suburbanite or 'yuppie', social man and woman must have always held fond sentiments about his or her immediate environment. Part of the great and renewable strength of nationalism, therefore, has been its ability to press-gang patriotism into active service. It is difficult, of course, to dislodge patriotism from nationalism now.[4] The identity of one is swallowed in the all-embracing arm of the other. This sometimes helps to protect many forms of nationalism, which may be otherwise unpalatable, from unreserved attack, because of the respect people everywhere have for love of the land of birth or adoption. In such situations it may be asserted that we and indeed most reasonable men and women, irrespective of where we situate ourselves on the political spectrum, would be loathe to condemn nationalism firmly, out of fear that we might thereby be condemning patriotism. If the two are separated – as indeed they ought to be – then, it is perfectly possible to display patriotism without hate or rejection of the 'other'.[5]

Finally, it is important to make distinctions in this very slippery field because we need to be constantly reminded of the necessary critical perspective on the elusive set of social and political behaviour we regard as expressions of nationalism. For example, such has been the success of nationalism in the modern world that, as Gellner puts it,

> A man must have a nationality as he must have a nose and two ears; a deficiency in any of these particulars is not inconceivable and does from time to time occur, but only as a result of some disaster, and it is itself a disaster of a kind.

> (Gellner, 1983, p. 6)

The possession of something called *nationality* – a resource which is some-times converted into a commodity – is now perceived as a necessary part of the definition of a person and is widely assumed to be inextricably interwoven into the individual's personality. This is no mean success of a modern credo and whether we are impressed, supportive, critical or even hostile to its cause, we have to admit this glaring fact.

Smith seems blinded by this success. His position appears to be that because nationalism has been successful and the rationalist's dream of a world governed by universalistic principles has not been realized, then, the former is to be preferred to the latter. His argument seems to rest on the following premises: ethnic awareness has always been part of human communities; what-ever has always been with us has a greater claim to authenticity and truth than whatever has been recently fashioned as a result of human reason. Ethnic consciousness and organization are, therefore, to be preferred to any alternative perception of organization of human communities.

Patterson, on the other hand, is not taken in by nationalism's universal suc-cess. He does not wish to succumb to the lore of the ethnic or communal option. His stance is that the development of nationalism in the modern world is a fall-back on reactionary ideas and forms of social organization. In his empirical case-studies of the Chinese in the English-speaking Caribbean, Patterson attempts to demonstrate how people may use ethnicity to their economic advantage and, equally, may abandon this kind of identity when it is to their economic advantage to do so. Patterson's basic plea is for a return to, or a reassertion of, the Stoic tradition of universalism and the rejection of ethnic particularism or chauvinism.

The choice may not be as easy as Patterson appears to think. Indeed, it may be particularly difficult in circumstances where ethnic or racial minorities live constantly under a dual injunction to respect the democratic majority and at the same time to keep within their own cultural enclosures (Dench, 1986). Posing the issue in this way provides a convenient occasion for turning from the broad distinction between nationalism and ethnicity to look a little more closely at the more precise question of the relations between national majorities and minorities. In the last section of this chapter I return to some of the points raised above, with the general view of relating the two sets of issues with which I am concerned here, namely, the relationship between nationalism and ethnicity, and the relations between national majorities and ethnic minorities.

National majorities and ethnic minorities

The problem of the relationship between national majorities and ethnic minorities is one of the many ways in which the larger and more general prob-lem of ethnicity and nationalism confronts contemporary societies everywhere.

It seems almost inevitable that this relationship must be one of profound inequality and it therefore raises fundamental questions for all kinds of communities in the developed and underdeveloped parts of the modern world, irrespective of their socio-economic and politico-ideological orientations.

The fundamental reason for this may be what Dench sees, not without justice, as the hypocrisy of the national majority which makes conflicting behavioural demands on minorities (Dench, 1986). National majorities require minorities to adhere to a national consensus, but on the other hand the same majority treats the ethnic minority differently from itself. The result is a situation as contradictory as the demands. A tension emerges between the pull towards communalism and the exhortation to integrate. Dench's solution is to give way to the temptation of communalism, and in this respect his position is much the same as that of Smith, which was outlined earlier.

Several considerations arise from these apparently realistic but all the same depressing observations of contemporary societies, nearly all of which have national majorities and ethnic minorities (Nielsson, 1985). I want to look very briefly at some of Dench's not uncontentious propositions and prescriptions within the overall context of the question of the communal option which both Dench and Smith, in their different ways, ask us to adopt as a realistic response to the crisis of the most sovereign association.

One pertinent question raised by Dench is whether ethnic minorities in liberal societies are ever in a position successfully to change their relationship with the national majority by surmounting social barriers, reducing injustice and promoting overall equality beneficial to themselves. In other words, is it possible for minorities in liberal societies to pressure the national majority to live up to the universalistic principles it preaches and thereby to come to share in the equality individuals within the majority society enjoy and are able to take for granted? The point could be expressed in another way: with respect to Britain, will people of West Indian or Asian backgrounds ever come to be regarded by the majority, longer established, white population as equals in those areas of life which matter?

Dench's answer is that this is unlikely for at least two reasons. First, whilst the majority population's behaviour is determined by communalist concerns, these are camouflaged by the universalistic principles it preaches. The most important of these is the injunction to uphold a national consensus which, in reality, amounts to nothing more than the communalism of the majority population. This is not called communalism, however, because whatever the values preached, they are the values of the demographic majority. Where this majority is also the *native* population, as in the United Kingdom, it may be assumed that if Dench is correct – and there is no reason to believe that he is not – then the majority's communalism can be very effectively concealed. Where the majority is not a native but a settler population, as in Australia, the 'communalism' of the majority population may be less well concealed and a more confused situation may obtain (Yuval-Davies, 1986).

Second, the elite in the majority society is likely to emphasize consensus and universalism at the national level because this gains the state/nation kudos in the international community. At the same time, however, the elite can depend on the majority population to control the minority through the insistence on supra-ethnic, national unity. The elite, Dench argues, loses nothing by this because the minority itself will support the majority population's credo of national unity and national norms in the hope that adherence to these will protect it. In the end, the net beneficiary of the situation is the elite. Fundamental structural and ideological factors, therefore, stand in the way of minorities being able ever to change the relationship between themselves and national majorities in the liberal, open societies of the West.

Dench invites us to explore with him some fascinating instances of how minority leaders have tried to surmount barriers set by majorities against any meaningful integration. These include interesting analyses of Canada's Pierre Trudeau and his handling of the French/Quebecois question; of the Irish Catholic John F. Kennedy and the question of civil rights in the USA; of the Georgian Joseph Stalin who completed the (tzarist) policy of Russification under the Soviet banner; of Benjamin Disraeli, the converted Jew, who laid the cornerstones for pre-Thatcherite popular Toryism in England.

Dench makes a number of important observations from these efforts by minority political leaders. First, these examples demonstrate how the exception simply proves the rule. The election of Kennedy to the presidency made non-Catholic white Americans proud of their proclaimed liberalism but the hopes he kindled for black Americans could only be realized by a son of the South, Lyndon Johnson, who was trusted by his fellow Southerners. Johnson was therefore able to negotiate the Civil Rights Act through congress in 1964 whereas it is doubtful whether Kennedy would have been successful on this front. The exceptional individual from the ethnic minority is successful, however, precisely because he draws upon the loyalty of his own ethnic community as well as paying lip service to the universalism which the majority society hypocritically preaches.[6] Failures which outrage the national or international communities (such as Stalin's atrocities) are blamed on the individual and the causes are traced to his background. Success of his policies, on the other hand, points to the magnanimity of the majority population and thereby vindicates its proclaimed universalism.

The main response, however, of minorities to majority domination is communalism. This tends to commit the minority to a policy of withdrawal from the majority society. The minority becomes, sensibly in Dench's view, sceptical of professions of universal norms by the majority. This response is sometimes coupled with an acquiescence to majority domination particularly in some prestigious or lucrative areas of social, economic or political life which the majority population considers to be its own preserve. Under majoritarian pressure, the minority, with a view to its own best interest, will agree to keep its head below the parapet.

Dench gives two examples from contemporary British society which are at the very heart of much of the discussion over race or ethnicity in Britain. He argues that Asians tend to accommodate themselves to, and take advantage of, the education system in its present form and therefore do well at school. Dench appears to be saying that Asians do not participate in the politics of protest but take as given the majority's domination in important areas of British society. West Indians, on the other hand, are confrontational, and therefore expect speedy reform of a system which will not change overnight. This point has now gained a degree of respectability in academic circles (Rex, 1979; Modood, 1988). And in this respect it is interesting to observe that the dangerously biased vocabulary of journalists and ideologues is being incorporated into academic discourse. The word *confrontation* is now generally used to describe the efforts of people to *resist* certain impediments to their lives, and the impression that groups of people (in this case, West Indians) set out to disturb the peace is being conveyed as the proper interpretation of their situation and any action in which they may engage.

Whilst the Asian response in Britain corresponds to Dench's prescription of a 'quiet clientship role' for ethnic minorities, the West Indian response corresponds to an unacceptable utopian path. Similarly, whilst the former leads to community (and presumably personal) satisfaction, fulfilment and success, the latter leads into the cul-de-sac of frustrated expectations. Further along the road the West Indian's cry of protest is transformed into an inbred, natural predisposition to disrespect authority. But, as we shall see later, it is not possible to reconcile this view with the relative patience of West Indians over social injustice and the willingness to adapt to majority mores and practices.

Dench is not short on advice to the academic community. He argues that theorists betray a tendency to encourage what he sees as a *confrontational* approach to overcoming the problem of ethnic minority status, rather than the more realistic 'minimal', 'accommodationist', or 'quiet clientship role' of which the Asian response in Britain is exemplary. His main concern here is that theorists must come to recognize that, contrary to what liberal proclamations may lead us to believe, what he calls 'utopian' prescriptions have no place even in the 'open' society. There is a need, therefore, to try to alleviate, cushion or lessen the pressure of rejection, inequality and injustice. Dench is careful to stress that he is not trying to present the rightist view of some commentators who raise fundamental objections to the demands of militant ethnic minority groups.

This is a just position for a theorist to adopt and to try to persuade those of us who are in the business of 'race relations' in Britain to take seriously. I for one readily accept that academics and intellectuals need to look at these matters with less populist zeal or less commitment to particular scenarios, and to be more concerned with the need to offer realistic and dispassionate analyses of the relationship between majority and ethnic minority populations. I do not, therefore, doubt Dench's sincerity and conviction, but, as Billy Graham used to be fond of saying, a sinner can be 'sincerely wrong'. And there are several reasons why I feel that, although Dench is not at all a sinner, he is sincere but wrong.

First, his outline is something of an oversimplification of the relationship between majorities and minorities in today's world. The differential perception and histories, for example, which exist between the majority white population of these British islands and the Asian minorities, on the one hand, and on the other, between the majority and the Afro-Caribbean population, are quite different. The lumping together of Asians and West Indians in Britain by academics and activists does not significantly demolish these differences. There are two important points that arise from this which I wish to comment upon.

It is widely acknowledged that members of these 'communities' are gener-ally treated differently by important private and public institutions, leaders and groups. The banker, it is believed, is more likely to treat the Asian favourably than the West Indian Afro-Caribbean person when a loan is applied for with respect to a business enterprise; the police officer is more likely to brutalize the latter than the former, whilst members of various fascist groups are more likely to attack the supposedly meek Asian on the street than the West Indian. The petty criminality of the youth of West Indian background is more likely to attract the attention of the media, academics and commentators generally than are the dishonest economic activities of some Asian businessmen. With regard to crime this differential treatment reflects the relative tolerance of society towards middle-class crimes and its abhorrence of working-class crimes. The class dimension of prejudice is therefore sometimes mirrored in the differential racial treatment to which African and Asian minorities are frequently sub-jected. There are, of course, plenty of other examples of the white majority's differential treatment of ethnic minorities.

This difference in attitudes towards Asians and West Indians is not signifi-cantly determined by the behaviour of either group – a point Dench recognizes with respect to the Maltese population in Britain. Of far greater importance than minority group behaviour are the *expectations* of the majority population. These not only condition the majority but, with time, also condition the minorities themselves into behaving in certain ways. Whether it is the com-pliant Jew in nazi Germany, or the African-American in the *ante bellum* Southern states of the USA, or the sojourn of black people in the West as a whole, the resultant stereotypical behaviour of the oppressed is nearly always, predictably, the same.

Moreover, the carelessness with which we sometimes aggregate the experiences of minorities in the 'open', liberal society in the West also tends to hide the very important *conduit* role of the majority white population. By this I mean to say that it is with the majority population that minorities establish social relationships rather than between minorities.

In Britain, for example, members of ethnic minorities develop important social relationships with people in the majority white population, but these are rarely established between members from the ethnic minorities themselves. Asians from East Africa and the Indian sub-continent marry whites, and Afro-West Indians marry native whites from the majority indigenous population. It is a social oddity, however, for members of these two minority groups to intermarry. White youths share in much of the popular music culture being developed by West Indians, and members from both communities relate to a popular mass culture expressed through sports and music to which they both contribute. The proximity of West Indian culture to the dominant white culture makes it possible for the majority population, particularly young and working-class people, to have much in common despite what may be described as widespread white middle-class animosity towards West Indians. On the other hand, the cultural distance between the majority white population and the Asian communities appears to attract an appreciable middle and upper class or (as Dench would say) elite respect and awe. With regard to popular culture, however, only cuisine appears to link the majority popular mass and Asian communities.

Difference is nonetheless a crucial resource for the Asian communities, not merely in the sense of maintaining an identity in an alien culture, but also in the sense that they do not appear to pose a threat to the elites of the majority population. It is, therefore, not surprising that it is mainly elites in, for example, academic institutions, public bodies and economic enterprises who give almost unqualified support to the artificial preservation of *difference*. There are, however, some crippling weaknesses in the argument that *difference* will promote social peace because Asians keep their heads low and do not upset the majority white population. In the first place, the Asian businessman's ability to compete in the area of the economy traditionally occupied by the native petite bourgeoisie (such as small shopkeepers) has indeed given rise to hostility against members of the Asian community. This is, of course, far from Dench's *sensible* minority keeping a safe distance from areas of activity that members of the majority population may see as their preserve. The strident demands by militant Muslims for separate schools for their children, particularly their daughters, the burning of Salman Rushdie's *Satanic Verses*, the support of the late Ayatollah Khomeini's *fatwa* calling for the murder of the author, and similar occurrences, do not confirm Dench's accommodation thesis.

In their prescription of the communal option for Britain many writers seem not to take into account the fact that the close proximity of West Indian and majority cultures is a potentially vast resource which could be tapped by Afro-Caribbean politicians if they were to mobilize ethnicity in the ways being encouraged by Dench. The paradox of this situation is that on the whole, people of West Indian background in Britain no longer seem aware of the fact of cultural proximity. Like other minorities, they appear determined to create an ethnic community which is in every way distinct from the majority population; that is, a community based on *difference*. But it is arguably the case that West Indian *similarity* to the majority population is at least a resource of equal strength as West Indian *difference* from the majority.

Apart from a differential colonial experience and the fact of being human beings, the single most important commonality that exists between Asian and Afro-Caribbean communities in Britain is that of racism. But this too is a differential experience, as I indicated earlier. This essentially negative experience places members of both minorities on a common ground which sometimes encourages political alliances. So far, however, this has remained a political relationship and it is in the nature of things that such relationships are merely temporary. For example, if immigration, which continues to be a major concern for Asians, ceases to be a political football between the parties, and if class considerations were to become more important than colour discrimination, then this political understanding between minorities is likely to disappear. Moreover, the assertion of cultural difference and preservation as the central issue of contestation is likely to undermine this political alliance. Each 'racial' minority may also come to seize upon what may appear to be immediate benefits from exploiting its own so-called 'racial advantage' or, indeed, 'racial disadvantage', differentially imposed by powerful elements in the white majority.

These are some of the complications in the majority/minority relationship which escape Dench's framework. And there are reasons for this. Dench's recognition of only homogeneous, undifferentiated, groupings is reflective of a far wider view amongst many commentators on race relations in Britain. Minorities, elites and majority populations are all perceived in this simplistic, undifferentiated fashion. Dench insufficiently appreciates that there are classes, religious affiliations, gender or age groupings with interlinkages which undermine the simple distinction of national majority and national or ethnic minority. Where these are mentioned, it is with a view to showing how they serve to hide what appears for Dench to be the fundamental divide in contemporary societies, namely, national majorities and minorities. The scenario he presents comes close to the apocalypse of Ronald Segal in which a race war on a world scale seemed imminent in the 1960s (Segal, 1967). Sadly, it is also difficult to step aside from the almost inevitable conclusion that arises from Dench's work, namely that it is best for the world's peoples to find their 'own kinds' and settle exclusively with them. How this may be achieved will always be a mystery.

The example of Dench's elite will serve to illustrate this point. Surely it does not make much sense to speak of the elite of a national majority as if it were a single, homogeneous social unit with identical interests. If it is admitted that there may be conflicting interests within an elite and that there may therefore be several elites in the majority population, then it must be reasonable to expect differential treatment of, or perspectives on, the minorities. Similarly, elites in the minority population or populations are likely to have different interests. The political result is likely to be several kinds of elite alliances. Such complexities provide some space for a variety of actions on the part of both majority as well as minority populations even where the conditions are as sharply defined as Dench wants us to believe.

My second main reason for questioning Dench's framework is that its treatment of the majority/minority national relationship ignores the major areas of confrontation in the post-World War Two world. It is, of course, true that his concern is with what he calls the 'open' society. But, quite unconsciously, he seems to assume that the 'open' and liberal society is to be found only in the white majority world of North West Europe and North America. Apart from this inexcusable error – after all, no academic can be allowed to enjoy the right to be as ignorant as it was once acceptable and convenient to be – there are two important points to be borne in mind here.

First, the experiences of minorities in the white and non-white worlds must be reversed if we are to understand the complex situation of the contemporary world with regard to majorities and minorities. Where whites are in the majority and non-whites in the minority the situation is one in which the minorities are dominated. Where, however, whites are in the minority and non-whites are in the majority the economic and social dominance of minorities over majorities pertains. This was, of course, the general situation throughout the pre-World War Two colonial world. Political independence for the states of Africa, Asia and the Caribbean has served to hide much of the ethnic or racial dimension of this inequitable relationship. Colonialism, like feudalism, makes no attempt to hide naked domination; post-colonial imperialism does, chiefly by operating from behind the public scene, in economic, not obvious military or even political, institutions and relationships.

There is at least one other situation which must be considered in any comprehensive treatment of the relationship between national majorities and minorities. This is where the host society is in a minority to the recently settled ethnic majority. Recent developments in Fiji provide us with both a topical and a fascinating example of this kind of socio-political situation. In both May and September 1987, the military under Colonel Rabuka felt compelled to assume power on behalf of the indigenous ethnic *minority* against the recently settled Indian *majority* population. In this situation the new majority is not itself the military conqueror but has grown and prospered under the aegis of the colonial power. The Fiji situation is therefore interesting because the indigenous population has not been effectively wiped out of existence, as occurred in other parts of the world since the age of European exploration and settlement. Here the now reluctant *host* community is still very much alive but is presently the minority to the majority, recently *immigrant*, population. The complex set of problems thrown up by the Fiji situation does not fit easily into a simple framework of homogeneous national majorities and homogeneous minorities. Of course, this applies also, to one degree or another, to alternative models which have sought to explain the relations between majorities and minorities.

Finally, whilst Dench's analysis is a welcome caution to those who too readily offer idealistic solutions to complex problems in the field of 'race relations', his analysis too cavalierly dismisses whatever merit liberal humanitarianism may have with respect to the survival of ethnic minorities. I would argue, contrary to Dench, that the survival of minorities depends, in the circumstances he outlines, very much on minorities and men and women of goodwill in the majority population constantly reminding the majority as well as social, economic and political elites of the universal, liberal, 'open' traditions of which they are (hypocritically or otherwise) proud and to which the progressive elements in the majority society are striving. After all, society is not a once for all given construct which never changes. As Brotz points out in a punching review of Dench's work, the pessimism he expresses with respect to the majority population in a free democracy may be unwarranted (see Brotz, 1988).

The case of the African diaspora is a good example of how a highly visible but economically weak people can creatively forge political alliances with other minorities, as well as with members of the majority population, for its survival. The firm hold on the liberal persuasion that is boldly stated in the abolitionist motto – 'Am I not a man and a brother too?' – summarizes a perspective of the human condition which seems to transcend communalism. This perception is that of all people being able to embrace the politics of protest where necessary in order to fashion a better world for all groups. This may be utopian; it may be a dream. But where has any progress been made without there first having been a dream? Indeed, it may be argued that if the voice of protest which West Indians in Britain represent was to be silenced, then Dench's Asian communities whose educated sons and daughters reap some of the benefits of protests would be amongst the people most immediately affected.

In other words, it may be hypothesized that if a political economist were to take a dispassionate look at the British situation in the narrowness that too often informs current race relations studies and the coverage of events by the media, he or she would conclude that in terms of contributions to *society as a whole* the West Indian makes a disproportionately large one. West Indian contribution to music, literature, sport, theatre and politics is rarely commented upon as a contribution to the development of the greater whole, the British community in a general sense. Sometimes even the symbolic values of these attainments are denied the West Indian communities. My suspicion is that these aspects of the question are not taken into account because any dispassionate assessment would reveal that individuals in the theatre, music, sport and so forth provide very many individuals in the majority white community with more than a good living. It is tempting, therefore, to suggest that there is a silent understanding in many circles that we should speak of contributions being made to society as a whole by specific groups but 'contribution' is assumed in this context to indicate, solely, the ability to seize an opportunity. It would seem to me that this is so because of the competition between different races and ethnic groups which is being unleashed in the post-imperial era, particularly as the experience of nazism and fascism fades.

I find this exercise of comparing groups – of people of African and sub-continental backgrounds in Britain – to be distasteful and it is ultimately damaging. But it has to be faced because it is constantly being made either directly or indirectly in nearly all areas of British life. The comparisons I have unhappily drawn here are not made in the spirit of one group scoring against the other's weakness but, rather, to support my contention that these comparisons may be highly dangerous and may bode ill for good relations between non-white minorities in post-imperial Britain.

But, of course, this situation is not unconnected to relationships of power. The contestation involved is to do with access to the soul or sympathy of important social elements in the majority population on the part of minorities, as well as their sense of security. On the part of the majority itself, the contestation is to do with gaining the support of one or the other of the main non-white minorities. A victory scored on this front ensures control. Outcomes can be interesting: West Indians whose culture derives largely from Britain achieve something of a neutrality, at the very least, on the part of a majority working class weary of its own traditions of protest and small elements of the intelligentsia that may be knowledgeable about the Caribbean or are inclined to abhor the communal option; Asian exclusivity may gain the sympathy of elements of a weary majority middle class concerned about its comforts and happy to have a new social element to maintain the shops and other services, as well as members of the intelligentsia who perceive the communal option as being an endless resource. The willingness to be happy with the one and unhappy with the other may have to do with a deep-rooted desire to know and predict behaviour on the part of groups that control the life-chances of others.

In other words, there may be something to the view expressed by some West Indians that whilst it is their communities which protest openly against injustice it is Asians and whites who get the jobs created as a result of such protests. There may also be something in the view of several members of these same communities who condemn the West Indian for rocking the boat with his noisy protest while they themselves develop their careers in a world made a little more *tolerant* through the very protest they condemn on *racial* grounds.

There are several reasons why this view of the matter cannot be taken to be the whole truth, but I will mention just one of the most obvious ones. The Asian voice is no more mute in the sounds of protest in Britain than is Afro-Caribbean behaviour unlawful. It is fashionable for Afro-Caribbean people to be portrayed as unlawful, protesting and anti-authority, whilst Asians are seen as the complete opposite. But this is not innocent; nor is it new. Where the two peoples came into contact through the experience of British colonialism it was common to read statements such as the following from the *Report of the West India Royal Commission, 1897*:

> The labouring population of the West Indies is mainly of negro blood, but there is also, in some of the colonies, a strong body of East Indian immigrants, and the descendants of such immigrants. The negro is an efficient labourer, especially when he receives good wages. He is disinclined to continuous labour, extending over a long period of time, and he is often unwilling to work if the wages offered are low, though there may be no prospect of his getting higher wages from any other employer. He is fond of display, open-handed, careless as to the future, ordinarily good humoured, but excitable and difficult to manage, especially in large numbers, when his temper is aroused.
>
> The East Indian immigrant, ordinarily known as the coolie, is not so strong a workman, but he is a steadier and more reliable labourer. He is economical in his habits, fond of saving money, and will turn his hand to anything by which he can improve his position.
>
> (Sadler, 1901, p. 800)

Here the very different historical experiences of two peoples are confused: for indentured labour from India the prospect of land in the West Indies was an attraction; for the African ex-slave the same land represented slavery and degradation. Of course, the situation was more complex than this. But the purpose in referring to these differential experiences is in order to ask whether some of these views are not being reproduced in Britain today, to the detriment of both non-white ethnic minorities, as well as, in the longer view of things, to the detriment of interest of the country as a whole. Whilst the reasons why the media convey these popular images in the ways that they do may be understandable, for academics to accept them as the truth is to fall mightily short of the responsibility of questioning received wisdom. After all, received wisdom carries with it, almost inevitably, much of the misunderstanding, prejudice and ignorance of the past.

No reasonable person who is familiar with 'race relations' matters in Britain, however, would deny that Afro-Caribbean protest has led to at least a general questioning of long-standing assumptions regarding social justice and certain institutions of the state in Britain. This is a credit to the indigenous British white population for having created a framework within which this is at all possible, as well as to those who have dared to carry the protest forward. The many and varied *general* questions raised by the Brixton riots of 1987, and reflected in the *Scarman Report*, illustrate this point well (Lord Scarman, 1987).

A major point of which Dench seems unaware is that minorities faced with the pressures of majority domination stand in a unique position to contribute to the whole and thereby to establish a place for themselves in the national community. After all, the population composition of all societies is constantly changing and Britain is one country which demonstrates this more clearly than most.

In other words, I wish to argue in contradistinction to Dench's main thesis. Far from there being a liberalism which puts great store by universalistic norms, the spokespersons for majority white Britain have a clearly expressed preference for communalism. With respect to state agencies this has come about from two easily identifiable sources. First, from at least the period of the Dual Mandate in Africa, there has been an appreciation in British ruling class thinking of the fact that it is easier to effect control in complex societies by the recognition of what M. G. Smith calls the 'plural society' (Smith, 1974) through the simple mechanism of 'divide and rule'. Second, with its decline in world status, post-imperial Britain has slowly but surely come around to seeing merits in overt nationalism. And in the present age it seems inevitable that this new British nationalism is destined to be part of the world-wide phenomenon of ethnic nationalism. But these are matters for discussion in chapter five.

The communal temptation

There are some important questions that Dench, and others who support his kind of analysis, avoid. Mention of just two of these may suffice here. First, why is it the case that the general message to West Indians in Britain is that their lowly position in society derives from a weak sense of communalism? This is sometimes accompanied by the seemingly benign encouragement for West Indians to stress their ethnicity as being their only, or their most sure way of overcoming racism in the majority population. It may be asked whether the insistence for West Indians to become a more easily recognizable group in terms of residence and location, cultural norms and belief systems, is in fact as benign as it at first sight appears. In other words, West Indians are encouraged to mobilize those aspects of their ethnicity that distinguish them from the majority population. Consistent with this kind of exhortation, which runs the risk of ethnic exclusivity, is the encouragement to Asian groups to keep within the cultural pens all Asians are wrongly believed to want for themselves.

In this regard we may note that West Indians in Britain are not quite as 'non-communal' as is widely assumed, nor are Asian groups quite as 'communal' as we are so often led to believe. Indeed, one point brought out in the discussion over the Rushdie Affair from late 1988 is the fact that, contrary to a widespread view reflected by Dench and several academics, all Asians do not necessarily wish to lock themselves within an arrested sense of ethnic solidarity (see, for example, Ali, 1989). It may be argued that an attempt to construct a new national British identity for all may present many Asians with the opportunity to depart from the communal response to adaptation that they have shown in many of the places where they settled, particularly during the hostile imperial age and which, contrary to a view widespread in Britain, was not a successful strategy to pursue.

The second important set of questions which Dench does not broach is the danger the communal option represents for all in Britain, but particularly minorities. In the majority of cases this option has meant severe punishments for groups that adopt it. In Britain this option may now seem attractive because it offers immediate economic rewards as well as the blessings of leaders at every level of society. What we cannot afford to forget is that this option also holds out the best prospect for the insane butcheries we see, on the television news almost every evening of the week, taking place in other parts of the world where society is organized, not on the basis of common, universal norms (however imperfect these may be), but on the basis of communal affinities. Paradoxically, neither Dench nor those who would support the communal prescription for modern societies see the demands for differential treatment on communal lines as militant and confrontational minority behaviour. On the other hand, however, demands for universal norms to be upheld are readily dismissed as confrontational, as if there are not indeed some social practices which demand confrontation. Whilst protest may help to correct present injustice, it must be obvious that the deliberate construction of communalism in an unjust and potentially racially divided society is a recipe for disaster in the not too distant future.

There is, therefore, a profoundly moral question involved in the discussion of these matters. In the first place, the doctrines of nationalism and communalism implicit in much of the debate around ethnicity implies a moral attitude. If we accept that these forms of organizations are the best for humanity, then we are also wont to argue that they have deep and lasting roots in the distant past. Similarly, if we stand in total opposition to these forms of organizations for humanity, then we can easily be led to argue that precisely because the urge towards communalism or ethnicity was basic to the earliest forms of human societies, it is likely to be less relevant to the complexity of a present which has obviously not been entirely of our making.

The worldwide ethnic revival, particularly since the decline of European colonial empires after the Second World War, has not only gained adherents among the young – the main vehicle of nationalist fervour – but also in academic and intellectual circles. The works of Dench and Smith considered here seek to present the intellectual's commitment to the communal option, and they therefore represent the surrender to what I see as the communal/ethnic temptation. This is likely to be a grave danger for the human community as a whole, but particularly for the very ethnic minorities themselves in whose interests this option is ostensibly advanced.

Patterson's contribution to this debate is, first, the persuasive argument that the demise of universalism in the liberal society is part of a longer contention between the *universal* and the *particular* in Western civilization. The second aspect of his contribution is his stress on the argument that the recent restatement of ethnicity has been due partly to the intellectual and spiritual disillusionment with the record of historical liberalism and humanism from the nineteenth century (see also Agassi, 1984). The great strength of Patterson's analysis is his grasp of the importance of the universal principle which runs through the Western tradition of social, political and ethical thinking. Where Smith stresses the particular, Patterson points to the development of some universal criteria that underpin industrial society. For him the upholding of universal norms is linked to the freedom of the individual to choose and the rebellious disposition and unease of the exile. It is the exile who breaks new ground and is both creative and innovative.

In addition, attention must be paid to the desire for comfort towards which both Dench and Smith point us. In other words, there is a great deal of comfort to be derived from the communal fold or bosom. And this seems to be a fundamental aspect of Dench's exhortation to minorities to embrace communalism instead of any other form of social behaviour. To be fair to both Smith and Dench, their persuasion is humanistic to a degree. It is humanistic insofar as we are called to our individual, particular watering holes. This necessarily narrows the vision. It is also a call that seeks to drown out the genuinely humanistic voice which demands sharing and democratic participation in a secular and tolerant social order.

The position of both Smith and Dench is deeply rooted in the Romantic tradition, which correctly pointed to the error of the sweeping generalizations made by eighteenth-century rationalists about human society. In Smith we hear the harshest voices of the Romantic response to the rationalism of the 'age of man'. Man, in the world of the Romantic, is not so much concerned with the rational as with his feelings about his traditions and customs developed over time. His world extends to his immediate fellows, environment and those who may be readily identified as being close to this community. All others are out-siders and therefore illegitimate – outcasts at worst, at best they belong to their own equally exclusive communities. The communal option, which originated largely from this tradition, presumes that humanity can be legitimately and properly divided into easily recognizable ethnic or racial categories. It seeks to deny that reason can be applied to the construction of communities that transcend our initial instincts or impulses. The communal option encourages us to establish boundaries around our ethnic enclaves and both to interpret as well as to change the world according to the lights of our particular ethnic visions.

Conclusion

What is clearly missing from this picture of the human condition is any 'image' of the possibility of a commonality informing human diversity. There is an absence of a vision of the possibility of us transcending the statal definition of our largest socio-political entity. What there is, however, is an image of a society in which each individual must of necessity belong to one state or another or risk becoming a pariah – the fate of the present-day refugee who must be herded onto boats and kept at sea by a civilized country.[7] The *communal option* to which we are thereby admonished does not even contain the vaguest echo of the universalistic message of the early cultural nationalists such as the German thinkers Herder and Fichte (Hayes, 1931). For all the emphases these gentlemen placed on German culture and the German language as the essential elements of the German nation, they also cherished the hope of a reconciliation between a variety of particular cultures and larger com-munities.[8]

In the specific case of post-imperial Britain, what we are left with is a large, empty social space which ought to be occupied by a shared sense of community that transcends specific differences such as those of culture or religion. But this is an appropriate point at which to turn to the question of the different forms nationalism may take, and the difficulty of classifying this amorphous social force which now tempts us with the communal option.

4

Traditional and ethnic nationalism

Introduction

Two principal propositions regarding nationalism and ethnicity, which arise from the discussion so far, are advanced in this chapter. The first is that the contemporary expression or resurgence of ethnicity, as the preferred form of community existence, marks a decisively new stage in nationalist doctrine and practice. The second proposition is that whilst no single-variable explanation can wholly account for such complex phenomena as nationalism and ethnicity, their re-awakening (with respect to groups with historic homelands in these islands) or awakening (with respect to recently settled groups) in post-imperial Britain is best explained as part of a much wider questioning of the ways in which power is presently distributed, and the manner in which it is exercised.

Two forms of nationalism

What Hans Kohn, the outstanding historian of European nationalism, called the 'age of nationalism' (Kohn, 1961, pp. vii–x) has indeed, in a general sense, come to an end. I would not, however, argue this case on the grounds implied by Kohn – namely, that the war against fascism, which was being fought at the time he was writing these words, would point men and women to the folly which flows from their blind faith in nationalism (see Wolf, 1979). It is not that Hegel's famous aphorism that 'history teaches that history teaches men nothing' does not contain a kernel of truth: it is, rather, simply that the social groups, classes, social elements, cliques and other groups contending over political power at any one place or time will use any means at hand to articulate and promote their immediate cause. Nationalism is one means of achieving an end and for every folly it may have led men to commit, the nationalist can point to several ways in which it can be said to have helped to promote a worthy cause.

As indicated earlier, not all that may be described as ethnicity is necessarily also nationalist. Of course, some phenomena that may be described as nationalist are also ethnic. But it is hardly enlightening to call all nationalist expressions ethnic. At least, these phenomena should not be so totally collapsed that they lose their individual identities. Their doctrines and their respective aims are lost if their identities are not retained. I would stress again that whilst ethnicity may have no claims whatsoever to anything resembling 'national' aspirations, nationalism nearly always sets its sights on achieving the political condition of a recognizable state. This nationalist vision or project entails the possession of territory, control over population and identifiable structures such as government, judiciary, army and police. The nationalist project also involves at least the rudiments of civil society such as religious bodies and schools. Nor is any nationalist project complete without at least the beginnings of an economic structure, including the production and circulation of goods, financial institutions such as banks to regulate the market, and the development and maintenance of infrastructures such as roads, rails, radio and other kinds of mass communications.

Traditionally, nationalism's main project has, therefore, been to effect a society in which political authority (the state) and the nation (the community) are co-terminous. Naturally, these units come in all shapes and sizes; some are landlocked, others are plagued by drought, while others are under constant threat by floods. Some are more viable than others; there are those that are unviable economic units while others are as large as some continents. At the beginning of the present decade 183 political units were said to be in existence, 168 of which were sovereign states and the others dependent territories (Nielsson, 1985, p. 25). The increase in the number of states in the post-World War Two period was, of course, the result of large-scale decolonization in most parts of the world.

There are several interesting idiosyncratic and comparative aspects about these states, but one truly significant point to bear in mind is the disjunction between the aim of the nationalist project and the actuality. There is a remarkable distance between the promise, hope or purpose on the one hand, and the actual historical performance on the other. In general, nationalism has not achieved the congruence of 'nation' and 'state'. Rather, a number of 'nations' have been brought under a single, and more often than not a highly centralized, political authority. It is true, as Acton observed in his celebrated anti-nationalist essay on nationality, that logically nationalism claimed to have 'resolved society into its natural elements' (Acton, 1907, p. 276). Had this claim been true, nationalism would have led, in France, to the 'break up of the country into as many republics as there were communes' (Acton, 1907, p. 277). But having destroyed, as they thought, the holding principles of the *ancien régime*, the revolutionaries could not go the whole way and allow total dismemberment of the community which had historically developed as France. Instead, 'a new principle of unity' (Acton, 1907) was required whereby the totality that was historic France could be held together. The 'notion of an abstract nationality' (Acton, 1907) which emerged was not so abstract (as Acton thought) as to abandon entirely the received notion of a political community; nor could the Revolution have wholeheartedly embraced the naturalistic beliefs of Rousseau (Hayes, 1931; Rousseau, 1954) because this would have involved a decrease, not an increase, in structured political authority. What was achieved was a retention of what had already been in existence prior to the Revolution, as Alexis de Tocqueville was to argue persuasively in the century which followed (de Tocqueville, 1955).

I am suggesting, therefore, that as with all great historical movements, nationalism has very rarely seriously sought to apply some of its own fundamental principles. The combination 'nation-state' has become a universal duo but there are few, if indeed strictly speaking there are any, places where the 'nation-state' exists. In other words, there are remarkably few 'nation-states' anywhere in the world. Nielsson's classification of the world's population according to what he calls nation-group attributes may be useful here (Nielsson, 1985). These he identifies as consisting of states with single nation-group states, one nation-group dominant states, one nation-group dominant states with fragmented minorities, bi-national states, and multinational states. In none of them, however, is there a total congruence of 'nation-group' and 'state', because even his first category is defined as being states in which the 'nation-group' accounts for between 95 and 99.9 per cent of the population.

Japan is sometimes pointed to as an instance where the nation and the state coincide. But there are Ainus and Koreans in Japan; and they are not entirely happy with their lot, denied as they are the rights that the majority of people in Japan enjoy. The Republic of Ireland and Iceland are also sometimes pointed to as examples of the coincidence of the community or collectivity we call the 'nation', and the political *ensemble* of authorities which, after the often vitriolic debates of the years after 1968 (Miliband, 1973, 1977; Poulantzas, 1973; Laclau, 1977), we may be nearly all now willing to call the 'state'. There is no need to quarrel over the possibility of this being so because the argument is not that such coincidence is impossible. The point is simply that it is the *exception*, not the *rule*, for the principal doctrine and purpose of nationalism – the congruence of 'community'/'nation' and 'state' – to be realized.

But this relatively new, and in many ways sophisticated, socio-political community introduced in the eighteenth century and particularly by the French Revolution, stopped short of the realization of the promise of its doctrine and purpose. Indeed, looked at in this way, it is possible to argue that the 'nation-state' has, in *practice*, resembled in some important respects the imperial systems that the new men and women with the new ideas of socio-political organization attempted to replace. The *principle*, however, of nationalism has remained that of attaining a congruence of the social community and the state. This has been true of both bourgeois and socialist/Marxist attempts to define or redefine 'national' boundaries (Zwick, 1983). Whatever the reason or reasons may be, it would appear that two important but contradictory suggestions emerge from this historical failure of nationalism to effect its principal and stated aim and thereby gain its desired legitimacy. Thus, although nationalism has been very successful in reshaping the world it found, as well as having its central tenets widely accepted without too much questioning, its success should not blind us to its historical failure.

First, nationalism's project is part of a wider contestation over political power and in the drive towards realization nationalists will call upon any set of perfectly natural factors to augment their cause. I will return to this point below. A second suggestion is that this failure of nationalism to achieve the coincidence of 'nation' and 'state' may be due in part to the impracticality of such an arrangement. It is difficult to imagine a world organized into states having boundaries drawn exclusively in accordance with whatever people believe distinguishes them from others. In other words, is it practical to think in terms of humanity's largest socio-political community – the 'nation-state' as we have envisioned it since the American and French revolutions of the eighteenth century – being organized around religion or language or 'race'? The question would seem to be particularly relevant today as the world's population becomes increasingly forced to share or to inhabit the same physical space, through economic opportunity, migratory patterns, accident of birth and so forth. Can the old ties of what we call 'race', ethnic affinities, language and the like continue to be stronger than the new bonds forged by industrialism and its attendant secular cultural imperatives? Or, is it the very facts of internationalization and secular society which are forcing groups of people to struggle for political positions around the old shibboleths? These are questions that have been with us for several centuries and are likely to continue for the foreseeable future. But whilst they have remained dormant during the first phases of nationalism, they are being raised in a new and dynamic fashion today by the rising tide of *ethnic* nationalism.

What must be stressed here is this: where *traditional nationalism* stopped short of trying to effectuate the congruence of 'nation' and 'state', *ethnic nationalism* takes over and expresses a desire to press forward. The adoption of this failed mission necessarily implies some fairly drastic changes in the composition and boundaries of any given state, and significantly shifts the basis of political legitimacy. In other words, *ethnic nationalism* amounts to a significant challenge of the present arrangements of state power wherever such a challenge occurs. This new type of nationalism, therefore, poses a threat to

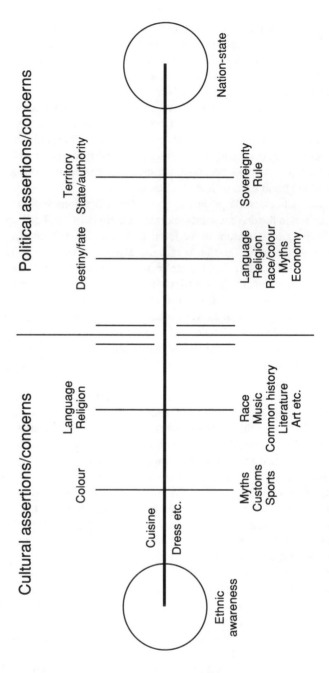

Fig. 4.1 The ethno-nationalist spectrum

all forms of traditional nationalism by seeking to take the nationalist call to its ultimate conclusion.

Ethnic nationalism, therefore, rather paradoxically, undermines the legitimacy of the so-called 'nation-state' by challenging *traditional nationalism* on its own grounds. The *new* nationalism calls for the tenets of the doctrine of the *old* to be strictly applied. It is not the case of nationalism being merely a modern expression of ethnicity as Patterson contends and as Smith implies. Rather, it is more a case of ethnicity, like other forms of early social consciousness and community (such as implied by language, 'race' and patriotism) being incorporated or press-ganged into service by the perversive force of nationalism.

Not all ethnic challenges, however, are necessarily to do with nationalism. Indeed, it is the very distinction between ethnicity and nationalism which reveals something important about the nature of their close relationship. Ethnicity runs along a continuum which displays various forms of cultural assertions or affirmations, to acts of defiance or defence, to more highly charged assertive or even aggressive political struggles, as indicated in Figure 4.1. In most of these situations ethnic nationalism does not necessarily pose a serious threat to the power structures of the traditional 'nation-state'. Indeed, with respect to the liberal-democratic state, some of these challenges may even strengthen the traditional nation-state by providing it with the opportunity to display some degree of toleration (Dench, 1986). It is where and when the cultural marks (for example, ethnic cuisine, dress, life-styles) on the continuum are passed, and the articulation of significant groups of people amounts to the demand for a state to coincide with the presence of these marks that we can say there is a situation of ethnic nationalism. The basis of legitimacy shifts to become self-determination for a given group, however they choose to define their ethnicity. The demand becomes that of the 'perfect' community of the nationalist dream – 'people' or 'nation' or community becomes co-terminous with the political authority, the state.

When such demands are made by groups hitherto silent or which in the past raised largely cultural issues, those in control of the state and who have most to lose from separation, betray the distinction between the historical development of the *nation-state* and its doctrinal claims by over-stressing the sanctity of the *nation* as single, whole and undivided. They appeal in the main to abstract factors which are supposed to have held all groups together all along, and the separatists are seen as the disturbers of the peace who threaten the fortunes and welfare of the people. *Ethnic nationalists* are usually not persuaded by this. And their righteous indignation usually carries more conviction than those of the *traditional nationalists* because the *ethnic nationalists'* claim is for the terms of legitimacy upon which the state rests to be implemented, namely, for the state and the people to be co-terminous. The logic, therefore, of the ethnic nationalist appears to be impeccable because the clarity and justice of his claim are more genuinely articles of the nationalist's first principles or raison d'être.

This new phase of nationalism is becoming everywhere more and more evident everyday. And this has been so in both the long- and well-established so-called 'nation-states' as well as in countries where newly independent and centralized states have emerged only since the decline of European empires. The redefinition of the nationalist project as *ethnic nationalism* has given new life to, and interest in, the search for the 'perfect' or preferred socio-political human community. Not only are new challenges presented, but some old problems which have long been dormant are being ploughed up afresh and forked over as new issues. Ethnic nationalism presents a new kind of agenda for a world increasingly unified by capitalist production, technology, markets and communication. The challenge this involves is thrust not only upon minorities but also onto majorities. For example, post-imperial powers in Europe such as France, Holland and Britain have had to reassess their relationships with each other, sometimes with minorities within their borders, and certainly with the rest of the world, particularly the post-colonial world. With respect to the reassessment of themselves, the majority population in these countries are having to reckon with the possibility of themselves becoming minorities, after 1992, in a more integrated European Community. The prospect appears to be most daunting for Britain (see, for example, Conservative Research Department, *Politics Today*, no. 17, 1988; Bennett *et al.*, 1989, as well as Thatcher, 20 September 1988). This is paradoxical because, from the perspective of the minority-majority complex, at the European level Britain perhaps stands to gain the most because of the widespread use, within the Community as elsewhere, of English as the language of commerce and finance, political discourse, and popular culture and technology.

Some common understandings of the 'nation'

After nearly two centuries of the active use of the word 'nation' to describe discrete communities, we still do not have a universally acceptable definition to employ. We have already noted this with respect to nationalism. But both 'nation' and 'nationalism' are problematic concepts. Whereas, however, it was not necessary to dwell at length on the concept of nationalism, it is of vital importance to do so in the case of nation. There are several sound reasons for this. First, the creation of this, the largest of human communities which demands our loyalty in multiple ways, lies at the very base of the philosophy of nationalism. Second, the nationalism which attempts to justify the existence and/or explain the characteristics of any nation may vary significantly. Moreover, even members of a given nation may also have fairly different understandings of what 'the nation' means. Third, as Rustow reminded us some twenty years ago, the nation 'has come to be accepted as the central political concept of recent times' (Rustow, 1968, p. 7). In the years following Rustow's statement the concept of the 'state' may have replaced that of the 'nation', particularly as this was largely a Marxist debate in which *structures* featured larger than *community*. There is, however, every sign that this has been a mere interregnum in the continuing reign of the concept of nation in political discourse. But this goes beyond the site of political disputation. In the world of rude, practical politics the ever-renewing energy of ethnic and national consciousness bursts out, disrupting established patterns of communities and posing new challenges for whatever forms of state there may be in existence. It is interesting to note that with respect to Britain, much of the debate concerning the present and future community welfare of 'new' ethnic communities is presented or formulated in terms of preservation of the cultural baggages with which they came to Britain. This, however, may have more to do with prevailing notions or definitions, or understandings, of the 'nation' in Britain than with any deep-seated disposition to preserve these baggages. For, whilst militant political nationalism may have escaped the Kingdom, we must not assume that there has been or is an absence of a sense of 'the nation' in Britain.

Of course, we nearly all have some notion of what we mean when we speak or think of 'the nation'. The difficulty is to get to grips with some essential elements which may have universal application. The word 'nation' is itself slippery and is now almost totally dislodged from its medieval origins (Snyder, 1954, ch. 1; Kedourie, 1985, ch. 1) and the word *nationality* is sometimes used instead of *nation* (Acton, 1907).

For example, Kohn argued that nationalities 'come into existence only when certain objective bonds delimit a social group' (Kohn, 1961, p. 3), but he admits that these bonds of themselves are an inadequate definition of the 'nation'. There is also the need, following the French nineteenth-century historian, Renan, for there to be 'a living and active corporate will' (Kohn, 1961, p. 18). And J. S. Mill argued that

> A portion of mankind may be said to constitute a Nationality if they are united amongst themselves by common sympathies, which do not exist between them and any others – which make them cooperate with each other, and desire that it should be government by themselves, or a portion of themselves, exclusively.
>
> (Mill, 1861, p. 295)

In both formulations voluntarism is the active ingredient necessary for the birth, and presumably also the continued existence, of a nation.

This *voluntaristic* perspective has the merit that it avoids any single, essential characteristic as being the definitive criterion of the nation. The stress on voluntarism may, however, be an overstatement but this need not be so. In the Renan/Kohn formulation it would appear that 'nation' is more strictly separated from 'state' than in Mill's formulation. In the former case, therefore, the formation of a nation may indeed be largely an act of will and so may be closer to Toennies' concept of *Gesellschaft*. In Mill's formulation the state and the 'nation' are perceived to be almost one and the same thing; in other words, he has in mind the 'nation-state' duo.

In both cases, however, I would want to qualify this voluntarist definition in the following ways. In the first place, although *will* is involved, it is rarely, if indeed ever, voluntary, either in the case of the formation of the 'nation' or especially in the case of the 'state'. This 'will' or voluntary determination to form a 'nation' must be understood in a very general sense, because there is usually no specific moment when it can be said that a collection of individual persons decide that they will form a nation. This 'will', if such it is, evolves over time and may be closer to Jeremy Bentham's theory of sovereignty. Bentham argued, contrary to the 'rights of man' theorists such as Thomas Paine and the French revolutionaries, that sovereignty is not a right but rather begins with *coercion* and only over time becomes a *disposition* (Parekh, 1973). The formation of the 'nation' and the 'state' may be seen in much the same way as Bentham argued with respect to sovereignty because it is not a 'natural' act but, rather, an act of deliberation.

Second, this *will* is more often than not of a distinctly political nature, which entails force and coercion, determined by an elite with a more or less clear programme of its own. The exercise of this *will* is an exercise of power, as discussed in an earlier chapter. But the creation of this association of groups of people is only part of an elaborate power game. It is necessarily a complex process whereby no one set of players can possibly understand the totality of the game. This is not a cynical view. After all, most games are far from cynical and the stakes demand heated contestation. The fundamental point about this particular game is that it has very little space or tolerance for disinterested spectators. It demands the loyalty and active participation of all.

These characteristics make the game appear deeply rooted in both human nature as well as human society. Thus, some of the notions we have when we 'imagine' what must be for most people a large, distant and impersonal entity (the nation), are said to rest on natural grounds while others are said to have evolved through human history. It may be useful to explore some of the ways in which nationalism forces us to perceive what Benedict Anderson very suggestively calls an 'imagined' community (but what most people have come to regard as a natural collectivity) – the nation. There are at least two important and immediately relevant reasons to do so. First, it should help us better to understand what may be occurring in Britain with respect to the formation and reformation of communal identities. Second, the exercise may point to how

Britain's new minorities are, or may not be, fitting into the emerging 'imagined' British community.

Race

Two relevant natural criteria for defining a nation are 'race' and territory. The racial definition holds that humanity's essential division into separate groups or communities is determined by common lines of blood and descent. The theory is a very simple one and herein lies its attraction. During the heyday of racialist theories, in the late nineteenth century, there were many supposed scientific yardsticks for identifying different races. But as these have been demonstrated to be bogus (Rex, 1986), contemporary racists may be wont to shift their arguments so as to give greater importance to such obvious differences as the colour of a person's skin. Sometimes culture and even quite trivial aspects of social behaviour are pointed to as differences based on something called racial types.

There are plenty of examples during the course of this century of nationalists who have taken this definition of a nation from the psuedo-scientific laboratory into political life, causing havoc and untold misery in the lives of many individuals and large communities. The nazis' mission of cleansing the German nation of abhorrent blood which led to the Jewish holocaust; the perhaps less dramatic but historically and socially far more long lasting, widespread and generalized practice in the Southern United States, until comparatively recently, of lynching black men; the philosophy and practice of apartheid in South Africa, are some of the more obvious examples of political action arising out of a definition and application of the racial definition of the *nation*. The annals of nationalism are of course replete with perhaps less well-known examples of humanity's inhumanity: the treatment of the Armenians by emergent Turkey before the First World War; the systematic liquidation of whole continents of people in Australia and New Zealand and in the Americas, are examples too often forgotten.

While we await important change, the 1990s open with South Africa as the only country in which the state officially declares and upholds racialism as its fundamental social and political philosophy. But it would be difficult to find a state today which does not treat both its citizens and its aliens according to some theory or crude understanding of racial differentiation. Of course, quite often differential treatment is presented in terms of legal and residential rights and obligations or explained in terms of social class. In such situations it is not usually difficult to see through these supposedly objective criteria.

Where there are clear phenotypical differences between majorities and minorities, the latter are likely to be at the mercy of the former. As noted, in colonies the reverse was more often the case, but the domination of the majority by the minority or minorities was firmly supported by unconcealed force. In the case of Fiji, to which we referred in the last chapter, obstacles may be placed before the majority due partly to its own exclusivity, which served this community well in the past but now appears to be an obstacle to its own further advancement. In other words, whilst in the past the Indian community in Fiji was no doubt strengthened by its strong sense of communal affinity, once it became the majority this no longer served its long-term interests. Communal affinity may strengthen a minority in a hostile environment, but a majority has the added responsibility of being fairly open and non-exclusive. In Britain the majority white population is expected to be tolerant and open because this is a moral responsibility in a democratic order. Minorities do not yet carry this responsibility because they are more *victims* than *masters* of the unequally shared environment. Where the relationship, however, changes and former minorities become majorities, they are faced with the same responsibility. In Guyana, as we shall see in a later chapter, although communalism was never allowed to develop, the 1960s witnessed the establishment of a political system which attempts to ensure that political power remains in the hands of the Afro-Guyanese population and the larger Indo-Guyanese population is pushed to the political periphery. It is generally agreed that the fears and hostility between Afro-Guyanese and Indo-Guyanese led to this sorry situation largely because it was believed that the new majoritarianism of the Indo-Guyanese population would jeopardize the security of the Afro-Guyanese population and the other minorities.

Contrary to widespread expectations, then, what we see around us is not the withering away of the legacy of a world contested on supposedly different racial considerations, but sometimes a more sophisticated application of this in many areas of social life. After all, there are several developments which would not have led only the humanitarian to expect that racial differences would become increasingly less significant. First, there has been mass migration, whether forced or voluntary, particularly over the last two centuries, which has thrown the world's population together in a way that has never happened before. Historically this mass movement has been largely *from* Europe to the rest of the world, but since World War Two it has been from other places to Europe. Then, too, there has been the increasingly mixed complexion of humanity – whether on a voluntary or on a forced basis. Kohn correctly observed that 'The great migratory movements of history and the mobility of modern life have led everywhere to an intermingling so that few if any nationalities can at present claim anything approaching common descent' (Kohn, 1961, p. 14). The continued attractiveness of *race*, however, as an important differential factor in human societies must therefore be understood as being more of a *political*, as opposed to a *natural*, preference. This political choice is better understood by political activists (for example, Sivanandan,

1983) than by some analysts (for example, Modood, 1988).[1] If this proposition is correct, then, it follows that the choice of racial affinity is not as obvious as is generally assumed, particularly in view of the fact that biologists have long dismissed the notion that there is a scientific basis for the division of mankind into definite groups called 'races'.

Part of the answer to the question of why 'race' continues to be an attractive definitive factor in human affairs may be precisely because of the momentous changes the world has undergone in recent decades. Outward, obvious differences are likely to be given ever renewed life in a time of momentous change which brings uncertainty. This benign reading would suggest that to maintain such differences is a strength or resource which brings comfort to some. It is this single point that Dench grasps well. The fact that such differences are also, in some circumstances, a source of immediate and crude power to particular groups is the other side of the coin which is too readily ignored by those who are sympathetic to the communal option. Again, the promotion of public discourses of all kinds within a framework which fails to take race as a potentially dangerous definition of the contours of debate, characterizes perceptions in both *black* and *white* Britain.

It is pertinent at this point to consider how territory may also be understood to provide a natural basis for the division of humanity into separate national groups. After all, some little comfort may be derived from the knowledge that not all the ills that are inflicted upon humanity in the name of the nation or nationalism can be brought to the door of racialism.

Territory

The nation is sometimes believed to be synonymous with the territory, the land upon which a group of people live. Frequently, the very name of the country is derived from the name of the people who settled on it and whose characteristics are closely associated with the land. The examples of the land of the Angles (England) or Deutschland (the land of the Germans) come readily to mind.

But territory can be understood in two very distinct ways. It can be taken to mean the physical land mass, such as Jamaica or England. A person born and brought up in a specific place or whose adoption to a new place has been pleasant or memorable in some way or other, comes to love the physical entity, the land, because the affinity to the place may root the individual within the wider cosmology. This can take on a graphic reality. A good example of this is the case of the Jamaican folk practice (taken from West Africa) whereby, when a child is old enough to understand, its umbilical cord, which has been kept hung from the ceiling of a room, is buried close to the home and the sucker of a tree planted on top of it. The 'naval' tree then becomes the responsibility of the child. This simple act links the child, symbolically, with his or her birth-place, to a definite piece of *terra firma*.

Of course, this kind of attachment of the individual to the place of birth or adoption is a perfectly natural human experience which is a crucial aspect of our relationship with our environment. Nationalism, as noted in chapter two, converts this natural attachment, this love of the land of birth, adoption or of the forebears, which we call *patriotism*, into a vital aspect of nationalist doctrine. Thus, a natural, human phenomenon such as patriotism has become the cornerstone of a movement concerned primarily with power. This is no doubt due to the enormous emotional or evocative powers knotted into our feelings about the physical space with which we naturally come to have a strong affinity. In nearly all nationalist statements, therefore, a piece of *terra firma* is focused upon as constituting the mother/fatherland to which a people is said to have belonged from time immemorial. Both time and space become silent, unprotesting, allies of the nationalist cause. Sometimes there is an absence of any continuity of occupation of the land, such as with Israel's claims in Palestine; sometimes a people, for example the Armenians, are so scattered that they are unable to have their claims taken seriously by the nation-states which have emerged in the last century or so; in still other cases, such as amongst Africans outside Africa, groups may have an affinity to the land but dismiss as foolish any real claims to precise territory. At other times political contestation is over excluding newcomers from land long settled by the forebears. In some cases the new settlers destroyed those who welcomed them, or conquered them. Sometimes, as in the case of Israel, the new settlers may resurrect aspects of the destroyed past in order to construct new nationalist myths to serve in an ideological defence of claims to the land.

Where the physical space being claimed is protected, or demarcated by such natural factors as sea, lake, rivers or mountains, the land and the people may indeed appear to be synonymous. And this identification may be reinforced in a number of ways. Common myths (such as the tale of St George and the Dragon or Morte d'Arthur in the case of England) or events (such as the defeat of the Spanish Armada or the Battle of Britain) help to form and renew something of a common bond or personality, filling out what used to be called 'national character'. Usually this 'national character' may include the peculiarities of how a people set about doing things, their social mores, prejudices and so forth. Sometimes these characterizations are largely self-imposed, such as the myth of the ill-organized, muddling-through English at the beginning of a war who become successful in the end (Dummett, 1984, ch. 1). Sometimes these are partly extraneously imposed and may occupy a lowly place in the pantheon of common symbols and myths of a people – but may be taken on board in order to deflect more severe abuse or repression. Crude characterizations of the Irish or the Jew in England may be cases in point.

There are instances in which the nation is believed to have come about, or been formed, by the territory itself. It is not that a people has given its characteristics to the territory, but the reverse. Such, it may be argued, is the case in the Americas where it is the fact of living on a large land mass which first linked together peoples of sometimes vastly different phenotypical and cultural backgrounds. Frederick Turner's famous thesis of geographical determinism in the formation of the American character, which has been amplified by Hollywood, is a good example of the kind of myth which may develop in such circumstances (Turner, 1962).

The second sense in which territory may be understood is where the presence of the state is involved. In this case the state is sometimes believed to have existed prior to the formation of the nation. Kohn believed that the single most important outward, objective, factor in the formation of the nation is indeed the territory. In some respects this resembles Weber's definition of the state as being where authority is exercised continually by an administrative staff which has a monopoly of legitimate force within clearly demarcated territorial boundaries (Weber, 1947, pp. 154ff.). It seems acceptable enough to say that whatever our understanding may be of the community we call 'the nation', it nearly always includes something of the notion of territory.

Where there is no obvious territory in evidence there is usually an immense effort made to *territorialize* the 'nation'. Zionism as a nationalist philosophy during the first part of this century was obviously an attempt to *territorialize* the Jewish faith. It is worth remembering that there was a possibility for zionism to have been territorialized on the borders between Kenya and Uganda (for a discussion, see Humphry and Ward, 1974, ch. 1) before it was realized in Palestine. There are relatively few cases where nationalists without a land on which to locate a state exclusively their own do not include this as part of the package of demands to be recognized by whatever mightier power there may be in the protracted game. It is possible, therefore, to speak of *diasporic nationalism* such as zionism (Dubnow, 1970) and Garveyism (Lewis, 1987). Diaspora nationalists yearn after a homeland which may or may not be realizable. Success depends partly on the strength of a particular group but of far greater significance is the interest of powerful states in the creation of a new state. In this respect the American and British interest in the creation of the state of Israel is a case in point. Conversely, it may be argued, an equally ancient people, the Armenians, have not succeeded in attracting support from the great powers. Armenian claims against Turkey most probably jeopardize, not enhance, US interests in the region. The claims of the Armenians include territory and population presently within the USSR. The Armenian claims may, however, be as strong or stronger than those of the more successful minorities such as the Jews.

Demands for the creation of new states are likely to receive a hearing in the international community where the claim is based on a notion of territorial or historic affinity. Despite the widespread discussion taking place over *race* there is a reticence to accept this as the most or the sole basis for the creation of new states in the international comity of nation*s*-states. Perhaps this has something to do with the defeat of the nazi experiment. Perhaps, also, because of this, *territoriality* has been ostensibly more responsible than race for wars and disruptions of settled communities in many parts of the world in the years since World War Two. And, of course, we do not have to look far for examples of the importance of territorial claims in the present century. The dispossession of Palestinians in the Middle East, the German question in Central and East Europe, the border peoples throughout most of Europe, Asia and Africa, the current tense situation in Central America between the former British colony of Belize and Guatemala and Honduras, disputes between Guyana and Brazil to the south and Venezuela to the north, are some examples of territorial and/or border disputes today, each with a baggage of justifications for its claims and counter claims. *Racial* claims, however, would appear to be more successful where these are made within the broadly accepted framework of established national boundaries. Thus, some democratic claims in Britain and elsewhere today are articulated in terms of racial considerations. Where these do not pose a threat to the sovereignty and territorial integrity of the established nation*s*-state, then, a hearing is frequently guaranteed.

Territorial disputes can frustrate relations even *within* countries as well as *between* countries which share common ideological norms and stand against the rest of the world on many questions of the day. In India, for example, one persistent problem that the Union has faced since independence from Britain in 1947 has been that of borders between the separate states. In a later chapter I shall consider this question more closely with respect to the Punjab. The Soviet Union and China on the one hand and on the other China and Viet Nam oppose each other's policies tenaciously on the international scene, although they have much in common through the sharing of a Marxist political and social ideological outlook. Their quarrels, when all the jargon and wrappings are removed, rest almost entirely on a nationalism based on territoriality.

Many wars have been fought, and unfortunately will be fought, over the question of control with respect to the physical space people inhabit. It seems a truism to say that even if the seeds of a 'nation' are sown on 'alien' soil there is nearly always the intention to transplant these onto a specified piece of land at whatever cost. No longer are there lands – perhaps apart from the Amazon Basin, South Africa, Australia and Palestine – where the more powerful can carry out genocide on a whole people in order to make space for others to settle. Contestation over known quantities of land, therefore, may be likely to become more intense, not less so. As settled and stable as the British population is, there can be little doubt that such contestation has become an important question in British politics. In the case of the oldest settled Britons, Scottish and Welsh nationalisms express a significant sense of territorial belongingness to these islands and so do not, in this specific sense, necessarily contradict English forms of nationalism although this is peculiarly *expansionist* (over the British Isles) rather than *contractive* as the others. The situation in Northern Ireland is, of course, lodged within this problem of territoriality as much as in the religious affinities of the people who live there.

In the case of people without 'homelands' in Britain, areas of settlement in the inner cities may come, with time, to impart a sense of *belonging* to a particular part of the country. These are, of course, likely to change from generation to generation and a kind of *nomadic* sense of territory may emerge. But, overall, the development of a sense of belonging and affinity to specific locales should have positive effects on the communities and may be reflected in such matters as policing, services and education. This is not, however, an invasion forcing the establishment of an Alfredian Danelaw – part of territorial England being occupied by invaders in order to maintain peace. It is, rather, likely to be a *symbolic territorializing* of the country's non-white population.

Religion

Cultural definitions of 'the nation' may vary from the sharing of such common factors as customs and habits, which are supposed to make up what is sometimes called 'national character' and thereby mark off one nation from another, to less vague factors such as language and religion. Perhaps because of the war against fascism, the stress on 'national character' has lost much of its respectability. This is not to say that it is not sometimes called upon to supplement more widely acceptable arguments. But it is true to say that in terms of the cultural arguments in support of a definition of the nation, language and religion generally continue to enjoy pride of place. It is worth noting that commentators from both the Right and the Left in Britain place much emphasis on *culture* as the proper definition of peoplehood (for example, Gilroy, 1987; also, Powell, 1988a). I propose, however, to comment briefly only on religion and language.

In the case of religion the claim seems to be that the sharing of a particular faith is a sufficient basis for the definition of 'the nation'. The oldest and most tenacious example of this is, of course, the Jews and Judaism. While the creation of the state of Israel in 1948 is a clear example of the nation-state claiming to come into existence as a result of the sharing of a common faith, it is only one example of this kind. The formation of the state of Pakistan in 1947 is another example of religion defining 'the nation'. During the post-World War Two years the Middle East has experienced the revival of what is generally called Islamic fundamentalism[2] and part of this has been a tendency to identify 'the Arab nation' with Islam.

There are of course several examples to point to with respect to the political dynamism which religion releases in the faithful even in an age which is supposed to be imbued with the objective spirit of science. The reliance on Islam as a defining national factor, the efforts of Israel to secure Jews from Christian/communist USSR and the remarkable feat of transporting the Fellashas from, again, Christian/communist Ethiopia in December 1985, are examples of how religion, like patriotism, has come to be the servant of nationalism in its quest to establish the community it calls the nation. It is easy enough in Europe to underestimate the importance of religion in the contemporary world if we ignore the religious divide in Northern Ireland and forget that it took several centuries for religion to cease being the essential divide in Britain and continental Europe. In short, the definition of 'the nation' in terms of religion is of as much importance in our contemporary world as it ever was in the less 'enlightened' days of yesteryear. We ignore this raw fact at our peril because the religious understanding of the 'nation' is likely to affect even societies such as the United Kingdom which (Northern Ireland aside) has long neutralized religion and expunged it from the field of active (as opposed to symbolic) politics.

The national British and international crises caused by the late Ayatollah Khomeini's call (*fatwa*) to all good Moslems in February 1989 to kill Salman Rushdie, because of the hurt his *The Satanic Verses* caused to adherents of the faith, constitute the most dramatic recent example of the continuing importance of religion in people's consciousness (see, for example, Weir, 1989; also, Alibhai, 1989). One thing that the Rushdie Affair, which closed 1988, opened 1989 and is likely to continue into the first years of the 1990s, forced us to re-examine, is the relationship between the certainties of a rationalistic secularism and the dogmas of religious intolerance. The ensuing debate brought onto the public agenda questions that were once settled between civil society and the state and their return should serve to remind us of just how fragile 'historic victories' of reason over fanaticism and irrationality can be.

It hardly needs to be said that the claim that religion defines a nation is unsatisfactory. Just as race is not a satisfactory definition of 'nation', nor is religion truly a definition of this large human community. Black Moslems in the US and Libyans have the Islamic faith in common but it would be absurd for them or for us to regard the two groups, separated by so much else, as a 'nation' in the commonsense understandings we have today of the word. Protestants and Catholics in Ireland not only share a common territory but, paradoxically, also a common religion. Nevertheless, the 'national question' in that beautiful island continues to be a bone of major contention – and one largely pivoted on, or symbolized by, the sharing of a common faith. In a later chapter, which examines the question of the Khalistan movement as it affects Sikhs in Britain, I will show how this question of religion in the United

Kingdom is of primary importance in the definition of 'the nation' for some people.

Language

Intellectually, perhaps the most respectable, or at least the most frequently attested, understanding of 'the nation' is that which claims that it is to be recognized by a people's sharing of a common language. This is by far the most widespread claim when it comes to defining 'the nation'. There are several reasons for its healthy longevity and popularity in the nationalist lexicon and propaganda.

First, the social and political contexts out of which this definition of 'the nation' arose in Germany and France were sufficiently powerful to give language a head start over other claims. The point may be expressed another way: language was the first social artifact to be press-ganged into the service of nationalism. Disciplined into this role from the very birth of nationalism, language has been rooted into almost every nationalist claim. Here nationalism benefits from our preference, developed during the revolution in the biological sciences in the last century, to give primacy of place to factors present during the birth or origins of a phenomenon whether it be social or natural.

Second, the claim made for language by the German Romantic thinkers such as Herder, Fichte and Schleirmacher that the language a man speaks shapes his personality, seems to be a force in the longevity of the claim itself. In the contemporary world, the fact that a person grunts or twitches the muscles of his face and can claim that his ancestors have always done so, is enough to signify the necessity of a break in whatever traditions he or she may share with millions of other human beings. Language becomes, in this sense, truly a Tower of Babel. That language may also result in a Pentecostal experience is something to be ashamed of, except in the marketplace where language is seen as a useful artifact in the exchange of goods. It is clear that for many the Babel confusion is to be preferred to the Pentecostal comprehension because a higher premium is placed on the comfort to be derived from an exclusivity than on the potential peace from a genuinely humane culture of sharing.

Third, the force of the claim that language may define a nation seems to rely largely on the fact that language is one of the most easily recognizable human experiences which both unites and divides. This means that it can accommodate or reject; it can be made to include or exclude. And in each such instance there is an abundance of equally justifiable claims which may be readily marshalled by adherents.

It is no wonder that language has played and continues to play a vital role in defining the 'nation'. In post-Renaissance and post-Reformation Europe, the development of territorially-based vernacular languages led to the most obvious identifying factor for a people after the destruction of the continental unity which had been held together by a dead but 'sacred' language – Latin. Anderson grasps and expresses this point remarkably well. Perhaps, however, the reason why language also became such an important and salient weapon in the armoury of the new Protestant and absolutist monarchs of the centralizing states was the very fact that it was language which had been used to control the supposedly faithful during the heyday of the Holy Roman Empire. So, in the rebellion, language had, of necessity, to play an important part. This too has been the case in the decolonized world of the post-World War Two era. In Africa and Asia, in the Pacific islands and sometimes even in the Anglophone Caribbean, the question of language becomes an important question for public policy or debate.

It is not surprising, therefore, that language is the common variable in both Marxist and non-Marxist, sometimes termed bourgeois, definitions of nationalism. Influenced as they were by German philosophy, French politics and British economic thinking, Marx and Engels – but particularly Engels – seem to have been captivated by those German philosophers who placed language at the very centre of their theory or understanding of nationality. Stalin, who was more a follower of Engels than of Marx, also stressed language as the central factor in the definition of the nation when he sought to address the problem for the Bolsheviks (Stalin, 1913; Kedourie, 1970, chs. 24, 25; Petrus, 1971). To appreciate the force and widespread popularity of the linguistic understanding of the nation it is important to understand something of the socio-political context from which it emerged.

In staking out the frontiers of the nation, the French revolutionaries stressed language as the decisive criterion of where the borders of the new Republic should be drawn. This was, of course, particularly important in areas such as the Tyrol and Alsace-Lorraine. In the construction of a national consciousness they were careful to give emphasis to the teaching and speaking of the French language as a crucial aspect of the process. The French state's interest in maintaining a national standard of French is, of course, still very much alive today. But already under the Bourbon absolutist monarchy there had been the development of a distinct French consciousness, and with the demise of the *ancien régime* the revolutionaries were able to build on the inheritance from this period, as de Tocqueville was later to argue. Language was important, therefore, both in the partially spontaneous emergence of a French nation as well as in the deliberate, nationalist, process of consolidating it around a new political authority, the republican state.

It was in Germany, however, that language perhaps first revealed its tremendous potentiality for forging an otherwise dispersed people together. It was here that Herder, Fichte, Schliermacher and others developed the theory that a nation is defined by the language a people speaks. Properly speaking, every people, these German Romantic thinkers held, was blessed with a distinct language of its own. A people, therefore, without a distinct language is not, strictly speaking, a people, a nation, at all (Kohn, 1961; Hayes, 1931). In Fichte's understanding of the nation, peoples with derived languages (such as English and French?) lack continuity between sense-experience and abstract ideas (Kedourie, 1985, p. 66). In Herder's view a man who speaks a language other than his own original tongue leads an artificial life and is, as Kedourie, speaking of Herder's thought, puts it, 'estranged from spontaneous, instinctive sources of his personality' (Kedourie, 1970, p. 64). By this token Afro-Caribbean people in Britain, and African-Americans, are not distinct groups of people at all because they have lost their original languages. However foolish this may seem, the extent to which this view informs much discussion over the conditions of Afro-Caribbean and Asian people in Britain is surprising. For example, the view is frequently expressed that Afro-Caribbean peoples' lack of success and Asian success in Britain is entirely, or at least largely, due to these groups' respective sense of cultural certainty. And language is, of course, a crucial component of general culture. This has tended to engender something of a vacuum in Afro-Caribbean life in Britain. Partly as a result of this perception, many groups from this segment of the population have embarked upon a quest to *find* or *develop* ostensibly distinctive cultural forms and modes of expression. On the other hand, many Asian groups have come to believe that their well-being in Britain depends entirely, or almost entirely, on the degree to which they can maintain their separate cultural identities. But the ethnic adventures upon which these groups are presumed to have embarked are not necessarily in their own best long-term interests nor those of British society as a whole.

But, aside from the broad socio-political context of its origins, how are we to explain the persistence and prominence of language in the definition of 'the nation'?

One plausible explanation is what Anderson alerts us to, namely, that with the collapse of the central pillars of feudal society, little remained for the emerging new social orders to be latched on to. The aristocracy had lost its 'national' legitimacy in most of Europe because it had *internationalized* itself over time through the mediation of the altar and the bedroom. Nor could the church provide a basis for the emerging orders because it was so closely associated with the old, feudal system. What, then, was left as the central holding factor in the emergent orders throughout Europe was the language of the people. This could be said to be truly national in character – something which many people shared amongst themselves and with none other. Throughout fragmenting Christendom, therefore, the vernaculars spoken by fairly distinct collectivities of the common people became the vehicles of mass communication, enhanced by the development of the printed word.

A second reason for the emergence of language as the prime consideration in the demarcation of one nation from another must have been the fact that language is the supremely human mode of communication and, notwithstanding the frequency of discord and war, men and women are naturally highly social and communicative creatures.

There are, however, some obvious flaws with the definition of the nation in terms of the language of a people. First, although people use language to communicate and are proud of this artifact, language of itself is insufficient in capturing what we ordinarily understand by the notion of a 'nation'. For example, one of the most far-reaching effects of European colonialism in Africa, Asia, the settled areas of the Americas and the Caribbean and other parts of the world has been the legacy of language each imperial power left behind. English, Spanish, Portuguese and French (if we put aside Chinese and a number of other Asian languages such as Bengali) are by far the most widely spoken languages as a result of colonialism and imperialism in the different regions of the world over the last three or four centuries. This legacy has helped to link peoples at different points of the globe, facilitating rapid communication, commerce, the transfer of technology and so forth.

Unfortunately, however, the sharing of a common language such as English has not helped to break down long-established barriers between groups who consider themselves to be different nations. Indeed, despite the sharing of a common language, the joke that Britain and the USA are two countries separated not so much by the Atlantic but by a common language, points to an important half-truth. Even with the spread of general education and a sense of shared values, the fact of speaking English has not been sufficient to limit the damage some politicians are capable of inflicting on the ideals of the Commonwealth. In short, the sharing of a common language has never been a sufficient force to foster what would ordinarily be regarded as a common purpose. This is true not only where people are divided by natural barriers such as oceans; it is so even in cases where people live in peace next door to each other (such as Canada and the USA, or the Anglophone Caribbean countries).

Second, even where communities may regard themselves as forming nations, far from there being a language which they share, they often lack such a language. The stress on language as the principal determinant of a nation often comes after the nationalist realization of self-determination, and the development of the national language comes after the existence of the national state. This was true in Norway. It is the present situation in many post-colonial states in Africa. In some situations a dying language may be recovered, such as modern Hebrew.

There is also the situation where nationalists may reconstruct basic aspects of a language or encourage its development through state patronage. A good example is that of nationalist Turkey abandoning the Arabic alphabet so as to reconstruct Turkish. One remarkable current example is the active support and encouragement given in Tanzania to the development of Kiswahili as the national language. Another example of options available to nationalists is where the very national language has to be the language of the former colonial power. English in a large multi-national state such as Nigeria is a good example of this situation. The same is true for the even more complex situation in India, where as the 1990s open militant Hindus are insisting that Hindhi should replace English as the national language. In the case of Mozambique, the political directorate decided in the 1970s to make two European languages the first and second languages in the country (Portuguese and English respectively). The variety of approaches to the language question seems endless.

What is evident in all these circumstances is not so much that language has any clearly demarcated position in defining a nation. Language is in no way self-evidently, obviously, a definition of a nation. In the nationalist enterprise its role is extraneously imposed. Language, like patriotism, religion, similarities and dissimilarities between people, has, with these, been forced into active service for and by nationalism. The claims made for them, or on their behalf, today are generated partly by the search for identity in an increasingly hostile, regulated and impersonal world. But it would seem to me that the motor that galvanizes these into a powerful force is the search for political power. This is demonstrated by the implicit or explicit desire on the part of nearly all nationalists to achieve the congruence of the 'nation' and the 'state'.

Despite these fairly clear shortcomings, it cannot be denied that something men and women in modern societies choose to call 'race', the land, religion and language are likely to be foremost in our minds when we imagine the large socio-political community we call 'the nation'. The combination of these will differ from place to place but once fixed in the popular imagination, both within a given 'national' community and without, it becomes difficult to construct alternative images of that community. For example, a person born of, say Pakistani parents in Dorset, who is subjected to much the same socialization process as any white English person, may be laughed at in Lahore if he or she claims to be British – even though the presumed recognition is based largely on colour. In some parts of the West Indies the same experience may await a similar person of West Indian parentage. In other words, a brown or a black British person is not yet part of the widespread and acceptable image, or landscape, of post-imperial Britain and the British by either the native population or the international community.

With respect to political life it does not matter so very much whether these understandings of 'the nation' are valid or invalid. What is of far greater significance is whether they are what we have in mind when we think of the 'nation', form attitudes towards others or take action to promote or defend particular interests of the 'national' community.

Classifying nationalism

Traditional nationalism has been variously classified according to broad historical periods, geographical regions and what some writers consider to be the main or essential characteristics of the phenomenon. These are, of course, sometimes combined. Here I wish to look very briefly at some of these classifications in order to see the extent to which they are relevant to the distinction between *traditional* and *ethnic* nationalisms.

How a writer may classify nationalism depends largely on the definition of the subject, and the moral attitude he or she brings to bear on it. It is not an exaggeration to say that the most stimulating works on the subject tend to be of an anti-nationalist persuasion. This may be due to several factors. For example, the ascendancy of the fascists and nazis in Italy and Germany, respectively, utterly destroyed the hope that the First World War had been the war to end all wars. Scholars interested in the phenomenon of nationalism were able to observe its renewed force and the misery it caused within Europe. In these circumstances the largely critical, oppositional perspective of that generation of scholars is perfectly understandable. They sought to understand nationalism, not with the view that they might assist its project but with the hope that it may come to an end. It was from this humanist background that Kohn said of the critical analysis of nationalism:

> Others will carry on, amplify and improve; future generations may view the age of nationalism in a different light. Their viewpoint will be determined by the great war in the midst of which this volume is being written, a war which is a consequence and climax of the age of nationalism and which can be seen as a struggle for its meaning.
>
> (Kohn, 1961, p. x)

It is hardly necessary to comment here on the variety of classifications there are and I will restrict myself to just three examples.

I commence with Louis Snyder's highly suggestive classification. Combining historical account with what he considered to be the essential characteristics of nationalism, Snyder outlined four broad periods. The first of these runs from 1815, the end of the Napoleonic Wars, to 1871, the end of the Franco-Prussian War and the completion of the Bismarckian unification of Germany. He called this *integrative nationalism*. The second period is marked by *disruptive nationalism* and runs from 1871 to 1890 – the end of Bismarck's helmsmanship in Germany. In this period the peoples of the multi-national empires in Europe became restless and sought their independence. During the first forty-five years of the twentieth century nationalism developed into its *aggressive* phase. Snyder's last phase of nationalism is rather non-analytical; it is described simply as *contemporary nationalism* (Snyder, 1954).

This classification has the merit of pointing to some of the main features of nationalism and locating them within specific historical periods, movements and events. If we accept that these are some of the main characteristics of nationalism then they could help us to understand something of its versatility and its capacity for adapting to different circumstances.

Snyder's schema is unhelpful, however, in at least one important respect. Whilst it is possible to see nationalism as an integrative, aggressive, and disruptive force in modern history and in contemporary societies, I am not sure that we can so neatly mark off historical periods in which one or the other of these characteristics clearly predominated. Rather, if anything, they tend to go in combination. The same nationalist movement or period may move from one of these phases to the next or, alternatively, intertwine all these characteristics into an intricate web. Thus, at any one historical moment since the late eighteenth century, nationalism may have exhibited all three characteristics simultaneously. After all, nationalism is nearly always disruptive, more often than not aggressive and not infrequently achieves the desired end of effecting a new politico-social integration around rearranged or new centres of power.

My second example is Minogue's classification of nationalism according to the stages through which a specific nationalist movement or experience may pass (Minogue, 1967). The first stage is what he calls 'stirrings' – where people become aware of themselves as being oppressed by foreigners, which then leads to a radical rediscovery of the past. The second stage is the 'struggle' – the very centrepiece, for Minogue, of nationalism. The final stage is the process of consolidation, which involves a shift in focus away from political to economic concerns.

Whilst Snyder's classification concentrates on the broad European experience, Minogue's is more concerned with nationalism in the non-European world of the post-World War Two era. This makes it appear more relevant at first sight, because it was in the colonies that traditional nationalism first received its renewed strength after World War Two and this should not be bypassed as just another example of the expansion of an essentially European experience. We must be ready to see that the spread of nationalism in the non-European worlds of Africa, Asia, the Pacific and the Caribbean, whilst carrying on a tradition largely derived from Europe, has left its own distinctive marks in nationalist annals. For example, nationalism in Africa and Asia has tended to intensify the politicization of all areas of society, and political institutions, such as the party and the presidency, have sought to establish a presence beyond their competence.

Minogue's classification, however, falls short of being adequate on at least two important counts. Attention is too narrowly concentrated on a particular manifestation of nationalism to have widespread application. It is not stated as a model built from the non-colonial world, but if we were to try to apply it to actual historical movements and events, it would appear that the model is derived from experiences such as those of the Thirteen Colonies of North America which developed from a political to an economic nationalism. Second, although Minogue admits that the true course of nationalism never did run smooth (for example, it is not always possible to attain consolidation), it must be noted that economic consolidation, or economic development, is often deliberately sacrificed for the sake of ostensibly firm political control. And political control remains perhaps the single most important concern for the overwhelming majority of politicians in, for example, the vast majority of African post-colonial states (Nellis, 1972; Goulbourne, 1979, 1987).

Kohn's classification is perhaps the simplest, most straightforward and in some ways the most relevant of the three that I consider here. He established a basic distinction between political and cultural forms of nationalism. In his view political nationalism was first experienced in Britain, then in the USA, France and Holland. This was not exclusively political nor economic in emphasis. However, the urge towards greater political democracy and the achievement of economic progress were the main characteristics of this first form of nationalism. Kohn recognizes that these, in turn, were brought about by the increasing strength of the Third Estate in these countries from an earlier period than was the case elsewhere.

Cultural nationalism, on the other hand, whilst again not exclusively cultural, was predominantly so and emerged where the middle classes had not developed or were very weak. Such were the experiences of the German principalities and the Slavs of East Europe. Kohn argues that amongst 'these peoples, at the beginning it was not so much the nation-state as the *volksgeist* and its manifestations in literature and folklore, in the mother tongue, and in its history which became the centre of the attention of nationalism' (Kohn, 1961, p. 4). This cultural assertion developed into political demands and the founding of new 'nation-states' throughout East and Central Europe towards the end of the last century and in the early part of the present one. The circumstances of the birth of these states, Kohn argued, made, however, for a quite different kind of nationalism from that experienced by Britain, the USA and France.

This distinction between political and cultural forms of nationalism has been a highly influential one. Kohn himself made the point that modern expressions of nationalism beyond the Anglo-American and European homelands have taken their cue, not so much from the *political* but from the *cultural* model. Writing in 1954 Snyder argued that the 'Kohn formula has served a generation of historians well, and there have been no significant attempts to alter or modify it' (Snyder, 1954, p. 122). Expectedly, this is no longer as true as it once was. It is, however, true to say that 'the Kohn formula' still echoes in some of the more recent theories which purport to explain the *conditions* of the Third

World. From conservative-liberal development writers (for example, Almond and Powell, 1966; Almond and Coleman, 1960), to radical and neo-Marxist theorists of underdevelopment (for example, Frank, 1969; Amin, 1976; Thomas, 1974); from hard-boiled orthodox Western Marxists (for example, Warren, 1980) to post-World War Two Soviet theorists of the so-called 'non-capitalist path' (for example, Brutents, 1977; Thomas, 1978) runs the familiar theme that perhaps the principal cause for the failure of the efforts of theorists, planners, administrators and politicians to effect development has been the absence of a dynamic middle class. Fanon was the first, however, to popularize this point of view in the post-World War Two period (Fanon, 1963). The absence of a middle class confident and innovative enough to transform political nationalism into economic nationalism in the vast majority of post-colonial states has undoubtedly had some influence on the highly parasitic or bureaucratic state forms that have emerged in many post-colonial societies.

Anyone who attempts to classify an amorphous phenomenon such as nationalism must be aware of the dilemma to be avoided. Classifications can be too general and can so conflate diverse experiences that the specificities that make them interesting and important are lost. The second danger is to over-stretch the essential qualities of a specific experience so that it can account for others elsewhere. Aspects of the classifications by Snyder, Minogue and Kohn are, of course, useful in any attempt to understand nationalism better. On a second reading, however, it would appear that the true value of these attempts is their reflection of the difficulty involved in establishing generally acceptable or applicable classifications. It is enough that they help us to establish points of contrasts, highlight some of the salient features of *traditional* nationalist experience and thereby quite properly remind us of its tremendous dynamism. The real danger is to see classifications as being more than what they are: to see them as establishing lasting and universally applicable categories rather than being a rough and convenient way of highlighting the main characteristics of complex phenomena.

The distinction I have sought to establish between the *traditional* and the *ethnic* forms of nationalism is, therefore, an attempt to highlight the major turn currently taking place in the continuing dynamic career of this perhaps the most powerful of modern social forces. And the premises on which traditional nationalism rested its case have been bequeathed to ethnic nationalism, which takes to its mission with an earnestness traditional nationalists never experienced. An appreciation, therefore, of the notions or concepts of race, language, territory, religion, and so forth as definitions of the *nation* should help us better to understand the demands of ethnic nationalists. It should also help us better to grasp the possible outer limits of the urge towards communal affinity in its most political form.

Nationalism and power in post-imperial Britain

These points bear directly on the discussion in the following chapters on ethnicity and nationalism in post-imperial Britain. Unlike Kohn's argument that Britain underwent a nationalist experience of a political nature, some writers would contend that the United Kingdom, particularly England, needs to rediscover itself. This is partly because of a need to redefine its national identity after the imperial adventure. It is also because, presumably, it has never had the kind of nationalist experience Europe had in the nineteenth century (for example, Nairn, 1981; Patterson, 1977). Whilst I believe Kohn to be correct here, it is nonetheless true to say that unlike her major continental neighbours, Britain has not undergone the conscious, deliberate and dramatic nationalist experience which commands attention. The long and slow development from disparate tiny kingdoms into a United Kingdom, through a mixture of conquest (of all England and later Wales) and compromise (with Scotland) and natural good fortune (being an island separated from quarrelsome continental Europe) there developed over several centuries an assurance of 'national' identity. With time and the experience and joy of establishing an hegemonic world order this British assurance passed into a common assumption. Unlike other peoples struggling to establish their identities, the British could stand aloof, certain in the knowledge that they knew, and others also knew, who the British were. The assumption became universally accepted. So much so that to a considerable degree and for a considerable time the retained contours or boundaries of earlier 'regional', 'national' or 'ethnic' communities were largely hidden from the rest of the world and to some extent from the British themselves as they gloried in their industrial, financial and military domination of the world. What were obvious divisions amongst the peoples who inhabited the island were submerged and became dormant. But these differences, such as language, regional variations, customs and traditions, were never delivered the final death blow, despite England's cultural and economic supremacy (see Daly and Troup, 1989).

Three developments during the post-imperial years were to give new life to these and to help to reshape them into becoming potent forces in a new Britain. The first of these, as we know, was the impact of the war itself. It delivered the final blow to Britain as the dominant world power. Her decline had started from the nineteenth century with the emergence of a united Germany and, after the Civil War in the first half of the 1860s, a resurgent and rapidly industrializing USA. And in the post-World War One period the USA and the USSR emerged to take the places Britain and France had occupied from the seventeenth century.

The new forms of world domination found no need for colonies as such. The qualified anti-colonialism which had grown out of the American Revolution and the strident anti-colonialism of the Soviet Union combined with the nationalist movements in the colonies of European powers to render colonies anachronistic. During the years after the Second World War independence has been thrust upon even those countries which did not desire it. The right to self-determination has become an obligation. And this has completed a historical cycle of nationalism which calls for legitimacy to be sanctioned through and within the framework of the 'nation-state'.

The aftermath of World War Two also brought the loss of both Britain's and France's world-wide empires. It may be argued, however, that whilst France quickly adjusted to its new position, Britain has taken a much longer time to do so and Thatcherism may be seen as part of a delayed adjustment. The experiences of defeat on home grounds, the establishment of Vichy, the Resistance, defeat in Indo-China and in Algeria, helped in the birth of Gaulleism and a rejuvenated French nationalism, powerful enough to embrace both left and right. Whilst being able to recognize the winds of change in Africa, Britain in the immediate post-war years appears to have been numb to the same winds of change at home.

The loss of empire was not initially a painful experience for Britain because of the circumstances in which this took place. These included, in the main, negotiated, constitutional decolonization and even where wars of liberation were fought – such as in Kenya, Malaysia or, more recently, Zimbabwe – in the end the overwhelming majority of new and independent states have been proud to be part of the British Commonwealth of nations. Through these processes Britain has retained a paramount status whilst the former colonies have become respected members of the world community of 'nation-states'. In effect, the ex-colonies have been able to transform themselves and display the (British) ability for political compromise. Much goodwill remained (and probably still remains despite what is widely regarded by Commonwealth members as Margaret Thatcher's, paradoxically, non-British behaviour) between the former colonies and Britain. No doubt this has been partly due to the good grace with which Britain accepted that the habit, or game, of painting the map of the world red was finished. But, then, there was no great horde of barbarians, no Attila the Hun, threatening the frontiers of the metropole of the empire. Nor was there any contiguous stretch of land which Britain shared with the colonized peoples. Once again the fact of being an island on the north-west rim of Europe helped. Britain was able to disengage from empire with a minimum of loss of face. After all, no loss of traditional British territories was involved in the process. She has also been able to maintain a position on the second rung of the league of nations and, as the Falklands/Malvinas war against Argentina demonstrated in 1982, Britain is still a force to be reckoned with.

I am not, of course, trying to minimize the effect of the loss of empire on Britain's reduced economic and political standing in the world. The point is simply that in general terms Britain does not appear to be as traumatized as she might have been expected to be by the experience of decline. She certainly revealed the symptoms of being dazed from these blows, but not knocked out. There have been, however, many kinds of delayed reactions to the multiple blows. One of these is the questioning of national identity or identities.

I would suggest that the second significant development in the post-war years which has affected Britain in an important way has been the entry and settlement of a visible population of non-white people on this island. The presence of black and brown people, particularly the former, has acted as a catalyst to bring home to Britain its changed circumstances and the need for redefinition.

The migration route in the empire was one-directional. Cosmopolitan or Island Britishers were free to roam beyond fixed boundaries within the empire as missionaries, soldiers, travellers, adventurers, traders or administrators. Colonial peoples were British subjects but were constrained in their movements. Of course, West Indians, Indians and Africans roamed as soldiers, workers, missionaries, educators, clerks and the like but within confined space sometimes regulated in terms of occupations. And of course the public schools, Oxbridge, the LSE and the Inns of Court were destinations for some sons of the middle and upper classes in the colonies but theirs were only temporary sojourns, planned to enable them to acquire something of the 'superior' cultural baggage of the British.

With the end of World War Two, however, the barriers to movement within the enclosure of the decolonizing empire became less rigid. To rebuild Island (as distinct from imperial) Britain, cheap labour was required and a historical departure occurred. Just when the empire was coming to an end, therefore, the new needs of its different parts became apparent. Crucially the metropole itself needed the cheap labour the colonies provided. The process of migration became complicated. It became multi-directional. Moreover, nationalists were at the same time negotiating for political independence. Whites in the metropole left for regions of white settlements – South Africa, Australia, New Zealand, North America. They also continued to go to the non-white world as explorers and sometimes as settlers. Non-whites within the empire came to the centre, Britain. Destinations, expectations and patterns of settlements became highly differentiated, reversing much of what had been received wisdom during the heyday of empire. It was 'discovered' that black people could work well in cold climes and not all whites in Africa wanted to return to the 'mother country'; black and brown people whose experience had taught them that they were British found themselves on uncertain grounds.

Not surprisingly, at first all parties assumed that the stay in Britain would follow the pattern of earlier journeys. Migrants expected to stay for a few years, then to go back with the wherewithal to improve themselves. The native Britishers had seen colonials come and go as sailors, soldiers and, of course, students. A combination of factors, however, dashed these hopes and expectations. The limited time frame within which immigrants were operating proved much too short for many, and soon their temporary visit developed into settlement. The state rediscovered that British meant something else too: it meant being white. As Britain began the pull inwards away from empire and Commonwealth, immigrants had to decide for themselves too whether they would become permanent settlers. The 1962 Commonwealth Immigrants Act seems to have helped to settle the minds of people already in Britain as well as Asians in Britain's East and Central African colonies. Whilst continuing to live in Africa, some Asians chose to remain British subjects when independence was gained by the African population, and by the end of the 1960s the repercussions of this began to have an impact on Britain itself as these Asians with British nationality rights were either discouraged from staying in, or were deliberately expelled from, Kenya and Uganda, respectively.

The third development which has significantly affected the nation's sense of its identity is the European integration movement. The Single Europe Act due to take full effect in January 1993, and such events as the revolution in Central and East Europe, and German unity in 1988–90, are momentous changes which offend traditional British reticence and insularity. The age of insular innocence, to paraphrase Norman Tebbit's statement quoted in chapter two, is rapidly passing and the nation is being called to play a major part in the new Europe. I shall return to this point in the next chapter, but it must be noted that, like Tebbit, many in the Conservative government of Margaret Thatcher and in the country at large see the new challenge as a threat to British sovereignty and identity.

I wish to argue, then, that at least three significant developments in the post-war period have slowly pushed into the forefront questions which were made largely irrelevant or which lay dormant during the days of empire and British hegemony. These developments provide us with an unprecedented historic opportunity to create a new and enriched Britain. In a time of momentous change and uncertainty it is not surprising, however, that what is a resource is confused for uselessness and potential strength is then taken for potential decay of the national fabric.

Traditional nationalism which, as I pointed out earlier, never had a safe and stable home in Britain, now finds expression in a number of contradictory ways. I would include in this category, for example, the economic nationalism of the Labour party, the anti-EEC stance of some of its prominent figures and the party's *de facto* agreement with the Conservative party's policies, if not attitudes, over immigration and nationality. But these expressions of the late appearance of traditional nationalism in Britain are analysed in a later chapter.

For now it is enough to note that the more easily identified expressions of nationalism in post-imperial Britain have been much more of the *ethnic* than of the *traditional* kind. But, as I argued earlier, ethnic nationalism has inherited the historical mission of traditional nationalism. And ethnic nationalism in Britain takes many forms. Kohn's distinction between the political and the cultural manifestations of nationalism may be of some use here. In general terms, there are any number of *cultural* expressions of ethnic nationalism as well as the more vibrantly *political* ethnic nationalism as defined in earlier chapters.

In the latter case there is a commitment to break down the *de facto* multi-ethnic, multi-national state into actual discrete communities where state and community are co-terminous. These developments are, of course, relevant with respect to the growth of the Scottish Nationalist Party and Plaid Cymru in Wales. The decade of the 1970s was the most spectacular for the SNP (Webb, 1977; Fusaro, 1979). The 1980s has witnessed a decline in both their fortunes and those of Plaid Cymru. The taking of three seats each in the 11 June 1987 general election, as well as the poor performance of the Conservatives, the party of government, in both Wales arïd Scotland, are important developments that would suggest that these nationalist parties may be on the rise again. The winning of a strong Labour seat in Glasgow by the SNP in the life of the present Parliament, the willingness of opposition parties to participate in a convention over a separate Assembly for Scotland and, despite Labour's obvious strength in both Scotland and Wales, the party's willingness again to place devolution on the national political agenda, are so many factors which point to the possible resurgence of a vibrant nationalism in Scotland.

With respect to forms of cultural ethnicity, it should be said that elements within the minority population seek to establish their difference with the majority whilst the majority itself encourages this for a variety of reasons many of which are concerned with control and power as well as the security which comes from having a certainty of self-identity. The optimism that imbued the progressive view of history led thinkers of an earlier age to believe that advance in science and technology, communication, trade and production on a world scale would be so many factors which would enable humanity to transcend the enclosure of the 'nation state' and usher in true internationalism. This was as true of Marxism before the building of 'socialism in one country' under Stalin from the 1920s, as of many liberals in the nineteenth century. Not only have subsequent developments not borne out liberal and Marxist universalist and humanitarian expectations, but the very idea of internationalism today seems almost as utopian as Sir Thomas More's imaginary world. In situations of either cultural or political nationalism, a serious challenge to the status quo is thrown down, but this may be used by the majority for a successful retention of established power structures.

Conclusion

The fortunes of the Nationalist Party in Scotland and of Plaid Cymru in Wales are cases in point. And these can be discussed in terms of ethnic and traditional nationalist manifestations and power relations. First, the expressions of *traditional* as well as *ethnic* nationalism in Britain seem to be concerned, in one way or another, with the maintenance of the *status quo ante*. I mean this not only in the sense of there being those who wish to keep alive something of the splendour and glory that was Britain, but also the desire to return to a pre-World War Two British Island situation in which the population was, supposedly, *racially* homogeneous. The sense of loss, the inability so far to fashion a new international role for herself and the loosening of many bonds which held the internal structures together, find a variety of expressions. The desire to return to the *status quo ante* expresses itself also in terms of the project to reconstitute independent political authorities in Britain. This is essentially nationalist in the ethnic sense in which I have defined it. There is, therefore, a longing to return to a pre-Union, pre-united island; in other words, independence for Scotland and home rule for Wales. These kinds of demands are at the higher end of the spectrum of ethnic nationalism because there is a demand for the political authority over these areas to coincide with the territory and the ethnic groups who have lived in Scotland and Wales since time immemorial.

The questioning of the present political order also include racist and populist kinds of expressions such as Powellism and economic nationalism as represented by the Labour party. It is the transition, however, from traditional nationalism to ethnic nationalism, as represented by the two major political parties, which forms the basis of discussion in the following chapter.

The second profile which emerges from this consideration of nationalism, and to which I wish to turn in chapters six and seven, is that which concerns non-white minorities without claims to historic homelands in Britain. The politics that emerge here represent another type of ethnic nationalist expression being articulated in post-imperial Britain. Naturally, migrants continue to have an interest in the welfare of the countries from which they come. The extent and intensity of this interest in the life of 'back home' are dependent on several factors. For example, if the initial reception in the new country was hostile and continues to be so, then it should not be surprising that contact with life 'back home' is not merely maintained but developed into a resource. Alienation from British society of young people born of West Indian parents means they might feel closer to the West Indies, which they may never have seen nor necessarily understand, than to Britain, the country they do know and to which they do belong. Sikh youths in Britain may feel pulled towards the events taking place in the Punjab not only because they are alienated from Britain, their new home, but also because of events in India itself. Nonetheless, the absence of any encouragement, to see Britain as 'home' must be a powerful message in itself to such youths that the original homeland is of primary importance and must, therefore, be defended.

Chapters six and seven are concerned then to see how and why ethnic nationalism, expressed in terms of religion, race, territory and so forth, in what are regarded by many in the indigenous white population as 'far off' lands may continue to affect people in this country. This is because, as noted in chapter four, ethnic nationalism is no respecter of place and does not need to be confined to any one physical location in the way that traditional nationalism had to be territorially located. Ethnic nationalism, therefore, may be able to impart greater strength to small, relatively isolated communities surrounded by large majorities. And it is at least partly for this reason that the diasporic politics of ethnicity and democracy have continued to attract the attention and demand the energies of minorities from the former empire. Before, however, turning to these questions, I wish to look first at the problems of transition from British empire to British nation as part of the search for certainty of identity by the white, national majority, as represented by the central state.

5

From *imperial* British to *national* British

Introduction

The discussion in this chapter hinges on two propositions that are central to the notion of the communal option. These arise from the variety of ethnic nationalism which is emerging in post-imperial Britain. The first proposition is that the development of nationalist expressions in British nationality and immigration laws before the 1960s tended to be as a series of reactions to nationalism in the dominions and colonies. There was, therefore, an initial reluctance on the part of both the British Conservative and the British Labour parties to embrace nationalism and nowhere was this more clearly expressed than in legislation regarding nationality. By the same token, when change was perceived by these parties to be desirable, the specific forms of nationalism they emphasized have been clearly expressed in the debates over nationality laws. In the case of the present Conservative ministry its greater emphasis on *ethnic* nationalism is also strongly expressed in the crucial sphere of education.

The second proposition is that, whilst the main tendency of the Conservatives has been towards ethnic nationalism and the Labour party's has been towards traditional nationalism, in the end both parties have articulated almost identical types of nationalism during this transition from empire to nation. This convergence of Labour's traditional nationalism with the Conservatives' ethnic nationalism is a clear indication of a remarkably unified British response to the challenge of the post-imperial age. The convergence on this point, how-ever, is not always seen in its proper focus because of the parties' claim to uphold universalistic norms. But the rhetoric of leaders, particularly when in opposition, and the legislation their respective parties have enacted while in office, reveal little party political difference on this crucial question of national identity.

Reluctant nationalists

After all, one of the most crucial and persistent questions that post-imperial Britain has had to face is that of how to define the *nation* in terms that respect both past responsibilities and present realities. On the one hand, British politicians and governments in the post-imperial age have been concerned to demonstrate to the world that they will respect past commitments to people in what would now appear to be 'far-off' places, as a result of having been the premier colonial power for several centuries. And on the other hand, the loss of, or retreat from, empire has forced governments to define the nation's responsibilities more narrowly. Consequently, like her former colonies, Britain herself has been very much concerned with questions of national identity. This transformation from *empire* to *nation* has not been as traumatic for Britain as might have been expected. It has not, however, been an entirely smooth transition.

This is so despite the fact that nationalism in post-imperial Britain has taken various forms. First, there are some well-known forms of extreme right-wing political expressions of a predominantly English-based nationalism. Enoch Powell is no doubt the undisputed and fulsome expression of this particular genre of nationalism. It is hardly necessary, here, however, to comment extensively on Powellism as a factor in British, and particularly English, politics since the late 1960s. Much has already been said about the phenomenon (for example, Foot, 1969; Nairn, 1981) to which a once promising politician gave his name and who now appears, even to members of his own party, as something of a 'false Festus, he who bore the name of shame'.[1]

There is also, of course, the right-wing nationalist expression of the Monday Club in the Conservative Party, and various fascist groups such as the National Front, outside the party (Miles and Phizacklea, 1979). Moreover, there has been what is generally referred to as the New Right, a hotch-potch of individuals and groups. We are wisely warned to be cautious about compressing these groups too tightly together (Parekh, 1986, p. 33; Keegan, 1986, p. 45). For example, Parekh identified three characteristics that members of the New Right tend to share. These are the recognition of the decline of Britain since the last war; the pervasive nature of this decline which affects such areas of national life as the economy, morality and politics; and the agreement that the decline can be stopped by a radical programme (Parekh, 1986). It must be noted, however, that much of what is generally described as *new* is really quite *old* and has certainly run the gamut of ethnic nationalist feelings at least from the debates over immigration from the non-white Commonwealth in the late 1950s.

The second main feature of nationalism in post-imperial Britain is, of course, the nationalist movements in the 'Celtic fringes' of Britain. This type of nationalist expression is particularly relevant with respect to Scotland and Wales. These are the northern and western rims, or peripheries, of the island to which the various waves of later continental conquerors and/or settlers pushed some of the earliest inhabitants of these islands in a series of protracted struggles. Again, a great deal has been written about these forms of struggles for autonomy or independence in the United Kingdom and it is, therefore, quite unnecessary to go into them here (Hanham, 1969a; Webb, 1977; Fusaro, 1979). Suffice it to note that, although Scottish nationalism reached its apex in the 1970s, its rumblings have a long history. For example, the Scottish Office was established as early as 1885 as a way of muting demands for more attention to be paid to Scottish, as distinct from British, affairs (Hanham, 1969b). The main point, however, is that the present insistence for Scottish independence from England (and the rest of the United Kingdom) is very much a post-imperial phenomenon.

There is a third variant of post-imperial nationalism in Britain. Whilst the Labour Party exhibits a traditional type of nationalism and the Conservatives have shown an ethnic nationalism in the post-imperial period, both parties embrace quite unexpected and inconsistent forms of nationalist economic policies. As the economic crisis in Britain deepened in the post-imperial period, Labour has tended to preach more vigorously an economic nationalism that calls for less investment abroad by British capitalists and less foreign capitalist involvement in key areas of the British economy. The Conservatives, particularly under Margaret Thatcher in the 1980s, have opened the national doors wide for foreign investment. Whereas, therefore, the nationalist aspects of Thatcherism are clear enough in the political sphere, in the economic domain this nationalism is far from obvious. There is, in other words, quite a distance between the highly charged nationalist approach to the Falklands/ Malvinas crisis and the more liberal approach to general economic policy. Mrs Thatcher's famous speech in Bruges, Belgium in September 1988 was, of course, also delivered in the spirit of the Falklands: it was meant to be seen, and has been seen, as a British nationalist response to a perceived growing bureaucracy in Brussels bent on thwarting legitimate aspirations of nation-states within the Community. The former Conservative prime minister Edward Heath's pro-European statement in May 1989 in Belgium, which aimed to counterbalance Mrs Thatcher's anti-European manifesto, opened the debate within the party over the desirability of Britain losing her identity for a more general European one. The contradiction, ambivalence or tension within the Conservative party over national or wider European identity remains evident as Britain and Europe enter the decade of the 1990s.

But in the economic sphere the party's sense of nationalism is far from clear. For example, the ministry of trade under Leon Brittan opted for the Egyptian Fayeh Brothers against the British Lonhro of Tiny Rowland in the take-over of the House of Fraser/Harrods in 1985. Westlands helicopters went to the Americans rather than to the European partners in 1986, thereby providing Michael Heseltine with a crusading cause in what many believed was a bid for future leadership of the Tory party. In early 1988 the majority shares in Britoil went to Kuwaiti interests amidst much national discussion over the desirability of this development. The fact that by October 1988 the Thatcher government was willing, under pressure, to demand that the Kuwaitis sell off some of their 22 per cent ownership of Britoil, does not negate the main point here, namely that the Conservatives have embarked upon a highly inconsistent nationalist path.

On each of these issues Labour has put up stiff resistance against the government. Thus, by early May 1988, as foreign interests in the British economy appeared to be increasing, Lord Young, the then secretary of state for trade and industry, was himself expressing fears over Kuwait's £3.3 billion interest in the country's largest company (*The Independent*, 5 May 1988, p. 1). The Kuwaiti Investments Office's 22 per cent share in Britoil was referred by the minister to the Monopolies and Mergers Commission. Another example of a shift in attitude towards uncontrolled competition in 1988 was the support given by John Banham, director-general of the Confederation of British Industry (CBI), over Nestle's £2.1 billion bid for the chocolate firm Rowntree. Banham's argument was that since British firms cannot freely make similar bids for Swiss companies, Nestle should be referred to the Commission. And Sir Gordon Borrie, director-general of the Office of Fair Trading, was reported to have complained that ' . . . few foreign acquisitions of UK companies had been referred to Monopolies', even though he agreed with the government's policy on competition (*The Guardian*, 6 May 1988, p. 14). These criticisms of the Conservatives' open-door economic policy were valuable support for Labour's more traditional nationalist position on the question. Obviously, part of the reason for Labour's nationalist stance is to do with the antics of a party occupying the opposition benches. But a reading of Labour's publications, particularly the party's manifestoes and speeches by its leaders in the post-Wilsonian years, suggests that the party's opposition arises from a commitment to a strong economic nationalism.

The particular aspect of these three manifestations of post-imperial nationalism in Britain that I want to focus upon is the state's definition, or understanding, of who may be considered to be 'British'. This concern with the nation's identity is perhaps best understood in terms that have been, and continue to be, expressed in nationality and immigration laws in the post-imperial period. I should, however, caution that my interest in nationality and immigration laws lies in the *perceptions* of the British nation articulated by politicians, rather than in the legal provisions per se.[2]

As noted in earlier chapters, historically Britain eschewed that type of militant nationalism that had a strong economic or political bias. The country was largely untouched by the waves of militant traditional nationalist fervour that swept over her continental neighbours from the French Revolution in the late eighteenth century to the reshaping of Europe after the two world wars. This is not to say that there was any absence of patriotism in Britain. But, as noted earlier, patriotism is not necessarily nationalism. Nor was there an absence of the feeling of racial superiority. But the feeling of racial superiority has been shared with all West Europeans in their relations with other peoples, and it also pre-dates the rise of nationalism. The confidence she had in herself, based on political stability, industrial, financial and military strength, made militant nationalism irrelevant in Britain, from at least 1713 with the signing of the Treaty of Utrecht (which followed the Union with Scotland some six years earlier). The new conditions of the present century, however, in which Britain has lost her position as the premier power in world affairs may have provided the basis for the rise of nationalism. But even in the post-imperial period when the country's long decline has become clear to all, the two parties of government have embraced nationalism with that reluctance to disturb the status quo which is deeply rooted in the British evolutionist political tradition since the comparatively quiet but important Revolution of 1689.

British nationality and immigration laws before 1962 strongly reflected this reluctance. Until the British Nationality Act of 1948, there was a common set of assumptions regarding nationality throughout the British empire. The basic understanding was that all who came under the crown's power were British subjects. The British Nationality and Aliens Act, 1914, for example, sought to define British citizenship for an empire which was, naturally, scattered, multi-racial and multi-national. Rushed through parliament during the first week of August as Britain was about to enter the Great War against Germany and her allies, the Act sought to consolidate the law relating to British nationality as it had developed piecemeal over the centuries. The cabinet papers of the period reveal nothing about the government's thinking on the matter. But the chief concern of the Liberal government of the day may well have been over the free and unfettered movements of aliens, rather than an attempt to sharpen the definition of who was and who was not a British subject.

In brief, the Act defined those who were to be considered to be British, the means whereby an alien could be naturalized, and how he or she could also lose the status of being British. Of all persons who came into close proximity with British jurisdiction, only persons born on a foreign ship whilst in British territorial waters were excluded from consideration as British. In sharp contrast to post-imperial British nationality law, the Act seems to have been concerned with who could be *included*, rather than who should be *excluded* from being part of the Pax Britannica.

From the point of view of the question of nationalism or its absence, the definition of 'natural-born British subjects' was not only generous – if *generous* is the appropriate word in this context – when compared to current provisions in British nationality laws, but also extremely brief. Qualifications for being included in this category were, first, that the person was born within the crown's 'dominions and allegiance'; a person born outside these domains but whose father was British by birth or naturalization; and persons born aboard a British ship within or outside British territorial waters. There is a noticeable absence in the Act of any reference to Britain as a physical or geographical location or entity. The central principle or definition of 'British' was perceived to be allegiance to the crown, and the importance that a specific territory – the British Isles – was later to assume in nationality legislation was conspicuously absent.

Generally, until 1948 these provisions were maintained throughout the empire and Commonwealth, with necessary local variations. When Ireland gained her independence from Britain in 1918 the laws were so amended that Irish citizens retained their 'British subjects' status. By an act of 1935 Ireland refused to recognize these provisions. But as late as 1946 the Home Secretary and the Secretary of State for Dominion Affairs made a point of Eamon de Valera's strong objection to Irish citizens being referred to as British subjects. In a joint memorandum to the cabinet these ministers stressed that the Irish nationalist leader 'has gone so far as publicly to stigmatise as an impertinence the claim of the United Kingdom Government to treat Eire citizens as British subjects' (Cabinet Papers, July 1946, p. 4). Quite clearly, Irish nationalism was forcing citizens of the newly independent state into new directions of loyalty. Britain, on the other hand, wished to hold on to the old sense of loyalty. In the case of post-imperial Irish migration to Britain, the nationalist equation is no longer as simple as in the 1930s. For example, the nationalist de Valera's concern over distinguishing Irish citizens from British subjects contrasts interestingly with a statement in 1988 in a Coventry local newspaper. Under the heading 'Irish Citizens' it was reported that,

> Too late for our Christmas issue, Dr Owen O'Grady, who gave no address, wrote to our office about the Nationality Act, suggesting that the Irish community has been given the wrong information by the Citizens Advice Bureau about Irish people becoming British citizens. Registration has to be done before December 31.
> Also too late, we had notification from the Irish Centre of a seminar on the subject, to be held in Birmingham on December 20. It arrived on December 22, the same day as Dr O'Grady's letter.
> So in the last few days of registration we've been unable to help, although Coventry has a big Irish community.
> (*Coventry Citizen*, 31 December 1987, p. 4)[3]

The difference in the attitudes expressed by a non-immigrant nationalist leader in the 1930s and those expressed by a concerned immigrant group in the late 1980s over the question of nationality, reflect the fluidity of the notion of national community.

In the decade before the post-imperial age commenced, the white Dominions as a whole sought to gain more control over their own affairs and thereby to establish their equality with the 'mother country'. Not surprisingly, this desire expressed itself particularly in the closely related areas of citizenship and immigration laws. In 1931 the Dominions – Australia, Canada, the Irish Free State, Newfoundland, New Zealand and the Union of South Africa – were given, by the Statute of Westminster, the power to enact their own citizenship laws.[4] This was going one step further in the direction of giving the Dominions control over their populations, or, expressed another way, the British citizens who were domiciled within their respective territories. In 1918 all the Dominions were allowed by the imperial government to restrict emigration into what were rapidly becoming exclusive *national* boundaries, though still under the aegis of the Pax Britannica. Britain was the only member of the club who did not lay down such restrictions. Instead, she proclaimed an open-door policy to members of the empire – both Commonwealth and colonies. Although in later decades some British politicians were able to make much ado about seeming liberalism, it must be stressed that Britain's position at this time was not reached out of any feeling of liberalism. It was a response to changes that threatened to wrench out of her hands control of the right of people to move within the empire.

For example, it was important for Britain that members of the colonies and the Commonwealth were, first and foremost, British citizens and only secondarily citizens of one or other of the Dominions. As the Home Secretary, Chuter Ede, told Parliament when introducing the second reading of the 1948 British Nationality Bill, after 1914 'there came into existence an almost identical set of laws in several countries of the British Commonwealth' (Hansard, 1947–8, col. 386). Members of the empire, irrespective of race, colour, ethnic group, religion, physical location within the imperial pen, were invited to take for granted a common citizenship status.

But this common status meant different things to the different members of the empire. At the very centre was Britain herself, with her people enjoying the freedoms that had been won over many centuries and are commonly associated with citizenship status. The people at the centre of the empire enjoyed more or less, depending on class locations, the freedoms and rights that we nearly all expect in a democracy, such as the vote, the right to form unions, the freedom to assemble, speak and publish within the framework of the law. No restrictions existed on movement of people, within either Britain or the empire. And people from the various parts of the country went to whichever part of this vast

British imperial world they chose, where economic opportunities existed largely for themselves, moving on again when fortunes changed or sufficient prosperity was secured to make for a better life, preferably in one of the Home Counties of England.

Beyond the centre of the empire were the white Dominions. In these territories, full or near to full political rights as they pertained to internal matters were also enjoyed but differentially. In the predominantly white populated Dominions – Canada, Australia and New Zealand – the power to control immigration allowed local politicians to keep out non-white peoples from their territories. Where they allowed non-white people to settle, they were careful to restrict the numbers. In Britain itself there were attempts to control the entry and settlement of non-whites (Rich, 1986, ch. 6). In several of the colonies British officials were given instructions from Whitehall to restrict departure for Britain.[5]

Racial considerations in all areas of social, political and economic life, were taken almost to the limit in those societies where white settled but the population remained predominantly non-white. India was an exception to this. Apart from administrators, soldiers, missionaries and the like, Europeans did not earmark India as a region for settlement. The subcontinent was perceived more as a region for *exploitation* than one for *settlement*, to employ a suggestive distinction from the debate over plantation economies in the Caribbean (Best, 1968; Beckford, 1972). Rather, an interesting development occurred: Indian labour followed the British to various parts of the empire (Saha, 1970; Tinker, 1974; also Dabydeen and Samaroo, 1987). And this effected Indian settlement overseas on an unprecedented scale under the aegis of the British political banner.

In the Union of South Africa, Africans lost all their civil and political rights; they had earlier lost their economic rights when the whites settled there. In East and Central Africa, particularly Kenya and Northern and Southern Rhodesia, the African population was similarly denied the rights enjoyed by white settlers. Only during the last years of British rule did Africans in East Africa gain any political representation. Moreover, wherever in East and Central Africa and Asia Indians, Chinese and Europeans inhabited the same territory, they were allocated political rights according to their 'race'. In Fiji, for example, representation on the Legislative Council was made up of equal numbers of Indians, Europeans and Fijians from early in the century (Ali, 1982). Comparing the centre of the empire with the colonies in 1956, Rita Hinden *et al.*, on behalf of the Labour Party, concluded that

> An essential difference between the history of Britain and that of the colonial territories is that in the colonies the colour identifies the class.
> (The Labour Party, 1956, p. 14)[6]

This was perhaps less true in the cases of India, West Africa and Uganda than in the vast majority of the colonies.

It is well known that even the few legal/formal rights Africans had, particularly in East and Central Africa, were grossly abused. Asians brought from what was then British India to East and Central Africa enjoyed only limited rights. For example, in Kenya they were largely excluded from the land. Salaries, residence, schooling and almost every area of life were segregated along racial lines by the settlers, supported by the central imperial power. Senior positions in the civil service, the army, the police, economic enterprises and so forth, were reserved for whites. Some of these posts went to whites from Britain, others went to the white settlers.

In these respects the West Indies, Britain's oldest colonies (with the exception of Ireland), came somewhere between the Dominions and the colonies in Africa and Asia. Although the white plantocracy continued to dominate the legislatures in the region, representation based on race was not introduced after the abolition of slavery in 1838. Property and education were the bases for elected representation in the free assembly (in Barbados), the Court of Policy (in British Guiana) and the legislative councils (first established in Trinidad at the beginning of the nineteenth century) in most of the other territories. Of course, until the introduction of adult suffrage in the 1940s, these bodies were dominated by governors and their white nominees. But by the mid nineteenth century both the mixed and black people of wealth and education were gaining access to the representative or legislative bodies in the region. The majority population, mainly of African and Indian descent, did not, however, enjoy full political rights until 1944 when universal adult suffrage commenced in Jamaica and spread, during the next quarter century, to all the British possessions in the Caribbean. Thus, although colour and racial discrimination existed in the region and still does, Hinden *et al.* argued for the Labour Party that the West Indies 'provide an example of the solution to some major problems of the plural societies' (The Labour Party, 1956, p. 17) because they had developed societies in which 'Character and ability have gradually superseded colour as qualifications' (The Labour Party, 1956, p. 16) and, moreover, the European and African populations had become significantly mixed.

These different situations, therefore, meant that the common status of members of the colonies and Commonwealth had little or no meaning for the vast majority of people until the last thirteen years of their existence, that is, the years between 1949 and 1962. This was a brief period when Indians, Pakistanis and West Indians came to the centre of the empire as citizens in order to improve their material life. Between 1949 and 1962 then, the common status and the freedom of movement were tested by the colonial peoples. For the first time in the long history of the empire, people from the peripheries were moving to the centre in modest numbers. This made population movement in the empire a two-way process. As we shall see later, this was to be one of the most important factors to help put an end to Britain's reluctant nationalism.

Before the abandonment of her reluctant nationalist posture, it was understood that any change in nationality laws by either Britain or one of the Dominions should be preceded by consultation with members. The cumbersome nature of the system of consultation deterred members from making amendments because the result was not worth the effort. Nonetheless, through the imperial conferences, the precursor of the Commonwealth heads of government meetings, there was encouragement for the system to work, with respect to formal nationality laws. At such meetings Britain represented herself and the colonies as one entity, whilst the Dominions represented themselves as individual emergent nation-states on a more or less equal footing with Britain.

The essential requirement on the part of all parties was loyalty to the crown. In this respect Anderson is surely correct to point to the pre-nationalist and dynastic origins of the United Kingdom and place this beside the example of the USSR, as well as to hint at the apparent paradox that these states may be the precursors of 'a twenty-first century internationalist order' (Anderson, 1983, p. 12). It was certainly something of this pre-nationalist spirit that informed the 1914 Nationality Act as well as subsequent acts before the 1960s (The Labour Party, *National Executive Committee*, 1946–84 (1971)).

There is perhaps no other piece of legislation in British legal history which more clearly reflects the emerging tension between nationalism in the Dominions and colonies and Britain's attempt to hold this spirit at bay, than the British Nationality Act of 1948. This Act was to become a watershed in British nationality legislation. It reflected the concern to maintain the common status whilst recognizing the necessity for newly emergent nation-states to exercise their independent rights in international relations with regard to who would be citizens and who aliens.

The Act retained the imperial definition of 'British' and in fact extended this. Whereas under the 1914 Act a person was British by virtue of natural birth (generously understood) or by the process of naturalization, under the 1948 Act a person could become a British citizen or subject by virtue of being a citizen of a Commonwealth country. The search for a new formula that would capture the meaning of 'British' was found in the new expression 'Commonwealth citizen', and it was hoped that as the colonies became independent they would join the scheme. As the Home Secretary told members of the House during the committee stage of the Bill.

> We are dealing with one of the manifestations of growth inside this living democratic organism, the British Commonwealth of Nations. I am sure that we are all exceedingly anxious that the older self-governing Dominions shall be entitled to feel that in our eyes as well

as in their own, they have attained full nationhood. I am sure that we are quite as anxious that those new countries to whom self-government has been recently granted by this country shall also feel that inside this Commonwealth, they are not merely welcome but are recognized as being sovereign states with the rest of us, and that we treasure their adherence to this great family of nations.

(Hansard, 1947/8, col. 1024)

The principal concern, however, of the Attlee government was to undermine nationalist intentions. I have already alluded to the Irish nationalist attitude towards Britain's description of citizens of Eire as British subjects. The British ministers concerned with these matters were sensitive to such nationalist sentiments and at one point in the discussion over the question of a new British nationality act, stated, a little incredulously from the vantage point of today when we more readily recognize nationalist claims and aspirations, that:

This is possibly no doubt due to objection to the term 'British subject' as such – but in the main it rests upon the fact that the status of British subject connotes an allegiance to the Crown which is wholly inconsistent with Mr. de Valera's conception of the position of Eire in relation to the Commonwealth.

(Cabinet Papers, July 1946, p. 4)

The major threat to the common status of British subject was to come, however, not from the militant Irish nationalists, but from the seemingly calm and loyal Canadians. In the year after the Second World War ended, the Canadian government exercised its power to legislate over who would be considered to be citizens of the Dominion of Canada and who would not. This caught the imperial government by surprise. After all, Britain and her empire had just fought a war against fascism in Europe and Asia. And in 1937, after one of the imperial conferences, it was agreed that the traditional common status as defined by the imperial parliament would be upheld by all the Dominions. Moreover, part of the understanding throughout the Commonwealth was that no government would act without first consulting the others. Canada, however, decided to act unilaterally and to establish its own nationality law, which was to come into effect on 1 January 1947. The British cabinet papers for the years 1946 to 1948 reveal something of the concern of leading participants in Britain's attempt to seize the initiative from the Canadians and try to save the *status quo ante.*

The first step in this process at cabinet level was taken by the Home Secretary and the Secretary of State for Dominion Affairs in their joint memorandum to the cabinet in July 1946. The first suggestion to the cabinet was that Britain should participate in the new system of nationality law implied by the

Canadian act. These ministers wanted Britain to concede to the Irish government's wish not to have Irish citizens considered as British subjects, but they
also wanted Ireland, as well as India, Burma, Southern Rhodesia and Newfoundland, to be invited to the proposed conference of Commonwealth experts
who would consider the pros and cons of a new system. The most important of
their recommendations, however, was that Britain's participation in the new
scheme should result in the

> creation in United Kingdom legislation of some form of citizenship
> which would be the *gateway* through which the status of British
> subject would be conferred upon the inhabitants of the United King-
> dom and . . . upon the inhabitants of the colonies.
>
> (Cabinet Papers, July 1946, p. 4; emphasis added)

This was because the Canadian law ran directly counter to the system of
citizenship throughout the empire. As Ede explained to the cabinet and later to
parliament, under the traditional system the status of British citizenship was
conferred upon the individual 'directly without reference to local citizenship'
(Cabinet Papers, August 1946, p. 1). The Canadian law was reversing this procedure. An individual would be first a Canadian citizen, and only secondarily
would he or she become a British citizen. Ede feared that this new principle
would jeopardize the common status throughout the empire and, rather
prophetically, warned the cabinet that

> there is a danger that one or more of the Dominions may in the future
> be disposed to drop the common status altogether and give way to
> demands from within for completely separate nationhood.
>
> (Cabinet Papers, August 1946, p. 1)

The recommendation, which was later supported by cabinet and parliament and
was enshrined in the 1948 Nationality Act, was for citizens of self-governing
states within the empire to be British subjects first and then become citizens of
particular states within the family of British Commonwealth States. In this way
both principles – of common status and the right of the dominions to enact their
own nationality laws – were temporarily held in balance.

This was attained largely through compromise, achieved at the experts' conference in London in February 1947. But like most compromises it had a short
life. Indeed, in 1949 Ireland left the Commonwealth, and in 1961 the inhuman
system of apartheid made it impossible for the Union of South Africa to remain
a member of a growing Commonwealth which was also becoming less exclusively white. After the independence of India and Pakistan in 1947, the decades
from the 1950s to the 1970s witnessed one country after the other in Africa,
Asia and the Caribbean becoming politically independent, sovereign states.
Some of the new nation-states that had come under the British flag as colonies,

condominiums, protected or trust territories, went their own ways. For example, Egypt, Sudan, Jordan, Palestine and Burma have kept their distance from Britain and from the overwhelming majority (of nearly fifty) former British colonies that have transformed themselves into the free association of states called the Commonwealth. Each state within the Commonwealth has, however, enacted its own independent national citizenship law.

Consequently, as during the imperial age, a variety of practices exist within the Commonwealth today. In most of these countries 'Commonwealth citizens' are distinguished from 'aliens', but in the majority of cases the distinction is merely nominal. In some, however, the distinction is an important one because 'Commonwealth citizens' may enjoy certain rights. For example, in Kenya or Tanzania, or India and Bangladesh, it is inconceivable that a 'Commonwealth citizen' should be allowed to vote without first becoming a citizen of these countries. In Jamaica, on the other hand, a 'Commonwealth citizen' may vote in general and local elections after one year's residence, as in Britain. In like manner, most Commonwealth countries do not permit dual citizenship. In the Commonwealth Caribbean dual citizenship is the norm, with the possible exception of Trinidad and Tobago. In some member countries 'Commonwealth citizens' require visas whilst in others they do not.

It may be suggested that these differences most probably reflect the variety of nationalist perspectives that emerged and developed in different parts of the empire during the struggles for political independence. For example, the relative absence of militant nationalism in the Commonwealth Caribbean may account for the generosity of its laws. On the other hand, the deep national awareness in most other parts of the post-colonial world may help to explain their relatively stringent laws regarding nationality.

Of course, there were other factors involved. For example, the fact that nearly all colonial societies were deliberately rooted in racial division of one kind or another did not mean that, simply because the colonial power was being removed, the various peoples would automatically come together to live in harmony. Rarely has nationalism developed to the extent that it has been able to embrace Europeans, Africans and/or Asians. In Africa, Tanzania is perhaps an outstanding example of nationalism achieving this embrace. But even here most of the small body of white settlers departed after independence, and more than half the Indian population followed suit, having opted for British nationality (Tandon, 1973). Following the deliberate sabotage of the economy by white settlers as they departed from Mozambique in the early 1970s, Zimbabwe embarked on a policy of encouraging white settlers in the 1980s to stay and regard themselves as Zimbabweans. But given the antipathetic forces towards this aim it would be surprising if it were to succeed, although there appears to be a small minority of whites who have stayed on to settle as Zimbabweans and may be willing to abandon their Rhodesian identity. The

Asian communities that sprang up throughout East and Central Africa under the British have also diminished through migration. The *new* Europeans and *new* Asians in Africa have established different relationships with Africans and with the continent. This is because they have returned, or more likely migrated, to the continent not as settlers but as people with needed skills, as investors, and so forth. Most importantly, they have been invited by African governments and institutions, rather than by an imperial government, to occupy the positions they have taken.

The force of nationalism in the colonies, which was just about to reassert itself after the interruption of the 1939–45 war, was grasped in a limited way by some members of the British cabinet, as reflected in the debates over the 1948 Nationality Act. Ede gave two examples to parliament to explain the difficulties the Dominions were facing: first, he argued that when

> we are dealing with great, thriving countries like the Dominions, with their legitimate ambitions for nationhood, it can be well understood that this kind of problem is one which confronts them acutely.
>
> (Hansard, 1947–8, col. 389)

A second reason, according to Ede, for recognizing separate nationality laws within the Dominions was 'because many of their inhabitants are not people of British descent' (Hansard, 1947–8, col. 389) and therefore find the word *British* 'irksome'. Ede warned that the old term 'British subject' could prove 'detrimental' in Britain's relations with people of French descent in Canada, or of Dutch descent in South Africa.

The conjuncture marked by 1948, therefore, held out two possibilities: that proposed by the Canadian measure and the other represented by the compromise enshrined in the British Nationality Act. By the end of the 1960s it was abundantly clear that the Canadian principle had not only won the day, but had been overtaken by the forces of nationalism throughout the empire. This included Britain herself. As one nationalist, Enoch Powell, was later to argue,

> economic conditions in Britain, coupled with the enormous capacity of air transport for shifting large numbers of persons, opened up the imminent prospect that a movement hitherto negligible would become so massive as to alter substantially the composition of the population of Britain. If this was not to happen, it would be necessary so to alter the law of nationality of the United Kingdom as to detach the right of entry and abode from the status of British subject and attach it to a narrower category, however, defined, of those who *belonged* to the United Kingdom itself.
>
> (Powell, 1968b, p. 41, emphasis added)

It is necessary, therefore, at this point to turn from 1948 and the principle of the common status, the last stand of the reluctant nationalists, to looking at the two variants of nationalism which have since informed British policy on nationality and immigration.

Labour's traditional and ethnic nationalism

The attempt by the Labour government to undermine the Canadian initiative between 1946–8 must be seen in terms of Westminster's traditional abhorrence of overt nationalism and the preference for compromise to save a situation, in this case the *status quo ante*. The outcome was also typical of the kind of traditional nationalism the Labour party has developed in response to Britain's changing position in the post-imperial age.

By Labour's *traditional* nationalism I mean to suggest that the party has sought to embrace and advance nationalist justifications for their policies that were articulated by nationalists in the past, particularly where new political communities were emerging out of older, imperial ones. Traditional nationalism was necessarily multi-national or multi-ethnic both in its emotional appeal and in the political organization (the nation*s*-state) to which it gave rise. This was not, however, the case with respect to its doctrines. The nation*s*-state construct, as argued earlier, has therefore rarely been made up of only one ethnic or national group. In the retreat from empire to nation this point was consciously or unconsciously grasped by Labour. The party has articulated a *traditional* nationalist perspective in its policies regarding the kinds of political communities it desired to see emerge out of the empire. There have been three dimensions to the party's understanding of a multi-national political community of which Britain would be part in the new world that was emerging out of the empire.

At the international level of state blocs Labour preferred a multi-national community rather than a dramatic and total severance of all bonds. The party's answer, therefore, to the demise of the empire was twofold: it welcomed this inevitable change and encouraged the colonial peoples in their struggle for freedom. But at the same time the party wanted the new nations to become members of an expanded Commonwealth of nation*s*-states with Britain at its head. This was, of course, consistent with the new imperialism – what Kwame Nkrumah christened 'neo-colonialism' – which did not require colonies in order to thrive. Indeed, it called for politically independent states as the norm and an expansion of the international market for the stronger capitalist economies to have free access to national and what used to be monopolized colonial markets. The pressure for this came principally from the traditionally anti-colonial USA and it accorded well with the economic interests of major American multi-national firms seeking new areas for investment and new markets. Paradoxically, the American anti-colonial tradition and US business interests, therefore, complemented the already strong anti-colonial movements throughout the empire and the USSR's as well as the Labour party's support for these movements.

There were, nonetheless, several examples of Labour's deep and quite genuine commitment to the idea of a multi-racial, multi-ethnic, multi-national Commonwealth; an international community embracing a multiplicity of politically free peoples. For example, the party was far less willing than the Conservatives to join the European Economic Community (EEC) and thereby weaken the economic, cultural and historic links with the Commonwealth. But in 1988 two events were to change Labour's position on Europe dramatically. On 8 September the president of the EEC Commission, the French socialist M. Jacques Delors, received an enthusiastic ovation at the Trade Union Congress at Bournemouth when he spoke on *Europe 1992: The Socialist Dimension* (Delors, 1988). Margaret Thatcher's anti-Brussels speech at Bruges on 20 September was a strident British nationalist response to Delors' integrationist, and socialist, vision of Europe. With the elections to the European parliament at Strasburg only months away, the Labour party moved quickly to build a strong pro-Europe platform. And in the June 1989 elections, Labour replaced the Conservatives as the main British party in Strasburg (*The Independent*, 20 June 1989, p. 8). But just as the Conservatives have a small group in support of Britain's withdrawal from the Commonwealth, so Labour has long had a small group willing to withdraw from the EEC that would prefer instead to strengthen some of the country's historic links with the Commonwealth. Consistent with its pro-Commonwealth stance, therefore, the main criticism Labour levelled at the Conservatives over the 1962 Commonwealth Immigration Bill was that it undermined 'the unity and strength of the Commonwealth' (The Labour Party, 1961, p. 115), because the Macmillan government had not consulted the prime ministers of member states and was thereby acting unilaterally.

This theme has been a regular refrain in Labour's opposition to successive Conservative governments' unilateral action over matters that affect the Commonwealth. Of course, this is partly the politics of opposition. But at the end of the day, there can be little doubt that at the very least Labour's commitment to the smooth working of the Commonwealth is a deeper one than that of the Conservatives. The 1986 and 1987 annual heads of state conferences in the Bahamas and Canada, respectively, revealed Margaret Thatcher's determination that Britain does not need to go even half-way to achieve Commonwealth agreement over the most crucial issue facing its members in the late 1980s, the question of sanctions against apartheid South Africa. At the end of the Canada summit Rajiv Gandhi of India expressed the view that the Commonwealth may not need Britain's membership at all. This is, of course, quite ludicrous. But the Indian leader's statement reflected the distance between Labour's hope and the reality of Britain becoming the respected and trusted head of a harmonious Commonwealth of independent nations. This commitment to the Commonwealth ideal was convenient for the party for at least two reasons. First, it helped to overcome the paradox of a socialist party being in government at the very centre of the empire during a period of rapid decolonization. Labour sought, however, to avoid landing on either of the horns of the dilemma of empire or socialism (where socialism is understood to negate empire) by an appeal to traditional nationalism in a rather curious way. The party appealed to what it understood as the *humanitarian* spirit of the British people in order to effect a benign, socialist, imperial policy.

Rita Hinden, secretary of the Colonial Bureau of the Fabian Society, clearly expressed the dilemma the party faced and, in the 1940s and 1950s, suggested ways of avoiding it. In *The Labour Party and the Colonies* (1946) she argued that, whilst socialism implied an end to empire, socialists could not simply up and leave the colonial peoples in their conditions of poverty and backwardness for which Britain was responsible. Whilst she recognized the anger of the colonial peoples at the British for their presence she cautioned against too rapid a departure or too strict an application of the principles of democracy in what she and her colleagues called 'plural' societies.

Nevertheless, she failed to grasp the full weight of nationalist feelings when she argued, correctly, that independence did not mean an end to poverty and backwardness, but implied, perhaps unwisely, that because of these problems British departure may have to be delayed. In other words, she failed to realize that most nationalists, understandably, preferred independence to an economic well-being based on the oppressor's benevolence. Even in Jamaica, where the nationalist movement was not only comparatively moderate but also deeply divided, Norman Manley stressed this point as early as 1938. At the launching of the nationalist People's National Party that year, Manley argued thus:

> There is one straight choice before Jamaica. Either make up your minds to go back to crown colony government, *benevolently shepherded in the interests of the commitment of everybody in the country*; or have your voice and face the hard road of discipline, developing your own capacities, your own powers of leadership.
>
> (Sherlock, 1980, p. 99, emphasis added)

Assessing the successes and failures of political independence in Africa in 1976, Julius Nyerere, then president of Tanzania, argued much the same case as Norman Manley had done nearly four decades earlier. Nyerere concluded that,

> Despite all the horrors that we have seen in independent Africa, I still
> assert that it is better to be ruled oppressively within a free nation, than
> to be part of a colonial empire, however mild its rule may be.
>
> (Goulbourne, 1979, pp. 249–50)

If at the centre of the empire, rational and well-intentioned men and women
could afford to discuss the future of what was the British empire, in the peripheries nationalism was establishing its own programmes. It is a credit to both the
nationalist leaders in the ex-colonies and the Labour leadership of the pre-
Wilson years, that a respectful retreat rather than a routing occurred at the end
of the days of empire.

The second dimension to Labour's traditional nationalist conception of the
post-imperial political order was the multi-ethnic or multi-racial composition
of the new states the party hoped would develop. This, in turn, has two aspects:
first, there was the encouragement of nationalists in the colonies to effect
multi-racial states; and, second, as the non-white population of Britain became
more visible, there was the admonition to the British electorate to see Britain
as a multi-racial society.

Perhaps the best illustration of the first of these points is contained in
Labour's Colonial Policy: The Plural Society (1956) prepared by Rita Hinden
and other members of the Fabian Bureau whilst the party was in opposition.
Throughout the empire, different peoples distinguished by such factors as
language, religion, colour or 'race' had been thrown together for one reason or
another. There was, in short, hardly any society in the empire that was clearly
homogeneous by these criteria. In some the situation was less mixed and therefore sometimes less complex than in others, but they all shared a common
experience of being mixed in one way or another. In some places the population was made up of Africans and Europeans, or of Indians and Africans; in
most cases there were people from several 'racial' backgrounds. There was
also the situation where British imperialism had superimposed itself on an
already highly complex heterogeneous social structure. British West Africa
and India were, of course, outstanding examples of this. Where people were not
divided by 'race' or colour, they were divided by religion, language, customs
and so forth.

The general view, therefore, that Britain has no experience in exercising
political control over a heterogeneous society is far from the truth. What is true,
however, is that the expertise for this kind of political management was developed in non-democratic colonial contexts; not here at 'home'. Moreover, racial
subordination was a major pillar of the imperial system. The British as the
central political authority, therefore, had the opportunity to provide a central
principle which could unite a huge segment of humanity. The great failure of
European civilization,[7] however, was not to use its privileged historical

position to elevate humanity. Instead, whatever had divided mankind was exploited to the full in order to effect control and subservience. But it is hardly necessary to dwell on these failures. They are obvious enough, almost half a century after the process of decolonization began with the independence of India and Pakistan in 1947.

What is worth remarking on is the high expectations held by Labour about the ability or willingness of the colonized peoples immediately to make right decades, in some cases centuries, of injustice. The 'plural' societies of the empire were more or less required to transform themselves overnight from societies rooted in racial hatred and hostility, religious bigotry, linguistic divisions and so forth, into 'healthy', democratic societies in which each ethnic group is allowed to cultivate its own value systems whilst contributing to a common 'national consciousness'. According to the 1956 Labour Party position paper, cultural and social pluralism 'enriches mankind, adding colour and contrast to each society and stimulating progress through controversy' (The Labour Party, 1956, p. 30). The drafters and indeed the party recognized, however, that for loyalty to the nation to exist, two prerequisites were necessary:

> first, the consciousness of belonging to a nation must become so strong that all the people, of whatever race or colour, will feel themselves to be 'Kenyans', 'Tanganyikans', 'Rhodesians', 'Malayans', 'West Indians' or 'Fijians', rather than only, or primarily, Europeans, Africans, or Chinese, or whites, blacks, browns, or yellows; secondly and consequently, political control and organization will increasingly be based on the expression of the will of the nation, each member of which is regarded as an individual and equal human being, and not as a member of a racial group. In this process every vestige of the idea of racial superiority must be utterly destroyed.
>
> (The Labour Party, 1956, p. 30)

These ideas are, of course, lofty and laudable. The essential problem was that the colonial peoples who were just about to win their political independence were being asked to do what the imperial power with very much more material resources did not do. In some of these societies, such as those in the West Indies, the colonial power was almost entirely responsible for establishing foundations on which these societies were to develop. Even if Britain were to be partly excused for some of the injustices which developed in colonial Africa and Asia, the same excuses cannot be made with respect to the Caribbean from where so much was taken and so little returned. After all, whereas the British, like other European powers, in the nineteenth century built empires in Africa and Asia on top of existing feudal systems, in the case of the Caribbean European powers terminated the indigenous peoples and constructed new social orders, in their own (self-perceived) images, on a *tabula rasa*. If in some places the imperial power introduced unjust social structures, in others such structures which already existed were compounded by the imperial presence. And from this perspective it was surely unrealistic to expect the nationalists who were about to assume political power to correct, overnight, multiple ills that had been left to fester under a largely indifferent and cynical imperial order.

It was envisaged, for example, that the constitutional arrangements that were necessary for democratic institutions and practices, would have to be so defined that democratic participation of the minorities' interests would not only be recognized, but also enshrined in the constitution. Whilst correctly recognizing that the notions of 'partnership' and 'multi-racialism' in Africa, 'suggest racial difference rather than human identity' (The Labour Party, 1956, p. 31), the Labour party was willing to recommend that the majority Africans should be enfranchised only gradually. In this way the African would slowly come to a position of 'equality' with Europeans and Asians. It is difficult today to believe that such developments were being prescribed for the African in his or her own country.

The general idea was to have both democratic and communal representation alongside each other. The main problem, as the drafters of this document saw it, was that if universal adult suffrage were to be introduced, then the Africans would outnumber the Asians and Europeans combined. And to add insult to injury, the Africans were not necessarily educated. On the other hand, property or educational qualifications for enjoyment of the franchise were likely to 'appear to non-Europeans as devices to maintain white supremacy' (The Labour Party, 1956). Having ruled out the only potential power Africans could utilize in a democratic manner, namely the vote, and recognizing that socio-economic power rested with the European and Asian, the party argued that it was up to these minorities to accept Africans as equals.

The party, nonetheless, recognized that a crude majoritarianism would hold sway eventually. Thus, it argued that Africans would inevitably constitute the majority with influence in any democratic system on that continent. In Fiji, however, it was argued, 'democracy will give a majority in influence to people of Asian origin' (The Labour Party, 1956). Similarly, in Malaya, the indigenous Malay people would be outnumbered by the Chinese and Indians. In other words, in these different situations the development of democracy entailed something of a loss for the indigenous populations: majority Africans making major concessions to the European and Asian minorities; in Malaya and Fiji, the indigenous peoples being relegated to minority positions. In all these situations, however, very different developments have taken place since independence. In Malaya the indigenous people are asserting themselves against the Chinese and Indians. Recently, the most dramatic events in this respect were the Rabuka coups d'état of 1987 in Fiji. These events were triggered by the coming to office of a party dominated by Indians whose forebears migrated to the islands under the British.

In Africa the relations between the groups were more decisively resolved within the first decade of political independence. In the three East African territories of Uganda, Kenya and Tanzania, political independence came with universal adult suffrage because the African won the argument for majoritarian democracy. For them the new order meant taking seriously the principle learnt from the imperial power itself – 'one man, one vote'; the will of the majority should be supreme. Nationalist leaders were therefore able to make it a require-ment that non-Africans should decide for themselves whether they wish to remain as British citizens or as Kenyans, Ugandans or Tanganyikans (Tanzanians after union with Zanzibar in 1964). Britain retained the responsi-bility of providing a home for those from the Asian minorities who chose to remain British. Political independence was, essentially, an African struggle and therefore an African victory. Some Asians and Europeans did, of course, throw in their lot with the African population (see, for example, Ghai and McAuslan, 1970, ch. 2). But where this occurred it was individuals rather than as groups of people. From the perspective of the African majority the demon-stration of commitment was, therefore, required of these groups. In general, the demand for this demonstration by politicians came in the form of a requirement to declare a preference for specific African or British nationality. This was a logical conclusion of the practice of segregation under the British. Under its political aegis no common human affinities were engendered or encouraged; there were separate worlds of *Europeans*, *Asians* and *Africans*.

Within the first decade or so of political independence, nationalist govern-ments, following the restrictive practices of the former colonial regime, applied severe pressure on Asians, particularly those who had not opted for the new national citizenship. Whereas in the colonial period Asians, like Europeans, were a minority group, with independence, as Tandon noted, they became a dual minority: a minority in Africa and a minority for Britain (Tandon, 1973). Through the processes of Africanization in Kenya and Uganda and national-ization in Tanzania from 1967, the Asian minorities were rapidly deprived of the strong positions they had enjoyed in the economies of these countries. The result was mass exodus. The Asians were caught between two large and powerful forces: by the emergent and generally progressive nationalism of the hitherto oppressed African population, on the one hand, and on the other by the nationalism involved in the transition from empire to nation which was unfold-ing in Britain.

The Labour party focused particular attention on Tanganyika as a model for the 'plural' societies of colonial Africa. Indeed, in introducing the paper for adoption at the 1956 conference of the party, Driberg also welcomed the young Julius Nyerere, the founder and leader, for the next quarter of a century, of the Tanganyika African National Union (TANU) to the meeting. At the time of writing and adopting this position paper in 1956, Labour seemed to welcome the fact that although there were only 20,000 Europeans and 80,000 Asians living in Tanganyika and over 7,000,000 Africans, they all had the same number of representatives on the legislative council. Clearly, although all men were perceived to be equal, some men were more equal than others because the democratic rights of the individual were being determined according to his or her 'race' or colour.

But Tanganyika could not have developed into being the healthy 'plural' society Labour hoped it would become. Whilst it is true that the country has not experienced the dramatic expulsion of British Asians that occurred in Kenya in 1966 and in Uganda in 1971–2 under Idi Amin, about half of the Asian population of Tanganyika migrated after independence. Tanganyika can be proud of her record on ethnic and racial matters, where the laws of the country have tried to ensure that the various peoples who claim to be Tanzanians are accorded equal security, rights and responsibilities. For example, the electoral process is open to all citizens irrespective of race or colour or tribe, and all governments under the leadership of Julius Nyerere (from 1952 to 1985) included members of both the European and the Asian communities. Again, however, these were individuals who saw themselves as Tanganyikans and identified with the majority African population. In this regard contemporary post-imperial Britain has much to learn from the Tanzanian political leadership.

The third dimension of Labour's traditional nationalism as expressed in her post-World War Two perspective of a healthy society, has been its vision of Britain herself in the post-imperial age. It is interesting, however, that nowhere throughout the discussion of the 'plural societies' in the colonies did the party raise the same set of questions with regard to Britain. This cannot have been due to the absence of non-whites in Britain, because by 1956 the Asian and West Indian populations were growing. The absence of discussion at this time over the implications of a racially heterogeneous Britain was most likely due to several factors. For example, there was the expectation on the part of the new migrants themselves that they would not be establishing themselves permanently in Britain. Moreover, in the past waves of non-white migrants were rapidly absorbed, marginalized, or, especially with respect to people from the Caribbean, they returned (Phillips, 1974; May and Cohen, 1975) due to their relatively low numbers.

As the 1950s drew to a close, however, and the decade of the 1960s took on its own peculiar post-war features, Labour faced the prospect of confronting the Conservative Party's opposition to non-white peoples coming into Britain. From before this date, members of the Conservative Party had been opposed to the entry of black people and the issue had been debated in government circles (Layton-Henry, 1984). Whilst by the late 1950s the Macmillan government recognized that there was a 'wind of change' blowing over the continent of Africa, it also recognized that it might be politically wise to put an effective stop to non-white migration into Britain. The 'wind of change' was supposed to be blowing in Africa, not in Britain.

This involved Labour in a number of exchanges over questions of alleged immigrant crimes, diseases and the overburdening of local and social services (The Labour Party, 1962). The party called for an end to discrimination and prejudice against the newcomers and generally struck the note of integration. Of course, much of this was the work of a party in opposition. But these professions of concern also contained genuine feelings and commitment to the creation of a more just society in Britain. This commitment was borne out in 1965 by the Labour government's legislation to curb racial discrimination which established a race relations board, and its setting up of the Commission for Racial Equality in 1976, with government funding. Since the 1960s Labour in office at Whitehall or in Town Halls in the areas of large non-white settlement has continued to champion the cause of tolerance and integration. The common assumption has been that with some goodwill the peoples from the colonies would be able to fit in somewhere within a well-established national community. Overall, although less sceptical than the Conservatives about the efficacy of legislation to change social behaviour, Labour was not over-anxious to take fast legislative measures to curb discrimination in public life, partly because of the fear that this might alienate voters.

In the 1970s and the 1980s this tune changed. There seems to be a twofold position being held by the party. In some local areas, the party seems to have moved from supporting that bland kind of integration which meant that minorities should abandon their cultures and embrace that of the majority, to embracing some of the legitimate (cultural) demands of minority groups. At the national level, however, the party retains its traditional notion of minorities integrating into the whole, as evidenced by the persistent opposition by the national executive to *black sections* in the party (Shukra, 1990). In a sense, therefore, the party seems to be going in two directions simultaneously. At the national level there is the respect for the *traditional* form of nationalism which requires that all people who claim to have their home in Britain see themselves as integral parts of the national community and not as separate entities. It is a desire for individuals to constitute the membership of the party and nation rather than recognizing racial group membership of a national organization. But at the local level, where activists are closer to the demands of various minority as well as the majority communities, there has been the desire to recognize and encourage groups to perceive themselves as *different*. Of course, an important consideration here is the increasing importance of the ethnic minority vote in a number of constituencies in the inner cities. Another significant factor which must be borne in mind is the fact that very many politicians from the ethnic minorities have themselves made a dramatic appearance in the Labour party in the 1980s, at national but especially at the local level (see Ali, 1988).

But, undoubtedly, the notion of being British for both Labour and Conservatives has been expressed in the nationality laws of the land in the years since 1948. Labour strongly opposed the 1962 Commonwealth Immigration Act which established an effective end to the free entry of non-white 'British' people into Britain. Nonetheless, in office between 1964 and 1970 the party did not change the law. Indeed, it sought to apply it more rigorously than did the Conservatives. This was admitted to the 1965 conference held in Blackpool where it was stated that 'It is the Government's intention to tighten up the regulations governing entry with a view to preventing evasion of controls' (The Labour Party, *National Executive Committee, 1946–84* (1965), p. 79). The party recognized, and indeed has always stressed, the contribution of immigrants from the Commonwealth, meaning non-white people, to the British economy. And the party has consistently argued that non-white, non-European, minorities must not be regarded as second-class citizens. Nonetheless, in the report of the NEC from which I have just quoted, the leadership of the party stressed the point that:

> At the same time it must be recognized that the presence in this country of nearly one million immigrants from the Commonwealth with different social and cultural backgrounds raises a number of problems and creates various social tensions in those areas where they have concentrated.
> (The Labour Party, *National Executive Committee, 1946–84* (1965))

This was to speak with a forked tongue.

Similarly, in 1971, Labour, again in opposition, opposed the Conservatives' 1971 Immigration Act which introduced the infamous 'grandfather clause' into British legislation. In office from 1974–1979 Labour did not, however, change the law with respect to what the party itself saw as a racist definition of British nationality and citizenship. Labour's statements on the issue, since being in opposition from 1979 up to the 1981 British Nationality Act of the Thatcher government are, of course, humanitarian and laudable. But if the past is anything to go by, it would seem most unlikely that a Labour administration in the 1990s will attempt to change the racial definition that has become an essential aspect of British nationality laws. This is now part of the state's response to the post-imperial experience and the political risks for Labour may be perceived by its leadership to be too high.

Even so, I would suggest that Labour's position on nationality and the membership of the nation falls within the broad traditional nationalist mould. Admittedly, however, this tendency must be qualified by the party's upholding of the ethnic definition of membership of the British nation, as set out in nationality laws, whenever in office at Whitehall. The major responsibility that the party has failed to assume is that of providing the kind of leadership which would create for the majority white population the spirit necessary in the country to construct a new national identity which embraces all individuals *qua* individuals rather than as groups.

Ethnic nationalism and the Conservative party

But it is important to balance the Labour Party's relatively poor post-1948 record against the *ethnic* emphasis given in the Conservatives' definition of the nation. This ethnic nationalism of the party has been expressed principally through nationality laws, and debates at the party's annual national conferences. Any reading of the debates over immigration and the legislation enacted by Conservative Party governments on both nationality and immigration reveals the important differences on this point between the two parties of government. Labour's commitment, pusillanimous though it may be, is rooted in a tradition of internationalism which is part of the struggles of the working people. The Conservative Party's claim to have the interest of the nation[8] more at heart than its rival is in this regard correct, because the party has shown far less hesitation in trying to fashion a new British definition than has Labour in the post-imperial age.

In contrast, therefore, to the Labour Party, the Conservative Party has consistently placed the emphasis on the *ethnic* dimension in its expression of a new definition of the British nation. The party has shown comparatively little regard for the possible feelings of the international community. Indeed, the Conservatives sometimes seem to be determined to show how little they are concerned about the views of the international community as far as 'race relations' matters go. But then, the Conservative Party has not been under the same degree of pressure as Labour to demonstrate either to the country or to the world that it is maintaining any universally held principle. This is true in two respects. First, little seems to be expected of the Conservatives in the area of 'race relations' and much seems to be expected from Labour. Whatever little the Conservatives do is likely to be seen in a positive light and much that Labour may do from time to time is seen as falling far short of the desirable. In this situation the parties are forced to adopt public *postures* which are sometimes contrary to actual achievements when in office.

Secondly, the pressures within the parties pull the majority membership and leadership in opposite directions. Labour is pulled towards a greater sense of internationalism, resulting in greater emphasis being given to, or toleration shown towards, minority issues, particularly in the local branches of the party. In the Conservative Party, on the other hand, the pressure seems to be in the direction of total exclusion of non-whites or, failing this, ignoring the presence of people who may be different in any way from the majority population. A stiff upper lip and blind determination to demonstrate a grand ignorance have sometimes appeared much more important than any impression of racial justice being seen to be done. This is one interpretation that is sometimes given of the party's well-known 1979 election poster which depicted a young Afro-Caribbean male with the caption 'Labour says he is black, Conservatives say he is British'[9] (Layton-Henry, 1984).

Consequently, there is a general view abroad that the Labour party is 'easy' or 'soft' on immigrants – the code word for non-white people who have settled in Britain – whereas the Conservative party is perceived as being 'tough' and therefore 'realistic'. The Conservatives' own expression of the same view is that it is the only party which offers the electorate a 'realistic and logical' option. Willie (later Lord) Whitelaw, a darling of the party, speaking as shadow Home Secretary, told the Tory conference in 1976 that

> The Conservative Party has always been the party of realism and common sense. Our nation's sorry plight under Socialism today demands, indeed cries out, for such an approach from us at this Conference. *Nowhere do we need these virtues more than in the complex and emotional area of immigration and race relations.*
>
> (The Conservative Party (the National Union of Conservative and Unionist Associations), 1976, p. 45; emphasis added)

These are common themes at nearly all party conferences: the country's problems emanate from the manner in which the socialists have mismanaged, misguided or even withheld the truth from the country, and the direction pointed by the Tories is the only sensible way in which to go forward. Whatever may be claimed or believed, however, about the party's immigration and nationality policies and measures when in office, it cannot be denied that they have indeed grasped an aspect of the problem the majority white population faces in the post-imperial period, which is to define for itself a new 'national' identity. What is inadequately understood by the party, to paraphrase Marx, is the fact that although men and women make their own history they do so in the context of their past. This failure, partly bred of ignorance, is all the more remarkable since the Conservatives place such stress on the past. But it is obviously a very *selective* past to which the party points with respect to the question of British nationality.

The Conservatives have sought, then, to articulate a relatively unambiguous position regarding a new definition of 'nationality'. This clarity is, however, more in evidence when the Conservatives are in opposition than when they are in office, just as Labour's utterances of adherence to a non-ethnic definition of the nation are more vibrant when the party is in opposition than when it is in office. This is an important qualification to the Conservatives' understanding of the 'nation' as expressed through debates and legislation over nationality and emigration in the post-imperial age.

Another qualification is that it must be constantly borne in mind that the Conservatives, although not a party prone to the same high degree of public dispute in its ranks as is the Labour party, sometimes at conferences expresses a wide range of views over these matters. Indeed, reading the debates on immigration at annual conferences from the 1950s to the 1980s, it is impossible to ignore the clarity of a very small minority's opposition to the party's views. I will give just two examples of this.

The first of these is the contribution of Nigel Fisher, MP for Surbiton, to the debate in 1961 over the restriction of Commonwealth immigration. He admitted that if 'the tens of millions from the Asian Commonwealth came to Britain, as they have a perfect right to do today, then of course we could not absorb them all' (The Conservative Party (the National Union of Conservative and Unionist Associations), 1961, p. 23). But he went on to contrast immigration from Ireland, Asia and the West Indies and concluded that the 'threat from Asia' was only a potential one and that there were more Southern Irish citizens entering Britain than there were West Indians. In Fisher's view, any attempt to stop migration from the Commonwealth would 'look like colour legislation'. Perhaps the most important point he made in his short speech was to link the colonial question which was debated at length with respect to East Africa at the conference, with the question of immigration and the kind of society Conservatives were aiming to develop in post-imperial Britain.

> I make this plea to the Home Secretary: Do remember that we preach partnership in Africa; *let us practice it in Britain.* For us as the leaders of the greatest multi-racial Commonwealth the world has ever known, good race relations are really absolutely essential. We have got to be colour-blind if we are not going to lose the Commonwealth. So let there be no hint or thought of colour discrimination in any of the measures you propose.
>
> (The Conservative Party (the National Union of Conservative and Unionist Associations), 1961; emphasis added)

The second example is that of Peter Leyshon from Rhondda, Wales. Speaking against a motion presented by Enoch Powell at the 1972 annual conference of the party, Leyshon reminded members that he was a member of 'a racial minority in this country. The majority of you people in the audience came to this country a long time after my people' (The Conservative Party (the National Union of Conservative and Unionist Associations), 1972, p. 76). He referred to the settlement of different groups of people in these islands, including the Picts and the Celts. He then went on to speak against a motion presented by Enoch Powell over the Tory government's welcome of the Ugandan Asians:

> ... we have in our party – and let us not forget it – something that is Egyptian in its style. We have a scarab. A scarab was something which the Egyptians believed was religiously very important, because it symbolised to them the sun. It was in fact a beetle which rolled up in a ball of dung, and I say that we have in this room someone who could best be described as a dung beetle, who is rolling a ball of dung for no other purpose than to use it as a weapon against the leadership of his party.
>
> (The Conservative Party (the National Union of Conservative and Unionist Associations), 1972)

Similarly, there have been outspoken persons at conferences concerning the colonial question and the kind of society that leading Conservatives would like to see emerge in the ex-colonies. At the 1961 conference the outgoing colonial secretary, Iain MacLeod, who had left a favourable impression on African nationalists, made a moving speech in defence of Britain's colonial policy and the transition from colony to Commonwealth. He clearly understood what was less easily grasped in the 1950s by the Fabians, when he stressed that

> ... I believe in the rights and duties of men, and that means of all men. But do not ever fall into the error of assuming that, because you give a man better housing, because you improve the health services, some-how that will satisfy his craving for basic political rights. It cannot do. Indeed, it is bound to sharpen it.
>
> Remember also that however great your services may have been to a country, however noble the contribution we have made in the five continents of the world to the developing countries has been – and it has been noble – that will never always be accepted as a reason why automatically you should govern.
>
> (The Conservative Party (the National Union of Conservative and Unionist Associations), 1961, p. 25)

Essentially, however, the Conservative Party's main contribution to the search for a new definition of post-imperial British nationality has been to give it an ethnic dimension. Nowhere has this contribution been more clearly demonstrated than in the 1962 Commonwealth Immigration Act, the 1971 Immigration Act and the 1981 Nationality Act. These have been the acts which mark the most important steps in this ethnic direction in the post-imperial period. Significantly enough, they have all been passed by Conservative governments. The details of these measures are too well known to require repeating here. Suffice it to say, therefore, that the 1962 Act marked the abrupt end of free entry of people from non-white Commonwealth countries into Britain. And the term 'new Commonwealth' was to become more familiar as a code term for non-white people. It is also worth noting that this new political label has tended to encourage the thinking that the countries of the 'new Commonwealth' have only recently established connections with Britain. This, of course, is far from the truth. Some of these 'new' Commonwealth societies (such as several of the Caribbean countries) were established by Britain herself in the early part of the sixteenth century and part of India was under British control (East India Company) long before the formal establishment of the British Raj in 1857. There is little that is *new* about the New Commonwealth. The term denotes the new post-imperial/colonial relationship between Britain and these countries but it helps to hide the centuries-*old* relationship between Britain and the non-white peoples she once governed and exploited. The change in the relationship provided, however, part of the justification for a voucher system which was introduced. Intending migrants now had to prove that they had a job to come to. Only dependents, such as a wife and minors, could join the head of the family.

From the perspective of a new British nationality, therefore, in the post-imperial period, the discussion which took place at the Conservative 1961 annual conference is very revealing and therefore warrants a closer look. Councillor D. Clarke of Hayes and Harlington moved the following motion, which provided the basis for discussion:

> That this Conference expresses its concern at the very serious problems being created by the uncontrolled number of immigrants flowing into the United Kingdom. It asks Her Majesty's Government to take action quickly on this matter.
>
> (The Conservative Party (the National Union of Conservative and Unionist Associations), 1961, p. 26)

The councillor[10] started by stressing that he was not calling for a stop to immigration on the basis of colour and pointed out that of the forty motions on the issue presented to the conference by delegates from different parts of the country, only two mentioned colour. Nonetheless, the case both he and those in support of the motion presented, amounted to the strongest rejection of the principle of free entry into the United Kingdom, particularly from the non-white Commonwealth. Although Irish immigrants were mentioned, they were not seen as presenting any of the social problems immigrants were depicted to be bringing into the country.

These problems, which several speakers referred to throughout the debate, included the increased demands made on an inadequate stock of housing, adding to an already overcrowded country, crime, poor hygiene and contagious diseases. T. F. H. Jessel from Peckham, South London, added:

There is also the beginning of an educational problem. I am on the management committee of several primary schools and some of the headmasters and headmistresses are saying that a considerable number of Cypriots and [sic] Pakistani and other children are arriving who speak no English and have to be taught, and this takes up disproportionate teaching time and effort with the result that other children's education suffers.

(The Conservative Party (the National Union of Conservative and Unionist Associations), 1961, pp. 27–8)

Frank Taylor from Moss Side, Manchester, was particularly incensed by his observation that immigrants were sponging on the social services. Speaking of an unemployed black man and his family, Taylor railed: 'You and I are keeping him and his wife and about six delightful piccaninnies around his knees' (The Conservative Party, 1961, p. 29). At the same time he was most worried about immigrants being able to hold onto jobs ' . . . if economic winter comes' (The Conservative Party, 1961). The Home Secretary, R. A. Butler, who was one of the more liberal-minded Tories of the immediate post-imperial period (Rich, 1986, ch. 8), in rounding off the debate, took up this point when he argued that Britain must look to the 'rainy day' when unemployment may return. Taylor concluded that there were three things which must necessarily be done: integration of those immigrants already here, 'send the bad hats home' and restriction of further immigration 'until we have digested what we have here already' (The Conservative Party, 1961).

But the question of integration was not a point welcomed by Norman A. Pannell, a Liverpool MP. He argued that, quite apart from the housing question, immigrants posed a danger to health and morals and by the births of unwanted children. He wanted conference to face up to the facts and admit that

These immigrants are not necessarily inferior to us but they are different – different not only in colour but in background, tradition and habits. But there are only two alternatives: they must either be fully integrated into our society by intermarriage, by intermingling of their blood with ours throughout the population, or they must form minority groups set apart from the general population – a sort of second-class citizenry. Either alternative is, in my view, unfortunate.

(The Conservative Party (the National Union of Conservative and Unionist Associations), 1961, p. 30)

He argued that no society has ever been able to solve what he called 'this problem' and it should not be allowed to develop and be faced by future generations. These are themes which were taken up by Butler in his closing speech on the matter, but more importantly by Enoch Powell after 1968.

Whereas, however, Powell was, from time to time, to shift the thrust of his attack from all non-whites to those who were more likely to *swamp* British culture, Pannell found offence in the presence of both people with a different culture and those with similar culture to Britain's. Here was an early rejection of both Asian *exclusivity* and Caribbean *integrationism*. For him it was the fact of *difference* which mattered, and difference in this context could surely have no other meaning than a dissimilarity of people's *colour*, particularly with respect to people from the Caribbean.

Another theme mentioned by Pannell and which was to be taken up by Powell in the 1970s is that of the relationship between Britain and the Commonwealth. Pannell argued that

> The old Empire has gone and a new Commonwealth has arisen – a Commonwealth of free and equal nations. All, with the exception of this country impose restrictions on immigration from other parts of the Commonwealth. It is time that we recognize this equality amongst the free nations of the Commonwealth by introducing into this country the same restrictions on entry that all the others apply to us.
>
> (The Conservative Party (the National Union of Conservative and Unionist Associations), 1961)

This attempt to redefine British responsibility, by pointing to the alleged practices of other Commonwealth countries, was taken up by Enoch Powell at the 1972 annual conference of the party. Speaking about the admission of the Ugandan Asians whom the Heath government had just allowed into Britain, Powell argued that Britain had only the same *moral* responsibility as other nations for the British passport holders fleeing Idi Amin's Uganda. In his view

> ... when the East African countries became independent there was no suggestion, let alone undertaking, in Parliament or outside, that those inhabitants who remained citizens of the United Kingdom and Colonies would have right of entry into this country ... the practice of international law which requires a country to re-admit or admit its own nationals applies in our case only to those who *belong* to the United Kingdom and not to other Commonwealth citizens, whether classified as citizens of the United Kingdom and Colonies or not.
>
> (The Conservative Party (the National Union of Conservative and Unionist Associations), 1972, p. 72; emphasis added)

In Powell's view, Britain had less responsibility for the immigrants than their 'true home' countries, such as India. Councillor Hogarth, from Bournemouth, asked whether it would not have been wiser for the government to have asked Asian Commonwealth countries, 'where the language, the food and the climate are familiar' (The Conservative Party (the National Union of Conservative and

Unionist Associations), 1972, p. 74) to accept 'these refugees'. On each occasion that there have been expulsions of British Asians from Africa – 1966 from Kenya, 1972 from Uganda and 1976 from Malawi – similar outcries have been heard from the right of the party. These have been equally vigorously opposed by speakers at the party's annual conferences. And the debate in mid-1989 in parliament and the media over the future of the non-white population of Hong Kong after 1997 serves as a reminder that the situation is a continuing one.

But the interesting point is that although the governments of both parties usually claim to live up to the responsibilities of the country, at Conservative party conferences the motions from the right usually get the support of the leadership and eventually find their way into legislation. Thus, the entry in 1968 of Kenyan Asians encouraged the party when it returned to office in 1970 to enact the 1971 Immigration Act. This related citizenship and immigration in a manner that had not hitherto been done. The Act brought into play the notion of 'patriality'. This meant, first, that people outside Britain who were able to claim close contact with the United Kingdom, by virtue of having had a grandfather who was born in this country, could gain entry.

Second, people outside the United Kingdom who could not make this claim but held British passports, could not automatically gain entry. It was to this new law that Enoch Powell's motion to the 1972 annual conference of the party addressed itself. He called upon the government to maintain the party's policy on the question, which was basically that not only should there be an end to immigration from what was now being called 'the new Commonwealth', meaning the non-white Commonwealth, but also that there should be encouragement to those already here to leave voluntarily.

By the late 1970s, therefore, both parties were coming to view the legislation governing issues of immigration and citizenship to be far too complicated. The Labour government of James Callaghan began the process whereby Britain would attempt to systematize her nationality laws after a period of thirty years under the 1948 Act. In the government's Green Paper of April 1977, it was argued that the chaos in the legal provisions over these matters warranted major reform because they 'have caused confusion and have encouraged the belief that our immigration laws contain elements of racial prejudice' (Home Office, 1977, p. 9). What Labour started was completed by the Conservative government in 1981, when the present British Nationality Act was passed. The concern with racial prejudice was not quite as sensitive as Labour's stated intentions. Consistent with its usual stance, Labour has declared its commitment to amend the present British Nationality Act whenever the party is returned to office (The Labour Party, 1981) but, as hinted earlier, it is doubtful whether such changes will incorporate what the party presently describe as 'racist' legislation.

The new act, which came fully into effect at the end of December 1987, provides for two categories of British subjects: those who are citizens of the United Kingdom and have the right of entry and settlement in this country; and those who are British Overseas subjects. This latter group does not have automatic right of entry into the United Kingdom. This sounds very much like the distinction Enoch Powell made at the 1972 annual conference between British citizens who have rights of entry and those British citizens who do not have such rights. Thus, although his motion was defeated by the mounting of an amendment which congratulated the government for taking responsibility for the Ugandan Asians, at the end of the day Powell and his supporters had their demand met by the state.

The 1981 British Nationality Act, therefore, firmly placed the nail in the coffin of a British nationality which included more than people who have had long physical contact with these shores. If nationalism in the white Commonwealth and the black colonies brought the Pax Britannica to an end, then between India's independence in 1947 and the 1960s, the decade of decolonization, the changing concept of British nationality has buried the notion of the *civic Britannicus sum*. The legislation, if only by implication, now recognizes a distinct, territorial entity of Britain and a much clearer understanding of who is likely to be considered to be 'British' is also established. In arriving at this juncture, two aspects of a longstanding non-nationalist tradition have been abandoned.

The first of these is that the acquisition of nationality by birth, the doctrine of *ius soli*, is now significantly modified. Whereas it was enough for a person to have been born on British soil or in British territorial waters, to be regarded as British, this is now no longer sufficient. The person must also have been born to parents of whom one is a British citizen. The second aspect of the tradition which is now abandoned is the sense of responsibility which Britain held onto during the period of imperial decline. From 1961, however, the Conservative party had made it clear that Britain was willing to take this step as she prepared for a new, post-imperial definition of her role in the world. An *ethnic nationalist* definition of the membership of the nation was consistent with this new posture. And on this T. F. H. Jessel of Peckham must have the last word. His statement is, not surprisingly, full of obvious inaccuracies and false assumptions:

> We hear a great deal about the traditional rights of the people who come into this country from the Commonwealth. I do not think it is a particularly long-standing tradition. It dates mainly from the 1870s and the 1880s when people went out to chance their arm in the old colonies and of course they had to have the right to return. But this has now been extended to hundreds of millions of people who all have a perfect legal right to come in quite regardless of how many come,

quite regardless of whether they can be properly housed and quite regardless of the social problems they may create. The whole situation makes nonsense and to many of us there is an overwhelming case for restricting immigration without delay to all people, regardless of colour and creed. The question is not whether it should be done but when and how.

(The Conservative Party (the National Union of Conservative and Unionist Associations), 1961, p. 28)

Retreating into the laager?

Sooner of later, Britain was bound to achieve the full retreat from *empire* to *nation* and, as a historical transition, it cannot but have been difficult for everybody concerned. And perhaps it was inevitable that in the process of effecting this rupture Britain would be involved in betrayals and the shirking of responsibilities. In particular, minority groups both in Britain and outside have found themselves paying a disproportionately high part of the cost incurred in this transition. Unfortunately, the aftermaths of the transition continue to have relevance for developments in this country. It may be worth considering, however, briefly, some of those likely to impinge upon the life of the nation for the foreseeable future.

First, there are still some small territories that entered the 1980s and may probably enter the next century under the British political aegis. These places have different kinds of relationships with Britain and no doubt Britain's response to their needs will vary from place to place. In the Caribbean, territories such as the Turks and Caicos Islands remain under British protection within the context of the British West Indies Act of 1966. This means that, whilst these islands enjoy a degree of internal autonomy, their defence and foreign relations are taken care of by Britain. In South America Britain holds onto the Falklands/Malvinas and after controversial military manoeuvring in the area in late 1987 to early 1988, Britain appeared prepared to go to war as in 1982 over the question of her suzerainty of the islands. In Europe itself there is Gibraltar, over which Britain and Spain, as members of the EEC, decided in 1987 to cooperate. The British loyalty to the unionists in Northern Ireland remains a firm one for both Labour and Conservatives. This would appear to put aside for the foreseeable future the unification of that island, despite the sensible calls in 1988 from the Irish premier, Charles Haughey, as well as Ken Livingstone and Tony Benn, for discussions to commence in order to begin the countdown for Britain's departure from the emerald isle – the first British colonial possession.

Presently, the most pressing and immediate problem for Britain in this respect is the vexed question of Hong Kong, which will revert, by treaty, to

China in 1997. It seems unlikely that even the massacre of reformist students in Peking during the first weekend of June 1989 will greatly affect the timetable of British withdrawal. The massacre, which the Chinese authorities denied took place, shocked the world and had an immediate impact on the British public. Not surprisingly, the British government expressed 'revulsion and outrage' at the event. But in a series of interviews covered in the press, on television and radio, as well as in responses to questions in parliament in early June, the then Foreign Secretary, Sir Geoffrey Howe, adamantly refused to commit his government to any decisive action which would disturb the agreement for peaceful handing over of the territory to China in 1997. The most the government was prepared to do was to 'relax' the immigration rules for civil servants and businessmen with assets to come to Britain. One reason frequently given by Sir Geoffrey for this cautious approach was that

> ... we could not easily contemplate a massive new immigration commitment which could more than double the ethnic minority population of the United Kingdom.
>
> *(The Daily Telegraph,* 7 June 1989, p. 1)

Why this of itself would be undesirable was never explained. But the statement makes perfect sense from the perspective of the ethnic nationalist who regards the presence of non-white minorities in Britain as a kind of external disturbance of the body politic and social.

At the same time, however, a Gallup Poll revealed that 42 per cent of the British public would support measures to allow people from the colony to enter Britain *(The Daily Telegraph,* 7 June 1989, p. 1). Throughout June the crisis in China deepened and the people of Hong Kong stepped up their demands for consideration to enter Britain as a *last resort.* Steadily, public opinion appeared to change in favour of those who argued that the immigration rules should be changed so as to give people in the colony the right of entry to Britain.[11] Paddy Ashdown, leader of the Social and Liberal Democrats, was reported as '. . . virtually a lone voice in the Commons . . . calling for the bulk of Hong Kong citizens to be offered refuge in Britain' *(The Daily Telegraph,* 7 June 1989).

What Britain's *actual* position will be when the people in these territories are forced to make a choice of either remaining under changed political authorities (for example, Chinese, Argentinian or Spanish) or coming to the United Kingdom is, of course, to be witnessed in the 1990s and the century around the corner. But the grounds have largely been prepared. People with acceptable ethnic backgrounds are likely to be welcomed under the present nationality law whilst those with unacceptable ethnic backgrounds are likely to be denied a home in Britain.

Such, however, are the vagaries of politics that it should not be surprising if the British government of the day were to accept members of the latter group in the 1990s as the Heath government accepted the Ugandan Asians in the 1970s. If there is a political point to be gained from acceptance then this outcome may very well become attractive. The central state's welcome of the Ugandan Asians was probably largely determined by the Heath government's concern to demonstrate Britain's declared humanitarianism and expose the 'barbarism' of the formerly favoured Idi Amin. Whilst a similar scenario may occur in the 1990s with respect to Hong Kong, two considerations would suggest some important qualifications: first, China, the world's largest country in terms of population, cannot be ostracized in the same way as smaller nations. Second, and more importantly, Britain will no doubt be concerned about her own increasingly complex internal, domestic racial/communal situation, as Geoffrey Howe's statement quoted above implies. The implication is, of course, that the entry of so many non-whites will cause social disruptions and racial antagonism between non-whites and the native white population of Britain.

But one major characteristic of this is likely to be a sharpened contestation between minorities themselves. For example, the *old* 'Asians' groups (from the Indian sub-continent) and the *new* 'Asians', the Chinese, may find themselves pitched in an ethno/racial competition as in parts of the Far East. Additionally, the entry of people from Hong Kong may very well present an opportunity for the government of the day to absolve the state and the majority white population from any responsibility for the increasingly chronic racial situation in Britain by making a good gesture towards the people of the colony. Moreover, whilst this is not an argument in support of exclusion, the new group(s) will most likely be professionals and businessmen whose success may be utilized as support for the view that racism is not a hindrance to the country's minorities.

A second aspect of the transition from empire to nation which is likely to continue to affect developments in Britain is the very fact that inside the United Kingdom itself minorities which came here during the period of imperial decline find themselves still effectively excluded from membership of the nation. One of the main reasons for this, although not the only one, is the construction of the British *nation* in such a manner that it has to be understood in purely *ethnic* terms. It is less of the *traditional* understanding of the *nation* as represented in the earlier post-imperial age by Labour, and more like the *ethnic* perception of the national community, as represented by the main body of the Conservative party and, contrary to Dixon's assumption (Dixon, 1983, p. 6), pre-dates Thatcherism. In a strictly formal sense, non-white minorities settled in Britain have been able to secure membership of the nation: many are British citizens either by birth or by registration and enjoy the formal rights of all citizens such as the right to vote, to become members of political organizations, and so forth. The *tangential* or peripheral relationship envisaged by this perception of the national configuration is crudely expressed by Figure 5.1. It may be noted that recently settled white groups (for example Poles, Ukrainians and Jews) are perceived to be members of the British nation, while the non-white groups, whether defined in terms of colour or religion, are external to the national community. There is little or no understanding here of the experiences of a person or of persons who may, for example, be Afro-Caribbean/ Rastafarian/Welsh and/or (strictly) English; nor is there here any appreciation of the existence of those who may be Muslim/Hindu/Sikh/Asian and, at the same time, be (strictly) English/Welsh and/or Scots. These various combinations and, indeed, very much more complex ones, do exist. To date, however, such individuals and groups are ejected from the national community and must find places for themselves outside the boundaries of the British nation.

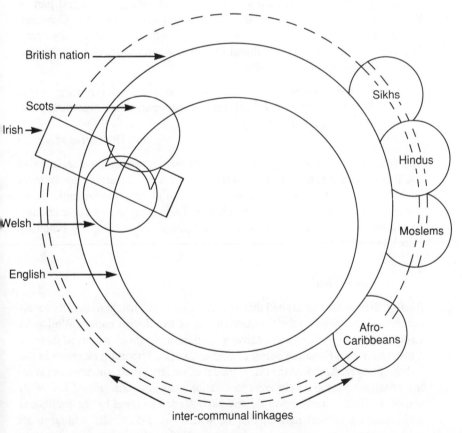

Fig. 5.1 An ethnic depiction of Britain

Thus, therefore, a variety of groups and individuals with mixed backgrounds are being constantly excluded from the national community and their humanity must be found in communities external to the mainstream of the society into which they were and are being born. The rejection I am speaking of here is that to which Enoch Powell, as we noted earlier, gave eloquent expression: a non-white person born and bred on British soil is not English, Scots or Welsh by virtue of such a natural process. One brief example should suffice here. When the Prime Minister, Margaret Thatcher, stressed in her famous Bruges speech on 20 September 1988 that 'Our [Britain's] links to the rest of Europe, the continent of Europe, have been the *dominant* factor in our history' (Thatcher, 1981, p. 1) she was, of course, pointing to an important fact. But the history of Britain over the past several centuries has been marked more by her overbearing presence elsewhere in the world than by her Continental appearance and concerns. It is no doubt for this reason that the Prime Minister has insisted that whilst Britain's future rests with being an integral part of Europe, the country's destiny does not lie exclusively with the Continent (Thatcher, 1988, p. 3). It ought, however, to strike us as strange that the Prime Minister of a so-called multi-cultural Britain can, forty years after the landing of *SS Empire Windrush*, boast that

> . . . the story of how Europeans explored and colonized and – yes, without apology – civilized much of the world is an extraordinary tale of talent, skill and courage.
>
> (Thatcher, 1988, p. 2)

This is not merely a case of gross insensitivity and historical injustice. It is also a telling statement to the effect that when the leader of the nation's government spoke of Britain and the British she had in mind only the collective consciousness of the majority white population. This perception of contemporary Britain, as we have seen, has been more openly and forthrightly stated by Enoch Powell.

Conclusion

Finally, then, it may be argued that a crucial aspect of Thatcherism is its development of the party's *ethnic* understanding of the British nation. Whilst the Labour party, as we have seen, converges on the same point, it arrived there by a different route. From the outset of decolonization, important elements in the Labour party realized that the plural model of society posed a number of pressing problems for the newly emergent nation-states in Asia and Africa. With respect to Britain itself, however, the party tended to stand by the traditional understanding of nationalism, that is, where the nation-state embraces all groups within a specific territorial boundary. Nationality and immigration laws enacted or administered by Labour governments have upheld an ethnic understanding of the British nation. Little has been done to develop what Hinden called 'national consciousness' in Britain. The Conservatives, on the other hand, have been quick to assert an understanding of the nation but this has been a strictly *ethnic* one. It has also been generously enriched by legislation. As suggested throughout this discussion, this has been so especially in the increasingly divided field of nationality and immigration. The ethnic understanding of the British nation, however, is not restricted to this field. In particular, the 1988 Education Act exhibits Thatcherism's dual task of unifying the British (white, European) nation whilst keeping at bay or on the periphery non-white minorities. I want to look a little more closely at the dilemma that this dual task involves. Before doing so, however, it is necessary to examine two examples of diasporic politics.

6

Diasporic politics: Sikhs and the demand for Khalistan

Introduction

This chapter examines the Punjab/Sikh problem within the framework of ethnic and traditional nationalism outlined in the previous chapters. In particular, the discussion here extends my contention that as the British nation continues to be defined largely in ethnic terms and thereby excludes the legitimate membership of non-white minorities, groups recently settled in Britain are wont to look to their original homelands for security and a sense of certainty. The mobilization of their own distinctive ethnicity will be one important way of asserting difference. This is, however, only part of the story. The second part consists of the kinds of developments occurring in these homelands themselves. The Khalistan question, therefore, serves to illustrate how ethnic nationalism can be aroused and mobilized in support of events in places that are physically far away from the new home of settlement. The important point to bear in mind, however, is that the flames of Khalistani ethnic nationalism are being fed by two fires: exclusion from the British national community, and the dynamics of developments 'back home' in the Punjab. And the political pressures released by these heated situations are perfectly compatible.

In this examination of the painful situation in the vast and diverse land which produced Gandhi and Nehru, I want to draw attention to three aspects of the Khalistan question as it relates to Sikhs in the United Kingdom. These are, first, the origins and development of the demand for an independent state of Khalistan in the northern Indian state of Punjab; second, some aspects of the nature of the work in which some groups that support the cause engage themselves within Britain, and in this respect the analysis focuses upon the Khalistan Council up to 1988; and third, the vision some Sikhs in Britain have of an independent Sikh state in their 'homeland'.

The dramatic storming of the Golden Temple at Amritsar on 5 June 1984 by the Indian army alerted the world to the demand by Sikhs for an independent state of Khalistan. It was also the single most important event that helped to galvanize the demand for an independent homeland as well as leading to the brutal killing of the Indian prime minister, Indira Gandhi, a few months later, on the morning of 31 October. But there are, of course, several other kinds of grievances expressed in defence of the demand for an independent state of Khalistan. These include a number of territorial, economic and linguistic grievances, which the Sikhs feel the central Indian government in Delhi has consistently failed to address adequately since independence from Britain in 1947. These grievances were, however, insufficient cause for the Sikhs to demand independence from India. The invasion of the Golden Temple provided the hitherto minuscule minority of Sikhs who had raised the question of separation, with the sufficient cause they had lacked.

The Khalistan crisis is only one instance of the highly complex and volatile relations between the central, union, government and the states in post-colonial India. I do not intend here to explore the kinds of politics to which these troubled relations give rise. My reason for looking at the Khalistan question in this discussion is to consider how recent events in India may possibly affect the political behaviour of the Sikh community in the United Kingdom. Such a focus will help to highlight the growing importance of diasporic politics as a specific form, or expression, of ethnic nationalist solidarity across the boundaries established by the community of nations-states.

There are, of course, various grievances advanced by Sikhs in India and Britain, in order to justify their demand for an independent Khalistan. Most of these grievances, and certainly all the important ones, may be conveniently organized around the fourfold categorization of the nation and/or nationalism and related issues discussed earlier.

Territory and economy

The longest standing set of problems in the Punjab has been of a *territorial* kind. The point is strongly borne out in the *Anandpur Sahib Resolution* of October 1973, which is regarded by some Sikh spokesmen as their Magna Carta (Bhullar *et al.*, 1985, p. 12).[1] A very brief statement of Sikh demands, the Resolution was agreed at an All-India conference under the leadership of the main Sikh party, the Akali Dal, at a time when the party was itself in opposition to a Congress state government in Punjab. In 1978 the Resolution was amended at another Akali All-India conference at Ludhiana. At this time the Akalis led a coalition government in the Punjab but did nothing to put the Resolution into effect. This led two of the most incisive analysts of developments in the Punjab to conclude that the Akalis did not, at this time, take the Resolution seriously (Nayar and Singh, 1984, p. 23). Nonetheless, after the present troubles in the Punjab began, the then leader of the Akali Dal, the late Sant

Harchand Singh Longowal, negotiated yet another version of the Resolution. There will be occasion to return repeatedly to this document but for now I wish only to comment upon the emphasis it placed on the recovery of traditional Punjabi lands as an integral part or aspect of the Sikh nation.

The first political claim of the 1982 Longowal version of the Resolution was for the lands lost in the various divisions of the Punjab since independence to be returned to a newly reconstituted Punjab. With the partition of British India at independence in August 1947, the larger West Punjab went to the newly formed Islamic state of Pakistan, and East Punjab went to India. The division, not surprisingly, caused mass disruption and the transportation of people in a two-way flow across newly drawn borders. In the process the traditional or historical Punjab was divided, resulting in much loss of life and property, due to communal conflict between Moslems fleeing India for Pakistan and Hindus and Sikhs fleeing Pakistan for India. There was also the loss of much else that the Sikhs hold dear. Many sacred shrines including, significantly, the birthplace of the founder of the faith, Guru Nanak, were lost to the new Punjab, across the Pakistan border.

It seems Sikhs both then and now accept this as fate and have no intention of recovering these in any reconstituted Punjabi/Sikh state. The quarrel the Sikhs have is not, therefore, perceived to be with Pakistan, but with India. Indeed, some leaders who are calling for an independent Khalistan would argue that the holy places of the Sikhs in Pakistan are respected by the Moslems whereas Hindus in India do not respect the gurdwaras (Sikh temples). This may be a tactical position on the part of Khalistani leaders. After all, it would be most unwise, politically and otherwise, to challenge the power of the Indian state and that of Pakistan simultaneously. It matters little here what the reason may be, but Khalistani leaders are generally careful to make clear that they have no quarrel with the state of Pakistan. They seem quite unconcerned to recover lands lost with the 1947 partition in which the Sikhs were undoubtedly the major losers (Nayar and Singh, 1984, p. 21); as farmers in British India they were particularly affected by the vacating of land for new settlers.

The dispute with respect to territories goes back to the creation of new states based on linguistic boundaries which Congress adhered to, at least in the decolonizing and early independence periods under Pandit Jawaharlal Nehru. This perception of language is a good example of how the linguistic definition of a nation, discussed in chapter four, is honoured in varied circumstances. The creation in 1966 of Haryana, which established a buffer between the national capital Delhi and Punjab to the south, and to the north Himachal Pradesh between the troubled Indo-Chinese border state of Kashmir and Punjab, also resulted in loss of territory for an already reduced Punjab. The territorial demands, of what became the moderate Akali Dal by 1982, include the return of some areas lost to newly created states in which the national majority Hindus vastly outnumber the pockets of Sikhs. These pockets presently exist principally in Haryana, Himachal Pradesh and Rajasthan. The territorial demand, therefore, includes a rejection of corridors linking pockets of either Hindu or Sikh populations. This was, however, one possible solution from the perspective of the central government in Delhi in the 1970s.

Moreover, the Sikhs have claimed that in every division and subdivision since 1947 the central government has been able to so arrange matters that the Hindu majority of the region has been able to safeguard their interests whilst those of the Sikhs have been gravely jeopardized. The argument is that whilst some people have not even claimed state status they have been granted it, unlike the Sikhs who have protested repeatedly for such status within the Union. In this regard there is constant reference not only to states carved out of historical Punjab, but also to the new states of Andhra Pradesh, Karnataka, Kerala and Tamil Nadu in the deep south.

One vital aspect of these territorial claims has been the demand for the return of the post-colonial state capital of Chandigarh, built after the loss of the traditional areas, including Lahore, to Pakistan as part of the 1947 settlement. In 1966 the Shah Commission recommended that Chandigarh should become part of the new state of Haryana. Sikhs argue that this is against the precedents set within independent India: where new states have been created out of older ones, the capitals have remained with the older state. Such, they argue, was the situation with respect to the city of Bombay when Gujerat state was created in the west out of Maharashtra, and also with the city of Madras when the state of Tamil Nadu in the south came into being.

It is believed that the opposition to this led to a compromise whereby Chandigarh would become a Union Territory under direct rule from Delhi but with the state assemblies of both Haryana and Punjab being housed in the city (Tully and Jacob, 1985, p. 44). The situation deteriorated to the point where one prominent Sikh leader who was not a member of the Akali Dal, Darshan Singh Pheruman, died from his fast which was designed to coerce Mrs Gandhi into conceding Chandigarh to the state of Punjab. When, soon after this dramatic event in 1969, Sant Fateh Singh threatened to burn himself to death over the matter, Mrs Gandhi forged a compromise in January 1970 whereby Chandigarh would be given to Punjab after five years in return for the Hindi-speaking areas of Fazilka and Abohar, which would go to Haryana, linked by a narrow fifty-mile corridor through Punjab. The terms were never fulfilled and in 1981, under the leadership of Sant Harchand Singh Longowal, a new *morcha* (peaceful mass demonstration) was started, organized around the demands of the Anandpur Resolution. This acted as the catalyst to the present problems in the Punjab (Bhullar *et al.*, 1985, p. 22; also Tully and Jacob, 1985, ch. 7).

Intricately linked to the question of territory have been a number of important economic factors. These have given urgency and weight to the Sikhs' demands over Punjab's boundaries. In their view these claims substantiate their point that they have suffered a net loss of resources and are likely to continue to do so under present arrangements within the union.

Undoubtedly, the most urgent and significant of these economic grievances is to do with water. Every Punjabi will inform the enquirer that the name of their homeland, Punjab, means the land of the Five Rivers. But Punjabi/Sikh nationalists today argue that the state has been reduced to the land of only two rivers. The claim is that fertile hills, mountains and most of the waters have gone, first to Pakistan and later to Haryana and Himachal Pradesh (Bhullar *et al.*, 1985, p. 23). Mention is not made specifically of the water dispute between Punjab and Delhi in the Longowal version of the Anandpur Resolution but comes under the general head of state control over state resources and the exclusion of the centre with respect to these. At the very time of the Resolution's reformulation in the early eighties, however, Sikh nationalists were arguing that:

> The river water dispute forms today the most important politico-economic issue in the Punjab. It has become source [sic] of tension between the state and the centre and has embittered relations between Sikhs and Hindus. Unless the situation is handled in a Statesman-like manner it may assume serious proportions, as it affects the present and future generations of crores[2] of Sikh farmers and industrialists.
>
> (Bhullar *et al.*, 1985, p. 23)

The argument is easy enough to understand. Most Punjabi Sikhs earn their living from the land as farmers, and the Punjab is properly regarded as India's bread basket (see, for example, Kumar *et al.*, 1984). It follows then that the state depends heavily on its water for irrigation. Sikh farmers and militants, however, claim that interference by the union government, through the State Reorganization Act of 1966, not only removes Punjab's control over this vital resource but has led to an unjust allocation, from the centre, of the state's water. They argue that 76 per cent of the water from the Beas and Ravi rivers goes to Haryana, Rajasthan and Delhi, and only the remaining 24 per cent is left for use in the Punjab. Moreover, it is argued that this supply is inadequate for the demands of a successful agricultural system. Farmers have, therefore, to pay expensively for the diesel and electricity necessary to pump underground water – which is being overexploited – to meet the requirements of irrigating over three million acres (Bhullar *et al.*, 1985, p. 27). The farmers' fear is that this unjust distribution of water will result in the Punjab becoming a desert. Thus Bhullar and his associates ask:

How can Punjab develop feelings of patriotism and nationalism[3] in the light of this gross injustice meted out to the state in the allocation of water and energy of its own rivers?

(Bhullar *et al.*, 1985, p. 29)

Another economic grievance has to do with the industrial development of the state. The Green Revolution of the 1970s has not been complemented by a comparable industrial transformation of the Punjab. For example, it is argued that whilst the state produces about 14 per cent of India's cotton, only 2 per cent is processed into manufactured goods in the state. The case with sugar-cane production is said to be the same.

Speculation over the reasons for this situation in the state vary. For example, a plausible explanation suggested by one observer is that Delhi has been cautious about encouraging industrial development in the Punjab because the state is too close to the Pakistan border (Shackle, 1984, p. 11). Another view is that, should the Punjab experience heavy industrialization, its agricultural output would decrease (Pettigrew, 1985, p. 13). From the perspective of the centre these may very well be legitimate reasons for a policy of limited industrial development in the Punjab. To Punjabis, however, there must seem to be a more sinister reason in these circumstances, namely, a deliberate plan to undermine the well-being of the state and particularly of the Sikh community.

A radically different view is offered by Tully and Jacob. They argue that at the time of the attack on the Golden Temple in 1984 industrial investment in the Punjab was growing at a rate of 8.4 per cent per annum and that this was twice that of the national average (Tully and Jacob, 1985, pp. 47–8). Their contention is that the state was rapidly being developed into a modern urban state, being the fifth most urbanized in the country.

Perhaps, however, the answer lies in the very success of the Punjab. As Tully and Jacob, amongst others, have observed, being the most prosperous state in the country, having carried forward the Green Revolution, the Punjab attracted non-Sikh immigrants from eastern India. Moreover, whilst Sikhs have controlled farming, the merchant class are mainly Hindus. It should not, therefore, have surprised Tully and Jacob (1985, p. 48) that the Resolution should place so much emphasis on the state helping the small and middle farmers whose land holdings are being fragmented. Nayar and Singh, however, readily grasp the limits placed on the Green Revolution in the Punjab and the impact of this on the Sikhs (Nayar and Singh, 1984, pp. 22–3).

These problems are compounded by the complaint that the state has become a producer of raw materials within the Union and has to purchase manufactured goods at higher prices than she is able to sell her own products. This is, of course, the classic situation which exists between Third World producers of raw material and the industrial, developed North. The scenario is well known: whilst the producers of primary or agricultural goods find that their products diminish in value on the world market, goods for consumption as well as those necessary for improved productivity, which have to be purchased from the manufacturing North, become progressively more expensive as they are produced increasingly with a higher input of capital over labour (Emmanuel, 1972).

Such adverse terms of trade may seem inevitable in a country the size of India with varied conditions but, again, given the very special conditions of the Sikh population in the country it is not surprising that many should see this as being the result of discrimination from Delhi. This is particularly so when there appears to be no lack of financial resources in the state itself. After all, another complaint is that only about one third of the deposits placed in Punjab banks are actually invested in the state (Pettigrew, 1985, p. 12). These developments placed a block on employment opportunities for the young. They are also seen as part of a wider process whereby the Delhi government is believed to be seeking ways of restricting opportunities for Sikhs.

Restrictions on the free entry of Sikhs into the armed forces is, perhaps, the most important aspect of this nation-wide curtailment. In 1974 the union government effected measures whereby the armed forces would be more representative of the diverse Indian population. This, perhaps otherwise perfectly reasonable policy in a heterogeneous society such as India, made some Sikh leaders believe that Sikh young men were being discriminated against. Although the Sikhs make up only about 2 per cent of the Indian population, traditionally they contributed, after the 1847 Indian Mutiny, a disproportionate 10 per cent or more of the armed forces. For example, Major-General Bhullar claims that the recruitment of Sikhs has fallen from over 30 per cent to 1.5 per cent in the armed forces since independence (Bhullar *et al.*, 1985, p. 32). This may, of course, be an exaggeration. But there is general agreement that the Sikhs make up at least 10 per cent of the army.

Tully and Jacob argue that this policy has never, however, been implemented rigorously. They also seem to accept the army's claim that Sikhs have not been rushing to sign on, particularly since army life is rough and the Punjab has become prosperous and therefore offers preferable careers in civilian as compared to military life (Tully and Jacob, 1985, p. 49).

Nonetheless, any attempt to recruit on a percentage basis rather than on the basis of individual merit was bound to be perceived by Sikh leaders as being to the community's disadvantage. They have, therefore, argued that the union government has denied their community the chance to serve the country in one of the vital areas in which Sikhs have long excelled. Implied also in this policy, from the perspective of the Sikhs, is a mistrust on the part of the central government of the loyalty of the Sikhs. As a people quite correctly proud of their contribution to what is India today, this is, indeed, a grave insult, particularly, but not exclusively, to the devout Sikhs.

Language and religion

And yet, these broadly economic and territorial considerations which form the background to the present crisis in the Punjab are not as important as the questions of language and religion. These are, understandably, sensitive issues which touch the Sikh community throughout India and the diaspora. Both issues are vital to the definition of Sikhism, and given the threat to the traditional territory since independence, it is hardly surprising that both the Punjabi language and the Sikh faith should be undergoing something of a revival.

The policy of Congress under Nehru was to allow the spontaneous creation of new states in the Indian union, provided the new states were established along linguistic boundaries. Thus, a number of new states were created in independent India. Usually, of course, whilst it may not be difficult in some places to determine the main language, in others the opposite was the case. With respect to the Punjab, the crucial 1950 population census which was to form the basis of linguistic boundaries, returned a very mixed situation. Many Hindus, who were born and had their roots in the Punjab and for whom Punjabi was the mother tongue, stated that Hindi was their mother tongue out of fear of a Sikh dominated state being established in Punjab.[4]

This complicated the situation in at least two important respects. First, the Hindi-speaking population increased from 13.61 per cent in 1921 to 55.54 per cent in 1961, whilst the Punjabi-speaking population decreased from 54.08 per cent to 41.09 per cent over the same period (Bhullar *et al.*, 1985, p. 19). Second, the choice of Hindi as the mother language of Punjabi-speaking Hindus in the state left Sikhs with the feeling that they were the only defenders of the common regional language. It must be borne in mind, of course, that the development of Punjabi as a written language was due, in the first place, to the writing of the Sikh Guru Granth Sahib (the Sikh scriptures) in Punjabi and the Sikh revival at the turn of the century. The close association or identification of Punjabi Hindus with the Hindi language and Sikhs with the Punjabi language tended to confirm the union government's view that the demand for a Punjabi Suba (where the language would determine the boundaries of the state) was a communal demand. And this demand ran counter to the secular aims and concerns of the founding fathers of Congress and leaders such as Nehru who had no sympathy for the religious definition of states within the union.

Nonetheless, after several *morchas*[5] over a period of twenty years starting in 1955 the demand for a Punjabi Suba was partially achieved in 1966, but with a greatly reduced Punjab. Sikhs speaking Punjabi were now in a 60 per cent majority in the state as a whole but this was not necessarily so in the cities where, according to the 1971 census, Hindi-speakers significantly outnumbered Punjabi-speakers (Shackle, 1984, pp. 4 and 10; Sinha *et al.*, 1984, ch. 1).

Migration was to erode further this partial victory of the Sikhs for a Punjabi Suba. Between 1966 and the 1980s it has been estimated that the Sikh majority decreased to 52 per cent in the state (Shackle, 1984, p. 11). This seems to have been due to both the inward migration of Indians from other states and the outward migration of Sikhs. The latter continued the migratory process started after the 1947 partition, to Canada, the United Kingdom and the Middle East where employment prospects were better than in the Punjab. At the same time, whilst there was little heavy industrial development in the state, some small industries, linked to the dominant agricultural economy, were established and, as noted earlier, these attracted Indians from less well-endowed and less prosperous states within the union.

Another aspect of the language question is the complaint that the education system discriminates against Punjabi in states where there are sizeable populations of Sikhs. Sikh militants argue that instead of making Punjabi the second Indian language to be offered in the schools, the choice has been for a South Indian language to be taught. The claim is that this policy is followed in states that have little or no South Indian population at all (Bhullar *et al.*, 1985, p. 32). The Union government, however, in its White Paper on the situation in the Punjab issued on 10 July 1984, argued that this particular complaint has been redressed by making Punjabi the second language in states with sizeable Sikh minorities such as Haryana, Delhi, Himachal Pradesh and Rajasthan (Nayar and Singh, 1984, pp. 141 and 176).

Without doubt, the most important complaint the Sikh population has against the union government is to do with their religion. Indeed, it may be argued that without the feeling of a threat to Sikhism the Punjab problem might possibly not have reached its present dimensions. Obviously the religious problem is a large issue with many aspects to it. Not all of these are relevant to this discussion and I will therefore limit myself to a consideration of just three aspects.

First, the Sikhs have complained that the government discriminates against their religion by refusing to grant what they see as purely religious and therefore reasonable demands. Several examples are given of this situation. One of these is that the government refuses to declare Amritsar a holy city while at the same time granting this status to cities such as Varanasi and Kurukshaetra which are held to be holy by Hindus. A second example is that the government is not willing to give permission for a radio transmitter to be installed in the Golden Temple at Amritsar which would be used solely for the transmission of devotional songs to Sikhs outside India. Sikh militants have argued that the objection cannot be due to financial constraints because the Sikhs would them-selves stand the cost of the project. Another example of this kind is that since the last of the Ten Gurus, Guru Gorbind Singh, established the Khalsa in 1699, no government in India has tried to interfere with the carrying of the kirpan (a knife) by a baptized Sikh. The union government, however, has tried to limit the length of the kirpan, and this is seen as a gross interference with the religious practices of the Sikhs.

The union government's response is contained in the White Paper of 10 July 1984 (Nayar and Singh, 1984, Annexure H). With respect to the demand for 'holy city' status to Amritsar, the White Paper stated categorically that 'The grant of "holy city" status as such to any city is not in consonance with the secular nature of our Constitution' (Nayar and Singh, 1984, p. 173). There is something of a government concession, however, in its claims to have placed restrictions on the selling of tobacco, liquor and meat in February 1983 in the vicinity of the Golden Temple and other holy places in Punjab. In the Hindu cities referred to by the Sikhs the restrictions were imposed by local authorities. With respect to broadcasts from the Golden Temple, the government claimed that the Shiromani Gurdwara Parbandhak Committee (known by its initials, the SGPC), which oversees gurdwaras in the country, refused to take up an offer by the All India Radio service. The government could not, however, permit private broadcasting facilities to any group. On international flights the government would not allow kirpans because they are weapons. It would, how-ever, allow kirpans with a maximum length of nine inches and with blades of six inches maximum length.[6]

These are, of course, important demands in themselves with, perhaps, wider implications than many Sikh militants would care to admit. For example, they reveal the tension that exists between the imperatives of a secular state and the religious life, particularly since many Sikhs would deny that there can be any meaningful distinction between politics and religion. Nonetheless these demands are considered to be minor by Sikh militants compared to the two other demands to which I now turn.

The first of these concerns the management of Sikh gurdwaras in India. The Gurdwara Act was passed in the 1920s under the British and this enabled the setting up of the elected SGPC which became responsible for the running of the gurdwaras. One demand made by the Sikhs, therefore, has been to have those gurdwaras not under the management of the Committee to become so. Pre-sumably, the defence of this demand on the grounds of religion is that Sikhs would thereby be better able to preserve their faith and a united religious com-munity living in different parts of the country. Part of the complaint in this respect is that the central government interferes in the management of the gurdwaras by amending the Act without first consulting Sikhs themselves. It is also claimed that the central government sponsors candidates for elections to the committees of the gurdwaras in order to control these crucial Sikh meeting places.

Obviously this issue is one that is of vital importance to the government because of the central place the gurdwara occupies in the Sikh community. The White Paper is very brief on this issue. It states:

> On February 27, 1983 the Prime Minister announced that Governments of the States where the gurdwaras are located and the managements of the gurdwaras would be consulted to arrive at the consensus needed for enacting such a legislation.
>
> (Nayar and Singh, 1984, p. 174)

The strongest objection Sikhs have to the activities and assumptions of the central government in this respect is the description of their faith as being part of Hinduism in the post-independence national constitution. Article 25 of the 1950 Constitution described Buddhists, Jains and Sikhs as Hindus. With respect to their faith, therefore, Sikhs have demanded that the Indian Constitution be amended so that they are recognized as a separate nation with its own identity. They do not wish to be confused with the Hindu majority and want to be seen and treated as equals with them.[7]

The government's response has been that far from the Constitution discriminating against the Sikhs, Article 25 'was in fact a recognition of that identity' (Nayar and Singh, 1984, p. 177). The White Paper also points out that this was a new issue brought into the negotiating process late in the day. Even so, it is argued, whenever the government has asked for specific recommendations there have been none forthcoming from either the Akali Dal or the SGPC.

Irrespective of the pros and cons, however, Sikhs have come to feel that the aim of the Hindu majority in India is to absorb all minority religions into its fold. Hinduism, they argue, has indeed been able to re-absorb Buddhism and Jainism. Understandably, therefore, Sikhs have felt that their separate and quite distinct traditions may be eradicated through the process of Hinduization. To this end, they believe, the Delhi government encourages militant Hindu groups such as the Rashtria Sewak Sang in their anti-Sikh activities. Many also felt that Mrs Gandhi's public appearances at Hindu celebrations and her respect in the public eye for Hindu ceremonies when inaugurating bridges, canals and the like, all tended to encourage Hindu hegemony. Many devout Sikhs, therefore, began to see such public displays, or favour, as the signs of an arrogant resurgent Brahminism throughout India.

Since the storming of the Golden Temple, many Sikhs, both in India and outside, have come to believe that the creation of Khalistan is the only means whereby they can attain their goals. The Anandpur Resolution itself did not go as far as this. It did, however, place great stress on the need for a Sikh renaissance with respect to devotion, writing, baptism, and study groups in schools, colleges and universities (Dalit Sahitya Akademy, n.d., p. 11). Moreover, events since 1984 have pushed both the Akali Dal and the SGPC further towards the camp of the militants.

The road to Amritsar

These territorial, linguistic, economic and religious grievances and claims of the Sikhs in the Punjab were well known in India before the *morcha*, started by Sant Harchand Longowal, then leader of the Akali Dal, in 1982. Events between 1982 and 1986, however, were to bring these demands to the attention of the world.

The storming of the Golden Temple in June 1984 marked the turning point in the relations between the Sikhs and the central government in India. It is, therefore, of crucial importance to understand this momentous event from the perspective of the Sikhs. There are at least two very sound reasons for doing so. The first is that the world, through the mass media, has been able to understand something of the position of the Indian government, particularly from its fairly comprehensive White Paper of 10 July 1984. The second reason is that it is always more difficult to understand the position of the minority in situations of this kind than it is to understand that of the majority. This is particularly so with respect to the Sikhs since the majority population and the central Indian government appears to have the overwhelming sympathy of the world community. In the Sikh psyche the storming of the Golden Temple, or, in military parlance, 'Operation Blue Star', was their first modern holocaust. The widespread murders of thousands of innocent Sikhs throughout India which followed the assassination of Mrs Gandhi in November 1984 is considered to have been the second holocaust (Sikri, 1985; Sandhu, 1985). For a people with a strong tradition of militancy when provoked, these events are seen as amounting to a challenge, a rallying call to defend the faith.

But holocausts are not new to the Sikhs. Indeed, their faith emerged out of a situation of physical conflict in which India was subjected to conquest (by the Moslems) and alien rule (by the Moghuls). Both militant and devout Sikhs tend to see the initiation of the *Khalsa* (the defenders and promoters of the Sikh faith who undertake baptism) by the Tenth and last Guru, Gorbind Singh, as the point of departure in the emergence of the Sikh nation (Kapoor, 1984, p. viii; Devinderjit Singh, 1986, pp. 17ff.). After all, Sikhism, or the Sikh *panth* (path), is a religion and a way of life which, not unlike Christianity, originated at the junction of many pathways.

Certainly, the Punjab and Sikhism stood in the very real and physical pathway from Central Asia to India as a whole. Here, in the Punjab, the people were subjected to the cruelties of conquerors who came by the north-western land route, such as the Greeks, the Persians and the Afghans. A second pathway was and remains the warrior-saint traditions of the Sikhs. These seem to be an offence to the more tolerant and pantheistic Hinduism and the imperial-minded Islamic faith from the north-west. In short, Sikhism came into being as a protest against the tyranny of the conquering Moslem faith led by a powerful military and political force against a pliant and tolerant ancient faith, Hinduism.[8] Sikhs are, therefore, proud that they have been the defenders of the freedoms of a continent against foreign domination and as such have developed a martial spirit proud of liberty and the freedoms of all peoples. Devout and militant Sikhs, therefore, confront a dilemma when the government of India claims that it must promote and defend a secular and universalistic state. Because both *spiritual* and *political* authorities in Sikhism are intricately intertwined, the Sikh has difficulty accepting the distinction made between these by the central state, particularly since this state appears to be dominated by members of another faith – Hinduism.

Deeply ingrained in the belief system of the Sikh is, for example, that view which is contrary to early Christian teaching, namely that the afflicted individual should turn the other cheek to the aggressor. Guru Gorbind Singh taught that the Sikh must always be ready to defend the oppressed and the carrying of a *kirpan* (a sword/knife) by a baptized Sikh is more than a symbol of the Sikh's willingness to carry out this duty. It is not surprising, therefore, that all Sikh spokespersons stress the necessity for force to be used against force – but always as a last resort. Violence, per se, is not seen as an evil. Rather, it is seen as a necessity under certain conditions because there seems to be a sensible belief that reason alone will never be allowed to govern social action. The position seems to be similar to the utilitarian view that an action is neither morally good nor bad but can be judged only according to its capacity to increase happiness or pain. But with this stress on opposition to tyranny, there is a corresponding stress on responsibility and discipline and these are perceived to be more important than justice for all. Sikhism is therefore essentially a *defensive* belief system and way of life. It stresses the need to *defend* what is and so appears to be limited in its perspective of what *ought* to be the universal norm. But it is more relevant to look more closely at the storming of the Golden Temple and what this meant for Sikhs both in India and in the diaspora.

There are various accounts of the storming of the Golden Temple (for example, Kapoor, 1984; Tully and Jacob, 1985). A narrative account of the event itself is, therefore, hardly necessary here. Suffice it to say that on 5 June 1984 several thousand Indian troops surrounded the complex known as the Golden Temple in Amritsar and a blockade on news reporting was imposed on events in the Punjab. The following day an estimated 15,000 troops confronted militant Sikhs who had earlier occupied or taken refuge in the Temple. The troops were under the command of generals who had served against Pakistan in 1965 and in Bangladesh in 1971. These included, Major-General Brar, Lt.-General Dayal who drew up the plans for 'Operation Blue Star', and Lt.-General Sunderji who was in overall command. The fighting went on for some three to four days before the staunch resistance of Sant Jarnail Bhindranwale and his supporters was overcome. It is believed that nearly 120,000 troops of the crack 4th Division, Guards and Bihar Regiments, supported by the central reserve police force, the border security force and the Punjab police force as well as a Gurkha battalion were involved in the fighting.

The storming of the Temple complex, which covers a sizeable area of about 72 acres, resulted in the widespread destruction of the Harimandir Sahib (the Golden Temple itself which is situated in the Sikh baptismal lake), the Akal Takht (the religious-political centre for the Sikhs), the *langar* (kitchen/eating area), the guest houses for pilgrims and so forth. It is difficult to know, since there was a curfew in force, how many people died, but some Sikhs believe there were over 3,000 people who died during the attack (Kapoor, 1984, ch. 1). Tully and Jacob are more cautious and speak of 1,600 souls who have not been accounted for in the official figures.

The union government of Mrs Indira Gandhi claimed that the Temple complex harboured Sikh terrorists who posed a threat to security in the state. Militant Sikhs of all political persuasions, both in India and abroad, saw the storming and occupation of the Golden Temple, and the thirty-eight other Sikh temples of historical importance throughout the state, as the culmination of the central government's attempt to liquidate their religion. Even non-practising Sikhs, such as the distinguished writer Kushwant Singh who said of himself that he has 'always felt more strongly as an Indian than I have as a Sikh' (Nayar and Singh, 1984, p. 9) felt that under the circumstances he had to return to the president of India the badge of honour bestowed on him some ten years earlier for services rendered to the nation. To understand how this tragic situation came about it may be useful to give a bald outline of some aspects of the rapidly deteriorating conditions of daily life and politics in the Punjab after 1981–2 to 1988.

First, the launching of the *morcha* by the Akali Dal leadership under Sant Harchand Singh Longowal on 26 July 1982 involved peaceful mass demonstration to force the union government to concede the demands of the Anandpur Resolution. Several thousand volunteers would go to the Akal Takht, say their prayers and by demonstrating court arrest. This, of course, brought the demonstrators and the police into direct confrontation. In itself this was bound to cause a great deal of aggravation between devout Sikhs and the police.

The important point, however, is that prior to the commencement of the *morcha* Sikhs had been complaining about police brutality in the state. Many had complained about the general breakdown of law and order and the excesses of the police – a complaint which is fairly widespread throughout India. In the Punjab this situation was compounded by what many Sikhs believed to be the deliberate favourable bias of the police towards militant Hindu groups, such as the Arya Samaj, Jan Sang and the Bhartiya Janta Party. There are several accounts of alleged atrocities committed against Sikh farmers and others by the police (Bhullar *et al.*, 1985, pp. 34ff.). Here in Britain it became commonplace, particularly between 1984 and 1988, to hear on the news or read in the newspapers accounts of daily atrocities in the Punjab. In some cases the police are said to be the culprits and at other times the culprits are said to be groups of extremist Sikhs.

Second, in these circumstances it was perhaps inevitable that the initiative would pass from the relatively moderate Akali Dal to more radical and militant leadership. After all, the demands of the Akalis were made within the framework of an Indian union and there was a willingness to compromise. The police atrocities, the activities of militant Hindu and Sikh groups resulting in the breakdown of law and order at a time when the central government seemed if not incorrigible then certainly slow, were some of the factors which prepared the ground for more radical and militant political initiative.

This was to be provided by a young and charismatic Sikh priest. Born in 1947, Sant Jarnail Bhindranwale gained a presence in the Punjab as a serious and committed preacher of the Sikh faith after 1978. As the *morcha*, started in 1982, went on and police harassment and militant Hindu and Sikh activities increased, a more insistent voice could gain ready attention. Bhindranwale spoke out against corruption, the arbitrariness of the police and the ineffective Akali Dal. It is believed by Sikh spokesmen that Congress leaders, in order to undermine the Akali Dal leadership, encouraged the emergence of Bhindranwale by giving him maximum coverage in the media. There seems to be evidence to support not only this but also the view that Bhindranwale was a creation of Mrs Gandhi's Congress party (for example, Nayar and Singh, 1984, ch. 2). A large number of Sikhs believe, however, that his message and vision of Sikh rejuvenation was a simple, clear one which the majority of Sikhs could understand and therefore they rallied to his cause. Irrespective, therefore, of how the Sant embarked upon his brief but stormy public career, he was soon to become the focal point of protest against the police. He also became the symbol of militant Sikh pride against what is taken to be an arrogant Hinduism propagated by a Congress leadership with an eye to the general elections which were to be held by January 1985.

Additionally, the deteriorating situation in the Punjab led to the public humiliation of many Sikhs who were not necessarily supporters of either the Akali Dal or of Bhindranwale. The catalyst in this highly charged situation was the checks made by the police of vehicles entering and leaving the state to attend the Asian games in Delhi in November 1982. Longowal had called upon his followers to go to the games and demonstrate there for the rest of Asia to see the plight of the Sikhs. Naturally, the government could not allow this and the police took harsh measures to keep all Sikhs out of the capital. A number of prominent Sikhs were stopped in this way and humiliated. Their loyalty to the nation was questioned. The story is that after this a number of ex-military officers decided to join Bhindranwale at the Akal Takht in the Golden Temple complex where he had taken up residence out of fear for his life.

It would appear that when it became known to Bhindranwale and his supporters that there were serious plans afoot to storm the Golden Temple, General Shubegh Singh, a hero of the Bangladesh war in the early 1970s, began to train his comrades in preparation for the assault. There is a thesis that insists that this was the real cause for the massive attack on the complex because of the serious military implications for the Indian army. But Tully and Jacob cast doubt on this by their insistence that the general's letters to his son during those trying days do not reveal a man preoccupied with such matters but simply a man deeply worried about his family (Tully and Jacob, 1985, ch. 10).

The storming of the Golden Temple marked the turning point in Sikh–central government relations. The deed was condemned by Sikhs everywhere and overnight all the complaints against Delhi took on a new meaning for Sikhs both in the Punjab and abroad. It is important, therefore, to mention very briefly some of the immediate aftermaths in India.

First, in November 1984, within months of 'Operation Blue Star', Mrs Indira Gandhi, whose personality had dominated Indian politics for two decades, was assassinated by two of her guards who were both Sikhs.[9] Her son, Rajiv, succeeded her immediately despite his comparative inexperience in national politics and his earlier protestations about not having any political ambition. He very quickly established his own presence by calling national elections for January 1985, and his Congress party returned with a majority. Like his mother after her authoritarian rule under Emergency regulations in the 1970s, Rajiv lost the general elections in 1989 to a coalition. The new ministry was led by a former finance minister bearing the name of V. P. Singh and although not a Sikh himself, his government was more sensitive to the Sikh/Punjab situation within the context of the union. Rajiv's conciliatory public attitude in the months following his mother's assassination did not, however, immediately stop the killing of thousands of Sikhs in the *communal* violence between Hindus and Sikhs, which followed the assassination of his famous and widely respected mother.[10] There are those Sikhs who believe that whilst Rajiv Gandhi was giving public assurances that there would be no backlash against the Sikh community in India for the death of his mother, his Congress party was deeply involved in organizing communal violence (see, for example, Devinderjit Singh, 1986, pp. 39ff.). Another grievance of the Sikhs is that Rajiv Gandhi did not set up a commission to investigate who carried out the killings. Various independent bodies, however, went ahead with their own public investigations. These included the Citizens for Democracy (who made a detailed report of the situation in 1985), and the People's Union for Democratic Rights and the People's Union for Civil Liberties, which carried out a joint investigation and reported in 1984. There was also the Citizens' Commission which likewise reported its findings in 1984. The reports of concerned citizens in India have been published abroad and have helped to highlight the condition of the Sikhs in India, a sub-continent which touches the lives of so very many peoples elsewhere in the contemporary world.

Third, there have been two important events which, in early 1985, presented a ray of hope for peace in the Punjab. In the first instance, Gandhi and Longowal signed an accord whereby the central government would set up a commission of enquiry into the communal violence in which several thousand Sikhs lost their lives, return the city of Chandigarh to the Punjab, and remove the ban on Sikh groups such as the All India Sikh Student Federation. Basically, the accord attempted to reassert some of the principles of the earlier award made by Mrs Gandhi whereby some villages in Punjab would be given to Haryana in return for Chandigarh.

The second encouraging development in 1985 was the victory of the moderate Akali Dal under Longowal's leadership in the state elections in September. There was a reported 65 per cent turnout at these elections. At the time it was widely believed that this indicated a desire for reconciliation on the part of the majority of Sikhs. The importance of this was the seeming lie it gave to the scepticism with which many greeted the accord. The elections seemed to be a vindication of both Longowal, who was coming under increasing suspicion by more radical Sikh groups, as well as Gandhi whose proclaimed sincerity was always in question amongst militant Sikhs. Some believed the son was deeply implicated in the mother's decision to storm the Golden Temple (Devinderjit Singh, 1986, p. 41) and there are those who believe that Longowal was but a stooge of the Congress and went as far as he did with the Anandpur Resolution demands because he was pressured by more devoted or sincere Sikhs in the Akali Dal leadership. Certainly, after the taking of the Golden Temple Longowal became the prisoner of the central government. He had failed to move towards the union government before Bhindranwale outmanoeuvred him and Mrs Gandhi had failed to come to his rescue early enough by making more significant concessions.

The situation in the Punjab in 1988 suggested that the sceptics of 1985 had won the day. In the first place, there were those who believed that there was little sincerity in Gandhi's professions of peace and goodwill towards the Sikhs. For example, the elections did not stop the state of emergency in the Punjab and from all accounts most Sikhs appeared to believe that this was against their best interests and safety even in their own homeland. Longowal was assassinated, quantitatively filling just one point in the increasing fatal statistics of the state. The powers of the police increased, stimulating desperate action by individual Sikhs in various parts of North India. From the reports we receive in the media in Britain and from India it is difficult to see how life in the Punjab can be anything but nasty, brutish and short. And it would be bad enough if this were merely for those men who articulate demands and carry arms. But ordinary men, women and children are caught up in this seemingly ever-spiralling whirlpool of conflict mixed with mayhem.

Under these conditions the civilian Akali Dal government of Chief Minister Barnala, who succeeded Sant Harchand Longowal, could hardly be expected to operate as a normal government. The interests of the central government were always too much to the forefront in a situation of extreme confrontation to allow the normal process of government. The police force of Superintendent Rebiero, the officer in charge of law and order in the Punjab, has remained active but insufficient to stem the tide of disorder. In the first half of 1987, therefore, the Delhi government disbanded the duly elected government of the Akali Dal, which it had supported earlier, and imposed direct rule from the centre.

The main paradox of this supposed solution to the Punjab crisis is that arbitrary rule in Punjab came just before the signing of the accord between Prime Minister Gandhi and President Junius Jawardene of Sri Lanka over the conflict between the Tamils and the Sinhalese peoples on the island. In this situation Gandhi was prepared to recognize the disparity between national unitary aspirations and the legitimate demands of the Tamils for autonomy in the Northern and Eastern regions which they inhabit. Gandhi was unable to bring the same degree of resolve to the problems of India itself and the Sikhs were very much sensitized to this. The imposition of direct rule in the Punjab in 1987 seemed a significant departure from any attempt to find a lasting solution to the crisis in the state.

It is important to bear in mind that for many Sikhs both in India and abroad the story is not as simple as this. They see their future, and that of the Punjab and of the Sikhs, as being with a united India. These alternative points of view can only be mentioned briefly in an account of this kind but there are, of course, a number of texts that give the opposite view of the situation. The first of these is obviously that of the government itself. In its White Paper the government argued that Punjab had been subjected to three years of agitation organized by the Akali Dal, 'strident communalism' and violence by extremists, anti-national sentiments, criminality and so forth. In Delhi's view the situation was being exploited by secessionist movements based abroad, some of which had an interest in the disintegration of India. Between 1981 and 1984 there were a number of meetings through which the government tried to placate the Sikhs, but these came to naught. The government complained that one of the main reasons for this was that when 'some issues appeared to have been settled, new issues were raised, thereby frustrating the possibility of a settlement' (Nayar and Singh, 1984, p. 177).

To one degree or another, close observers of developments in the Punjab have elaborated one or the other of these points. One strong view agreed by a number of commentators is that the Sikhs' demands may be best perceived from the perspective of communalism (for example, Kumar *et al.*, 1984). Kuldip Nayar argues, in his 'Preface' to his joint work with Khushwant Singh (1984), that

> Punjab's tragedy is that there are no Punjabis any more in Punjab – only Sikhs and Hindus. The only Punjabis left are outside the state. And even they are now getting divided according to their religion. I am writing this book in the hope that by placing before them, and the rest of the country, a true record of events they will act to save this endangered species.
>
> (Nayar and Singh, 1984, p. 7)

Another writer contends that although the thinking of Delhi was 'amateurish' and there was brutality unleashed by the militants in Amritsar, it was a situation in which all sides were caught in a vicious power game.

> Each party in the conflict regarded the other as a particularly vicious species of humanity. Rational thinking was out: every Sikh was a terrorist, so the Hindus believed; every Hindu, an agent of the imperial power at Delhi, so the Sikh imagined.
>
> (Butani, 1986, p. ix)

Yet another view of the Punjab/Sikh problem is that all the *dramatis personae* are to blame for allowing the situation to degenerate to the level it did so that the storming of the Golden Temple became inevitable. Tully and Jacob argue that Mrs Gandhi acted too late in a sensitive and explosive situation, and that the Akali Dal leaders, particularly Longowal, were too cowardly and failed to turn against Bhindranwale and condemn terrorism at a time when the situation might have been saved. For Tully and Jacob it was in this situation that the deputy inspector-general of police, A. S. Atwal, was killed within the complex of the Golden Temple on 23 April 1983. They argue that if either the prime minister or the state authorities had acted at this moment against Bhindranwale and his men, such action would have gained widespread Sikh support both in Punjab and throughout the country.

Advancing a pro-Akali view, Sinha *et al.* contend that the Punjab crisis is not one over national integrity, insurgency and communalism, as the government White Paper makes out, but rather that 'Punjab is a victim of a dirty game played by New Delhi' (Sinha *et al.*, 1984, p. 18).

Perhaps the most severe view of Sikh and Congress leadership during this period has been that of Khushwant Singh. Well known for his critical posture towards religious fanaticism and his commitment to secularism and rationalism he argued, in the 'Preface' to his co-authored book, that he does not

> ... accord any special sanctity to places of worship and none at all to those misused by being converted into fortresses and providing sanctuary to fugitives from the law. I hold both the Akalis and the government guilty of the desecration of the temple long before the final denouement that took place in the first week of June 1984. Akalis allowed, knowingly or unwittingly, free passage of arms to the temple and by their reluctance to condemn terrorist activities, encouraged them. The Government cannot be exonerated of the charge of criminal dereliction of duty in failing to prevent these weapons and criminal elements getting inside the temple.
>
> (Nayar and Singh, 1984, p. 9)

In Khushwant Singh's view the divide between Sikhs and Hindus in the Punjab has been brought about by the Akali leaders' lack of leadership qualities; they are described as 'a short-sighted, self-seeking group of men of limited political ability and lack of foresight with a penchant for over-playing the game of brinkmanship' (Nayar and Singh, 1984, p. 12). His most damning remark on the leadership provided for the people of the Punjab is worth stating in his own sharp words:

> The drama of the Punjab is a tragedy played by poltroons with the common people watching it as silent spectators. In the final act players come off the stage to set the theatre on fire.
>
> (Nayar and Singh, 1984, p. 14)

But these are not merely the sharp words of an angry man. It is difficult to read the batch of books, pamphlets, leaflets and media reports published in India in the wake of the events of 1984 without being moved by the strong desire of Indians of varied backgrounds to see the wrongs done to the Sikhs righted as well as to see the union survive.

Where the Punjab crisis goes to from here cannot be predicted. However, there is, first, the hope of very many people, both in India and outside, that a solution can be found whereby the aspirations of the Sikhs are realized and, second, the desire of others that the unity of India, for which the Sikhs themselves sacrificed so much, may be maintained. But these are contradictory hopes. The first requires recognition that many Sikhs believe that the situation is such that to remain in the India union is to sanction their demise. This is something that the central government and the majority of Indians cannot accept. Nor, however, can they afford to take the demands of concerned Sikhs lightly. In short, the situation in 1988 gave little sign of hope for the immediate future. Clearly, the problems of the Punjab, the Sikhs and indeed India as a whole, demand sophisticated political leadership and much goodwill on the part of all concerned. After all, a new state of Khalistan in the region will have far-reaching implications not only for India but also for the international power blocs in the region.

This brief outline of the Sikh grievances against the union government in India provides the basis for a consideration of the British connection in the unfolding story of Sikh diasporic politics with respect to the demand for an independent Khalistan, carved from what is the existing union of India.

The British connection

There are several aspects of the British connection with the Punjab crisis that are relevant to the overall discussion. The first of these is the kind of colonial relationship that the Sikhs had with the United Kingdom during the days of the British Raj. This was one of Britain's *special relationships* with a colonized people. In her practice of the philosophy of 'divide and rule' Britain developed different kinds of relationships with colonized peoples in her multi-national, multi-racial, multi-religious empire. For example, apart from that with the Sikhs in India, there were, amongst others, those with the Tamils in Sri Lanka, the Ibos in Nigeria, the Bugandans in Uganda, and the Maroons in Jamaica. The special relationship between the colonizer and the colonized in these varied circumstances came about for different reasons. Perhaps, however, the single most important common feature that these groups shared was the belief that they were indeed *different* from the rest of the colonized within their respective countries. During colonial times this preference, or special relationship between the colonizer and a section of the colonized, sometimes meant special favours for members of the preferred group. In return, the British gained the loyalty of a martial, educated, or entrepreneurial element within the population of the colonized. In some cases the imperial power was simply exploiting longstanding pre-colonial divisions, in other cases it was creating new divisions. Irrespective of their origins, however, the imperial power tended to nurture, and thereby reinforced, any division which seemed likely to make politico-military and market controls, the prime considerations of any empire, more secure.

With political independence, however, the once preferred group finds itself, to one degree or another, in a somewhat uneasy relationship with other members of the new 'nation' state. Typically, the preferred group was a minority of the total population of the former colony. In the new conditions introduced by political independence, this minority status is transformed so that the rule of democracy, or any other form of majoritarianism, is wittingly or unwittingly directed against the hitherto privileged minority.

In one sense, therefore, the post-independence period becomes a cold day of reckoning. The new situation demands an unusually high degree of good will on the part of the majority population as well as sophisticated political leadership either to integrate the minority and/or to develop sufficient social and political space in the *nation* so that the minority can feel that it has a secure future. There is hardly anywhere in the post-colonial or post-imperial worlds where this can be said to have occurred to date.[11]

In the case of the Sikhs, the former special relationship with Britain remains of some importance. Thus, after a trial referred to below, Jasvinder Singh, spokesperson for International Sikh Youth Organization (ISYO), argued that the trial was bound to damage relations between Britain's 400,000 Sikhs who 'have always cherished a long historical relationship with the British people' (*The Guardian*, 22 December 1986). This relationship dates from the Indian Mutiny of 1857, in which the Sikhs supported the British against the rebels. By this action, the Sikhs demonstrated that they were prepared to let bygones be bygones because the British had a decade or so before reneged on the treaties entered into with Sikh leaders.[12] The Punjab was annexed in 1849 and when Whitehall took over the governing of the country from the East India Company after the Mutiny, Punjab became part of the new British Raj. The Sikhs were never again to see the glory of the days when their Maharaja Ranjit Singh ruled over larger Punjab.[13]

After 1857, however, the Sikhs became a highly favoured group. The two most noticeable and important political aspects of this relationship were the granting of fertile farm lands in the newly irrigated canal areas of North India, and large-scale recruitment into the army. This preferred treatment drew upon two principal Sikh virtues – their skills as farmers and as warriors. Such a favoured position within the British Raj helped to single out the Sikhs as a distinct group, despite the spirit of a united India promoted by the British[14] for their own imperial purposes.

Not surprisingly, therefore, there are contradictory interpretations of the basis of Sikh 'ethnic' or 'national' awareness. Devout Sikhs, understandably, emphasize the teachings of the Ten Gurus, commencing with the founder of the faith, Guru Nanak (1469–1539) and ending with Guru Gorbind Singh (1666–1708) and their holy scriptures, the *Guru Granth Sahib*, as the foundations of their faith and therefore their nationhood.[15] On the other hand, nearly all secular works on Sikhs or the Punjab stress the favoured treatment received from the British as the real and practical basis of Sikh identity. In this view, the preferred treatment of the *keshadhari* over the *sahajdhari*[16] Sikhs (Kapur, 1986, ch. 1) widened the gap between those Sikhs who did not cut their hair and who carried a sword and those who did not adhere to these aspects of the religion.

The disagreement here may be over the quite different questions of *origins* and *development*. In other words, there seems to be little dispute that without their preferred treatment by the British during the latter's occupation of the subcontinent, the Sikhs may not have developed the sharp sense of their difference from the rest of India that they have done. The economic and other privileges they gained from the special relationship set them apart from other Indians.

At the same time there can be no denial that the set of beliefs to which Sikhs adhere emerged over a period of two centuries, prior to the founding of the British Raj. The Hindu revival led by the Arya Samaj in the 1870s which tried to bring Sikhism back into the Hindu fold triggered instead Sikh reaffirmation of their distinct identity from the Hindus. Again, in the 1920s mass agitation led to the state conceding control of the gurdwaras to the *keshadhari* Sikhs.

The two points of view are not, therefore, as irreconcilable as they may at first appear. The first view claims that prior to the British presence there was a break with Hinduism, particularly the development of a monotheistic belief by the Gurus and the founding of the *Khalsa* by the Tenth Guru. The alternative position stresses the conditions of the development of the faith under the British Raj. Without preferred treatment by the British, Sikhism may very well have been imbibed by the all-embracing and tolerant Hinduism of the vast majority of Indians. According to Khushwant Singh, Sikhism was able to distinguish itself from Hinduism by a rejection of hegemonic Brahminism and 'the tyranny of caste'; and it was more successful in the former than with the latter (Nayar and Singh, 1984, p. 19; also, Nayar, 1966, ch. 3), but it was British policy of preferential treatment that provided the sufficient factor for the development of a separate identity.

During the British preparation to quit India, Sikh leaders raised the question of an independent Sikhistan for much the same reasons as the Moslem League under the leadership of Mohammed Ali Jinnah raised questions about the desirability of a state for the Moslems – Pakistan. Militant Sikhs today find it difficult to forgive leaders of the community during this crucial transitional phase, for failing to opt for their own independent homeland.[17] If there was to be Pakistan for the Moslems and Hindustan for the Hindus, then there ought to have been Sikhistan or Khalistan for the Sikhs. According to this view, India is not a secular state at all, but the state of the Hindus, and the Sikhs and followers of other faiths in India have been deceived.

There are at least two reasons to suggest that this judgment may be a little harsh. First, it is understandable that in the euphoria over an independent India, Sikh leaders would choose to go along with Nehru and the Congress leadership. These leaders grasped the advantages of the secularism that has emerged as part of the ethos of the contemporary state, particularly in a multi-lingual country such as India. The promise, then, was that in such a state all Indians would be treated equally, irrespective of religion, and there was no good reason not to give the experiment a chance. Second, as Khushwant Singh points out, one set of reasons for the silencing of the demand for an independent Sikhistan in the 1940s had to do with the Moslem factors in Indian politics. These were the presence of the Moslem League and the spectre of Moslem fundamentalism. Since, historically, Sikhs have always sided with Hindus against Moslem fundamentalism, it was not unexpected that Sikh leaders should have turned to Congress rather than to either the League or the option of Sikhistan.

The policy of the alien rulers was no longer to 'divide and rule' but to 'divide and quit'. It is one of the ironies of British imperial history that the British presence had indeed created a viable model of unity which the new rulers, including Sikh leaders at that time, wanted to retain and work with. This is, however, a contentious point to which I will return when I discuss the vision of an independent Khalistan entertained by Sikh nationalists in the United Kingdom.

A related second major factor in the British connection to the Sikh/Punjab situation which must not be overlooked is the international dimension of the problem which no doubt must interest the former imperial power. On the one hand, Britain seems still to be committed to the ideal of a viable Indian union, if only as part of the long upper-class British romance with the sub-continent so well illustrated in contemporary British films. India as a political reality, as distinct from a geographical expression, is largely Britain's creation and she is still proud of this achievement.

On the other hand, with respect to international relations, there may be a more immediate and pertinent reason for Britain to pay keen attention to developments in the sub-continent. Whilst Britain may have good relations with India and whilst they are both prominent members of the Commonwealth, it must be remembered that both countries are members of the two major opposing blocs of states in the world today. India is the major ally of the USSR in South Asia and since 1981 Conservative governments have done much to strengthen Britain's *special* relationship with the USA, the then major international competitor with the USSR in South Asia as elsewhere.

The creation, therefore, of an independent state on India's northern boundaries would have significant implications for the political balance in the region. This would be so not just for India and Pakistan but also for the Soviet and NATO states. Since partition in 1947, India and Pakistan have seen each other as the main enemy; they have fought two wars (1965 and 1971) and their border is a permanent potential source of explosion. Moreover, Punjab shares the common border between India and Pakistan as well as the disputed Jammu and Kashmir state which, in turn, borders on China to the north. An independent state in this part of Asia could provide the Western bloc countries with the possibility of a very substantial presence in the sub-continent. It may very well, therefore, have been perceived to be in Britain's interest to have a major card which she could play, should it become necessary, in the then power game between East and West or even with respect to India itself, particularly since India is highly critical of Britain on a wide range of questions from sanctions against South Africa to the freedom of Khalistan militants to move around freely in the United Kingdom.

The struggle for, or the existence of, an independent Khalistan espousing religious fundamentalism, is not likely to gain the support of the Soviet Union against a friendly India. Nor are militant Sikhs likely to look to the Soviet Union for necessary support against India. On the other hand, the USA's only ally in the region, Pakistan, may very well welcome a companion, particularly if this companion sees religion as its fundamental principle of cohesion. Religion has been the main weapon used against the Soviet Union and communism in very many countries in the world.

Looked at from this perspective, it is hardly surprising that the government of India, in its White Paper on the Punjab problems, should point to foreign parties which it seems to suspect may have no interest in the unity of India. In particular, the White Paper points to the fact that supporters of the Khalistan demand are allowed to organize in North America and Britain. This raises some important questions which are best treated below in the context of the problems Sikhs in Britain have to confront as a result of the Khalistan demand and the politics which have arisen in India, particularly since 'Operation Blue Star' in June 1984.

The third and perhaps most immediately important aspect of the British connection is domestic. There is a sizeable body of Sikhs living in Britain.[18] Most arrived here during the crucial period when Britain was about to revert from its imperial to national standing in the world. But, like many other Asian groups, there have been pockets of Sikhs in parts of the country from the turn of the century. Moreover, many Sikhs in Britain are from East Africa. Irrespective of their specific background, however, they carry the collective memory of being Sikhs and having had a special relationship with the former imperial metropole as soldiers, police officers and so forth. They respected what they saw as the strength of the British, and in turn many believe that the British respected them for their martial spirit, unconventionality and enterprise wherever they settled in the empire. It is not surprising, therefore, that for many people with only a passing knowledge of the vast and complex Indian sub-continent, the typical image of a person from the region is that of the distinctive keshadhari Sikh lionized by Kipling and by contemporary films in the West.

Both the historical relationship between Britain and the Sikhs and the size of the Sikh population in the United Kingdom in the post-imperial period combine to give Sikhs in Britain a very distinctive voice outside the homeland. Moreover, the majority of the non-white population of Britain have their origins in the sub-continent and so there is a ready audience for the airing of grievances relating to the region. The views of the Sikhs, therefore, over developments in the Punjab cannot be lightly dismissed by either India or Britain. The general point which emerges from these considerations is that the attachments to both the homeland and Britain are likely to be strong, reinforced as they are through family ties, sentiments, origins, a distinctive history and religious beliefs.

This attachment to both Britain and the Punjab appears to be shared by first and second generation Sikhs in Britain. Asked their nationality, many Sikhs will say they are British citizens. When asked 'what nation do you feel you belong to?', the same individuals will say 'Sikh', 'Khalsa', or 'Khalistan' and 'Punjabi'.[19] This suggests that there is, therefore, an understanding of a distinction between belonging to a 'nation-state' and belonging to a 'national community'. The first clearly denotes the legal status of the individual and the second relates to the actual community in which he or she, for a variety of reasons, feels at home.

Like most major religions, such as Judaism, Christianity and Islam, Sikhism has its holy places. If Christianity and Judaism share Jerusalem as their holy city and Islam has Mecca as its own, then Sikhism has its Amritsar in Punjab. And in Pakistan there are, as noted earlier, other important holy places associated with the history of this comparatively young religion. Irrespective of where Sikhs go, therefore, the Punjab is likely to remain a place of special importance in their collective memory.

Migration invariably nurtures memories of 'home' but the duration or strength of such memories are dependent on two other important factors. The first of these is the nature of events which occur 'back home'. The second is the kind of reception experienced in the new home. Sikhs in Britain, as elsewhere, have established stable, prosperous, self-contained communities with a strong sense of their separate identity. The initiation of the *Khalsa*[20] by the Tenth Guru, Gorbind Singh, was meant to single out the Sikh from others. Hence, many Sikhs in the diaspora have become particularly proud of their distinguishing physical features which include adherence to some or all of the Five Ks. It follows, then, that the sad events in the Punjab are bound to have an immediate effect on such a conscious, proud and successful people with strong diasporic relations both in the industrialized and in the underdeveloped countries.

If the *reception* experience of the Sikhs in their new home has been such that alienation from the majority host community's cultural norms sets in, then it is to be expected that the homeland of their religion and their forebears would become more important. In this respect it would be naive to think that Sikhs in Britain do not suffer, to one degree or another, from alienation since this is the common, though differential, experience of all non-white groups that have settled in post-imperial Britain. If this is a correct observation, then it would also be correct to assume that one of the reasons for strong support in the Sikh community for the demand for an independent Khalistan must be the disenchantment with British society itself. Whatever may be the merit of this view, it certainly finds support with the Indian High Commission in London (Interview, 10 August 1987).

Naturally enough, any sense of insecurity in this country tends to encourage articulate Sikhs to support the demand for an independent and secure homeland in the sub-continent. An independent homeland promises a safe place for a possible day of repression in the adopted homeland. Of more significance, however, is the fact that an independent Khalistan promises a greater sense of security for the immigrant's religion. This must be of tremendous importance to the immigrant in a country where the majority faith is a different religion. Below I look a little more closely at some of the specific reasons why some Sikhs in the United Kingdom support the demand for Khalistan as well as at some aspects of the impact of these developments on the Sikh population in Britain.

The point here, however, is that the demand for greater security of the *homeland* is bound to strike a responsive chord amongst people who have recently undergone a migration experience and are still committed to the welfare of the country from which they came. The very experience of being migrants in what was once the centre of the empire has meant that events in the Asian homeland are likely to impinge upon their lives in ways which are not welcomed by either the host society or the immigrants themselves. These experiences are many and varied. For example, the Indian government's decision to impose visa restrictions on all British citizens visiting India is a policy which Sikhs feel affects them most acutely. Certainly the newspapers carry enough reports of cases in which individual British Sikhs are subjected to harsh treatment in India largely because the Indian government, by imposing at various times a state of emergency in the Punjab, has been treating all Sikhs as if they were all terrorists. These states of emergency have affected British Sikhs adversely, cutting them off from relatives by making visits difficult. Another pressing problem seems to be the frequency of requests from the Punjab to relatives in Britain to help in whatever way possible because of the problems in the state. The Anti-Terrorism Act is also another cause for concern for the Sikhs, in much the same way as it is a cause of worry and stress for the Irish people in mainland Britain.[21] Such developments are likely to continue to affect Sikhs settled in Britain as long as the problems of the Punjab and Sikhs remain unresolved by Sikh leaders and the central Indian government in Delhi.

One further example should be given here. This is the fear that the Sikh population in the United Kingdom could be used, so to speak, as a political football between the Indian and British governments. This concern expresses itself in various ways, but particularly with respect to the extradition of Sikhs from Britain to India and the treatment of Sikhs in the courts in the United Kingdom. Quite understandably, the Indian government is very worried about the support separatists and terrorists in India may receive from abroad, as its 1984 White Paper reveals. And the kidnapping and killing of the Indian consul in Birmingham in 1981 by Kashmiri separatists has obviously forced the Indian government to be careful wherever there are sizeable populations of minorities with grievances against Delhi living abroad. Indeed, it is believed by many Sikhs that the Indian government has gone to great lengths and is spending a considerable amount of money on keeping a close watch on the Sikh community in Britain. The announcement by the Home Office in 1987 that it wants to make itself more aware of the religious and political organizations of Britain's minorities may also have been seen in much the same light as the Home Office's new-found desire to become knowledgeable about the religious and political affinities of minorities. The desire of the state (whether Indian or British) to keep a close watch on minorities such as the Kashmiris and the Sikhs living in this country may become a cause for concern.

In this respect it is believed by members of the Sikh community that there is collusion between the Indian and British governments politically to control the Sikh population in the United Kingdom. David Pallister, a writer on home affairs for *The Guardian* newspaper, expressed the point well in a report on the life sentence[22] passed on Sulikhan Singh Surai, president of the Gravesend International Sikh Youth Federation, for conspiracy to murder, in 1985, another Sikh, who was a member of the Congress party of Rajiv Gandhi:

> Other smaller militant groups exist in Britain who espouse the armed way to a separate state. As part of the British and Indian response, a new extradition treaty is soon to be signed which will make extraditable a wide list of offences that attract more than twelve months in prison. It will be the first time that a Commonwealth country has negotiated a treaty outside the Fugitive Offenders Act, which covers all Commonwealth countries.
>
> (*The Guardian*, 9 May 1987, p. 2)

The trial of three Sikhs in Leicester in 1985–6, accused of conspiracy to kill Rajiv Gandhi during his visit to Britain, is seen as a clear example of the close watch the police keep on the Sikh community in Britain.[23] In brief, two undercover policemen, named as Tom B. and Ian S., posing as hit-men of proven record in the IRA, appeared to have enticed three Sikhs in Leicester to employ them to kill Rajiv Gandhi whilst in Britain in October 1985, for the sum of

£60,000. These Sikhs – factory owner, Patmatma Singh Marwaha, a company director, Jarnail Singh Ranuana and a dyer, Sukvinder Singh Gill – were introduced, during the course of what defending counsel Mike Mansfield described as a pub chat, by another police officer, John, to the would-be assassins. When Marwaha realized that the plot was serious, Tom and Ian having impressed on the plotters the severity of the punishment they inflict on turncoats in such situations, he tried to dissuade the others. He was therefore found not guilty of conspiracy to murder. Ranuana, who had offered an extra £10,000 if the plot were successful, and Gill were, however, found guilty although, as Mr Justice McCullough pointed out in his summing-up, these men were entrapped. Indeed, he was reported in the following terms by *The Guardian* reporter, Paul Hoyland:

> It was of little or no importance whether John had originated the idea of killing Mr. Gandhi . . . What counted was that Ranuana and Gill had adopted the idea.
>
> *(The Guardian*, 22 December 1986, p. 2)

The police officers were commended by the judge for their action, particularly for arresting the plotters three days before the visit of the Indian prime minister, in spite of Mike Mansfield's argument in defence of Gill that the police had 'breached in an unprecedented operation' (*The Guardian*, 22 December 1986) the Home Office guidelines on undercover work. Indeed, the judge went on to reprimand the accused for bringing 'dishonour on the Sikh population in the United Kingdom' (*The Guardian*, 22 December 1986).

Another example of the injustice some Sikhs believe they face in Britain as a result of a perceived collusion of the governments of India and Britain was the Home Office's decision in 1984 to refuse permission to Jasvir Singh to enter the United Kingdom (*The Guardian*, 7 January 1985). A nephew of Sant Jarnail Singh Bhindranwale, Jasvir Singh was eventually denied leave to re-enter Dubai where he had lived and worked. Before his lawyers could present their case in the civil courts, he was whisked away by military aircraft from the Philippines to India although there was no extradition treaty between India and the Philippines. Reportedly, Singh had not been, nor been in contact with, his uncle for some considerable time before his death at the Golden Temple in June 1984. Nonetheless, the Indian government saw him as a threat. And in the view of concerned Sikhs in the United Kingdom the Home Office also chose to see a close political connection between the nephew and the uncle.

The 'collusion', therefore, between governments – if such indeed are the relations between the Indian and British states – seems to involve the former pointing to individuals who are deemed dangerous for the union of India and the latter delivering or excluding them from Britain. India is understandably concerned about its unity. And Britain, with her continuing experience of

Ulster no doubt always casting a shadow over state deliberations of this kind, is concerned about the activities of separatists from anywhere using the country as an external base for undermining another, albeit often disagreeable, member of the Commonwealth. Cordial relations between Britain and India become, it appears in these circumstances, more important than the maintenance of the rights individuals in a liberal democracy are expected to take for granted.

The defence of minority rights on the basis of ethnic affiliation raises some perplexing questions for democratic principles and practices in very many societies, including Britain, today. Aspects of these are considered in chapters eight and nine. It is pertinent, however, to turn at this point to a consideration of some of the questions raised earlier regarding the Khalistan movement in Britain.

The origins of the demand for Khalistan

As may be expected, there are at least two separate, though not necessarily contradictory, accounts of the origins of the demand for an independent Khalistan. One account emphasizes episodic demands for a separate Sikh state in the Punjab. As indicated, the question was raised during the negotiations over Britain's withdrawal from India in the 1940s (Nayar, 1966, ch. 3), and Kapoor give definite dates on which this demand was made – 1946, 1958, 1972, 1978 and 1984 (Kapoor, 1984).

It appears that the demand was first given dramatic support by the All India Sikh Students' Federation on 15 August 1972 when the Federation organized a demonstration in Jullundur. In 1978, as the Punjab issue began to gain momentum again, the Dal Khalsa (a radical Sikh organization) was founded and at its first meeting in Chandigarh made the demand for a Sikh state. In June of the following year another group of radical Sikhs formed the 'revolutionary' Akali Dal and they also called for a Sikh state.

According to Kapoor, after the storming of the Golden Temple, Sikhs 'all over the world unanimously demanded a Sikh state' (Kapoor, 1984, p. 76). The desecration of the Golden Temple also led to the formation of two 'governments in exile', both based in London.[24] And in July, a month after the storming of the Golden Temple, the World Sikh Organization was founded in New York, under the leadership of Major-General Jaswant Singh Bhullar.[25]

Another account of the history of the demand for an independent Khalistan is given by members of the Khalistan Council itself which is based in West London. In late 1954, Davinder Singh Parmar, who apparently comes from a family which was already prominent during the reign of Ranjit Singh in the nineteenth century, came to London and immediately began to propagate the view that there should be an independent Khalistan. On his departure from

India he was encouraged by the then Akali Dal leader, Master Tara Singh,[26] who told Parmar to 'make some noise abroad' (Interview with Parmar, 1987) about an independent Khalistan. Soon after his arrival Parmar held a meeting in a gurdwara at 79 Sinclair Road, Shepherd's Bush, which some fifteen to twenty members of the gurdwara of the same address attended. Parmar remembers being called a madman by one member when he raised the question of an independent Khalistan. Only one person supported his call. Parmar nonetheless continued to write to the newspapers and discuss the matter with fellow Sikhs; he also wrote and distributed leaflets about the question. It was not, however, until 1970, when Parmar and Dr Jagjit Singh Chohan met in London, that the Khalistan movement was formally launched.

Dr Chohan, first President of the Khalistan Council or the government of the Sikh state in exile, had just arrived from Punjab when he met Parmar. Chohan, a medical doctor by profession,[27] claims that he had come to London with the blessings of Fateh Singh, the leader of the Akali Dal, to raise support for an independent Khalistan. As Minister of Finance and Planning during the Akali-led coalition government in Punjab, Chohan knew Parmar's brother who was also a minister in the government, and Chohan was advised before leaving home to contact Parmar on arrival.

The Khalistan movement was formally launched in London at a press conference held at the Waldorf Hotel in the Aldwych, opposite the offices of the Indian High Commission which are situated in India House. At first the Council's membership consisted of two medical doctors (Mangat Singh and Chohan) and Parmar himself. Both Chohan and Parmar admit that at the time, support for their cause in the Sikh community in Britain was negligible. They were regarded as 'madmen' by devout Sikhs in Britain and their demand for an independent Khalistan was unheard of in India.

However, in October 1971, just before the start of the Indo-Pakistan war over Bangladesh, Chohan visited the birthplace of Guru Nanak, the founder of the Sikh faith, in Pakistan. He made some remarks about an independent Khalistan which were taken up by the media in Pakistan. The result was that for the first time people in India heard about this demand and the name *Khalistan* began to circulate. According to Parmar and Chohan, the reception of the idea in India was much the same as earlier in the United Kingdom: almost every Sikh man and woman was against the idea of an independent Sikh state. Nevertheless, at least the name, *Khalistan*, became recognizable.

These details are generally corroborated by publications of the government of India. In a *Note* prepared by the home ministry (Nayar and Singh, 1984, pp. 142ff.), Dr Chohan's launching of the Khalistan movement in London is described as being accompanied by 'wild allegations of oppression of the Sikhs in India' (Nayar and Singh, 1984, p. 143). Whilst at Nankana in Pakistan for Guru Nanak's birthday celebrations, Chohan is reported to have made an 'anti-

India statement which was highly played up by the news-media in that country' (Nayar and Singh, 1984). The government stressed that the Akali Dal, both in the UK and in India, distanced itself from Chohan's statements and that he was suspended from the party by its leader, Fateh Singh, in November. The *Note* describes separatist leaders such as Chohan as 'frustrated and out-of-power politicians [who] found a convenient and handy slogan in the demand [sic] for Sikh Homeland' (Nayar and Singh, 1984). It is important to note, however, that of the leaders of the Khalistan movement in the UK, only Chohan has had any significant political experience in India.

There was, in the view of the Council, a twofold initial response to this in India. First, the central government ignored the demand because they refused to believe that it was serious. Second, Hindu nationalists in the Punjab sought to demonstrate that the demand for an independent Khalistan was ludicrous and anti-unionist. According to Chohan and Parmar this exposure at least helped to make the concept of and the demand for Khalistan more widely known and, in their view, this was a gain for their cause.

As noted earlier, it was the storming of the Golden Temple, however, which gave life to the demand for an independent Khalistan. Overnight, this single event transformed the situation. The Anandpur Resolution, which stood at the centre of Sikh demands from the 1970s, suddenly appeared to be redundant to many Sikhs both in India and outside. This is one important point on which the two accounts of the origins of the demand place great stress.

Whilst one account places emphasis on the Indian roots or locations of the origins of the demand, the other stresses how the demand gained ground amongst the Sikh community outside India. The government of India's White Paper on the Punjab situation mentions a number of groups in India. These include the Dal Khalsa, Babbar Khalsa and Akhand Kirtani Jatha as well as the Khalistan Council. The first of these, the Dal Khalsa, is said by the White Paper to be based mainly in the United Kingdom and West Germany. The White Paper also lists a number of atrocities for which the organization is said to have claimed responsibility, such as the hijacking of an Air India aircraft in September 1981 and the killing of the deputy inspector-general of police, Atwal, in the Golden Temple complex in 1983. The Babbar Khalsa is said to operate chiefly from Vancouver in Canada and, like the Dal Khalsa, the organization is said to seek support from Pakistan. The government argued that Babbar Khalsa would be founding a Khalistan Liberation Army. The Akhand Kirtani Jatha, the followers of Sant Jarnail Bhindranwale (Nayar and Singh, 1984, ch. 1) is described as supporting other organizations and was supposed to be active in both the United Kingdom and Canada.

Tully and Jacob argue that the government had no real evidence that these groups were in fact involved in terrorist activities and that groups based outside the country had little influence on events in the Punjab. In particular, they point to the silence of the White Paper on the then president of India, Zail Singh's connections with Dal Khalsa in its formative period (Tully and Jacob, 1985, p. 210; also Nayar and Singh, 1984, chs. 1 and 2).

What is important from the perspective of this account is not the authenticity of whether the demand for an independent Khalistan was first declared in India or in the United Kingdom. Rather, the relevant point is that the events in the Punjab have had and are likely to continue to have a dramatic and immediate effect on the Sikh population in the United Kingdom. This is an example of how nationalist politics follow groups of people as they move from one place to another, thereby intimating to us that shared values and histories are greater binding forces than the sole claim of affinity to historic homeland.

The leadership of the Khalistan Council

It is crucial, therefore, to consider the nature of the leadership the Khalistan Council provided in Britain for the Sikh community during the years under consideration, a large section of which is believed by leaders now to be sympathetic to the demand for an independent homeland. It is necessary first, however, to say why attention is being focused upon the Council rather than on the other groups.

First, the Council saw itself as the legitimate government of the Sikh state of Khalistan but because this state is not yet realized, of necessity, it has been a government in exile. As such the organization suffered all the drawbacks of a 'government' without a territory to govern. Nonetheless, there have been ministers responsible for particular areas of state whilst Dr Jagjit Chohan was the president. Secondly, the Khalistan Council, as noted earlier, was the first group to give direct and dramatic call for independence from India in the post-independence period. This gives it a pre-eminence above the other groups that emerged after the agitations started in Punjab in the 1980s. Third, as may be seen from the group membership of the Council, several Sikh groups exist, many of which support the demand for an independent Khalistan. Nearly all of them, however, are less accessible than the Khalistan Council. Moreover, being a federal body, concentration on the Council has the merit that it focuses on that aspect of the activities of these groups that is of interest here, namely the demand for an independent homeland for the Sikhs.

The Council does not see itself as a political party. Leaders are quick to point this out. They insist that it is a body that seeks to represent the interests of all Sikhs. Thus, as of 1987 the Council had a membership made up of representatives from most of the Sikh organizations. This includes the World Sikh Organization of which Parmar is the UK president, the Panthic Committee, the International Sikh Students Federation and so forth.

The United Kingdom branch of the Akali Dal, under the leadership of

Mohindar Palsingh Dhillon from Coventry, is also a member of the Council. This support by the Akali Dal of the movement for an independent Khalistan is in itself a significant comment on how events in the Punjab are influencing Sikhs in the United Kingdom. Sikhs in this country understandably enough feel that they must support those who are struggling for the security of the faith 'back home'. The support Sikhs 'back home' receive from British Sikhs may also be evidence enough to suggest that leadership has passed from moderate hands to men of radical persuasion or that moderate men have been radicalized by the attack on the Golden Temple.[28]

Relations between the Council and the Akali Dal in the Punjab are not necessarily the same. As late as September 1987 the Council was attacking the Akali Dal in India for introducing division into Sikh ranks. In a strongly worded statement the Council argued that

> Sarbat Khalsa is the supreme decision-making assembly of the Sikh nation, and the supreme source of its unity. No individual or group, however powerful or influential it may be, has the authority to reconsider the decisions taken by it. Any attempt to do so is nothing but an affront to its authority, designed to create divisions in the nation.
>
> (*Khalistan News*, No. 6, September 1987)

The Akali Dal leaders, the statement went on to say, consistently betrayed the Sikh struggle over the past twenty years 'by putting forward attractive-looking but unrealistic and impracticable targets before it' (*Khalistan News*, No. 6, September 1987).

Through its membership the Council keeps in touch not only with the Sikh communities in this country, but with Sikhs in India, as well as in other parts of the world such as Canada, the USA and Indonesia. Relations may be maintained with the homeland and the rest of the Sikh diaspora through the memberships of existing groups. Like the Congress party, some of the other political parties in India gained a degree of representation abroad when members migrated. For example, the membership of the Akali Dal on the Khalistan Council must give it the chance to develop and maintain contact with Sikhs elsewhere, through the utilization of already established channels of communication.

Another important means of communication between groups, particularly in the Sikh diaspora, has been through the organization of international meetings which leaders of Sikh organizations attend. At these meetings resolutions are passed regarding the problems Sikhs face both in India and elsewhere. The first 'international convention of Sikhs' was held in New York in April 1981 and there were reportedly over 200 delegates in attendance. The third convention took place in Slough, Berkshire between 17–19 April 1987 in order to build unity in the Khalistan movement. On this occasion the Council was able to call on various groups for their support; in his keynote address the president, Dr Chohan, mentioned, among other groups, Babbar Khalsa International, Akhand Kirtani Jatha of the United Kingdom, the Sikh Youth Movement, the World Sikh Organization, the Dal Khalsa International and the International Sikh Youth Federation, as having 'rendered invaluable and selfless help' and admitted that 'the Council would have been non-functional had it not secured the co-operation of the various jathas in the United Kingdom' (*Khalistan News*, April 1987, p. 7).

At these meetings fraternal groups from other minorities in India are also invited to attend and to speak. This is in accordance with the general policy of the Council to encourage cooperation between minorities. At the Slough convention there were speakers from the Azad Muslim Conference, the Indian Muslim Federation, the Jammu and Kashmir Liberation Front, and an 83-year-old Dr Phizo spoke on behalf of the Nagas. There were also Afghan speakers from various Mujahiddin organizations.[29] This aspect of the Council's work was further stressed in its call for Moslems and Sikhs to work together to bring pressure to bear on British politicians. The Council has identified 75 parliamentary constituencies in Britain in which the Moslem/Sikh vote could be decisive and argues that

> Politically, the friends and relatives of both communities back in South Asia are constantly suffering from vicious harassment and persecution at the hands of the Indian Hindhus . . . Obviously both communities stand to gain in terms of political influence by evoking a common policy in British politics.
>
> (*Khalistan News*, No. 6, September 1987, p. 2)

A third means of communication and type of activity open to the Council within the Sikh diaspora has been its publications. These include the publication of the People's Union for Democratic Rights/People's Union for Civil Liberties joint report into the causes and aftermaths of the riots which took place in Delhi after the murder of Indira Gandhi in early November 1984. The Council claimed that since this report could not be published in India it had a responsibility to do so in the United Kingdom. Perhaps more important than such occasional publications was the founding, in April 1987 of a monthly journal, the *Khalistan News*, which was published in both Punjabi and English.[30] This carries reports of developments in India and among Sikhs in the diaspora, as well as the Council's views and comments. There was also a *Khalistan News Service* which provided the media with the Council's views on matters affecting Sikhs, the Punjab and the sub-continent generally.

It is important to consider a little more closely the kinds of support the Council appeared to enjoy. Its principal support came from existing groups, particularly since the Council did not wish to become a political party itself.

Perhaps, not unexpectedly even if it is a little paradoxical, the Council seemed to work according to the model of political organization first developed by the Congress Party. This type of political organization sought to unite all kinds of political groups and became attractive to nationalists throughout the empire. To a significant extent, the single party systems in many post-colonial states in Africa were developed from this Congress model. In a similar manner to the nationalist parties in Africa and the Indian Congress party, the Council sought to unite in a fairly loose way groups with different interests and timetables, agendas, beliefs and political philosophies. The single requirement for membership of the Council appeared to be the support for an independent Khalistan.

There was a second and perhaps far more important source of strength for the Khalistan Council in Britain. This is the gurdwara, the central Sikh institution established in all Sikh communities. The gurdwara is more than a place of worship. For example, a major feature of Sikhism is the institution of the *langar*, or kitchen, which welcomes not only adherents to the faith, but anyone who enters, with a meal. It is also the place where discussions over matters affecting the community will take place. In short, the gurdwara is the central social, political and religious institution for Sikhs. For the faithful living abroad, it is not surprising that the gurdwara becomes a central, multifunctional meeting place where the weary may renew his/her strength through mutual companionship and worship.

The support, therefore, of such a body must be crucial for the success of any would-be Sikh political organization. As noted earlier, in India one important Sikh demand involves the question of whether these gurdwaras should be controlled by devout Sikhs themselves or by nominees of the central government. In the Punjab the complex of the Golden Temple, comprising the Akal Takht (which deals with temporal/political matters) and the Harimandir Sahib (the temple for worship) is the focal point for the rallying of Sikhs. It is undoubtedly this that encouraged Dr Chohan to submit a resolution at the Slough convention calling for the Council to affiliate with the Panthic Committee of the Akal Takht Sahib in order to 'derive validity, courage and resolve from the affiliation' (*Khalistan News*, April 1987, p. 1). Without the support, neutrality or silence of leaders such as Professor Darshan Singh, head of the Akal Takht, the various political Sikh groups will be significantly weakened. It is, therefore, important for these groups, like any other leader abroad, to secure the support of the religious leaders in Amritsar.

There would appear to be strong support for the demand for an independent Khalistan amongst members of some gurdwaras in Britain. Having said this there is cause for caution. Whilst many Sikhs may want to see an independent Khalistan, this feeling remains largely dormant and untranslated into active political support for the Council. It was the storming of the Golden Temple that made the demand appealing to many Sikhs. As this event recedes in time many will probably revert to a position of support for the union of India which, from a distance, may appear more attractive to many Sikhs. Of course, much depends on the ability of the Council's leadership to make political capital of the anger and alienation of Sikhs before the events of 1984 fade.

There is a second reason for being cautious. It would appear that the loyalty of the estimated 1250 or so gurdwaras in Britain goes first to a specific group which may then give or not give its support to the Council. This arises partly from the umbrella nature of the Council's organization. For example, the radical International Sikh Students' Organization, until recently led by Dr Parget Singh and which in 1987 came under the leadership of Dr Rai, is believed to be supported by the more radical gurdwaras in the country. More radical than the older leaders of the Council, it would appear that the organization prefers to move faster in agitating for a free Khalistan than the older men of the Council such as Chohan and Parmar. The group's loyalty to the Council does not appear, however, to be in doubt and therefore the Council will probably gain the support of radical gurdwaras via more militant organizations.

There are several reasons why it is very difficult to measure the numerical strength of the Khalistan Council in the Sikh community in Britain. It will suffice to mention three here. First, since the Council does not seek to become a political party it is expected that, apart from those who hold particular ministerial portfolios, individual membership does not appear to be at a premium.

Second, Sikh leaders tend to stress quality over quantity. They draw upon their history as an example of how relatively few dedicated men and women can achieve far more than the many who lack conviction and courage. Radical Sikhs stress that it must be remembered that their faith was itself founded by Guru Nanak in the fifteenth century, in the midst of foreign invasion and repression. But the distinctive features of the Five Ks were established by the *saint-soldier*, the Tenth Guru, Gorbind Singh. Amongst radical Sikhs Gorbind Singh appears to be regarded as second in importance only to the founder himself, Guru Nanak. This admiration is due to Gorbind Singh's soldierly qualities and his teaching that a member of the *Khalsa* (a baptized Sikh who observes the Five Ks) must be prepared to defend at all times the oppressed against the oppressor and must be willing to use force as a last resort (G. Singh and A. Kaur, 1986). Thus, under extreme provocation the Sikh is expected to resort to arms in defence of his or her rights; additionally he/she is also expected to defend others too weak to do so themselves.

This background seems to have a profound impact on the present generation of radical Sikh leaders who are convinced that the central government of India can no longer be trusted to act in good faith with respect to Sikhs and other minorities. In the circumstances it would appear that very many believe that their true strength lies not so much in numbers as in the quality or support the

Sikh nation itself gives to the struggle for independence from India. In this regard, too, radical Sikhs point to the disproportionately high contribution of Sikhs to the movement for independence from Britain.

A third factor which helps to explain the difficulty in measuring the support the Khalistan Council receives is this. It must be recognized that the general support for the demand for Khalistan is a *reaction* to events which, in the view of one Sikh intellectual who advises the Council and is keenly aware of its weaknesses and strengths, may be insufficient to sustain the movement. The tendency for the movement to react to the decisions and actions of the Delhi government is also seen as a weakness. According to this view the movement should be ahead of Delhi and should be able to determine the pace of developments in Punjab, thereby reversing the present situation.

The impression must not be given that all gurdwaras or all Sikhs in Britain support the demand for Khalistan. There are very many *individual* Sikhs who condemn the storming of the Golden Temple but who do not feel that this should lead to the severance of the Punjab from India. They would argue that there is still time and room for accommodation within the union and that an independent Khalistan would not be a viable proposition.

There are also some *groups* that would not support the demand for an independent Khalistan. The Congress party, which has branches in the United Kingdom, is, naturally, against the demand. Whilst this is not unexpected, it must be borne in mind that some Congress members are Sikhs from the Punjab. The same is true for some members of the various communist parties who would be unable to stomach the strong emphasis placed on religion by the movement as a whole. Some Sikhs active in the Indian Workers Association in Britain would stress the need for India to remain united. Of course, some orthodox Sikhs would say that many of these people are not *true* Sikhs because they do not stand ready to defend their religion against attack. But if a Sikh is to be defined in this way only, then it is not difficult to claim that nearly all Sikhs support the demand for a free Khalistan.

The principal organizational aim of the Council, therefore, is to bring together all parties that see their task as achieving independence from India for the Sikhs. In this respect the Council seeks to act as the central vehicle for the demand of Khalistani nationalists and its leaders believe it is enough that member organizations are committed to the cause of an independent Khalistan. One implication of this, however, is that the Council is made up of independent groups which may from time to time espouse conflicting aims and tactics. There are two crucial aspects of these differences which are likely to become more important if the Khalistan movement gains momentum and an independent state of Khalistan seems likely to be carved out of the Indian union. These are to do with, first, the methods of achieving such a state and, second, the kinds of future envisaged for an independent Khalistan.

The glow of freedom

In nearly every tract on the Punjab question Sikh leaders and intellectuals refer to Jawaharlal Nehru's betrayal of the Sikh people. Reference is usually made to his recognition that the Sikhs deserved 'special consideration' and his statement that 'I see nothing wrong in an area and set-up in the North wherein the Sikhs can also experience the glow of freedom' (Pettigrew, 1985, p. 9).[31] The perceived betrayal lies in Nehru's inability or, as Sikhs see it, his unwillingness to live up to his statement so that Sikhs could also enjoy 'the glow of freedom' for which they had sacrificed more than others. In addition to the points that I have already discussed above, this feeling of betrayal must be borne firmly in mind when considering the vision of an independent Khalistan which members of the Council articulate. I turn now to this important aspect of the discussion which Council members feel is very poorly understood by the public at large.

First, an independent Khalistan would seek to present itself as a model for the new states leaders believe are likely to emerge out of the break up of the post-colonial states of South Asia. The demand for an independent state of Khalistan is seen as part of a much wider demand by the people of India for 'the glow of freedom'. When this glow is realized in the Punjab others in the region will also want to experience it. Indeed, the condition of other minorities such as the Moslems, the Jains, Christians and Buddhists, the Nagars, the Kashmiris, the Tamils and so forth, all point to a general questioning of the relations of power in India. This question being posed by minorities defined according to such factors as religion, region and language will inevitably lead to the break up of the union, because the union was founded on faulty premises. And the birth and development of more representative states in the sub-continent will be the result. The vision of a free Khalistan includes the introduction in the region of a model of state organization which others may choose to emulate in this massive restructuring of states in the region.

Complementary to this model of state reorganization is the vision of a peaceful South Asia based on new *nation-states* – as distinct from the traditional nation*s*-states – which would voluntarily come together in a loose union or confederation. The model that leaders have in mind is the present EEC. They see a need for stress to be placed on *economic* rather than on *political* unity. Similarly to the terms set out in the Anandpur Resolution for good relations between the union and state governments, the Khalistan Council leaders believe that the powers of the centre should be strictly limited to certain inter-state matters such as the regulation of trade. Their position is much more radical, however, than that suggested by the Akali leaders in the Anandpur Resolution. The central authorities would be so limited in their functions that it would be difficult to speak of a central government at all. If this were to exist, it should be so limited in its powers that the centres of decision-making rest with the states. This new relationship may mean that decisions would no doubt take longer to be arrived at but they would be democratic and would have the support of the parties who agreed to them in the first place. The Khalistan Council argues with conviction that it is not possible to govern a country as large and diverse as India in any other way. In their view the retention of British India under the Gandhi *dynasty* is a travesty of the justice that the various peoples of the country deserve.

Third, contrary to a general impression, the vision of a free Khalistan is that it will not be a theocracy. The model of theocracies offered by the Moslem world is rejected in favour of a democratic secular state.

Two important qualifications, however, follow. One is a critique of political and juridical democracy as received and practiced in India and South Asia generally. Some members of the Council are in favour of a system of pro-portional representation to remedy aspects of the system whereby winners take all to the exclusion from government of the defeated. They believe that the simple majority electoral system unfairly excludes the defeated party in political contests.

Another aspect of this is a critical approach to the adversarial system of justice received from Britain. Instead of there being two opposing sides to a contest in court, leaders would like to see village or people's courts. In these courts the community in which the accused lives will be able to judge him or her and pass sentence. In this way, Council leaders believe, justice may best be served because there would be less chance of the culprit escaping punishment and the offended will see and feel that justice has been done. Part of the justi-fication of this non-adversarial system of justice is the need to see the guilty punished, instead of escaping their fates due to their ability to pay for good defence lawyers.

The second qualification is that Khalistani leaders feel that the Sikh religion needs state protection. They argue that Sikhism is under threat partly because it has no state in which it commands prime religious consideration. Sikhism is also a comparatively young religion and to develop it needs political patronage. Thus, although an independent state of Khalistan would not be a theocracy, the tenets of Sikhism would have the legal sanction of the political authorities. There is a recognition that politics and religion must not be as strictly separated as in Christian West Europe, North America and other secular non-communist societies.

Leaders of the Council insist that the precise forms that the secular state of Khalistan, which would seek to promote and protect Sikhism, would take are still subject to extensive discussion. The feelings are that the immediate objec-tive is to achieve the goal of seeing the creation of an independent Khalistan, then to have national discussions and referenda over the form of state to be established. The constitution, for example, could be framed in much the same way as was the Indian constitution in 1950 – three years after political independence from Britain. Most leaders are careful not to speak about a future constitution for an independent Khalistan. The more secular-minded leaders tend to speak of the merits of a system without a written constitution, such as the British constitution.[32]

There are, however, significantly modified versions of this model of a free Khalistan. In one gurdwara in the Midlands where I interviewed about twenty orthodox and militant Sikhs, the modifications resulted in a much more militant vision of a free Khalistan. Members of the group were all young men with a knowledge of Sikh history and the faith to which they are deeply committed. Not surprisingly, they had not given as much thought to the kind of Khalistan they wanted to see as had the leaders of the Council. The position these young Sikhs articulate, however, may be more representative of the young than that of the older generation. If only for this reason it is, obviously, important to consider this briefly.

The vision of a free Khalistan which emerged from the various discussions I have had with this and similar groups in the region is that the state will be more of a theocracy than a secular democracy. It is not merely that Sikhism needs to be defended, it is that the very essence of the struggle for independence is wrapped up with the defence and promotion of their faith. Moreover, there is little or no distinction between religion and politics for some. And where there is a distinction there is little doubt that religion must come before politics.

Some of the political implications of this divergence of views may not be evident so soon after the declaration of the demand for a free Khalistan. But the tension between the desire for a secular state which sees the Sikh faith as the state religion and the desire for a state which for all intents and purposes resembles a theocracy, are likely to remain and surface, particularly if the demand for Khalistan is successful.

There is, however, one crucial difference between various groups and the Khalistan Council which is not likely to remain dormant. This is the question of violence. One point on which all groups and individuals appear to be clear is that violence in Britain in order to achieve ends in the Punjab is unacceptable. The argument is that the Sikhs have a quarrel with India, principally with the Indian government of the Congress party, and if any action should be taken this must be against parties to the quarrel in India. There is a strong view that Britain is a democratic and open society in which the Sikh faith is left alone, unmolested. Indeed, important concessions are perceived to have been made to the Sikhs such as the right to wear turbans instead of helmets and for baptized Sikhs to carry *kirpan*. This is the opposite, in their view, of the situation in India – the very country they fought to liberate from colonialism. Members of both the gurdwaras and the Council are particularly firm on this point.

The violence between various groups of Sikhs in Britain is viewed with grave concern by members of the Council. At the Slough convention Dr Chohan twice mentioned the question of violence. He argued thus:

> Talking about *modus operandi*, please permit me to say that I am more than aware that we Sikhs have been ordained, in our religion and in our psyche, to combat tyranny and pick up the sword when all other means have failed. It would be cowardice, in a situation of last resort, not to pick up the sword. I would go a step further and say that in those conditions not picking up the sword to combat tyranny would be collaborating with the tyrant. However, I cannot, at the same time, forget the sterling advice given by Birbal to Akbar. The advice was ... as you are only too well aware, that the best weapon is that which is effective in a given situation.
>
> *(Khalistan News*, April 1987, p. 6)

Earlier Dr Chohan had hinted at what he considers the present conditions to be when he stressed that he has 'lived with the belief ... that the battle of the pen is mightier and more fruitful than the battle of the sword' (*Khalistan News*, April 1987, p. 4).

Many of the Sikhs I had the privilege to speak with during the course of 1987, particularly those who are strong supporters of the demand for a free Khalistan, tend to believe in the teachings of Guru Gorbind Singh, namely that the good Sikh does not support violence but, if attacked, must be prepared to defend himself or herself. Dr Chohan has said that he himself does not believe in violence (Interview with Chohan, August 1987). Some members of the Council would, however, give much the same answer to the question as do the young men in my interviews. That is to say, the injunction to *defend* given by Guru Gorbind Singh should be obeyed if necessary against the enemy.

This, of course, returns the discussion to the central point of interest: the demand for Khalistan and the question of nationalism.

Khalistani nationalism

Essentially, the demand for Khalistan rests on the assumption that there is a nation which may be so defined and sensibly marked off from the rest of India. By implication at least, this is denied by the majority of Indians and enshrined by the 1950 Constitution which does not see the Sikhs as being distinct from the Hindu majority as the Sikhs would like others to see them. But there are very many Sikh men and women who are prepared to sacrifice their lives for the cause of establishing an independent state of Khalistan. For the Sikh nationalist there is an onus placed on all Sikhs to assert their national difference from the majority Hindu population.

As I stressed in the first chapters of this study, such arguments are usually based on racial considerations, territory, language and religion. Each of these should be considered in turn briefly and in light of what has already been said above.

Sikhs are not easily recognized from other Indians – the Five Ks apart – on the basis of markedly different physical traits, or what is called race. Their claim to be different from the inhabitants of the rest of India cannot be advanced on the grounds of racial or phenotypical distinction, fashionable as this may be, in some parts of the contemporary world. In this regard India may be more fortunate than several other countries and communities insofar as social and political disruptions are not justified on racial grounds. It is, of course, true that most Sikhs are Jats, the farming caste, and there may be an ancient racial factor to this. But in the main the caste/class configuration is of far greater importance in socio-political matters than race per se. It is not possible, therefore, to think in terms of a racial definition of the Sikh nation.

Earlier the other attributes of territory, religion and language were considered in terms of how they apply to the Sikh/Punjab question. There is no need to repeat these. The important point here is the nature of Khalistani nationalism. In other words, is this nationalism of the kind I suggest we call *ethnic* nationalism as distinct from the *traditional* kind? Another question follows from this: what are some of the possible implications of whatever answer there may be to this, not only for South Asia in general and for the people of Punjab but particularly for Sikhs in Britain and the diaspora.

The nationalism portrayed by the demand for an independent Khalistan comes closer to the *ethnic* nationalism paradigm than to what I called *traditional* nationalism above. The latter kind of nationalism requires no more than that the state has the loyalty of all the peoples who fall within the physical boundaries of the nation-state. Although this arrangement of social and political power is called the 'nation-state' the more correct way to express the relationship is 'nation*s*-state' because there is a multiplicity of 'nations' that come within the boundaries or jurisdiction of a given state. And, of course, the union of India or the notion of an Indian nation clearly demonstrates this situation.

There are some more specific reasons, however, for the argument that I am advancing. First, the language that unites Sikhs, Punjabi, is a language shared by more people than just the Sikhs. The Hindu people of the region also speak Punjabi as their mother tongue – census returns notwithstanding. Precisely, however, because it is a language shared by both Hindus and Sikhs and the former population is part of the overwhelming majority of the country as a whole, Punjabi has been politicized. One group (the Sikhs) claims it as its own whilst the other (the Hindus) rejects it. The choice does not, therefore, rest with the Sikhs. The majority Hindu population of the country has effected a narrowing of the community of declared Punjabi speakers. This is, of course, a classic example of how the majority in any population can force a minority to become an ethnic group because the choice of action rests largely with the majority.

The same may also be said of other distinguishing factors such as territory. The delimitation of the Punjab was largely dictated by circumstances outside the control of Sikhs. Players concerned with the larger field of contestation could use the situation to their own advantage. In the end the very territory occupied by Sikhs appeared so that all demands seemed to be communal demands and therefore ran counter to the supposed universalistic claims of the apparently disinterested central powers.

This rejection is accompanied by an attempt to undermine the single most important fact which makes Sikhs different from the majority of people in India, namely their faith. But it cannot be denied that Sikhs are indeed different in religion, cuisine and dress from the majority population. The *ethnicity* of Sikhs in India is therefore not difficult to establish. Nor is it difficult to establish in the UK and the rest of the Sikh diaspora.

Conclusion

The fact that Sikh leaders stress that an independent Khalistan would not be a theocracy nor a state inhabited exclusively by adherents of the Sikh faith, may suggest that a Khalistan state would be a *non-ethnic* state and therefore quite different from, say, Iran since the Islamic revolution in the late 1970s. The fact that it would be called *Khalistan* after the Khalsa brother/sisterhood would suggest, however, that the strength of, and adherence to, Sikhism would make the state of Khalistan co-terminous with the nation of Sikhs as defined by the single factor which unites Sikhs, irrespective of class, physical or territorial boundaries and so forth – their religion. Should this be achieved, then the Sikhs will indeed be in the pioneering group of those sets of people who may achieve statehood based exclusively, or essentially, on the tenets of *ethnic* nationalism.

It is necessary to relate more closely this excursion into Sikh diasporic politics to the general concerns of the discussion over the communal option for Britain. Before doing so, however, it is necessary to consider a second, but for comparative purposes quite different, example of diasporic politics amongst Britain's recently settled, non-European, population.

7

Diasporic politics: the demand for democracy in Guyana

Introduction

This chapter is something of a study in contrasts, because diasporic politics amongst Commonwealth Caribbean people in Britain are relatively inconspicuous. Indeed, the unpronounced nature of these politics appears in sharp relief against the political activities of West Indians regarding political life in Britain itself. The exilic or diasporic politics of people from the Anglophone Caribbean in Britain also contrast sharply with those of minorities from Southern Europe or South East Asia. This is not to say that there is an absence of groups and individuals in Britain who are deeply concerned about political life 'back home' in the Caribbean. The nature of the interest in these politics and their relatively low profile in Britain amounts, however, to something of a paradox for the observer.

An explanation of this apparent paradox is offered here. It examines, first, the Caribbean background to the politics of 'back home', or homeland politics, amongst West Indians in Britain and, secondly, it examines the kinds of support specific groups of Guyanese living in Britain give to the cause of democracy in the exceptional case of Guyana. Aspects of the kind of colonialism the region experienced as well as the political institutions and practices developed in the post-colonial period are necessarily involved in such an attempt. Attention is drawn, then, to the Guyanese situation because, of all Caribbean groups in this country, it comes closest to the experience of other recently settled communities in Britain which are deeply involved with the politics of their 'homelands' outside the United Kingdom. Finally, the nature of such involvement in diasporic politics will be related to the kind of communal option being pursued in Britain today.

Nationalism in the Anglophone Caribbean

The background to the exilic political behaviour of West Indians in Britain is perhaps best approached from the perspective of nationalism in the Anglophone Caribbean. My contention is that nationalism in the Commonwealth Caribbean has never received the vibrant and militant expressions it did in Asia and Africa. This is a similar experience to that of England, which did not undergo the militant nationalism France, Germany, Italy and other continental European countries underwent. But the reasons for this similarity of experience were quite different. In the case of England, the country's isolation from continental Europe and her dominant position in the world made it unnecessary to espouse militant nationalism. This indifference was reinforced by the political unity England imposed within Britain, as well as Britain's economic and military strength in the wider world which meant that the appeal of nationalism held out little or nothing for the dominant classes in the country. Indeed, militant nationalism in Britain could have jeopardized the dominant interests in the different *nations* of the United Kingdom. The political restructuring militant nationalism brings about would have disturbed the historic compromises reached between social classes across the national communities and within them.

In the Anglophone Caribbean, on the other hand, the very opposite set of factors tended to discourage militant nationalism. This is hardly the place to carry out the careful and necessary examination of the factors which have inhibited militant nationalism in the region. But essentially it would appear that the region's dependency and *weakness* vis-à-vis other states encouraged a strong non-militant nationalist tradition. As in England, the relatively strong internal social cohesion reinforced this tradition. The question of nationhood has not generally been, therefore, placed in a militant, forceful or unambiguous manner at the forefront of politics in the region. Militant nationalism, based on racial, territorial, religious and linguistic affinities has not significantly divided people from varied African, European, Asian and other backgrounds who today constitute the Commonwealth Caribbean. Several other factors also help to explain how this situation has come about.

These islands as well as Guyana have a common history which links them and makes the people of these countries easily recognizable as West Indians.[1] The people of the West Indies are, however, separated by the Caribbean and the Atlantic over a distance of more than two thousand miles from the Bahamas in the north to Guyana in the south east. The islands and people in the south east – generally called the Eastern Caribbean – are physically close and have long enjoyed well-established social and economic relations with each other. The hinterlands of Guyana and the oilfields of Trinidad have encouraged dynamic migration within the sub-region[2] (Richardson, 1983).

The Bahamas, situated just off Florida in the Atlantic, and Jamaica in the north-west Caribbean, have not had the same easy flow of inter-island communication. During the colonial period, it used to be easier for a Jamaican to meet a Barbadian in New York or London than for them to meet within the region. Apart from a very small group of businessmen, sportsmen and -women, diplomats, academics and students, it is still the case that West Indians in London or New York may get to know each other more easily than they would do in the Caribbean itself. The West Indies also boasts over a dozen sovereign states,[3] making the people of the region perhaps the most governed anywhere in the world in terms of the ratio of territory and population, but particularly the latter, to governments. There are less than six million souls in the Commonwealth Caribbean and if we exclude Guyana which is a little smaller than Britain, the land mass of these countries is barely more than Wales or East Anglia. Jamaica, Trinidad and Barbados, with populations of roughly under three million, one and a half million and one million respectively, account for the majority of people in the region. It is sobering to remember that the total population of the Commonwealth Caribbean is less than Haiti's nearly six million souls.

The main features of the region's history are well known. Indentured labour from conquered Ireland in the seventeenth century, followed for the remainder of the century and until 1838 by slaves from Africa, followed, in turn, from the 1840s to 1917 with what the English scholar Hugh Tinker, correctly, calls a 'new system of slavery' (Tinker, 1974; Cross, 1980), indentured labour from India. There were also white overseers from Britain and Ireland in the case of the older British possessions such as Barbados and Jamaica, and Spaniards, French and Dutch from continental Europe in places such as Trinidad and Guyana. In all these societies there were the mixed offsprings of blacks and whites – the mulattoes or coloureds. From the middle of the last to the middle of the present centuries there have also been small pockets of continental Europeans such as the Germans and Madeirans (generally called Portuguese in Guyana) as well as Chinese, Lebanese and others from Asia and the Middle East, settling in the region. Most have contributed to the emergence and development of a new kind of society, what the Barbadian poet and historian Edward Brathwaite calls 'creole society' (Brathwaite, 1971).

The *dependencia* economists of the 'New World Group', such as Lloyd Best and George Beckford, preferred to call the social orders which emerged out of these barbaric beginnings 'plantation societies' (Beckford, 1972; Best, 1968). This is because groups from different parts of the world were linked by the plantation economy based mainly on the production of sugar and rum from sugar-cane. The contention appears to be that even though the economy of the region diversified, for example shifting significantly to mining in Trinidad (petroleum), Guyana and Jamaica (bauxite) after World War Two, Caribbean society as a whole was formed during the heyday of the plantation and its ugly and dependent features remain, to paraphrase Beckford, a persistent reality for the region's people.

From the 1950s, however, the central contention with respect to the characterization of Anglophone Caribbean societies has been around M. G. Smith's theory of social and cultural pluralism. In a series of papers from the 1950s and the early 1960s Smith, a Jamaican social anthropologist, argued that Caribbean society is essentially divided by the social and cultural norms which we would ordinarily expect to hold or bind a society together (Smith, 1965, 1974). These would include such 'compulsory' institutions as the family, religion, language, marriage and so forth. His contention was, and remains, that each group of Caribbean people – African, European, Indian, and so forth – remains separate from each other through a plurality of these social and cultural institutions. Smith does not deny, as some of his critics accuse him, that there are social classes. But he does insist that the overriding factors in these societies are the plurality of social and cultural institutions and norms (Smith, 1974, 1984).

Smith's depiction of Caribbean society leaves us with a picture not significantly different from most post-colonial societies with a British past, and it cannot be denied that in the Caribbean 'race' and later 'colour' have been of profound importance. Anglophone Caribbean societies do not, however, generally present a straightforward pluralist situation, such as developed in many parts of the empire and may be developing in post-imperial Britain. Smith may be correct in alerting us to the diversity of Caribbean societies because in the euphoria of political independence leaders too readily dismissed the question of diversity in specific countries.[4] He has, however, been quite properly taken to task for stressing the point beyond reasonable bounds and thereby ignoring the perhaps more important factors that hold these societies together.

The case against Smith is, therefore, a strong one. Despite the most inhumane genesis, the Anglophone Caribbean people have evolved a society based increasingly on class. The importance of colour and race have given way to class in a manner which incorporates these older forms of differentiation. In recent years attempts have been made to sharpen the definition of Caribbean social class so that it does not exclude an understanding of race and colour because these have been very important ingredients in the emergence and development of classes in the region. Thus, some observers of Caribbean development would argue, correctly, that *race* is an essential element in the definition of classes in Caribbean society. This has been particularly true of Jamaica, which has received much attention over the past decade or so (Stone, 1985; Post, 1978; Gordon, 1987; and Beckford and Witter, 1982). Thus, it is still the case that in most of these societies the upper middle class is predominantly white or near-white whilst there are hardly any white people in the rural or urban working classes (the poor Germans of St Elizabeth apart). This is not a concession to Smith. Just as his admission that class differentiation does not make his theory of social and cultural pluralism irrelevant, so the admission that race and colour are powerful qualifications of class in the Anglophone

Caribbean does not mean that class has not become the single most important differential factor in these societies.

On the whole, compared to the vast majority of contemporary societies in either advanced capitalism or underdeveloped post-colonial societies, the Commonwealth Caribbean constitutes a distinct entity. And this is not held together by either a colonial power or the marketplace, the two agglutinating elements in Smith's plural society. Indeed, it would appear that what distinguishes West Indian societies from most post-colonial societies is the strength of certain central factors which have moulded aspects of different European, African and Asian cultures into Brathwaite's 'creole society'. This involves the merging of aspects of different cultures evolving over time into a new and distinct culture.

The point may be expressed another way: assuming that the marketplace and the production of goods for the international market were the only factors that originally characterized societies in the region, then it may be true to say that in the contemporary period social forces have emerged and led to a social homogeneity which the theory of social and cultural pluralism does not take into account. From this perspective it may be said that one of the most important achievements of the Caribbean people has been the transformation of the most abominable, crude and inhumane situations into a comparatively humane and contributing culture.

The 'creole society' of the Caribbean is, therefore, one which vindicates Hegel's view that the slave has greater potential for freedom than the master. Where the latter can only continue to oppress, the slave can look to a new dawn, a new hope. The slave has, as the St Lucian poet, Derek Walcott, implied, only one option and that is to rise from the nadir of a base degradation to a higher humanity.[5] As with British society (Hock, 1986), newcomers to Caribbean societies have made their contributions (*Jamaica Historical Review*, vol. xv, 1986; Cross, 1980; Dabydeen and Samaroo, 1987)[6] but there was an essential core upon which they built. Thus, although there are important differences between town and country life, between social classes in terms of shades of colour, speech, and so forth, when we see these in a comparative light there can be little doubt that these societies are, in the main, far from what we would expect in a society divided by social and cultural pluralism.

These general remarks lead to a number of more specific relevant points which should help us better to understand the relative absence of militant exilic politics amongst West Indians in Britain. Some of these may be mentioned briefly here.

First, West Indian societies are secular societies in which there is an attempt to treat people as individuals, irrespective of race, religion and so forth. Apart from the notable exceptions of Guyana and Trinidad, there are several common factors which hold the various communities together in civil society. Not even in these, however, are loyalty to the state and the rule of law determined by a prior loyalty to region, separatist ethnic, religious, or other communities. In the main, political ideologies are what justify the political divisions there are and social class – itself partly determined by colour – is what provides the basis for such divisions. These are quite different from social and cultural pluralism which leads to communal as opposed to class loyalties.

This has not always been the case. Indeed, a significant aspect of the development of these societies is the frustrated attempts to build white settler colonies in the region. The steady demographic change from a white to a black majority population which occurred from the seventeenth century was not originally envisaged. The settler colonies were intended for white men who would share many of the rights their compatriots in Britain enjoyed. This kind of colonial democracy *excluded* black people; like the helots of ancient Athens, both as slaves and initially as freed individuals black people were structurally placed beyond the pale of what was considered to be *civilized* society. The rights we have come to regard as the heritage of all humanity would, left to the white settler population, have become the privilege of the select few who happened to have the *correct* colour, namely the colour white. This kind of social and political agenda was not, of course, unique to the British West Indies but only in South Africa has it continued to receive full and unabashed implementation by the state.

Second, societies in the West Indies have evolved, rather paradoxically, democratic political systems which are as workable as anywhere else in the modern world. Apart from the well-known exceptions of Guyana and Grenada, elections are free and regular and governments are returned or turned out of office on the basis of their perceived or actual performance. In Jamaica, for example, election campaigns are usually plagued by violence between supporters of the two main political parties, the Jamaica Labour Party (JLP) and the People's National Party (PNP) (Lacey, 1977; Stone, 1983; Goulbourne, 1984). These elections, however, are free of military interference, and political malpractice (Figueroa, 1985) is perhaps far less widespread than in the USA. Neither political party has been able to secure a third term in office since universal adult suffrage and modern political parties were introduced in 1944 (see, for example, Stone, 1983).

In some of the islands the trend since independence has been towards the one-party dominant system rather than the two-party or multi-party system. Trinidad and St Lucia are good examples of this type of political democracy. In Trinidad and Tobago the People's National Movement (PNM), founded by the late Dr Eric Williams, remained in power from 1956, six years before independence, to the end of 1986 when a coalition led by a former PNM finance minister, A. N. R. Robinson, defeated the party at the polls. Much the same occurred earlier in St Lucia in 1979/80 when the veteran politician, John

Compton, and his conservative Labour Party was routed at the polls by a radical newly formed coalition brought together by men of differing political views such as George Hadlam, Peter Josey and Alan Louisy. Before this government could exhaust its mandate it was fragmented from within as the leaders jockeyed for power and then galloped off in different directions, thereby creating a political vacuum. Predictably, the Labour Party was returned without much of a fight after less than a full term out of office.

Generally, however, parties are returned or defeated at regular elections, making the region one of the most liberally democratic in the world. Its relative unimportance in the world, due almost entirely to its small size and domination by the American colossus to the north, has meant that the gains Caribbean society has made have tended to be generally ignored.

Some general characteristics of the Commonwealth Caribbean political tradition, which forms an essential aspect of the background of West Indians in Britain, may be summarized here. First, there is a profound respect for constitutional norms. This is reflected not only in the constitutions of the states in the region but also in the organizations of promotional and interest groups. Second, it is a political tradition which eschews militant nationalism. Political independence itself was won through constitutional means and in some cases the negotiations were protracted because of the relative absence of militant nationalist fervour. But it is from this perspective that it is possible to argue that the kinds of 'homeland' politics West Indians in Britain concern themselves with are situated within a relatively non-militant nationalist tradition.

For example, Commonwealth Caribbean political leaders have not had to flee their countries in order to save life and limb. Political exile has not been part of the Commonwealth Caribbean tradition. Politicians differ and party governments come and go but victors do not terminate their opponents as a rule. Nor is the opportunity to make a living denied opponents. Former West Indian politicians who have come to Britain, came as part of the general migratory process but not primarily because their lives were threatened by opponents or because they were denied the opportunity to make a living.

In recent years there have been some notable exceptions to this general rule. First, the deaths of Walter Rodney in 1980 in Georgetown, Guyana and that of Maurice Bishop in November 1983 in Grenada were painful departures from this tradition of tolerance. These events, therefore, remain nightmares in the collective memory of the Commonwealth Caribbean people. They marked a nadir point in the post-colonial political histories of Guyana and Grenada and are blots on the collective conscience of the people of the region. Second, after the election of Edward Seaga's conservative Labour party to office in November 1980, many supporters of the out-going People's National Party expressed the fear that they would lose their jobs in the civil service and para-statal institutions. Given the scarcity of jobs in the country it would appear that the operation of the *spoils-system* in Jamaica may have become more widespread in the 1980s but this kind of patronage has grown up with the party political system.

It is not the intention to leave the impression that state repression of individuals is not a constant threat in the Commonwealth Caribbean. Far from it. In 1968 the government of Hugh Shearer denied Walter Rodney the right to return to Jamaica in order to continue his lectureship in a regional institution, the University of the West Indies. Rodney found employment in Tanzania where, apparently, a West Indian government initially sought, unsuccessfully, through the Commonwealth connection, to have him declared a *persona non grata.*[7] The year 1968 was, of course, a year of international tension for governments in both the Eastern and Western bloc countries. In the West, including the Commonwealth Caribbean, governments were afraid of the new wave of militancy emanating from the United States as a result of the civil rights movement and the opposition to the war against Vietnam. In the English-speaking Caribbean the *black power* slogan which West Indians had helped to proclaim in the USA appeared to pose a threat to regimes. For example, Stokeley Carmichael (now Kwame Toure), himself a Trinidadian by birth, was refused entry into the country by Eric Williams. Rodney's ban in Jamaica was part of the response of the state to this general situation in the region as a whole. But there were other developments. Leading academics such as George Beckford had their passport confiscated, thereby restricting their movements. Guyanese academic and intellectual, Clive Thomas, and Ken Post the outspoken British political analyst, were also denied entry into Jamaica.

Moreover, following the Grenada invasion in 1983, which he supported, the prime minister of Jamaica, Edward Seaga, brought to parliament a list of names of well-known Jamaicans who had apparently visited either Havana or Moscow. These people, by virtue of having been to these two cities were, by implication, dangerous to the welfare of the country. In a society such as this in which the communist bogey is still very much alive and kicking, this political ploy was readily understood as an identification of individuals who could have been victimized by the state or by supporters of the ruling party.

Where the state is concerned, therefore, there can be no guarantee that repression will not be visited upon those who are perceived to be a potential or actual threat to entrenched interests. The Commonwealth Caribbean is no exception.

Fortunately, however, one consequence of the development of a highly democratic tradition in the region is that there are no questions being raised about the racial, religious, territorial or linguistic composition of the 'nation'. This would suggest that in most cases the *traditional* understanding of nationalism obtains and the *nations-state* triad is secure from the threats it faces in very many other parts of the world. The question of the composition of the 'nation' has been long settled. Unlike most parts of the colonial world – or, indeed, Britain herself – at the end of the imperial age, the question of the entity of the 'nation' was not seriously raised in the English-speaking Caribbean. There are, therefore, no efforts to form governments-in-exile or attempts to lead secessionist movements. The activities of people interested in the politics of 'back home' are restricted to propaganda and the demand in specific places and at specific times for greater democracy or agitation over very specific issues.

The general point I am making is that the various 'races' into which humanity has chosen to distinguish itself have through a process of compromise, of give and take, come to form a commonality in the Caribbean. In general terms, neither the Chinese nor the East Indian, neither the African nor the European need feel that separation from other races within the *traditional* nation*s*-state is a necessity for survival. Nor have minorities been forced to live *outside* the mainstream of society by the majority population. As Clive Thomas emphasized recently, West Indians have had to pay too dearly for their freedom to want to see it eroded.[8] By extension, the argument may be advanced that West Indians know only too well the price or value of the prize of freedom to wish to deprive others of it.

The British connection

The low profile, however, or exilic or diasporic politics amongst West Indians in post-imperial Britain has been determined as much by the socio-political background of the Caribbean as by the 'reception experience' encountered in Britain. I want to consider very briefly aspects of this *reception* which so shocked the first generation of West Indians in Britain and to which the second generation is sometimes still reacting.

First, I would suggest that West Indians have had to address themselves primarily to problems which faced them in this country. This left very little time to ponder about political events 'back home'. Of course, the first generation of West Indians in Britain was unfortunate in many ways but, unlike many other immigrant groups, it was fortunate that it never had to be concerned about the welfare of family, relatives, friends, neighbourhood and the like 'back home' due to any *political* repression from ruling regimes. The second generation has not had to be preoccupied with issues of Caribbean politics because these are largely irrelevant to their daily lives. The West Indian population in this country has already moved significantly away from the Caribbean and soon we may be speaking of *remnants* of the West Indies in much the same way that American anthropologists spoke of retentions of Africanisms in the Caribbean and North America in the 1940s and 1950s (for example,

Herskovits, 1970). But there are prominent West Indians in the UK who believe that, even in the distant future, alienation from British society may very well help reinforce a search for greater knowledge of and commitment to the West Indies. Of course, to a degree the worldwide revolution in telecommunications and comparatively cheap air travel make it less likely that there will be a total loss of links between the Caribbean and people of Caribbean backgrounds in Britain.

It should not be forgotten that British society, itself recovering from the ravages of war during the period of West Indian migration, had no time or place for the black man or woman other than as an *instrument* of labour. This was how the West Indies and the West Indian were known to British society. Almost total ignorance pertained in Britain with respect to the kinds of social order that had emerged in the Caribbean since the sixteenth century. It was a region of the world which had been important for Britain but was now a backwater. Interest had shifted to India and Africa, particularly after slavery and sugar declined in the West Indies. For much of the first half of the present century West Indian leaders were perhaps slow in recognizing the speed with which the great European imperial powers were fading and the emergence of the USA and the USSR as the new major world forces.[9] Williams' lament on the eve of political independence in 1962 expresses both these points well:

> Trinidad and Tobago attracted metropolitan attention only in periods of riot and disorder (1903 and 1937), only when the discovery of oil made it an object of interest to the British Navy and British capitalism, only when its invaluable natural harbour, Chaguaramas, made it a useful pawn to be traded by Britain against American aid in the Second World War.
>
> These developments apart, Trinidad and Tobago was merely a crown colony, forgotten and forlorn. No British statesman of substance was ever distracted by it from larger and more important issues, unless it was Joseph Chamberlain, and his connection with Trinidad and Tobago is probably the least reputable phase in his career. No British scholar found it worth his while to pay any attention to the history and potential of Trinidad and Tobago, unless it was Froude who came and went on a tourist visit leaving only froudacity behind.
>
> (Williams, 1964, p. vii)

Thus, whilst there was, for example, the School of Oriental and African Studies established in the University of London, there has never been a comparable attempt to get British islanders to understand the Caribbean. Indeed, only in late 1987 has the University Grants Committee decided to finance a permanent post at the University of Warwick. Although there have long been individual scholars with an interest in the Commonwealth Caribbean in British universities, the Centre for Caribbean Studies at Warwick is the first of its kind in the country. But, in contrast, the West Indian came with a certain knowledge of the people and history of the country of his sojourn.

Another important part of the baggage of the West Indian bound for Southampton or Liverpool, Heathrow or Gatwick, was the belief in being British. This may be difficult for the white Britisher to comprehend. The second generation of West Indians in the United Kingdom may also have difficulty in understanding the feeling or sense of being British which the first generation carried with them. On the one hand the second generation seems to reject all claims of being British and on the other makes demands on the basis of being British. This ambivalence towards the country will no doubt take time to be resolved. The ambivalence may, of course, remain indefinitely, because the behaviour of West Indians, in this as in so many other respects, is largely determined by the prior behaviour of the majority population.

But from the perspective of the first generation, being British was a fact to be taken for granted, almost as much as the settlers of the Falklands regard themselves as being British and find it difficult to reconcile themselves to Argentine sovereignty and citizenship. The difference is that the West Indian sense of being British was not born of any feeling of being isolated nor of any racial affinity, as is presumably the case with the British Falklanders. It was a sense of belonging, born of the long and close historical association between the 'mother country', England, and the colonies. This bond of a people to a state transcended such factors as creed, colour and physical location, and in some respects it is similar to feudal allegiance and loyalty. The bond or loyalty was akin to the Roman citizen who would carry his citizenship with pride throughout the empire. Discussions with first-generation West Indians in Britain reveal much the same sense or notion of citizenship. Theirs is a patriotic love for the lands of their births, be it Jamaica, Trinidad, Guyana and so on, which was not in conflict with a sense of loyalty to a greater England/Britain which was not restricted to these shores. This loyalty has, however, been betrayed and West Indians still feel the hurt caused by what Trevor Carter correctly describes as our 'shattered illusions' (Carter, 1986).

There are several aspects of West Indian history which help to explain this feeling of being British. First, in the struggle to abolish both the slave trade and the system of slavery, the acts of abolition and emancipation were passed in the British parliament. In the West Indies itself the local plantocracy opposed both the demands of the slaves who wanted their freedom and the humanitarian movement in England. Emancipation was therefore associated with a benevolent parliament which could be called upon by the ordinary people in times of extreme repression perpetrated by the local white plantocracy. After the famous Morant Bay rebellion in Jamaica in 1865 the plantocracy was also to demonstrate its confidence in the Crown when the Free Assembly voluntarily surrendered its powers to a governor from England out of fear of the black majority and the progressive mulattoes becoming a united block in the legislature, thereby undermining the planters' political domination.

Second, the experience of crown colony rule was to strengthen the view that whilst the plantocracy was against the Jamaican proverbial 'little man', the Crown wanted to help. In Jamaica it was the government of the crown which established a national system of elementary education in the 1860s, made it free in 1892, and sought to improve the agricultural productivity of the small farmers. Throughout the period of crown colony government enlightened governors fought an unsuccessful battle against the planters to raise enough tax to pay for elementary education, health and other services to improve the deplorable conditions of the ordinary people (Goulbourne, 1988a).

Third, it must be remembered that the West Indies, like the rest of the Americas, are new societies. European settlers and adventurers liquidated, intentionally or accidentally, the original populations, and new peoples were brought in from elsewhere. Although people in predominantly white societies are fond of referring to *black* people as *natives* when reference is made to the Caribbean, it must be firmly borne in mind that they are no more natives than are the majority of other West Indians. If 'native' has any distinctive meaning when applied to the African population of the region it must be in deference to the African's claim which he has laid to the lands of involuntary sojourn. And it is this claim, through sweat and adoption, which has made the region what it is today. It is perhaps only the Rastafarian who dreams of a messianic return to Africa.

This absence of *natives* has had a profound impact on West Indian sociopolitical thinking. It accounts in part for the further absence of any militant *nativism* in the politics of most of the societies in the region. Perhaps more importantly, however, it has meant that West Indians have seen themselves as just claimants to the Westminster/Whitehall political model of politics, government, administration and judicial institutions. In the not too distant past the essentially British foundations of major institutions meant that people also carried their British status in much the same sense that other settlers in the Americas have seen themselves as English, French, Dutch and so forth.

After all, the West Indies fell somewhere between being what Best calls *colonies of exploitation* and *colonies of settlement* (Best, 1968). Europeans perceived the former as mere locations where land, population and resources could be exploited and the wealth that was produced shipped back to the European metropolis. Much of the literature on the underdevelopment of vast regions of the New World attempts to explicate the processes involved in the construction and maintenance of these colonies of exploitation as Best and his colleagues perceive the matter. The colonies of settlement were, as the term suggests, established with a view to European settlers making them their homes and incorporating them into the socio-political systems of the 'mother country' – be it France, Spain, Holland or England. In the case of England, this was a joint venture undertaken by all the *British nations* but under Anglo-Saxon leadership.

The initial project of the British in the West Indies was not significantly different from that started on the North American continent. The region was settled very much in the same way as the North American colonies. It was only as the black slave population became the *majority* population that slowly the shift was made firmly in the direction of these islands becoming mainly colonies of exploitation. Even so, the institutions from Britain remained and took roots. For example, Barbados is considered to have the second oldest elected legislature in the world, due to this fact. The absence of autochthony in the West Indies accounts partly, then, for this longevity of British institutions (Munroe, 1973).

There is a further point to be considered with respect to the first generation of West Indians in Britain feeling British. This generation came *before* political independence was gained by West Indian islands. The process of decolonization had started, however, very much earlier. The formal and final countdown to political independence commenced in 1944 and full political independence for the region began in 1962 with Jamaica, and Trinidad and Tobago. Many West Indians who came to Britain before large-scale migration began after 1949, would have had the vote because they would have met the property or educational qualifications instituted under crown colony government in the region. Those who came after 1949, particularly from Jamaica, would have had the franchise under the 1944 Constitution. West Indians in Britain followed the progress of their islands' independence from the distance of the imperial centre. The main point here, however, is that when they came to Britain in the 1950s, their countries were British colonies and they came to England as British citizens. The subsequent legislation, as we saw in chapter five, to exclude West Indians from considering themselves British, has therefore received a mixed reception among West Indians. Some have experienced hurt and shame and have opted to deny this strong historical link between Britain and the West Indies.

This kind of reaction can take many forms. One of these has been to seek to re-establish links with Africa and the West Indies in a positive way and to try to rejuvenate a culture long denigrated by Europe. Others have met the rejection with quiet resistance. For example, there are West Indians who feel strongly that since they came to the United Kingdom as British citizens and were indeed British by birth, it is an insult to have to register under the immigration and nationality acts. And some have refused to register because to do so would be to accept that he or she was not in fact *already* British. The state's post-imperial redefinition of *British* is therefore a more complex matter than it may at least seem.

This feeling of being British did not mean that people could not be Jamaican or Trinidadian or Barbadian at the same time as being British. It was, so to speak, like being Welsh or Scots or English but also British. Being British did not mean that people had to forego or abandon every peculiarity based on regional variation, historical experience, colour and race, or even physical distance. This was what the educational system in the Caribbean had taught generations of West Indians and, apart from the church, there was, perhaps, no other institution which the West Indian held more dear than the school (Goulbourne, 1988a).

This view of the world has, of course, died. And it was dying at a time when migrant West Indians to Britain still held steadfastly to the vision of a multicultural, multi-racial, multi-national British world. The 1962 Commonwealth Immigration Act put an effective stop to West Indian migration to Britain, because, unlike the East African Asians, West Indians were citizens of the countries from which they were migrating, like Indians and Pakistanis from the sub-continent. The politics of passports did not affect West Indians at all. The year 1962 was also the year which marked, as noted, the beginning of the very final departure of the British imperial presence from the Caribbean.

The migrant West Indian felt that he or she knew something about the country to which he or she was coming in the 1950s and the 1960s. And what he or she knew was what was taught at school in the West Indies – a history and a social ethic which placed little emphasis on the basis of the communal option, and everything on the merits of universalistic principles and practices. On arrival, however, West Indians were nearly always taken aback by the differences they found on the ground. Many were surprised by the manner in which people at the centre of the empire lived[10] and quickly realized that their own ways of life were not at all inferior to those practised at the centre of the world which they were taught to look up to as superior. Most striking, however, to many new arrivants was the *overwhelming ignorance* on the part of native Britishers of the West Indies and West Indians.

The *reception experience* has therefore been something of a shock to the West Indian. It cuts against the very grain of his or her being, his or her beliefs, his or her historical experience. Most importantly, the West Indian's reception experience trod against that sense of what the good community may be like for a people who strongly believed in the universalistic values school and experience had taught them. And this was a sense of a *non-exclusive* community partly derived from Britain through church, school and political institutions but largely developed in the Caribbean during the course of a search for a new kind of social order to replace that of the slave-masters. In this respect, one of the most profound lessons the West Indian has learnt from slavery and indenture is that the good society cannot be one in which people are kept, structurally, apart from each other. Human nature is not necessarily good nor is it necessarily bad.

As noted earlier, the withdrawal of Britain from the imperial mission she had set herself, engendered a new definition of 'British'. Arising from this, however, has been the need in Britain itself for people to develop new values pertaining to self-definition. In the case of the second generation of black Britons an interesting conjunction was reached when radicals postulated the demands of separate identity and the state itself agreed that this was indeed desirable. For some time during the 1970s the two processes went on independently of each other and at first seemed to be contradictory. In their frustration bred of rejection at every level of British society, the once confident West Indian began to be enticed by the apparent comfort of the *communal option*. The psychic scar from which, the Kenyan political scientist Ali Mazrui argued in his Reith Lectures some years ago, all black people are prone to suffer in the West, began to sap the strength of the West Indian in Britain. And by the 1980s it had become clear that the move towards ethnic identity would satisfy both the state and the frustrated arrivants: many black spokesmen saw this as a positive identification for a generation of frustrated and alienated black youngsters whilst the state saw this development as a means of social control.

Two sets of factors, therefore, condition the exilic political behaviour of West Indians in Britain. One has been the non-militant nationalist traditions of the Commonwealth Caribbean and the kinds of politics in the West Indies which have emerged and developed from these. The second conditioning set of factors emanated from the unexpected reception experience in Britain by a generally hostile or unwelcoming society. The point can never be fully appreciated that the majority of West Indians came to Britain expecting that since their own culture derived partly from here they would, at the very least, not be despised and therefore begin to undergo much of the experience of social exclusion experienced less subtly under slavery. It is as if the overseers of the slaves and those planters who settled in the colonies of exploitation in the Anglophone Caribbean were forced through historical processes to adjust to the humanity of the slave but in the metropolis, in Britain itself, those who benefited most from the colonies of exploitation have on the whole never come to terms with *humanity in a black skin*. The post-imperial experience in Britain is, therefore, a time of reassessment and relearning for all who are caught up within it, partly through design but overwhelmingly through the accident of history. Sadly, however, initial persistent rejection, engendered in human greed and cruelty, and nurtured largely by visionless political and social leadership, will probably continue to hold us prisoners to the mistakes of even the recent past. This may, however, be a convenient point at which to convey a general impression of West Indian political groups in Britain.

Low profile of diasporic/exilic politics

These groups may be divided into at least two sub-types. First, there are those groups which are concerned with the politics of one or more countries in the Caribbean. These seek to inform, influence and gain support from countrymen and -women in Britain over and about the events taking place 'back home'.

Several of these bodies are organized around the interests of nationals of particular countries in the Caribbean. There are, for example, the Association of Jamaicans, the Trinidad and Tobago Association, the St Kitts-Nevis and Anguilla Association, the Antigua Nationals Association, the Dominica (UK) Association, the Dominica Overseas Nationals Association, the St Lucian Association and the St Vincent and Grenadines Association. These associations are in the main London-based groups; some have supporting groups or individuals outside London. These groups are by and large non-partisan bodies but, as may be expected, memberships overlap and individuals are members of 'national' as well as political groups which relate to the political life of these countries.

Some of these groups are more concerned with developments in specific countries than in the region as a whole. These tend to be support groups or branches of political parties in the Caribbean. For example, there are branches of Michael Manley's Jamaican People's National Party in London and Birmingham. There are also branches of the Guyanese People's Progressive Party of Dr Cheddi Jagan and the Working People's Alliance of the late Dr Walter Rodney as well as the ruling People's National Congress.

These branches in the UK help to articulate their parties' positions on given issues of the day, whether they are likely or not to affect people in this country. They also serve as reception points for West Indian leaders visiting the UK. Through these groups Caribbean leaders can reach some of their countrymen and -women who have settled in this country and who are still concerned about the affairs of their countries of birth or where they spent their formative years. During times of crises such meetings can provide invaluable propaganda forums for parties and governments in the Caribbean. This is so even though the West Indian population in the United Kingdom may not appear to be as important for Caribbean politicians as is the West Indian population in US cities. Most political leaders in the region seek the support of West Indians abroad. For some of these parties financial support may be important; for others, moral support is sought. In all cases, however, the careful attention given to the migrant West Indian population in Britain and North America reflects the strong connections between those who have remained behind and those who have migrated. The very founding of the PNP in 1938 was greatly influenced by Jamaicans who had migrated to the USA and by the experience of men who had lived in Britain (Nettleford, 1972; Sherlock, 1980). It is hardly surprising, therefore, that the party has tried to keep close links with Jamaicans in both countries. During the 1970s a crucial aspect of the then opposition Jamaica Labour Party's campaign against the radical government of Michael Manley's PNP was carried out almost as much in the USA as in Jamaica itself.[11]

These kinds of activities in Britain are hardly, however, the stuff of which exilic politics are made. These activities amount to little more than the natural interests in the affairs of 'back home' which would be expected of any group of people who have recently migrated from one country to another. Indeed, much the same kind of interest, even if to a different degree, may be found amongst other groups of migrants in Britain today. With respect to the Caribbean, it is not surprising that this interest is mainly amongst the older folks who carry with them a live memory of the politics of the past. Whilst it is unlikely that people of West Indian background will become as cut off from the Caribbean as individuals and small groups have done in the past, it may be expected that the kind of interest in the active politics of 'back home' displayed by the first generation of West Indian settlers will decline. This is not to say that people of West Indian background in Britain will not continue to have an interest in the region, but such interest is likely to be of a cultural nature and most likely only the exceptional political event or development will attract the attention of the people of Caribbean background in this country.

Some of the groups which have existed since soon after sizeable settlement, seek simply to keep nationals in this country in touch with developments 'back home', while others seek to elicit more active support for particular initiatives taking place in a number of countries or a specific country in the region.

An excellent example of a group which seeks to do both is the Caribbean Labour Solidarity group led by Cleston Taylor, a Jamaican who has been prominent in the trade union movement in London, and Richard Hart the veteran Jamaican politician. Hart is a member of a prominent family in Jamaica. He was one of the famous Four Hs – Henry, the Hill brothers, Frank and Ken, and Hart. They were the radicals of the PNP from its inception in 1938 to 1955 when the right wing of the party gained the support of its leader, the liberal-socialist Norman Manley, to expel the four. This group sets itself the task of informing West Indians in Britain about specific political and labour developments, and also seeks to secure the support of people in this country for specific issues in the region. The group's leaders are men and women committed to maintaining close links with individuals and parties throughout the region, including the non-English-speaking Caribbean. The group organize meetings and sometimes act as a lobby with respect to specific individuals and events. Two relevant examples of this aspect of its work have been the opposition to the 1974/5 Industrial Relations Bill of the Manley PNP government in Jamaica; and the second is the support sought since 1983/4 for Bernard

Coard and his comrades who were accused and found guilty of murdering the late Maurice Bishop of Grenada in 1983.

The exceptions

In conclusion, the several possible explanations for the low level of exilic politics among the West Indian communities in Britain may be classified under two headings. These are, first, factors which arise from British society itself. Second, there are those factors which arise from the development of what has been called creole society in the Commonwealth Caribbean.

I have sought to present the case that the West Indian population in Britain is not deeply concerned about *nationalist* politics either in this country or in the Caribbean. And yet, of the various minority groups which do not have a home-land in Britain, West Indians have perhaps the most salient political presence within England, relative to size. I have stressed that this is because the West Indian voice in Britain in the post-imperial years has been one of protest.

The politics of Guyana and Grenada are the exceptions which prove the rule that Commonwealth Caribbean politics have not been significantly divided along nationalist lines which demand fundamental rearrangements of established norms. In all the other Commonwealth Caribbean countries regular elections have resulted in the development of competitive party systems, either of a one-party dominant type such as in Trinidad or St Lucia, or of a regular turn-over type such as in Jamaica and Barbados. In the case of Grenada before the New Jewel Revolution of 1979 the government of Sir Eric Gairy was known for its dictatorial rule, which was more akin to the countries of Spanish America than the Commonwealth Caribbean. Similarly, the PNC government of the late Forbes Burnham and his successors has ruled uninterruptedly since 1964 but this long stay in office has been accompanied with loss of lives of opposition leaders, the most notable of whom has been the late Dr Walter Rodney. During the quarrels over doctrine amongst the leaders of the New Jewel Movement, the lives of the leader Maurice Bishop and his close comrades were taken as a result of ideological differences in October 1983. These unsavoury events run counter to the political traditions of the region. They also mark off Grenada and Guyana from the governments in the other English-speaking countries, both in terms of these two countries' more radical politics as well as the extent of their ideological and political 'extremes'.

In these circumstances it may be expected that a higher level of diasporic or even exilic politics amongst the Guyanese and Grenadian people in Britain exists, because Guyanese and Grenadians need to be concerned about the political life of their countries in a way that other Commonwealth Caribbean people need not be. But it is important to stress that the limited exilic politics that exist among the Guyanese people in Britain are not of the kind which demand separation of the Afro- and Indo-Guyanese people. The question must therefore be asked whether Guyanese abroad are divided according to race, colour, religion or the political ideologies of the parties to which they feel drawn, as people undoubtedly are in Guyana. It is not, of course, possible to answer these questions here. But it is possible to indicate some very general trends which reflect the perceived situation regarding politics in Guyana.

The situation as it exists in Guyana is a potential powder keg. As such it could be sparked off at any time, particularly as the standard of living continues to decline and the values which inform the day-to-day behaviour of social life touch the nadir point. The cases of Guyana and Grenada, as far as they are reflected in the politics of people living in this country, may very well be, however, the exceptions which prove the rule.

It is important to explain why I argue that these kinds of politics do not actually amount to what may be regarded as a significant level of exilic politics. This may, of course, change because there is now a growing willingness to recognize racism in countries such as Jamaica and Barbados (see, for example, Stone, 1989; also, Watson, 1989). It is pertinent, however, to relate the explanations I have offered here to the wider question with which this study is principally concerned. This is the question of nationalism and its communal impulse. In this respect it is necessary to look a little more closely at the exceptional case of Guyana and how the Guyanese people, and by extension the Commonwealth Caribbean people in Britain, may be affected by developments in Guyana.

The concern for democracy in Guyana

In many respects the exceptional case of Guyana proves the rule that, comparatively speaking, Anglophone Caribbean politics are not irreparably divided by either *traditional* or *ethnic* expressions of nationalism. If only for this reason, it is important to consider briefly the politics of this potentially rich country whose development has been truncated by the predominance of the People's National Congress (PNC) since independence in 1966. Two aspects of this exceptional case are of particular importance in the discussion here. These are, first, the support in Britain for the People's Progressive Party (PPP), but more particularly the efforts of the Working People's Alliance (WPA) to reintroduce into Guyana's politics the democratic principle whereby all racial groups participate actively. The second relevant aspect of these kinds of politics is the emergence and development of what the Latin American Bureau, in its special report on Guyana, calls a *fraudulent revolution* engineered by the PNC government (Latin America Bureau, 1984a).

In the first place it must be stressed that each of the three major parties in Guyana – the PNC, the PPP and the WPA – enjoys some measure of support or representation amongst the Guyanese community in the United Kingdom. As noted earlier, a number of political parties in the Commonwealth Caribbean have branches in this country and it seems likely that because of the special circumstances of Guyana, it would be natural for there to be greater representation of Guyanese parties here than of those from the other Commonwealth states in the region. Apart from the general background considered above, there are several other factors, however, which encourage the prevalence of exilic politics amongst the Guyanese communities compared to most West Indians in Britain.

First, the declining economic situation (Latin America Bureau, 1984a; Thomas, 1984) which accompanied PNC rule and the racial tension between East Indians and Africans have encouraged many middle-class Guyanese to migrate to the UK throughout the late 1950s and the decade of the 1960s. That outward flow of population continues to North America as the economic situation continues to deteriorate. The proportion of people with professional qualifications who migrated was likely to have been higher than for the other Commonwealth Caribbean states where political life was far less problematic.

Although there are no other situations in the Commonwealth Caribbean to rival the Guyanese case there were two other instances in the 1970s which strongly resembled Guyana's loss of skilled people. One was the migration of middle-class business and professional families from Jamaica during the late 1970s when the radical domestic and foreign policies of Michael Manley led many to believe that Jamaica was truly 'mashed-up', to use a Jamaican phrase or, in the equivalent English colloquialism, the country 'was going to the dogs'. This wave of West Indian migration, however, went in the direction of North American destinations. The second instance was that of the dispersal of Grenadian middle-class groups, both after the 1979 New Jewel Revolution and after the US invasion of the country in November 1983.[12]

Unusual as these situations undoubtedly were for the Commonwealth Caribbean, neither was as long sustained as the rule of the PNC in Guyana. Moreover, Guyana has the dubious distinction of being the only Commonwealth Caribbean state in which political unhappiness is a way of life for a large proportion of the people. Such factors tend, naturally, to encourage a comparatively high, or at least a noticeable, level of diasporic politics.

The PNC is, of course, represented through the delegation of about five at the Guyana High Commission in London. Through this channel the government/party views are made known to various bodies as well as to members of the Guyanese community. A prolonged financial crisis in Guyana in the 1980s has meant that the High Commission cannot always issue its newsletter. From time to time, however, it is able to do so[13] and the Commission at one time made available the invaluable *Guyana Update* which reprinted the news from 'back home' for interested individuals here.

The PNC also has a Regional Secretary in the UK, based in London.[14] Indeed, from the 1960s when Guyana was torn apart by racial strife between Indians and Africans, the PNC embarked upon an effort in the United Kingdom to encourage Afro-Caribbean people from the islands to settle in Guyana. Under the scheme land was to be cheap and indeed some individuals did go to Guyana. Overall, however, the scheme failed partly because the government did not provide the promised basic infrastructure such as roads, water and electricity. One prominent Afro-Guyanese told me that he continues to place much hope in the scheme for two reasons. First, he hopes that more Afro-Caribbean people faced by rejection in Britain will feel that they could make their homes in a country like Guyana with its abundance of land and potential wealth. Second, failing this development, he hopes that another racial group will settle in sufficient numbers so that the East Indian majority may be made irrelevant. In this way the racial vote, or the tendency for Africans to vote for African candidates and East Indians to vote for East Indian politicians, would diminish in the country and make Guyana a better society for all as is officially claimed to be the objective of the regime. No one race would need to fear domination from the other because none could be elected to office without the support of elements from the other groups. In such an eventuality the politics of the PNC would become unnecessary.

Another area of potentially important support for the PNC comes from the various attempts by prominent Guyanese in Britain to gather support for the regime's struggle against underdevelopment. In late 1987, for example, the return of Bernie Grant, Member of Parliament for Haringey, to Guyana on a brief visit and his reported concern for what he found there, has been frequently quoted as the kind of support the Hoyte regime needs. From time to time, therefore, individuals of Guyanese background in Britain attempt either to return to give support to the PNC regime or to nurture support for it in this country.

The PPP has perhaps a clearer voice of support in the Guyanese community. The party has a UK branch. In 1987/8 Lall Singh was secretary and Barry Sukhram was its chairman. The branch is able to keep members informed through its publication *Guyana Voice*, and through organized and regular meetings. Nearly all the items in the journal concern developments in Guyana and the Caribbean. These may involve differences between the PPP and the PNC government or the PPP and the WPA, or the combined opposition's objections to PNC activities, and so forth. For example, although the PPP has worked closely with the WPA against the PNC, in 1984 the PPP launched an attack against the WPA over what the party saw as a retreat from principled class struggle by the WPA (*Guyana Voice*, vol. 5, no. 2, 1985).[15]

Whenever Jagan visits Britain the branch also organize meetings for him to address the public, particularly Guyanese nationals, about politics 'back home'. Thus, in 1984 one issue of the journal informed its readership that

While in London Dr. Jagan made a call for Guyanese to join the struggle for their country. The *best* way this could be done would be to support *and* join the PPP group in the UK.

(*Guyana Voice*, vol. 5, no. 2, 1984, p. 13; emphases added)

The journal also informed readers that Jagan was off to the USSR for a holiday, returning to Guyana 'via Canada where he will be meeting with Guyanese nationals . . . ' (*Guyana Voice*, vol. 5, no. 2, 1984). Obviously, the views citizens of any Caribbean country living abroad may have about politics 'back home' are important to politicians because these are small societies which are closely integrated into the international community. But in the case of Guyana this is particularly so since Guyanese citizens abroad have the right to participate in general elections taking place in Guyana. The racial impasse and economic decline in Guyana, moreover, are such that many Guyanese both at home and abroad have been looking for alternatives to the entrenched politics of the PNC and the PPP.[16]

WPA support in the United Kingdom

It is in this context that support for the WPA must be seen. Whilst it is still very much a junior party to the two older protagonists, the PPP and the PNC, the WPA holds out a hope for the way forward in Guyana. There is of course no universal agreement on this, especially since it is not possible for the relative strengths of the parties in Guyana to be tested at the polls. Two recent assessments, however, of post-Burnham Guyana reflect the difficulty in assessing the party political situation in the country.

Baber and Jeffrey argue that change in Guyana may come through the intervention of the army. In this event, it is likely to act either to support Hamilton Green, the prime minister and the man to whom the military is partial, or it may act on its own behalf. Baber and Jeffrey tend to dismiss the possibility of the PPP ever coming to power peacefully and by constitutional means because it is unwilling to pursue an armed struggle for power. The WPA is seen in a similar light because although it has modified its Marxism in order to accommodate nationalists and patriots within the business community, it seems unlikely that the party could form a government without the active support of the PPP and this would be unacceptable to the USA. It is not surprising, therefore, that Baber and Jeffrey conclude their discussion of the Guyana situation on the predictable but nonetheless depressing note – 'We are not hopeful' (Baber and Jeffrey, 1986, p. 186).

A more optimistic assessment has been offered by the London-based Latin American Bureau. A year before Burnham's death, the Bureau argued that

> At present there appear to be only two forces in the society which are
> capable of inaugurating a new era of Guyanese politics. These are the
> Working People's Alliance . . . and the Guyanese Defence Force . . .
> (Latin America Bureau, 1984a, pp. 89–90)

It is important to note that in these assessments both the military and the WPA
feature prominently. Should the military act either in support of Green or in
support of its own hitherto politically unambitious colonels or sergeant-majors,
this would push Guyana farther from the mainstream of Commonwealth
Caribbean politics. It is true that in Grenada the army played, sadly, a
prominent and therefore visible role under General Hudson Austin in the days
preceding the American invasion (Latin American Bureau, 1984b; also,
O'Shaughnessy, 1984). It is also the case that in June 1980, during the long and
stormy campaign for general elections, the then prime minister of Jamaica,
Michael Manley, announced to parliament a hair-brained plan by some
Jamaica Defence Force (JDF) junior officers to subvert the constitution
(Stephens and Stephens, 1986, p. 231). But not only was this brought to the
notice of the prime minister by the JDF itself, but it was also stamped out by
the Force. Very few informed persons took the threat to have been anything
more than a joke.

But even such comic moments like these in Commonwealth Caribbean
politics are comparatively rare, despite Michael Manley's concern about the
military and politics in Jamaica (Manley, 1982, p. 201). So, should the military
in Guyana come to political prominence this would mark a further decline in
that country's blighted post-colonial experience. Should the WPA, therefore,
fail to develop a new type of politics to replace the perceived or actual racial
politics of the PPP and the PNC, the hope that Guyana's racial politics should
disappear will be pushed farther from realization.

It is important, therefore, to understand what the aims of the WPA are and
the nature of the support it receives in the UK. The two points involved here
may be best taken separately, provided it is understood that they are closely
linked.

It is proper to consider first the aims and tactics of the WPA in initiating
change in Guyana. It is not, however, necessary to outline the total programme
of the WPA because not all aspects are germane to the discussion. Briefly, the
party's aims are to institute a democratic and humanitarian socialism in the
country. Its *Principles and Programme* of 1978 remains the basic document of
the party. This document was meant to be a *draft* and therefore it has been
amended since its publication and the launching of the party in 1979. In this and
in subsequent statements on specific aspects of Guyanese politics and society,
it is quite clear that the party is fully aware of, and is willing to meet head-on,
one crucial problem that nearly all progressive parties operating under

conditions of Third World underdevelopment have consistently failed to confront. This is the relationship between democracy and socialism. In nearly all situations where regimes have declared themselves to be building socialism, issues of central planning, much rhetoric and ideological rigidity bordering on religious dogma have been brought onto political agendas not to complement, but to replace and frustrate, democratic principles and aspirations. Burnham's Guyana[17] undermined the democratic traditions of the Guyanese people and the PPP's Moscowite communism would appear to hold out, perhaps not the dictatorial rule of an individual, but control from above which would also stifle the creativity and democratic instincts of the people.

In the process of the struggle for democracy the WPA appears to hope that politics and state institutions in Guyana will be *de-racialized*. This process is, of course, necessary. The *Principles and Programme* is informed, however, by an understanding of institutionalized racism which seems to suggest that once the institutional supports of racism are removed, racism will disappear and class will become the primary consideration. The document is permeated with an understanding that racial consciousness is mainly the effect of colonialism, reinforced by the politics of the PNC and the PPP from the 1950s. The aim to overcome this is, of course, an important one. So too is the recognition that there is a contradiction between the *racialization* of political life and democracy. But the view that the divisions between the two major races, Africans and East Indians, is being negated by the development of a post-colonial petite bourgeoisie may be too simplistic. It is, of course, true to say that

> the concentration of economic and political power in the hands of the state bourgeoisie, and the growing use of that power to protect the interests of the bourgeoisie in both sectors, is creating the conditions for the assertion of sharper and clearer antagonisms.
>
> (WPA, 1978, p. 10)

But this assessment of the situation may underestimate the colonial legacy of racial practices upon which Burnham and the PNC constructed a state whose racial character goes perhaps beyond even Omi and Winant's reasoning on the matter (Omi and Winant, 1986).

In its efforts to make politics a non-racial matter, the WPA has attempted to develop a form of collective leadership which is quite new to Guyana and the Anglophone Caribbean. For example, the WPA is reluctant to project any single leader as the embodiment of the party and to avoid having any one of its leaders being singled out as its spokesperson. Clearly, this is an attempt to avoid the danger of having the party associated with the *race* of a leader – African or East Indian. In its *Principles and Programme* the party argued in support of its collective leadership principle that

The offices of Prime Minister and President will be replaced by a
Collective Executive Authority of the State in which the principle of
rotating chairperson is institutionalised *in order to discourage cultism
or racial or party patronage* at this level.

(WPA, 1978, p. 15; emphases added)

For example, although the late Walter Rodney was widely regarded as *the*
leader of the WPA, he was not officially so recognized. His untimely death,
however, on Friday 13 June 1980, in Georgetown, at the hands of the assassin,
exposed the essential drawback of this type of political leadership. The party's
senior leaders were insufficiently protected from a regime whose repressive
aptitude the party appears to understand so soundly. Rodney was blown up in
a car by means of a remote-controlled bomb whilst his companion, a soldier,
escaped and immediately left the country. As C. L. R. James was later to say of
Rodney's death, 'He never should have been there' (Alpers and Fontaine,
1982, p. 139), that is, as a leader Rodney had no business endangering himself
and therefore his party in this way. But to see this as being simply an act of
political immaturity is to miss the important point: for the WPA leaders had to
be seen to expose themselves to the same dangers as members of the party and
Rodney wanted to demonstrate that he too could be placed on the frontline
against the PNC's repression. The precise nature of the state's involvement in
this crime remains vague because the government refused to set up a
commission of inquiry into the matter. This reluctance, naturally, gives some
credibility to the widespread view that Burnham and/or the PNC was involved
in the removal of this major critic of the regime.

It appears that initially the groups which came together in the early 1970s
and later formed the WPA were suspicious of the very existence of political
parties because, as one member puts the point, in Guyana parties 'tend to
polarise the racial situation' (WPA, 1984).[18] This healthy scepticism of the role
of political parties in the region is not, of course, peculiar to Guyana. In
Jamaica, for example, the view is sometimes expressed that it is the very
existence of two equally strong political parties that is partly responsible for
that country's political violence, particularly since the mid 1960s (see, for
example, Stone, 1983; Lacey, 1977; H. Goulbourne, 1984 and 1985).

Although Marxist in orientation, the WPA is committed to the acquisition of
state power by peaceful and constitutional means. In tactics, therefore, the
party is pragmatic rather than dogmatic. This is a recognition of two important
aspects of the Commonwealth political tradition. First, there is a commitment
to operating within the constitutional framework in order to bring about fundamental changes to these structures. In this regard, oppositional political discourse in Guyana, like the rest of the Commonwealth Caribbean, is concerned
with the generally acceptable legal framework, even if this were instituted

through foul play, as it appears the 1980 Constitution did in Guyana. The WPA's 1978 *Principles and Programme*, formulated in the same year as Burnham's referendum over the founding of the first executive presidency in the Commonwealth Caribbean, committed the WPA to seek state power through a united Patriotic Front in order to overcome the country's varied problems. The party did not participate in the 1980 elections because of their undemocratic and fraudulent character. It contested, however, the 1985 elections and gained two seats in the legislature.

The WPA, the PPP and the PNC all claim to be socialist parties. In this respect, however, the WPA tries to distance itself from straitjacketed communist/socialist modes of behaviour. Theirs is a type of socialism which tries to learn from the political experiences of the past several decades. And these lessons include the geopolitical realities of the region. The people of the Commonwealth Caribbean, it is widely believed, will not easily accept any political party which seeks office through force and which would seek to abandon completely the historical links with the West, principally with Britain and the USA. It must be remembered that very many families in almost all the countries of the region have relations in either Canada, the USA or the United Kingdom. In any event, there is an awareness that 'better is the known devil than the unknown', so to speak. Thus, whilst the USA and Britain have exploited the region for their own ends, there is a sense in which the perceived 'openness' of these societies is to be preferred to the reported totalitarianism of the Soviet bloc countries. The one is familiar, the other is quite unknown.

Perhaps, however, the most dramatic reminder of the region's vulnerability was the US invasion of Grenada in 1983. This was an event whose significance could not have been lost on leaders in the region, particularly leaders with a *left of centre* programme who, from the perspective of Washington, are likely to be viewed as dangerous communists. The invasion was an open demonstration to all, including Britain, that the USA would be prepared to take military action against any seemingly progressive regime in the region. The fact that Grenada is a Commonwealth state made the demonstration all the more effective because this was the first time that the USA showed in the clearest terms possible, that in regional matters the so-called special relationship with Britain was quite irrelevant. Moreover, whilst the left of centre parties in the region tend to be ideologically and otherwise[19] closer to European socialist parties, the leaders of right-wing parties in the region tend to have a closer affinity with the USA. One of the lessons of Grenada, therefore, has been that radical parties in the 1980s must now consider seriously the military intervention of the USA in their internal affairs. Given the proximity of the Colossus of the North and its predatory relationship with the region, radical leaders cannot afford to alienate the USA. It is this realization that is partly forcing parties such as the WPA and the WPJ in Jamaica to reformulate their programmes in terms which, whilst not quite acceptable to the USA, are not perceived as cause for concern to its interests in the Caribbean. The *realism* of the WPA should be understood against this general background.

The support the party receives in the United Kingdom is, not unexpectedly, essentially of a propaganda nature. This is the same kind of support branches of all kinds of parties in the region receive from members or sympathisers in Britain. The WPA Support Group based in London holds meetings on the situation in Guyana. When members of the party visit London, for example, meetings are organized around specific current issues in Guyana and the Caribbean. In this way the Guyanese community may be kept informed about events in the country and the region from a political point of view which differs from those of the PNC and the PPP. The importance of this is readily appreciated when it is considered that the British dailies very rarely report Caribbean events. When the Caribbean occasionally gets a mention in the British media it is usually because of some natural disaster or the brutalities of one regime or another in the non-Commonwealth Caribbean. These meetings serve, therefore, to highlight particular issues and problems which Guyanese living in the UK may readily recognize and assess for themselves. The fact that all three major political parties are able to present their points of view is important in itself because this allows the person of Guyanese background to assess the situation for himself or herself.

Given the grave economic situation of Guyana from around 1978, resulting in severe food shortages which have since become a commonplace occurrence, support for political parties in Guyana is obviously important. The WPA support group, like supporters of other political parties in the region since the formation of parties in the 1930s, has therefore acted to gather financial support for the party to carry out its work in Guyana. In one circular the party pleaded:

> We have resolved to broaden and intensify the activities against the dictatorship in Guyana and abroad. But we can only do this success-fully with your continued solidarity and support. The party supporters and sympathisers in Canada and the USA have agreed to make a monthly contribution and we would be extremely grateful if you can make a similar monthly commitment.
>
> (WPA, 1988)

For most of its existence the WPA has had, for example, to survive in very adverse conditions. It is having to create a political space for itself from grounds hitherto held by either the PNC, the PPP or one or other of the smaller fringe parties to the right of centre or farther right of the political spectrum.[20]

The support group also maintains links with Members of Parliament who show an interest in developments in Guyana and may, therefore, be able to make available useful alternative information to influential individuals. These individuals include Lord Aylesbury, Jeremy Corbin, Lord Chitness and Tony Benn, some of whom were involved in the Parliamentary Human Rights Group's monitoring of the 1980 elections (UK, Parliamentary Human Rights Group, 1981). This kind of support sought here from Parliament stands, of course, within a long tradition of Members of Parliament becoming not only aware but also closely associated, since the struggle over the slave trade and the rights of the freedmen in the eighteenth and nineteenth centuries, with developments in the Commonwealth Caribbean.[21]

The WPA Support Group has done invaluable work in educating people in Britain about the situation in Guyana by circulating the party's press releases and publications such as *Day Clean*, and informing general opinion about the activities of the party in Guyana. For example, the November 1985 elections which the WPA decided to contest (unlike the 1980 elections) occasioned detailed WPA statements on the campaign, its strategy, the issue of democracy in the country and so forth. These were made available to the Support Group which was, in turn, able to keep interested individuals in Britain informed. Another example was the hunger strike of one of the leaders of the party in Guyana, the veteran politician Eusi Kwayana, in November 1987, over the chronic economic situation in the country which has led to shortages and the breakdown of normal life. Kwayana was made a Member of Parliament representing the WPA after the 1985 elections and he saw his hunger strike two years later as a blow for democracy. He wanted to alert international opinion to the undemocratic nature of the Guyanese state.

Unfortunately, however, neither the WPA nor its support group in the United Kingdom has been able to shift public opinion about Guyana significantly. It is in the nature of international politics that whatever is out of sight is also out of mind. The general silence in Britain over Caribbean events wittingly or unwittingly tends to support the regime in its undemocratic and authoritarian practices. Bad news is usually news for the media but even on this front the PNC has been successful in gaining from the *silence* over the bad news it creates for the region as a whole.

The politics of the fraudulent revolution

These developments speak, of course, of Guyana's exceptional position in the Commonwealth Caribbean. But Guyana's exceptional situation has several aspects. First, Guyana's difference from the rest of the Commonwealth Caribbean lies in her physical and cultural distance from the rest of the bloc of countries with which she is historically associated. She is part of the South American continent and, therefore, apart from Belize on the Central American isthmus, is the only English-speaking country in the hemisphere which is not physically an island. In *cultural* terms, however, these countries are islands, surrounded as they are by Latin cultures. Guyana's most immediate cultural neighbours include Portuguese Brazil, Spanish Venezuela and Dutch Surinam. Perhaps only French Guiana, and Surinam – itself separating Guiana from Guyana – can feel more culturally isolated in the Americas than Guyana.

Part of Guyana's past is very much wrapped up with her neighbours. Like Trinidad, Guyana came comparatively late into British hands. A Dutch stronghold from the early seventeenth century, both the British in 1665 and the French in 1708 made unsuccessful attempts to take over the territory. The territory was ceded to Britain by treaty at the end of the Napoleonic Wars and in 1831 the three countries of Berbice, Demerara and Essequibo (named after the major rivers of this well-watered country) became known as British Guiana.

But the country's pre-British antecedents sometimes return to haunt her post-independence leaders. Again, apart from Belize, Guyana is the only Commonwealth state which has border disputes with other states. These disputes are with Brazil, her giant neighbour to the south, and with the oil-rich Venezuela to the north-west. Venezuela claims 53,000 of Guyana's 83,000 square miles and Brazil lays claim to much of the remainder. In 1962 the Venezuelan government picked this dispute with the radical government of Dr Cheddi Jagan at the point when Britain was about to grant independence to the country. This was to revive an old dispute which had been resolved in 1899 with an award to Britain by an international arbitration tribunal (Latin America Bureau, 1984a, Appendix One).

Guyana has had other territorial problems during her less than quarter century of political independence. In 1978 the mass suicide of religious fanatics at Jonestown, in the remote interior of the country, shocked the world. The followers of Jim Jones, an American preacher, were given state encouragement to settle in the Venezuelan disputed region of Essiquibo and the commune became something of a state within a state. The mass suicide of almost a thousand devotees of the People's Tabernacle and the government's attempt to distance itself from the commune did not bode well for the country in the eyes of the international community.

Moreover, earlier, in January 1969, the secession of Rupununi presented Guyana with a major problem. It seemed that Venezuela was prepared to go to almost any length to undermine the authority of Georgetown. The demand for independence for the region was led by two wealthy white families, the Harts and the Melvilles (Greene, 1974, ch. 5). But Venezuela provided military support and sought to exploit the grievance of some Amerindians and a few whites, who may have been worried about being in a country governed by

Africans. The fact that the secessionists were supporters of Peter D'Aguiar's United Force party, and the fact that he provided them with legal assistance, suggest that Guyana's territorial integrity may be undermined by both external and internal forces. Apart from the invasion of Grenada by the USA in November 1983 and the repeated threat of invasion by Guatemala of Belize, this territorial insecurity marks off Guyana from the majority of Commonwealth Caribbean states.

A second factor that distinguishes Guyana from the rest of these states is the radical nature of her politics. It is true that the country's political system accommodates D'Aguiar's right-wing United Force and there are some even less significant right-wing groups which have appeared sporadically. But it was D'Aguiar's willingness in 1964 to enter into a coalition government led by L. F. S. Burnham which provided the opportunity for him and his PNC to bring about what many see as the *fraudulent*, rather than the world's first, cooperative republic, beginning in the early 1970s.

In general terms, however, all major parties in Guyana have claimed a place on the left of the political spectrum. The two major political parties in the country from the genesis of party politics in the 1950s describe themselves as socialist. The PPP, founded in 1950, and also led, by Dr Cheddi Jagan, and the PNC, founded in 1955 and led until his death in August 1985 by Burnham (a barrister), as well as the WPA, all proclaim some kind of socialism or the other. The third party in the country today, the WPA, was founded in 1979 by a younger generation of politicians such as the late Walter Rodney, Clive Thomas, Rupert Roopnaraine and the veteran politician Eusi Kwayana (Sydney King). The fraudulent victory of the PNC in 1973 convinced some groups that the PPP was unlikely ever to defeat the PNC and a number of groups started to coordinate their efforts against the PNC. These included groups such as the radical Ratoon, and Kwayana's Association for Social and Cultural Relations with Independent Africa (ASCRIA).

These three parties – the PPP, PNC and WPA – have all offered socialist programmes to the electorate. This gives a radical tone to Guyanese politics which is noticeably discordant with the generally conservative rhythm of Commonwealth Caribbean politics. The general profiles of three Guyanese political leaders will serve to illustrate this point. Some leaders and their parties declared themselves to be socialists during the early nationalist movement from the late 1930s in other Commonwealth Caribbean countries. For example, in Jamaica, the forerunner in party organization in the English-speaking Caribbean declared itself a socialist party in 1940, two years after its founding. Socialism for Norman Manley and the People's National Party (PNP) which he led from its inception in 1938 to 1969 when he retired from public life,was a very mild form of British Labour Party socialism. Nettleford expresses the point well when he argues that

> *Socialism* as understood in Jamaican politics may be said to have been
> the intellectual and moral 'creation' of the PNP egged on by a group
> of young nationalists and articulated in terms that suited the Jamaican
> palate by the *liberal* Norman Manley, the PNP leader.
>
> (Nettleford, 1971, p. iii; emphases added)

In Jamaica, therefore, the prevailing understanding of socialism propagated by
the socialist party was greatly influenced by British Fabianism and writers such
as Harold Laski and John Strachey and other contributors to Victor Gollancz's
Left Book Club.

In Guyana, in contrast, the founder of the nationalist movement, Cheddi
Jagan, states that Marx's *Capital* opened 'whole new horizons' for him during
his student days at Northwestern University outside Chicago (Jagan, 1971,
p. 54). Whereas in Jamaica and most of the rest of the then British West Indies
the early nationalist movement was led by members of the middle classes,
leadership of the movement in Guyana was won by men such as Jagan with a
radical perspective and programme. Having won the first elections held in the
country under universal adult suffrage in 1953, Jagan's 'communist-oriented'
PPP government was suspended by the Conservative British government after
133 days in office. Baber and Jeffreys sensibly suggest that 'it is interesting to
speculate whether, in the present geopolitical context of the continent, the PPP
would not be treated similarly today' (Baber and Jeffreys, 1986). The PPP's
leaders' known communist sympathies and leanings tended to cloud over some
of their sound and necessary social policies. These included a better deal for
rice farmers, trade union recognition by multi-national companies, lifting of the
ban on the free travels of radicals into British Guiana, and so forth (Jagan,
1971, ch. vi). After all, this is perhaps the major lesson of the Grenada debacle
and US invasion in 1983. In retrospect it seems obvious that at the height of the
Cold War between East and West it was undoubtedly unwise to have antag-
onized the USA and the waning imperial power, Britain.

These events not only placed Jagan and his government in a situation of
conflict with the USA and the UK but leaders in the rest of the British West
Indies condemned the leadership in Guyana for bringing the country and the
region into disrepute. Jagan was later to write with an impressive clinical
detachment, which perhaps comes from his dental training, of the ways in
which the nationalist founding fathers in the region condemned him and his
party (Jagan, 1971, ch. viii). These included Grantley Adams of Barbados and
Alexander Bustamante of Jamaica. In wry mood Jagan stated that 'We were
blacklisted by all the West Indian governments, *even* by the Eric Williams
government . . . ' (emphasis added) (1971, p. 185).[22]

The second Guyanese leader whose political profile runs counter to that of
other West Indian leaders in the years since the late 1930s is, of course, Linden

Forbes Sampson Burnham. Regarded in the 1950s as the socialist in the PPP, which he joined on returning to Guyana in 1949 upon completion of his training as a barrister in London, Burnham maintained throughout his career that he was a socialist. Indeed, for a brief while in the 1970s he was regarded as the foremost socialist in the Commonwealth Caribbean. No doubt this was because internationally, particularly in Africa, Burnham espoused socialist rhetoric and supported progressive nationalist struggles against Portuguese, British and South African colonial regimes. He assumed power first in 1964 and remained in office for the next twenty-one years. He died during a relatively minor operation in 1985 after establishing a regime built on corruption, fear and repression. The *Comrade Leader* Burnham apparently believed that he had a *destiny to mould*[23] Guyana into a socialist state in which the state controls the commanding heights of the economy, the ruling party is respected as supreme and the president of the republic enjoys dictatorial power.

Whilst, however, Jagan's socialism led him farther into the Moscowite camp, the *Comrade Leader*'s understanding of socialism led him and his PNC to a nightmarish montage of Stalinist *statism*, post-colonial African *presidentialism* and Latin American *caciquism*. These made his PNC regime most *un*-West Indian. It is true, of course, that in Grenada *Uncle* Eric Gairy cut an unconventional figure when compared to most Commonwealth Caribbean leaders. So too did the *Chief* Bustamante in Jamaica. In the latter case, however, the undemocratic tendencies of the *Chief* were held in check by the greater democratic instincts of the people, the PNP and, indeed, other figures within the *Chief*'s JLP itself. In Grenada the authoritarianism of *Uncle* Gairy was allowed to develop to the extent that the New Jewel Movement of Maurice Bishop felt that the only way to gain office was through a coup d'etat or, in terms of the leaders, a revolution which occurred in 1979. Sadly, this may be the only way out of the impasse in which Burnhamism has left Guyana. A consideration of this leads to the third distinguishing factor between Guyana and the rest of the Commonwealth Caribbean. It is instructive, however, to look briefly at one other Guyanese political figure before turning to the politics which gave way to Burnhamism.

This figure is of course the late Dr Walter Rodney. Academic historian, intellectual activist and, in the words of C. L. R. James, the 'brightest spark' struck in the post-colonial Commonwealth Caribbean, Rodney touched many individuals and people throughout the African diaspora as well as Africans themselves. A distinguished scholar who had spent all his mature years outside Guyana from the age of eighteen when he went to the University of the West Indies, Mona Campus in Jamaica, Rodney returned to Guyana from Tanzania in 1974. He had been appointed to a chair in the history department at the University of Guyana but the government intervened to stop him taking up the post. Committed to the cause of a just society in the country of his birth, however, Rodney resigned from his professorship at the University of Dar es Salaam and returned to Guyana. He soon joined with other radicals who were disillusioned with both the totalitarian PNC and the relatively ineffective Moscow-oriented PPP, to found the WPA.

Like Williams and James before him, Rodney had lived and worked in a number of countries gathering intellectual sustenance and widening his political perspective. He was unique, however, for a number of reasons. Rodney was one of a new generation who received not only their schooling but also their undergraduate training in the region. He also lived and worked in Africa in whose history he specialized at the London School of Oriental and African Studies. And he was, intellectually, an inheritor of the Pan-Africanist, anti-imperialist and radical traditions which had developed in the Americas since before the end of British and American slavery in the nineteenth century. He was the star of a generation who benefited from the achievements of the earlier generation of nationalists. This first generation of post-independence scholars, in its optimism, also adopted a critical posture towards the failures and drawbacks of the earlier nationalists. Rodney's intellectual and political engagement with the Guyanese situation during the last phase of his short life should be seen in this context. His major contribution towards the urge for a better society in Guyana must, therefore, be seen as part of the work of the WPA.

This leads, however, to a third major difference between Guyanese politics and the remainder of the Commonwealth Caribbean. Guyana is the only one of these countries in which East Indians constitute the overall majority population. In Trinidad, the other British colony in the region which encouraged Indian indentured immigration in the nineteenth century, the single largest ethnic or racial group is also East Indians. Here East Indians do not, however, constitute an absolute majority of the population. The combined populations of Africans, Europeans, Chinese and so forth, outnumber East Indians. In Guyana, in contrast, East Indians constitute 51 per cent of the total population and the Africans, who make up the vast majority in other Commonwealth Caribbean countries, account for 31 per cent. The mixed/coloured account for 11 per cent, the Amerindians for 5 per cent and 1 per cent Chinese and Portuguese each; the usual residual 'other' accounts for the remaining 1 per cent of the population.

No doubt these groups relate to the national 'community' called Guyana in different ways because they are inserted or have become included in this 'community' in different ways. The Amerindians were the indigenous people of the country who were subdued and colonized by the Dutch and then the British. They were hardly ever regarded as part of the 'national' community before independence. They lived largely beyond the pale of the new 'nation' which was emerging under these European powers and given its tone by creole Africans/coloureds. The support some Amerindians gave the 1969 Rapununi rebellion may also indicate that for some of them the new Guyana is as much a fictional creation as were the Dutch and British colonial communities. Theirs has been the experience shared by many other groups of people throughout the Americas, Australia, New Zealand and so forth where Europeans and others have settled during the last several centuries thereby blocking out the unwritten histories of truly indigenous peoples. Generally, these indigenous peoples are too small in number to put up a significant fight, even along nationalist lines. The essential problem for such indigenous minorities is that nationalism and democracy have effected an alliance which sees all forms of minority action and claims in antipathetic terms.[24]

The minorities arrived in Guyana throughout the long process of settlement and the creation of a 'nation' called Guyana. The Portuguese and Chinese people arrived initially as indentured labourers as part of an attempt by the plantocracy to resolve what they perceived, wrongly, as their labour problem. They had depended on slavery for their fortunes. With the abolition of slavery in 1838 throughout the British West Indies planters everywhere complained about the high costs of free labour and pressed for the imperial parliament as well as the local legislatures to find alternatives. Hence the 'new system of slavery' – indentured labour. When white Madeirans proved inadequate, the Chinese were brought in to resolve the situation. But difficulties between Britain and China over trade led not only to rebellion in the middle of the last century but also to the end of Chinese emigration to the British colonies. In any event, the Chinese and Portuguese populations quickly slipped away from the plantations to fill the gap in services and soon emerged as part of the creole Guyanese society.

By the latter part of the nineteenth century this was to become the essential social hub of the emerging society within the colony. Here the offsprings of the former slave owners who were mixed with the African slaves began to see themselves as the people whose home Guyana was. It might be expected that they should have led any nationalist movement which should emerge in such conditions but the group was small and, more importantly, sought to associate with the dominant white colonial officials rather than with the mass of their countrymen and -women. Of course, this was not unique. The behaviour of the creoles in Guyana was typical of the class throughout the British West Indies, not to speak of elsewhere.

The African population was seeing its majority swiftly diminished with the influx of East Indians who were replacing Africans on the estates. Their freedom enabled the ex-slaves to abandon these estates after 1838. But for the new arrivants the land was their salvation from a greater poverty in India. The sad part of the story is that the newcomers were being used to lower wages and thereby to establish the persistent antagonism between the two majority groups in the country. This was further fuelled by the planters' granting of lands to

Indians in lieu of a return passage to India – sometimes lands rented and cultivated by Africans. The situation, therefore, was not so much that the freed-men wanted to have nothing to do with the land but, as Richardson suggests, they very much wanted to secure some land for themselves (Richardson, 1983, ch. 1). Many creolized Africans believed, for example, that the medical treatment afforded the Indians, as well as the use made of them to break legitimate strikes by Africans for better wages, led to inter-racial animosity (Rodney, 1981, ch. 7). Later, the African was to organize to keep the East Indian out of the areas of public life which the middle-class, professional and urbanized African had come to believe was his preserve (Jagan, 1971).

It should now be clear that whilst the African arrived in Guyana as a slave, the East Indian arrived as an indentured labourer, partly through public funds. The system of indenture lasted from 1838 to 1917 when nationalism in India demanded an end to the inhumane conditions in which poor Indians were being transferred to various parts of the British empire to meet the needs of a number of brutal and brutish plantocracies.

This long and extensive wave of Indian migration may be seen as one in which Indians *saved* the economies of these colonies or as a system which *undermined* the Africans, Malays, Creoles and so on in their attempts to assert their dignity in a prolonged struggle between European capital and non-white labour. In Guyana, the plantocracy was able to create and perpetuate what became popular images or stereotypes of both the 'coolie' Indian labourer and the African, so that African and East Indian could see each other only in negative terms. In this process *Swamy* was transformed into *Sammy* and *Kewsi* into *Quashie*; the former fitted into the stereotype first constructed around the latter during slavery. Rodney explains this point clearly when he writes in his pioneering study of the late nineteenth and early twentieth centuries, that

> Planters created the Indian stereotype called 'Sammy' – taking the venerable 'swamy', steeped in a centuries-old religious philosophy, and reducing him to a mishmash of self-contradictory attributes: violent, child-like in dependency, hardworking, thievish, admirable frugal, and miserly to the point of self-neglect.
>
> The redoubtable Kewsi, having his origins in the fast-developing Akan polities of the eighteenth century, was in the West Indies a being called 'Quashie': indomitably lazy but cutting tons of cane and producing when workhorses failed in the Demerara mud; docile but requiring the amputation of his limbs to discourage resistance and flight. After slavery Quashie grew more lazy. True, he cultivated more provisions than ever before and he hazarded his life in the toil of the bush, but he never really worked satisfactorily – on the sugar estates – and therefore civilization was threatened.

When Quashie reproached Sammy with having come to undercut established plantation labour, the answer was readily forthcoming: 'Yes, you rascal neegah man: me come from India dis forty-six year: supposing me and me matty no come dis side fo' work, you rascal neegah been starve one time'. This retort could have had no basis in the experience of the Indians. They were in no position to know whether Africans were starving before indentured immigration got under way. But it was one of the self-evident truths of planter propaganda that the whole country would have been ruined had not the estates been saved by indentured immigration; and in that eventuality, the 'lazy nigger' would certainly have starved. As for the crudities of the typical African estimation of Indians, it is not in the least surprising that these should have been heavily influenced by prevailing planter misconceptions, given that even Creole African self-images were conditioned by white racist ideas. Ideological confusion and psychological oppression were as crucial to the maintenance of the plantation system as were the administrative controls and the final sanction of the police. In a heterogeneous society, the impact of racist perceptions was obviously magnified, and its principal consequence was to hold back the maturing of working class unity by offering an explanation of exploitation and oppression that seemed reasonably consistent with aspects of people's life experience.

(Rodney, 1981, pp. 180–1)

There are writers today, however, who choose to see this 'new system of slavery' in much the same way as the planters did and who argue that indentured labour from India actually saved the colonies from ruin (Saha, 1970). This point is, not unexpectedly, one of the cornerstones of post-colonial nationalism in Guyana. For example, in an article on the contributions of Africans and East Indians to modern Guyana, one historian wrote in the *Guyana News* that

Between 1838 and 1917 236,000 East Indians were brought to British Guiana. Their contribution to the development of the country in this period was profound. It was due above all to their efforts that the colonial economy was rehabilitated after 1838 and survived.

(*Guyana News*, January–April 1988, p. 3)

One of the main achievements of post-war Caribbean scholars and intellectuals living and writing either within the region or outside, is that they have been able to transcend these stereotypes and reveal the African and the East Indian in their true complexities, stressing such factors as the contributions of each of these major groups to the making of the contemporary Caribbean (for example, Dabydeen and Samaroo, 1987).

It was, however, the political exploitation of the fact of racial differences in Guyana by the PNC from 1955 which led to the institutionalized fraudulent revolution. Britain and the USA gave Burnham their support in the 1960s, and Burnham's own considerable political skills in outmanoeuvring Jagan at every step of a prolonged struggle for power emphasized the areas of tension between East Indians and Africans. Thus, between 1955 and 1961/2, Burnham became recognized as the leader of the African population and Jagan became identified as the champion of the East Indian racially conscious majority. Similarly, their respective parties, the PNC and the PPP, became racially divided particularly between 1957 and 1964. During these years the PPP under Jagan formed the government, while Britain 'prepared' the country for independence. But, as Jagan said of this period, the PPP was 'in office but not in power' (Jagan, 1971, p. 188) because the colonial office and the governor still held the real power in the land and exercised their powers more than seemed to have been the case elsewhere at a time when the imperial power was about to depart. The policies of the PPP, however, were not only denounced as communism by the party's detractors, but the African population also came to see these as aimed against them and promoting Indian interests. For example, the reform of the education system allowing for greater state participation was seen as a state action which could only benefit the Indians who were mainly non-Christian (Bacchus, 1969). Similarly, policies aimed at rural development, which was where the vast majority of Indians lived, were seen in the same light.

Moreover, Jagan's unwillingness to join the Federation of the West Indies, and his later scepticism of the Caribbean Free Trade Area Agreement (CARIFTA) – the Caribbean Community – have been seen by African Guyanese as the reflection of a fear that Guyana's Indian majority would be swamped by the far greater numbers of Africans in the member countries. Jagan has, however, argued his case quite differently. His opposition to federation and CARIFTA has been expressed in terms of his understanding of contemporary capitalism. Jagan argued that the rapid *growth* in the economies of the socialist Soviet bloc countries and a *decline* in the Western capitalist economies were forcing capitalists to expand national frontiers. Presumably this would increase growth. In any event the movement towards larger political and economic units – in Europe, South and Central America, and the Caribbean – was part of a US-inspired imperialist thrust. US multi-nationals wanted to replace the British, French, Dutch, Germans and Japanese not only in an enlarged European market but also in the Americas. The formation of CARIFTA in 1965 and its formal inauguration in 1968 by almost all the Commonwealth Caribbean states, Jagan argued, was therefore

> in keeping with the new strategy of US imperialism – the creation of
> Common Markets and Free Areas to benefit its multinational cor-
> porations and to rationalize and stabilize world capitalism and
> imperialism as a socio-economic system. It is not to be forgotten that
> L. F. S. Burnham, the chief protagonist of CARIFTA, had been
> brought to power in Guyana with the help of US imperialism and was
> committed to pro-imperialist domestic and foreign policies.
>
> (Jagan, 1979, p. 51)

The point of interest here is not whether Jagan's analysis of imperialism is
correct. Rather, what seems more germane in the context of Guyanese politics
is the apparent indifference or insensitivity to the charge by many African
Guyanese that opposition to a desirable greater unity and cooperation in the
region was based on a fear of Africans outnumbering Indians. Of course,
Jagan's insistence that federation and free trade were in the interest of the
imperialists may well be an expression of his deeply held communist views.
But, again, this is hardly the point. His apparently inflexible position, ultimately derived from Moscow's view of the world, allowed him to be driven
into a corner by the more cunning and less scrupulous *Comrade Leader*
Burnham.

For example, the fact that he was helped to power by the USA and Britain
did not mean that Burnham was not sufficiently astute to manoeuvre his way
out from these countries' control. Indeed, part of the problem for the PPP and
WPA opposition parties had been the fact that Burnham displayed an uncanny
ability to develop and strengthen a repressive regime at home whilst pursuing
a progressive and tenable foreign policy. Burnham alienated his erstwhile
friends in the USA and Britain by nationalizing the bauxite industry and large
plantations; he initiated development plans; and he gained the support of communist Cuba and radical Third World states, hosting the Non-Aligned Movement conference in 1973. In other words, to a considerable degree the *Comrade
Leader* stole both the thunder and the platform of the PPP whilst retaining his
racial support from African Guyanese and much of his *class* support from all
ethnic groups.

First, Burnham consolidated his racial support by ensuring that African
Guyanese tightened their hold on the offices of state. This was done in the first
instance by the pre-independence elections of 1964 in which a system of
proportional representation, devised by Britain, was used. According to this
system the whole country is treated, so to speak, as one constituency. The
parties nominate their candidates and the number of votes received by the party
determines the number of members they are allotted in the legislature. In 1964
the PPP won the elections again, with 24 seats to the PNC's 22 and the United

Force's 7. Jagan was, however, yet again denied office. Burnham was allowed by the governor to form a coalition government with the United Force. This gave Burnham enough time to consolidate his political position and, in the elections of 1968, the PNC won. This was achieved through the blatant rigging of the polls, using the *overseas* vote. The system allows Guyanese citizens living abroad to vote in elections taking place in Guyana. This has ensured PNC victories at the polls in 1973, 1980 and 1985. Like much that Burnham established, the overseas vote has so far survived him although its use in the last elections in November 1985 was said to be less blatant than in previous elections. All these elections have been condemned by national opposition parties as well as by international opinion.

Perhaps the second most important constitutional device the PNC introduced was the executive presidency in 1980 (P. Singh, 1983). This places Guyana in a company of its own within the Commonwealth Caribbean. Although Trinidad has a president, the office is restricted to the ceremonies of the formal head of state and executive power rests with the prime minister and his cabinet. The executive presidency of the PNC regime resembles that of the majority of post-independent African states in which the holder of the office assumes all powers of state, subjugates the legislature and the judiciary to his will and arbitrarily interferes in all areas of civil life. In short, there is a serious attempt to abolish the usual distinction between state and civil society. The end result, of course, is hardly ever a benevolent dictatorship such as could sometimes be expected of some colonial governors. Rather, the result of this type of uncontrolled executive president is a new type of dictatorship claiming a dubious legitimacy.

Moreover, the regime ensured that the major institutions of the state are controlled by Afro-Guyanese. This process involved the *Africanization* of the military and the police, and the strengthening of the hold middle-class Africans had on the civil service. These developments tend to heighten the racial contradiction because the occupational profiles of Africans and East Indians are accentuated: Africans control and man the state and ideological apparatuses as well as public sectors of the economy whilst East Indians control and own the private, particularly the rice-growing and trading, sectors of the economy.

Aspects of the racial political dynamics may be illustrated by a closer look at the issue of the civil service. It was traditionally a major occupation for the African middle class, particularly when the East Indians were kept beyond the civil and political boundaries of creole society. In the early decolonizing period the League of Coloured People (LCP), Guyana Branch, fought to ensure that those branches of the service opened to non-whites not sent out from Whitehall were kept as an Afro-Guyanese middle-class preserve (Jagan, 1971, p. 60; Greene, 1974, p. 36). This was in sharp contrast to the aims and objectives of the parent-body of the LCP based in London. Founded by Dr Harold Moody from Trinidad and having David Headley as its representative from Guyana, the LCP in London informed the Moyne Commission in 1938 that included in its aims were the following:

> To promote and protect the social, educational, economic and political interests of its members.
> To interest members in the welfare of coloured peoples in all parts of the world.   ˎ
> *To improve relations between the races.* ˎ
> To cooperate and affiliate with organizations sympathetic to coloured people.   ˎ
> (Memorandum from the League of Coloured Peoples, Moyne Commission, 1938, Colonial Office, 950; emphasis added)

Just as the LCP in Guyana in the 1940s defended the position of the middle-class African, so did the British Guiana East Indian Association (BGEIA) attempt to champion the interests of the East Indian middle class emerging amongst the rice growers and the small business community (Jagan, 1971, p. 60). The group's aim was to make an in-road into the areas of Afro-Guyanese middle-class employment.

Under Jagan's ministry between 1957 and 1964, wittingly or unwittingly, two developments in the PPP tended to reinforce these racial patterns of Guyanese politics. One of these was that the PPP became increasingly identified with the Indian population as more and more of its prominent non-Indians resigned.[25] Whilst Jagan gained the support of the Indian business community, the PPP steadily lost its broad nationalist appeal and was forced to modify aspects of its radical programme to satisfy conservative business supporters. A second development was the view held by increasing numbers of non-Indian Guyanese that the distribution of state patronage 'gave an unfair advantage to the Indian elements in the population' (Greene, 1974, p. 20). These developments increased the fears of the Africans for whom, as Dabydeen correctly states, 'Freedom from slavery saw a resolve never to be dominated again by other ethnic groups' (Dabydeen and Samaroo, 1987, p. 11) as they had been under the whites.

Second, despite Jagan's support amongst Indian businessmen, Burnham was able to strengthen his *class* support in several ways. In the first instance, the traditional areas of African middle-class domination were preserved. Political independence and the PNC's large-scale nationalization and centralizing programmes greatly expanded these spheres of employment. It would appear that almost half of the workforce in Guyana is employed by the state and the para-statals. As in post-colonial Africa, therefore, a sizeable state petite bourgeoisie has developed during the almost quarter century of PNC rule. This class may well come to see that their own immediate and longer-term interests depend on continued support for the PNC, whether under the lacklustre President Desmond Hoyte who succeeded Burnham in August 1985, or any one of a number of Burnham's lieutenants who are jockeying for his mantle and ultimate control of the presidency.

The prospect of Indian domination as the country approached independence in the early 1960s increased the fears, not only of Africans, but also of other minorities, and this encouraged support from the minorities for the then 'moderate' PNC. As Greene shows, the support given to the PNC in the 1961 and 1964 elections reflected strong support from the Chinese, Portuguese and other white minorities (Greene, 1974, ch. 2). This support broadened into the formation of the coalition government in 1964 of the PNC and the business-dominated United Force. As the sole party of office for well over two decades, the PNC has had to be reckoned with by the business community as the party of government. And as the prospects for the PPP to return to office disappeared under the blatantly undemocratic political system instituted by the PNC this fact has become more and more obvious.

More significantly, however, from the perspective of this discussion, the PNC managed to gain the support of prominent Indo-Guyanese figures. The example of Sir Shridath 'Sonny' Ramphal, the former outspoken secretary-general of the Commonwealth, is well known. Not only is he reputed to have enjoyed the confidence of Burnham but Ramphal was one of Burnham's most able attorneys-general and Foreign Minister. Mohamed Shahabbuddeen[26] was, first under Burnham, and until 1988 under Hoyte, Attorney-General and Minister of Justice; he was also a vice-president, deputy prime minister and chairman of the general council of the PNC. He came fourth in the government hierarchy. The general secretary of the party is also of East Indian background, Ranji Chandisingh, a former leader of the youth wing of the PPP. In short, of the thirty-four senior members of the party and state hierarchies identified by Baber and Jeffrey, seven have East Indian names, suggesting that at least this number are from that community (Baber and Jeffrey, 1986, pp. 97–8).

Reference to these members of the African-dominated PNC and government is not by way of saying that the East Indian population has anything close to adequate representation in the political life of Guyana. Far from it. After all, the East Indians constitute the majority population in the country. And if political life must be organized along racial lines, then it would be expected that the majority in these institutions would be from the Indian population. The general point, rather, is that despite the *racial* basis of politics and state relations in Guyana, the PNC has been able to outmanoeuvre Jagan and the PPP by acquiring some *class* support from the minorities as well as from the majority East Indian population itself.

The struggle for Guyana is therefore a struggle for democracy which attempts to override the division of race first introduced and nurtured by the British, as Eric Williams stressed with respect to Trinidad and Tobago but which is applicable to the Commonwealth Caribbean generally. As he stressed on the eve of his country's independence from Britain:

> Division of the races was the policy of colonialism. Integration of the races must be the policy of Independence. Only in this way can the colony of Trinidad and Tobago be transformed into the Nation of Trinidad and Tobago.

> (Williams, 1964, p. ix)

In a sense, the WPA is carrying forward this hope to create a society in which the differences between races which were cynically exploited for political control during the first twenty-five years of political independence may be reversed.

Traditional and ethnic nationalism

This is a convenient point at which to return to two general points that run throughout this discussion. The first arose in the course of the discussion over Caribbean politics and the second runs like a thread throughout the whole discussion. I have argued that exilic politics amongst the Caribbean people in Britain have been relatively inconspicuous. This has been so because of the absence of nationalist questions being raised in the region over territorial, racial, religious or linguistic groups claiming that they are distinct and separate nations from the rest of the general population. The situation in Guyana since the 1960s cannot, however, be discussed without reference to racial politics. Nonetheless, the exception of Guyana proves the general rule.

Throughout the period of racial tension and the African's control of the country through the PNC from 1964, only once has there been a suggestion that perhaps East Indians and Africans should separate and divide Guyana for the two largest racial and cultural groups in the country. This suggestion was advanced in the late 1960s by Sydney King (now Eusi Kwayana) but it was soon dropped because it failed to gain serious attention in either community. This supports the view that Guyanese of whatever racial background see themselves as being members of a community that cannot be meaningfully separated according to the fourfold affinities of race, religion, territory and language.

In 1988 East Indians in the Caribbean commemorated the one hundred and fiftieth anniversary of the commencement of their presence in the region. In Britain, as well as in the Caribbean itself, people of East Indian descent from the region are naturally examining their relationship with the Caribbean. The result of this examination will be of particular importance to Guyana and

Trinidad where the single largest racial/ethnic group is composed of East Indians. The region also celebrated the one hundred and fiftieth anniversary of the abolition of slavery as well as the fiftieth year since the 1938 rebellion which sounded the final death knell for British colonialism in the Caribbean. The region's statesmen and leaders cannot rest content on the record of the post-colonial experience. The lesson of Guyana's peculiar situation for the rest of the region is that without considerate leadership the racial factor could very well go beyond the boundary towards groups of citizens defining themselves in terms of *ethnic nationalism.*

This option must be a temptation to some East Indians from the Caribbean in Britain. Two developments in Britain may be encouraging this. First, the general emphasis on African culture by Afro-West Indians from countries such as Jamaica, Barbados, St Lucia and Grenada where the East Indian populations are very small. Quite unintentionally, this emphasis may discourage many West Indians from seeing themselves as *West Indians.* In other words, the majority Afro-Caribbean population in the Caribbean, Britain and wherever we might have travelled in the post-war years, must be aware of the hurt and injustice which may be unintentionally caused by the search for a clearer definition of an African past. This may occur if and where such a search is conducted in a manner which excludes the contribution to, and participation in, what we generally call West Indian or Caribbean culture and society by non-African groups.

The second development is not necessarily contradictory to the first. Several Indo-West Indians wish to reach out to Mother India in much the same way as Afro-West Indians wish to reach out to Africa. Most writers who have examined the records of slavery and indentured labour in the Caribbean would no doubt agree with Tinker's contention that the latter was a new form of the former system. The deprivation involved in these processes suggests that considerable mutual understanding is necessary for a peaceful and democratic Guyana to emerge from the debris of over two decades of racist politics by the PNC. Being a British colony the state was, of course, underpinned by racism prior to political independence and PNC paramountcy. The British, however, made little or no pretence about the racist nature of the system they established.

In Britain itself the *ethnicization* or *racialization* of the West Indian has meant that the East Indian who has been in the region for 150 years is rarely perceived as a West Indian. He or she is slowly becoming an *Asian* – a category which has meaning for Britain and her empire in East and Central Africa where a milder system of apartheid than developed in South Africa existed and required there to be separate estates of *Europeans, Asians* and *Africans* as the three elements of humankind.

Conclusion

If Guyanese Africans and Indians in Britain can work together for democracy in Guyana, then they are making a double contribution. First, they are defying the divisions between themselves deliberately created during the colonial period and exploited in the immediate post-colonial period by one group when it appeared that the other group was preparing to do the same. And, second, they would be actively undermining the *racialization* of all forms of social relations in post-imperial Britain which seeks constantly to compare and contrast, *negatively*, the people of African and sub-continental background. This has been part of a general process to reinforce or create new ethnic identities which, in turn, contributes to the attraction of the communal option.

8

Nationalism and the new pluralism in Britain

Introduction

In this chapter I want to relate to each other some of the central points raised in the last three chapters about historical/traditional and ethnic nationalism and diasporic politics. Secondly, I also want to set these points alongside what, earlier in the discussion, I called the new pluralism. Whilst I will discuss these points generally, I will pay particular attention to how Britain is affected by these phenomena.

Traditional and ethnic nationalism

There are, of course, many more pressing questions with which Britain has had to contend in this period than those I have raised in this discussion over ethnicity and nationalism. Questions, for example, relating to defence, economic recovery and adjustment in an increasingly competitive world system, education, internal social peace and so forth are all important problems which have exercised the minds of British statesmen and stateswomen since the Second World War. Each of these stands on its own as worthy of the extensive discussion received elsewhere. The question, however, of whether the less than five per cent non-white population of around fifty-six million Britons can become part or parts of the national community not only continues to have immediate and grave implications for other national concerns, but is likely to continue to be of paramount importance in the foreseeable future.

One way of describing the burden of this essay, therefore, may be to say that it has been to debunk Mishan's assertion, stated in chapter two, that the nation is spending too much time on matters pertaining to its conditions with respect to its own heritage of 'race relations'. On the contrary, it could be argued that whilst much valuable time, resources and money have been wasted on the construction of ethnic communities (including majoritarian communalism), too little attention has been paid to the more fundamental implications of this enterprise for all who inhabit these islands. We run the risk of ignoring the pitfalls of the communal option at the peril of the British national community – community understood in its widest, most generous sense. These pitfalls, I have argued, need to be faced and surmounted by both the majority and the minority populations which share a heavy responsibility for creating a *common British community*.

In this regard, I have sought to present the following points. First, I have argued that ethnic nationalism is emerging today as the central agglutinating, or binding, factor in a wide range of countries. Second, this wave of social consciousness is affecting post-imperial Britain as much as the post-colonial states which have emerged out of her empire since World War Two. I supported my case with three closely related historical and contemporary examples of this situation with respect to Britain.

One of these examples was the nature of party political responses to the very transition of Britain herself from empire to nation. Attention was drawn particularly to the development of nationality and immigration laws which, over a period of two decades, redefined the British nation in largely *ethnic* terms. I have argued that the Labour party took *island* or Lesser Britain into a fairly *traditional* kind of nationalism. To some extent the predominance of a traditional nationalist perspective may be helping the majority of the Labour party to make the transition from Britain's historical isolation to greater integration with continental Europe. On the face of things this attempt to embrace the multiplicity of what we still insist on calling 'races' seems liberal and even humanitarian. But the *ethnic* nationalist response of the Conservative party, which has evoked much anger and protest in the 1980s, not only faced the question of national identity more frontally but the party's rebels to the right of the political spectrum have also been able to set the tone of much party political debate on the changing concepts of nationality in the post-imperial age. The Labour party, to which the majority of non-whites looked for a fair representation of the situation, has consistently been politically beaten by the Conservatives on this crucial issue. Moreover, Labour has been only too willing to betray, for electoral purposes, its sense of a traditional nationalism and embrace the policies engendered by Conservative ethnic nationalists. But the *political* victories these developments entailed do not, necessarily, denote *moral* victories. In particular, these political victories have encouraged leaders at all levels of society to side-step the fundamental question of how a new national community may peacefully emerge in post-imperial Britain.

Another example in the discussion was the demand for an independent state of Khalistan, initially supported only by a handful of dissidents and by militant Sikhs. But this is no longer so. As the crisis in the Punjab deepened, from the mid to the late 1980s, Sikhs in both India and Britain have been gravely concerned about their security. One of the world's youngest and smallest major religions – its holy places, practices and traditions – has been perceived to be threatened with extinction.

The cause of defending the faith, which militant Sikhs in both Punjab and Britain espouse, reminds us that people are moved and propelled into action by vastly different feelings of affinities at different times. These are not confined merely to types of societies, as theories of development in the optimistic decades of the 1950s and 1960s sought to convey. In other words, the certainty, which once imbued nation*s*-states in the West with a confidence that our societies had settled the quarrels which led to national dissociation, is evaporating. The very developments that encourage mass migration in the post-World War Two, post-imperial age – revolutions in international transportation, telecommunication, technology, the openness of the market, and so on – have also been the very factors which provide the material basis for groups, or collectivities, of people to maintain close touch with, or *re-create*, historic 'homelands'. The speed with which news travels, the ease and cheapness of immediate communication, the search for a place to which groups can feel that they 'belong', are some of the forces that encourage the present growth in diasporic relations. And some of these relations are distinctly of a political nature and pertain to the definition of *peoplehood*. Where, in the land of settlement, the *reception-experience* is one of rejection, this rejection can develop to become the single most important determinant of diasporic politics, particularly where discrete groups carry with them a deep sense of trans-national ethnic identity. It hardly seems to matter whether this rejection is based on colour, culture, language, or religion.

I also drew upon an example from the Commonwealth Caribbean as it relates to questions of ethnicity and nationalism. I argued, first, that the overall Commonwealth Caribbean situation is one in which a multiplicity of peoples live in *relative* peace and have not generally mobilized ethnicity in order to secure political advantage. Paradoxically, therefore, these societies which have emerged from slavery and indentured labour, are engaged in the construction of social systems which probably come closest to the *desirable* multi-ethnic, or multi-colour, or multi-racial, national community. This general position was, however, qualified by the discussion of the Guyanese situation which is *not* conducive to the development of a peaceful and prosperous multi-ethnic community for the Guyanese people as a whole. It was also argued that this exceptional case within the Commonwealth Caribbean tended to *prove* rather than *disprove* the rule. In part this has meant that even the fraudulent revolution in Guyana under the PNC has been conducted with fairly strict observance of the rules of constitutional politics. Even the main opposition party, the People's Progressive Party, has from time to time supported the People's National Congress government founded and led by the late L. F. S. Burnham and presently led by Desmond Hoyte, Burnham's immediate successor. The importance of colour as an element of social class in the region, the dominance of people of African background in politics and the increasing dominance of people of Indian background in economic activities are significant factors in a number of these societies, particularly Trinidad, which may cause conflict in the not too distant future. There is, therefore, no place for complacence in Commonwealth Caribbean societies with respect to ethnic political mobilization.

Throughout the discussion, the essential point was to suggest that populations almost everywhere are being pressured, or are being asked or encouraged to organize themselves into what we would nearly all agree are societies or communities defined according to one or other *ethnic* characteristics. As many writers have argued, this sense of affinity is not new. Indeed, ethnic awareness is perhaps as old as the very first primitive communities established by men and women. For example, the strong awareness of ethnic solidarity exhibited by some ancient groups distinguished them from others, and made them *nations* in a sense that men and women today, who are familiar with one or the other variety of nationalist lexicon, would have no difficulty in understanding. The Jews distinguished themselves from their gentile neighbours by a monotheistic religion, the ethical teachings of their prophets and a profound sense of history. The Greeks had a similar ethnic consciousness of themselves based on a keen awareness of their moral and intellectual superiority over the barbarians around them. Jews and gentiles, Greeks and barbarians; such distinctions between the *us* and *them* were to become commonplace in human societies everywhere.

But until the emergence of mercantilist capitalism and the absolutist monarchies of Western Europe, it is more confusing than enlightening to speak about the *nation* and the *state* co-existing. Up to this point the marriage had not been seriously proposed, let alone consummated. States existed but rulers did not claim that their legitimacy to govern was based on any notion of a relationship between *people* and *state*. Here and there nations may have existed, and ethnic groups certainly flourished, but had little or no sense of political legitimacy emerging from them as a collective, as *the people*. Indeed, people separated by territory, language, religion and so forth, could all owe allegiance to a ruling family – as indeed all British citizens/subjects do to the present Windsor family in Britain. And it was not unusual for the royal family to be from a foreign dynasty and, like some of the early Norman and Hanoverian kings of England, ignorant of the language of their subjects. Neither *ethnicity* nor the *state*, as independent entities, are, therefore, new in human society. Nor are many of the claims ethnicity is making today.

What is, however, new is the nature of the claims being made in the name of ethnicity in the post-imperial age. Historically, it was *traditional* nationalism which made claims regarding the congruity of the nation and the state. It embarked upon a seemingly worthy project of reshaping the relationships and institutions of power so that the congruence of *nation* and *state* would be achieved. *Traditional* nationalism utilized long-established affinities such as loyalty, and natural feelings such as patriotism, in its determination to accomplish this revolution. To a very large extent *traditional* nationalism has been successful in its Herculean task. Equally, however, it has been singularly conspicuous in its failure to remould the world into its oft declared perception of its own image. The new world it created has been on the whole made up of 'mini-imperial' socio-political orders largely delimited by territory. In other words, aspects of the old imperial order that traditional nationalism sought to destroy have been merely reshaped and have become identified with nationalism.

The failure of traditional nationalism in this regard, however, has not deterred, but has rather encouraged, ethnic nationalism in its assumption of the quest for a perfect congruence between nation and state. In other words, the new type of nationalism which has become commonplace in the post-imperial period since the Second World War, like Acton's poet, wishes to find 'an innocent and contented people, free from the corruption and restraints of civilized life . . . ' (Acton, 1862, p. 270). This new ethnic nationalism may not have the Rousseauan naturalistic echo of Acton's statement, but ethnic nationalism by its very principles seems to deny much of what has been achieved during the age of traditional nationalism. Despite its failings, traditional nationalism left the door open for the possibility of new affinities being formed through common human experience.

In particular, by not completely eradicating the pre-nationalist assumptions of political authority, traditional nationalism left intact the practicality of different groups of people being under the same political umbrella due to long historical association. Thus, the nations of Britain have kept together despite strong ethnic sentiments in its historically quite distinct parts – of England, Wales and Scotland. By this same token, traditional nationalism has been able to allow for the creation of new zones of affinity for peoples of vastly different backgrounds. The rationalistic definition of the nation-state which some early nationalists sought to establish meant that, at least notionally, traditional nationalism envisaged membership of the nation-state in terms not dependent on an exclusive single *ethnicity*. This, of course, suggests that *traditional* nationalism was none too clear about its project. On the one hand it sought to construct a new socio-political order based on the marriage of the *nation*, or the people, and the *state*, but at the same time it also sought to establish an *abstract* principle or set of principles as the binding element of the duo. Nationalism borrowed, therefore, from two apparently contradictory traditions which followed upon each other in the eighteenth century. These were, first, the *rationalistic*, and second, the *romantic*. In the first an abstract definition which could embrace potentially conflicting aspects of humanity emerged; in the second the search was more for a sense of *feeling* and of evolved, well-established historic roots, as writers such as Alexis de Tocqueville and Edmund Burke earlier perceived. The subsequent lack of clarity has not only been reflected in the philosophy of nationalism but also in its practice, namely, the founding of nation*s*-states rather than nation-states. Thus, a variety of loyalties, often conflicting, logically irreconcilable and practically unrealizable, have bound different peoples together under traditional nationalism.

The nation*s*-states of North America and the Caribbean are clear examples of this situation. And it is one which can only be posed problematically: why should Afro-Americans not consider, seriously, breaking up the mammoth USA so that black Americans have a number of states exclusively their own for sovereign/political and cultural purposes? And why does the majority Afro- and Indo-Caribbean people so readily accept all people as members of the West Indian nation or nations who share a common heritage?

Second, tremendous accomplishments have been made in human societies under the organization provided by the coming together of two entities – the nation (community) and the state (political authority) – over the last three centuries or so.[1] These include artistic, intellectual, industrial, technological and other achievements. The dynamism of capitalism, which developed under the aegis of the nation*s*-state, has not been achieved under any earlier socio-political organization. It is not surprising that, contrary to Engels' optimism, the *nations-state* shows no sign of withering away under socialism. On the contrary, this form of the most sovereign and legitimate socio-political arrangement has been used in attempts to refashion societies in the Soviet Union, China and elsewhere. And this instrumentality of the *nations-state* has been much more deliberate in societies which have undergone a Leninist revolution – with the Leninist emphasis on organization – than under liberalism.

The main point here, however, is that it must be counted amongst the achievements of *traditional* nationalism that societies have been able to establish parts of the foundation of a more generalized organization of humanity. The existence of systems of mass communications (such as roads, rail and air travel, radio, television and films, the telephone, satellite, print), trade, production and so forth, have combined to undermine the very *nations-state* structures which enabled them to envelop the world in the space of, historically speaking, a very short period of time. In particular, the mobility of capital in the last century which so excited both liberal and Marxist writers, but especially in the post-colonial period, and the increased mobility of labour through *migration*, have helped to undermine the continuing relevance of the *nations-state* duo for vast sections of our present world.

These achievements may not have been attained through the deliberate design of traditional nationalism. Indeed, they were at least partially accidental to the enterprise of both the nation*s*-state and capital. Nonetheless they have established a broad basis whereby humanity can build towards a more tolerant tomorrow. Through migration, for example, the possibility of groups of people being held together exclusively through an affinity to the same linguistic, religious, 'racial' group becomes less tenable for all practical purposes. The other side of this same coin, however, is that *ethnic* nationalism has the potential of transforming such *positives*, at least initially, into their very opposites. In other words, the very opportunities we have for a more unified world are also the opportunities for each group in one part or the other of the globe to seek after its own kind at the other end, causing havoc sometimes for themselves, but mostly for others who, in turn, inhabit the space between themselves and those they seek out.

Ethnic nationalism's project of re-ordering the *nations-state* into the *nation-state* proper is nothing short of revolutionary. Should it succeed where traditional nationalism failed, then, the possibility of very many more states coming into being would be greatly increased. Of course, the number of states would depend on what groups of people would decide are their distinctive characteristics. For example, if language is used in this way then a state such as India could justifiably be divided into several smaller or larger ones than presently exist within the union. This would be true of many large states such as the USSR as well as smaller states such as Cameroon or Nigeria. In some places language would not be the distinctive factor. For example, in the United Kingdom the predominance of English is such that it is doubtful that language alone could be the driving force for the creation of new nation-states. But there are, of course, other factors such as territory, 'racial' affinity, long historical association, religion and so forth. Indeed, the only possibility for the creation of a new state in the United Kingdom in the foreseeable future seems most likely to be effected through religious affinity in Northern Ireland.[2]

Of course, not all forms of ethnicity are nationalist and therefore not all forms of ethnic expressions include the demand for the state and the single nation to be congruent. As I argued earlier in this discussion, most forms of ethnicity are unconcerned about this particular political project. In the main, although very many minority ethnic groups are defined by the majority population and this must obviously have (as the structural functionalists were fond of saying in the 1960s)[3] political aspects, nonetheless, the groups so defined most often do not wish to be separated from the majority. Only when there are definite gains to be made do such groups seek separation from majorities they have long lived with. For example, it is interesting that the single largest population of Jews is to be found in the USA rather than in Israel. It may be attractive for East European, Middle Eastern and Soviet Jews to wish to migrate to Palestine but this clearly is not so for American Jews. Another example is the desire of the Scottish Nationalist Party for separation from the rest of Britain. During the heyday of the Pax Britannica ethnicity did not, significantly, drive any group of Scots to this demand, no doubt largely because Scotland shared in the benefits of a worldwide empire (Hanham, 1969a).

But *ethnic* nationalism is no respecter of place, time or systems or political organizations nor of social, economic or political ideologies. The new ethnic consciousness we see or hear about every day seems to transcend all other forms of social affinity. It appears bent on organizing the world in an image entirely its own. In other words, ethnicity seems to suggest that for the individual human being to know and realize himself or herself, he or she must find the roots of his or her being within a specific *folk* and their distinct *ways*. Ethnic nationalism suggests, therefore, that ethnic affinity is a constant and not subject to change under new circumstances. Nor does it allow for the possibility of such change in the future. Should it therefore succeed in revolutionizing social and state structures not only would we have for the first time a world made up truly of nation-states, but we would also have humanity divided exclusively according to some supposed primordial affinity based on 'race', language, territory or religion. In this way some of the gains made under the nation*s*-state would be lost and a significant restructuring of populations would have to be undertaken.

This scenario is, however, only one of a range of possibilities. One other scenario could be that a multiplicity of nation-states based on ethnic affinities would lead to the bigger nations swallowing up the smaller nations. In this situation the implied democratic intentions of ethnic nationalism – such as Khalistani nationalists express – would be frustrated and political independence of small groups could become merely *formal*. Minorities could also be caught in a trap and become their own prison guards because they would be dominated by but prohibited from both formal and informal participation in the wider political life of majority groups. Such a world order would not institute any greater appreciation of democratic participation although it would provide more opportunities for elites through the very establishment of new states. This world order would, therefore, be very much like the dependent neo-colonial world of the present post-imperial age in which we live (Goulbourne, 1979 and 1987). In this case *ethnic* nationalism would not have improved significantly the political conditions under which the majority of people live.

It is conceivable, however, that the historical achievement of *ethnic* nationalism may be to undermine the *nations-state* in another way altogether and also bring about an age of greater democracy. The scenario I have in mind in this respect is the following. A world of ethnic nation-states would most likely be a world of small states. A few would perhaps remain large but most probably these would be about the same as today's medium-sized states such as Germany, France or Thailand. Some states such as these and Japan would probably assume big-power status. Superpowers would probably be out of the question in such a world if language is insufficient to unite large linguistic groups such as the Chinese or English-speaking North America. With so many states in the international system, they could conceivably become even less relevant as the basic units of determination of production, markets, and communication. Even law and order would conceivably become more difficult in many of the smaller states – as indeed is already the case with many small and poor states. In the situation of a drastically reorganized state system either we would be poised to make a rapid return to barbarism and anarchy or we would have the opportunity to establish larger political units through large federations and eventually world government. Such large political authorities, particularly if built from the bottom upwards, could quite legitimately see to *some* aspects of human activities which are already beyond the capacity of most nation*s*-states. It would be, in other words, in the interest of the vast majority of states to desire the construction of large political authorities in which they could have a legitimate voice. Weaker states could thereby more effectively moderate the power of larger ones than they presently do through the United Nations.

It is partly from this perspective, I believe, that the Scottish Nationalist Party's case for an independent Scotland can be sympathetically approached. Such a state, nationalists have argued, would be an active member in the EEC of which England is a member. An independent Scotland would also be a member of the Commonwealth. The two countries would maintain a common open border. Moreover, Scottish attitudes toward major international issues would have an independent voice so that Westminster would no longer be able to embarrass the Scots. One example of the kind of embarrassment SNP leaders would like to avoid was the African boycott of the Commonwealth Games in Edinburgh in 1986; SNP leaders argue that the boycott was due to Margaret Thatcher's decision not to support sanctions against South Africa and this had nothing to do with Scotland (Interview with John Swinney, 1987).

Another example may be drawn from the argument presented by Sikhs in their call for an independent state of Khalistan in the Punjab. Their spokesmen have argued that if post-colonial India were to be broken down into separate and independent states this would provide the basis for a more democratic and therefore healthier political situation in South-East Asia. Irrespective of size, states based on ethnic affinities, such as language or religion, could then enter voluntarily into new political arrangements with each other to effect a loose federation of all states in the region. In this way the minorities within post-colonial India would not need to fear Hindu majoritarian and cultural domination.

This vision of a more democratic and fair international order, constructed upon the nation-states proper, makes the *communal option* at the level of state organizations and relations seem more reasonable than it might first appear to many humanitarians who would see such a narrow nationalism as a threat to the human objective of global social justice and peace. There are, however, several other dimensions to this question. Some of these are apparent at the level of state-building within the international community of states whilst others are more clearly revealed at the level of well-established nation-states such as Britain, in which the *nation* is undergoing important changes. If we accept that it is sufficient for groups of people to feel that they share certain things in common and want to be separate from others, then we can easily enough envisage very many more nation-states being formed out of present nations-states.

Two intractable problems, however, present themselves here. First, for modern men and women to maintain a decent level of living, continue to develop technology and improve our understanding of the environment, there must be a limit beyond which it is meaningless to break down populations into discrete communities with their own sovereign political authorities. Second, the proliferation of mini-states would not *necessarily* ensure greater democratic participation for all. If small, ethnically defined states were to become the international norm, but each were to be sufficiently large to be viable, there would most likely be new minorities which would suddenly become more visible or might even be created by the new majorities in order to release new tensions and to try to resolve new contradictions. This suggests that – as Jesus said of the poor – minorities, we have always with us; conversely, we are, however, likely also always to have majorities. And with most new ethnic nation-states we could expect new minorities and a repetition of relations of domination and subordination over and beyond class domination. There would be, for example, minorities of English and Welsh people in an independent Scotland as well as Scottish minorities in other parts of Britain. Non-white minorities would be in all the largely ethnically defined states in Europe. In the event of an independent Khalistan, some non-Sikh Punjabis would no doubt want to retain their homes in a new Khalistan. These examples also suggest that – like individuals and groups within nearly all Britain's ethnic minorities today – individuals and groups within the new national majorities of a dis-United Kingdom would experience, simultaneously, majority and minority statuses, depending on their specific points of location at particular moments. Such experiences would invariably bring to the surface hidden dimensions of diasporic political relations and may trigger off ever downwards processes of disassociation.

The way to resolve relations of domination and subordination between majorities and minorities may not, therefore, be through *the politics of difference* which leads, eventually, to separation or disassociation. Rather, perhaps the best or more viable way, in most cases, to overcome the imbalance of social and political power which is involved in the majority/minority complex may be to strengthen democratic participation creatively. This approach has the advantage that it would build upon whatever may have become, through shared historical experiences, a common legacy. In this regard the refusal by both Afro- and Indo-Guyanese to consider the possibility of division of Guyana is a candid recognition of the need for greater democracy rather than consolidation of the ethnic group through the creation of new states which may now be seen as the panacea for present ills.

Ethnic nationalism which, as we noted, informs the important area of immigration laws, is unlikely ever to affect new minorities to the extent that they would wish to make claims of a territorial kind in Britain. The defence of neighbourhoods in Brixton, Broadwater Farm in Tottenham, Toxteth, Southall and so on should not be confused with territorial claims. Where ethnic nationalist inspirations are present within the black minority communities in Britain these are deflected by the politics of the original homeland, as the Khalistani issue illustrates in the case of militant as well as devout Sikhs. Within Britain, the ethnicity of non-white minorities is being asserted through demands for the new pluralism.

The new pluralism and nationalism

In chapter three I asserted that the new pluralism is at once optimistic and pessimistic in its prescription for post-imperial Britain. Its optimism was seen to lie in the very positive characteristics new pluralists find in the existence of diverse cultures in Britain. Whilst, however, the new pluralism does not set out, unlike ethnic nationalism, to be exclusive, nonetheless its emphasis on *difference*, and the high premium it places on cultural preservation, are likely to undermine the emergence and development of any commonality between groups in society. The new pluralism must, therefore, be distinguished from, first, the plural membership of the traditional nation-state described throughout this discussion, and second, what we generally understand as pluralism in the social sciences.

In earlier chapters I argued that traditional or historical nationalism has been characterized by a plural, not a singular, membership of the national community. In other words, the nation-state has historically been composed of any number of *nations*, but each has been willing to one degree or another to compromise aspects of their discrete culture, language and customs in the interest of whatever has been perceived as constituting the national community. Thus, the differences between people in Yorkshire and Wessex have been comparatively hidden when the national British community came into view. Even where differences were more acute, such as between Scots and English, the national community called British has held. My use of the word pluralism to describe the condition of the nation-state in its traditional form does not amount to a theory of pluralism because it is being used merely to highlight the fact of plurality as contrasted with singularity. In no way does its usage describe a situation in which difference becomes the main point of reference; on the contrary, difference is taken for granted but it is not assumed to be the proper basis for social and political association. Groups within the traditional nation-state are considered to be secondary to a series of factors – such as common language, values, customs and so on – which are derived from the various groups and are therefore owned by all. The use of plural member-ship of the national community is not, therefore, to be confused with the new pluralism.

The new pluralism presumably draws much of its inspiration, however, from one or more of the many concepts of pluralism found within the social sciences. Political pluralism and social and cultural pluralism (see, for example, Nicholls, 1974) are by far the most well known of these concepts and are obviously the ones which have influenced popular thinking. The first of these is deeply rooted in different, but related, traditions in British and American political analyses and the latter emerged and developed in the post-World War Two years in social anthropology and sociology. The American tradition, which goes back to James Madison's pessimistic view of groups (Hamilton, Madison and Jay, 1961), stresses that groups are a necessary evil. The large number of groups, however, representing sectional (for example, geographical) and sectoral (manufacturing, agricultural, mercantile) interests, would mini-mize the evil they could inflict on a republic. For most of the present century, pressure or interest groups came to be seen as an effective means by which individuals could influence the decision-making process and therefore strengthen democratic participation (see, for example, Bentley, 1967; Latham, 1964). For example, this confidence in the ability of groups to increase the level of participation in the political process was forcibly expressed by the late R. T. McKenzie who contended that the group ' . . . provides an invaluable set of multiple channels through which the mass of the citizenry can influence the decision-making process at the highest level (McKenzie, 1967, p. 262).

Unlike the American tradition, British political analysts such as Harold Laski, and historians such as G. D. H. Cole, celebrated the virtues of pluralism by stressing the primacy of the group over state sovereignty. Laski, for example, argued that ' . . . we have found that a state in which sovereignty is unified is morally inadequate and administratively inefficient'; and that the ' . . . more carefully the political process is analysed, the more clearly does it appear that we are simply confronted by a series of special wills none of which can claim any necessary pre-eminence' (Laski, 1921, p. vi). Laski's 'special wills' were placed, in the minds of British political pluralists, above Jeremy Bentham's utilitarian notion of sovereignty based on the submission to crude force and acquiescence; rather, sovereignty was seen to derive from the diversity of groups to which people belonged. Like the American groupists, British political pluralists conceived of the good socio-political order as being where classical liberalism, the freedom of the individual, could be realized within the multiple, overlapping and cross-sectional membership of diverse groups representing an individual's varied interests. These could be as a commuter with an interest in the transport system or as a voter with an interest in an aggregate body such as the political party.

Although the new pluralism uses the vocabulary of political pluralism, it must be obvious from these brief remarks that its advocates do not have in mind political pluralism when they glorify pluralism. In this respect, it is important to note that in Britain whilst many in both the non-white ethnic minorities and the majority, indigenous white population struggle to maintain their seemingly distinctive cultural heritages, there is no serious attempt to institute a political pluralism other than that of the traditional liberal persuasion. The demand for recognition of Black Sections in the Labour party and the formation of Moslem fringe parties in the Midlands are not serious demands for institutional pluralism in the political realm. The high level of awareness of political issues by voters of West Indian backgrounds and the high voting turn-out of voters of Asian backgrounds in the 1980s confirm the absence of any support for this kind of divisive politics in the country (Goulbourne, 1990). Indeed, the similarity in the political behaviour of all groups is one of the positive pointers to a more united Britain. The new pluralism in Britain does not, therefore, contradict political pluralism; there is in fact little or no relationship between the two concepts, despite frequent references to 'pluralist democracy' by new pluralists (Swann, 1985).

There is, however, a close relationship between the new pluralism and social and cultural pluralism. The latter emerged as part of a general attempt after World War Two to understand the rapidly decolonizing states of Asia, Africa and the Caribbean. The Dutch administrator F. S. Furnivall, who first formulated the theory of social and cultural pluralism, argued that colonial 'society' in the Dutch East Indies was characterized by groups of people who live in radically separate communities. People *mixed* as a result of buying and selling in the market but they never *combined* socially. These, then, were collectivities which were hardly 'societies' at all, because each group had its own separate cultural identity such as language, religion, schooling, marriage customs and so forth.

The theory of social and cultural pluralism is more closely associated with the work of the Jamaican social anthropologist, M. G. Smith. As noted in the previous chapter, Smith argued and attempted to demonstrate the validity of this concept in a number of theoretical essays and detailed empirical books on the Caribbean. Apart from the rigour and scholarship Smith brought to bear on the discussion from the 1950s onwards, his contribution was to show that the political dimension of plural societies was crucial to their existence. It was this central authority which held such societies together. Moreover, during the decades of the 1960s and 1970s the theory of social and cultural pluralism was refined by Smith – particularly his work on corporation theory (Smith, 1974) – and others (see, for example, Hoetinck, 1967; also, Kuper and Smith, 1969). Drawing on Maine and Weber, Smith argued that all collectivities, including the nation-state, are but different forms of corporations, which incorporate outsider groups differentially. The importance of Smith's work here, however, is the emphasis he places on the inherent relationship of superiority/subordination between groups in the socially and culturally plural society.

Just as the celebration, therefore, of pluralism does not entail any serious revision or challenge to traditional political pluralism, so too it does not mean that the new pluralists hope to institute social and cultural pluralism as the fundamental social philosophy of post-imperial Britain. The new pluralist, however, employs the vocabulary of pluralism from both these radically different traditions in the social sciences.[4] One result is a great deal of confusion over what is to be understood as elements of the new pluralism and what should not. This places a responsibility upon the adherents of the new pluralism to clarify the kind of pluralist society they envisage for post-imperial Britain. And this is not a trivial task. After all, the widespread appeal of the new pluralism suggests that the notion contains something of the germ which is likely to contribute to a fairer society; unfortunately, however, at present the new pluralism continues to point in much the same direction as the exclusive cultural conservatism of ethnic nationalists in Britain. This perspective has informed much of the efforts made and being made by the state to assert an ethnic nationalist community in Britain, as was illustrated by chapter five. If this sounds rather abstract, a realistic and dramatic illustration of the kind of construction of which I am speaking may be in order here. This is the 1988 Education Act. It illustrates perfectly the dual pressure of the ethnic nationalism of powerful groups in the majority population and the not contradictory pressure of the new pluralism, as represented by the *Swann Report*.

At one level the Act seems to uphold the principle of the unified nation*s*-state. This is clearest in the insistence that its principal provision is to establish a *national* curriculum to which all of the country's pupils are deliberately exposed. Clause 1 (2) of the Act seeks to provide for

a balanced and broadly based curriculum which
(a) promotes the spiritual, moral, cultural, mental and physical development of pupils at the school *and of society*; and

(b) prepares such pupils for the opportunities, responsibilities and experiences of adult life.

(Education Reform Act 1988, p. 1; emphasis added)

The *national* curriculum includes the *core* subjects of mathematics, English and science and the *foundation* subjects of history, geography, technology, music, art and physical education. With respect to the core subjects, Welsh in Welsh schools within the principality is the sole exemption with respect to mother tongue; in other words, the Welsh language replaces English in the principality. There is no recognition of newly established languages such as those from the Indian sub-continent which cannot claim legitimacy from either longevity of presence or a clear territorial base in Britain. This should be acceptable by all if such an effort were accompanied by a deliberate act of will to construct a national British community. After all, English is the language which unites all, or the vast majority, of all peoples who live in these Islands. But the former Secretary of State for Education, Kenneth Baker, who introduced the measure, refused to place any of the 'new' – non-European – languages onto the prescribed schedule of foreign languages to be taken in schools. The provisions for foreign languages emphasize such languages as French and German, and expectedly, this has angered many groups from the Indian sub-continent who would have preferred a choice between a sub-continental and a European language. Here is an opportunity for the state to satisfy non-antagonistic demands because, whatever the outcome, it is likely to be of immense benefit to Britain. The only reasonable objection here would seem to be one of resources and this could be overcome by qualifying provisos, such as the cultural composition of the school and the availability of trained teachers. It is possible, however, that the decision was influenced by the perception that the desire to see mother-tongues taught in the schools was part of a more general effort to maintain and reproduce a non-European culture on British soil.

A second aspect of the Act which has been the subject of much concern is the provisions for religious education. Clause 6 repeatedly stresses the requirement to have collective worship *on the school premises* and Clause 7 (1 and 2) points out that

in the case of a county school the collective worship required in the school by section 6 of this Act *shall be wholly or mainly of a broadly Christian character.*

. . . collective worship is of a broadly Christian character if it reflects the broad traditions of Christian belief without being distinctive of any particular Christian denomination.

(Education Reform Act, 1988, p. 5; emphasis added)

The Act further stresses that religious teaching

> shall reflect the fact that the religious traditions in Great Britain are in the main Christian whilst taking account of the teaching and practices of the other principal religions represented in Great Britain.
>
> (Education Reform Act, 1988, p. 6)

One reading of the reassertion of Christian religious teaching and the establishment of a national curriculum with its core and foundation subjects would suggest, then, a desire to strengthen a nationalist perspective of Britain. But the particular perception of Britain that is expressed threatens to push non-Christians to the periphery of the national community. In addition, the degree of centralization introduced by the Act undermines the traditional local control of education in the country which could, if imaginatively managed, provide a space for slight variations from the general norm.

Nonetheless, the reform has the merit of establishing a common basis for all to be exposed to the same subjects or the same schooling. This, surely, must be beneficial to the welfare of all groups in Britain. Additionally, if this provides the base from which educational performance may be better compared, then perhaps the Act will establish a basis for a more objective assessment of the role of the school in a rapidly changing society such as post-imperial Britain.

The strong opposition to aspects of the *national* curriculum suggests, however, that the government's understanding of society may be confined to the *ethnic* perception of Britain as being homogeneous in matters spiritual, moral and cultural – homogeneity understood exclusively as the community of the majority population. Naturally, such an ethnic nationalism stimulates, in turn, an ethnic response within minority communities. There is, of course, an assumption in the Act that there is a *common* notion of society shared by all. But the insult that some Moslems felt they have been forced to suffer and the resultant furore since 1988 over Salman Rushdie's book, *The Satanic Verses*, amounts to a suggestion that society in Britain means very different things to groups of people who occupy these Islands. I do not mean to suggest, as various organs of the media do, that the Affair has merely divided Moslems and the native population; some in the majority white population support the Moslem call for the law of blasphemy to apply to all religions and not simply to the teachings of the Church of England. Equally, there are Moslems and spokespersons from other ethnic minorities who have argued against such a retrogressive step. Others have, sensibly, suggested that state and religion should be entirely separated so that questions of this kind do not arise at all. Undoubtedly, the Affair has had a catalytic effect on a wide range of opinions *within* Moslem and non-Moslem groups in the country. And the series of protests over the publication of the book, its public burning by fanatical adherents to the faith, the late Ayatollah Khomeini's *fatwa*, and so on, have shaken many in Britain and stimulated them to re-examine secular and religious certainties. But little public good will come of this frightening experience if it does not stimulate a national debate around the crucial question of the kind of society post-imperial Britain is to become. For whilst this matter cannot be resolved by debate alone, it is public debate which will provide a basis for an eventual resolution. It cannot be expected, however, that both religious fanaticism and the intolerance it breeds as well as the toleration of liberalism can be equally satisfied (see, for example, Commission for Racial Equality, 1990).

Moreover, it must be noted that the policy of 'opting out', which introduces a *seemingly* democratic principle into educational choice, is a fundamental paradox in the Act. The 'freedom' of parents to 'opt out' of local government control whilst receiving state financial support undermines the nationalist pretensions of the Act. This reading of the Act can be denied only if it is maintained that the nationalist perspective which informs it is of an ethnic kind, that is, it is national only in the sense that it reasserts the nationalism of the majority ethnic, indigenous population. After all, ethnic nationalism seems so to delimit the membership of the national community that several groups in the country which may have formal British nationality and citizenship rights are regarded as illegitimate to the body social – though not the body politic.

The communal option, which both cultural-conservatism and the new pluralism justify, raises a number of questions, a few of which may be mentioned briefly here. First, there is the problem of increasing marginalization of the two major ethnic minorities without homelands in this country. This is being achieved through a variety of ways, but chiefly through the development of ethnic awareness. This ethnicity is based on perceived differences – such as racial, cultural and religious differences – which are redefining group identities. For example, as noted earlier, the West Indian is depicted as solely African whilst the *East Indian* person from the Caribbean is steadily but surely being transformed into an *Asian* so as to fit into a colonial category which is wholly alien to the Caribbean experience. West Indians of other backgrounds – Chinese, European, Arab, Indian – disappear entirely from view. If Chinese from Hong Kong were to settle in Britain in sufficiently sizeable numbers, individuals of Chinese descent from the Caribbean would, probably, be forced to assume a new identity which would deny their own experiences. More worrying is the fact that the only person who is perceived to be legitimately British is still only a person from the white majority population. When, therefore, leading politicians speak of 'the British people' it is difficult not to believe that they have in mind only the majority with historic homelands in Britain and Ireland. As noted earlier, Acts of parliament relating to a person's nationality make this understanding of who constitutes the *British people* abundantly clear to all despite the fact that there are some black soldiers in Ireland, and others fought in the Falklands/Malvinas. This official exclusion of Britain's non-white minorities from the general picture of the national community will continue to have several implications. These are likely to include an increased and prolonged attachment to the politics of the 'homeland'.

For those who can recall the threat of nazi Germany to the security of Europe and the world, the caution necessary when we seek to define ourselves in terms of our *differences* must be obvious. But the generation for whom this threat was very real indeed is passing away, and it seems to be becoming both *reasonable* and respectable, therefore, for us to think again in racial or ethnic categories. Class and *human* perspectives, in the main, receive less consideration. The new ethnicity underplays the *similarities* between groups of people. It must be assumed then that men and women in Britain today are superbly confident about the strength of the liberal ethos simultaneously to take the strain of heightened ethnic differentiation whilst groups and individuals freely take from a supposedly cohesive social entity we call society.

The encouragement for ethnic groups to embrace the communal option must appear, therefore, as part and parcel of the commitment to a future in which the non-white minorities have no place, or if they are to have a place this must be outside of the mainstream of social and political life enjoyed by the majority population. In this context, it is difficult to avoid the conclusion that there are those groups of leaders – not exclusively political – who would wish to see the communal model, as developed, for example, in East Africa under the empire, emerge in Britain. That model entailed that each so-called racial group should live apart, attend separate schools, belong to separate social and sporting clubs, participate in different areas of the economy and so forth. In short, the model demanded that the different groups of people in Britain enjoy only a *market relationship*: people of African, Asian and European backgrounds increasingly meet only where they buy and sell commodities.

I have argued that West Indians in Britain offend because, springing from a heritage which maintains ethnicity as a non-political resource, they unwittingly disturb the applecart of communalists. Where they *protest* this is converted by the media and many well-intentioned academics into *confrontation*, denoting a predisposition to disorder. It may also be suggested that the attempt to encourage some Asian and even West Indian groups to see themselves as utterly different from either the majority population or the other minorities is far from innocent. Not merely is it an attempt, wittingly or unwittingly, to recreate the imperial model of divide and rule, but it may be also an attempt further to marginalize these segments of the population. Developments since 1962 have shown that as Britain adjusts to her post-imperial condition her statesmen and women – decent folks all – have demonstrated an often alarming willingness to define more and more narrowly the status of being *British* in ethnic terms. And this ethnicity is determined largely by 'race' or colour, although cultural and territorial considerations are sometimes advanced in defence of a white Britain.

These comments lead to a second danger to the development of a fair society in Britain in which one individual treats another, and may expect to be treated by others, as first and foremost a person who shares common values, rights and responsibilities irrespective of the individual's colour or race. The negative demand that every non-white person in the country should have an ethnic stamp which silently, but effectively, denotes social status, may create the conditions for unhealthy competition and conflict. These would not only be, on the one hand, between the majority white population and the minorities but also, on the other hand, competition and conflict between the minorities themselves. As matters stand, at the highest level of political life there is a noticeable absence of a will to remove the question of non-white settlement and consolidation from the arena of politics. This may be unavoidable. But what is necessary is a national consensus over the rules of the game so that debates can be conducted in a non-racial manner. In this way at least people whose lives are involved would feel that they do not need to utilize the imperial model of *racial competition* between the disadvantaged themselves, and the majority population would not feel threatened by the presence of non-whites.

Third, the adoption of the communal option necessarily leads to an unhealthy situation for the country as a whole. This is not because *communalism* of itself is necessarily a good or a bad thing; it may be quite neutral. But the situation in which it could exist in Britain would most likely be one of discrimination based on racial consideration with respect to reward, punishment, and participation, as so many social indicators (for example housing, employment, criminal prosecution) already point. It is most unlikely that a series of mutually exclusive communities with little more than a vulgar market relationship between them would live together in peace and tranquillity. The economy and the political domain would remain a united force and competition would take place in these areas. With competition would come conflicts and even where some aspects may not necessarily be racially determined they would frequently be so interpreted.

Conclusion

These developments suggest, moreover, that diasporic relations will, for the foreseeable future, remain strong for Britain's non-white ethnic minorities. Separated from the main body of the national community, non-white minorities are likely to want to maintain close links with their historic homelands in the Asian subcontinent and the Caribbean. These may prove to be valuable links for Britain. Diasporic relations could, however, also be maintained in a largely negative way: minorities might continue, or come to see their security in Britain as depending on the links with states in Asia and the Caribbean. It may be suggested that this option holds out the likely prospect of political developments in the post-colonial world having an effect on politics in this country, as is the case between Britain and the militant Islamic states in the Middle East.

9

Conclusion: the need for a new national consciousness

In these concluding remarks I want briefly to consider some of the main dangers of this phenomenon, which I have called the *communal* response, to the challenge of community in post-imperial Britain. This communal response, moreover, is not contradictory to the position of either the exclusivism of the cultural-conservative persuasion nor to the patronizing liberal establishment, which upholds a dubious, because muddled, sense of justice through pluralism. Many groups and individuals, who see themselves as being committed to a progressive agenda, also support the communal response to the challenge of a national community. The first group pays too much attention to a narrow nationalism whilst the second often tries to avoid the question of nationalism altogether but, implicitly, supports or gives credence to the communal option through its own endorsement of the new pluralism. It is pertinent, therefore, to organize these final comments around the dangers these responses present as obstacles to the emergence of a fair and just national British community.

The new pluralism and post-imperial Britain

One fascinating fact about the communal option in Britain is that it has an appeal for the exclusivist conservative-culturalists as well as for the new pluralists. At least, the communal option does not contradict the views of either the new pluralists or the little Englanders. Whilst the intentions, hopes and arguments of those who hold these positions differ significantly, their visions of post-imperial Britain tends to converge on the same point – the suggestion that Britain is best served by adopting the communal mode of development. Replicating the tripartite world of colonial East Africa, the communal mode of development divides modern Britain into *white*, *black* (or Afro-Caribbean) and *Asian*. These and similar categories are now to be found on a wide range of application forms for jobs and the forthcoming national population census. Indeed, it is now obligatory to tick one of the boxes denoting a dubious ethnicity on many application forms. In other words, Britain is experiencing a sharp and sometimes frightening leap from an apparently benign colour-blindness to a hastily thought out bureaucratic recognition of differences. Whilst cultural-conservatives would refuse to see discrimination in so-called colour-blindness, the new pluralists would argue that the development of recognized categories, along with the now common statement by employers that they are 'an equal opportunity employer', is the way for overcoming discrimination.

There can be little doubt that very many in the majority white population in Britain would reject the exclusivism of cultural-conservatism and would be in favour, to one degree or another, of the new pluralism. This may be partly due to the grudging assimilationist perspective implied by some variants of cultural-conservatism whilst the new pluralism clearly rejects assimilation as the correct way to proceed. Whatever may be the case, it seems important here to point to some of the drawbacks in the more influential of these two general approaches, the new pluralism.

First, the new pluralism appears to assume that *social* pluralism is avoidable in a *culturally* plural Britain. In other words, it would seem safe to assume that where cultural pluralism is the norm, groups divided by their different, individual cultures will also form social groups to coincide with their cultural identities. It is not a question of ignoring or belittling cultural diversity. The point is simply that the new pluralism takes us up a blind alley, because it tends to undermine – quite unwittingly – the demands or struggles for *equal* treatment in the housing, employment and other markets. What the call for cultural maintenance by each ethnic group may logically entail is 'separate but equal' treatment. This kind of demand or preference is usually advanced by dominant groups in order to safeguard their already secure position. It is common knowledge that public policies emanating from such a public ethic resulted in massive injustice against African-Americans and today its remnants in the apartheid system in South Africa is about to be abandoned.

The assumption that social pluralism is not a natural consequence of cultural pluralism is consistent with other confusions in the new pluralism. There are, of course, several and I do not propose to treat them all. For example, the very use of the vocabulary drawn from discussions over theories of social and cultural as well as political pluralism, is confusing enough. Moreover, there is the confusion between the *description* attempted by theorists of social and cultural pluralism, and the *prescriptive* deployment of these concepts in the new pluralism. I want, however, to consider a little more closely two other confusions in the new pluralism.

The first of these is between the demand for social justice and the quite separate demand for cultural preservation. However justified the latter may be, it is not helpful to confuse it in the British context with the more general and necessarily continuous demand for social justice. There are plenty of examples of issues pertaining to preservation of culture pushing aside more important questions of social justice. The *Swann Report*, however, has been the perfect illustration of this. The Committee stated that its raison d'être was the concern expressed by West Indian parents over the poor performance of their children in school (Swann, 1985, p. vii; Rampton, 1981, p. 1). Whilst the Committee investigated this matter, much of the discussion it conducted or invited turned on the cultures of minorities, and perhaps the most interesting aspects of the report and its recommendations were to do with minority cultures and their preservation through the school system. Through protest over Salman Rushdie's *Satanic Verses*, the education of girls, the promotion of Moslem education, and so on, proponents of several cultural issues have come to use much the same vocabularies as those used to express demands for equality and justice in specific areas of British life. The central plank, therefore, of the new pluralism's platform is cultural preservation and assertion rather than the demand for equality and justice.

A second confusion has to do with the individual and the group. The new pluralism champions group rights but defends these with arguments traditionally advanced in defence of the individual. The group, therefore, takes on an individuality or individual personality in the new pluralism. This is unlike the earlier British pluralists, who assumed that individuals are free agents but need to realize themselves in group participation. The new pluralism is also unlike the American pluralist tradition in which the individual is perceived as the basic unit of the corporate group. In both these pluralist traditions the individual of liberal political and social philosophy may belong to any number of groups simultaneously and membership of these different groups is presumed to help him or her to be both part of specific communities as well as a citizen of a wider, more general national community. In contrast, the new pluralism appears to have no place for the individual. In the 1960s and 1970s, liberal social and political philosophy was rightly criticized for promoting the individual's rights to a point that those of the group appeared non-existent. It now seems that the new pluralism is determined to commit the opposite crime. The paradox is that the justifications proffered are drawn from the traditional liberal (individualist) defence – freedom of speech, assembly, publication, freedom before the law, representation, and so on. If therefore the new pluralism is to be taken seriously it desperately needs to develop a theory of group rights appropriate to contemporary conditions.

Finally, the new pluralism preaches difference and diversity to the extent that any notion of commonality tends to disappear from view. In this respect, there seems to be two flawed assumptions contained in the new pluralism. It is assumed that the social aggregate of the separate ethnic groups amounts to the whole and this whole is, or will, constitute the full expression of British society. The new pluralism further assumes that it is possible for groups to live peacefully together without having anything in common, apart from sharing the same territory and the simplest of exchange relations regulated solely by the market. The first of these assumptions is faulty because it is a truism that the aggregate is more than the individual parts; in this respect it seems not to matter whether these parts are strictly individuals or groups of individuals. The flaw in the second assumption is that the kind of social peace obtained in conditions where society is organized according to group *differences* usually requires some rather drastic preconditions.

One of these is an absence of democratic participation as it has developed historically and a high incidence of political instability. This instability perhaps begins with the need for a modicum of central regulation of peaceful relations (if only market ones) between groups or between individuals sharing the same territory. The states which have come closest in modern times to fulfilling this task in such conditions have been the colonial and the apartheid states. In the past imperial or feudal authorities established peaceful orders among varied groups occupying the same territory, but in these circumstances there was no notion that these groups constituted a national community; moreover, the relations of the market were relatively simple. In the modern world, however, where there is little or no sharing of what some theorists of social and cultural pluralism call 'compulsory institutions', such as customs, family, schooling, language, religion and so forth, if for any reason the state is weak, then there is likely to be political and social instability as one group or another vies for control of the instruments of state. Whenever any one group is successful in holding onto power, the state invariably becomes authoritarian. At best the end result is a cycle or rotation of authoritarian state, civil war, political atrophy or weak state, followed by a return to the *status quo ante*, and the recommencement of much the same cycle.

Institutionalized pluralism is often one way of trying to overcome the inherent problems in a country where there is little or nothing holding diverse groups together. This might involve enshrining in the law of the land certain constitutional rights pertaining to territory, historic sites, the use of language, religious freedom, and so on. The countries in which this device has been found to be necessary rarely enjoy social peace and tranquillity, because there needs be just one slight deviation from the letter of the law for conflict, which seems to be always lurking under the surface, to erupt and become contagious between members of different groups.

The witting or unwitting disappearance of commonality from the agenda of the new pluralists is, therefore, not a trivial matter. The response to this criticism is normally that British society has always been divided into ethnic groups. Again, both the new pluralists and the cultural-conservatives would find agreement here: British society has been made up of many and varied groups. The latter would argue, however, that because these groups were all of European stock their entry and settlement have been easily accomplished. On the other hand, the new pluralists would argue that whilst this was undoubtedly so, there is now a need for Britain to extend its traditional liberalism to embrace non-white, non-European minorities as they, ostensibly, are. What tends to be muted in both these positions is a recognition of the fact that entry and settlement for all groups have been fraught with difficulties and sometimes open and violent conflict. During the course of such conflict, as well as many others which were completely independent of ethnic considerations (such as class, regional or democratic interests), Britain developed a civic culture which has contributed massively to notions such as the rule of law, parliamentary sovereignty, individual freedom, and certain common assumptions about individual freedom and group tolerance in a wider social collectivity. There are, of course, many drawbacks in both the statement and the practice of these commonalities; they nonetheless constitute the basic essentials from which post-imperial Britain can strive to build a more fair society.

Beyond communalism and the new pluralism

As Britain enters the last decade of the present century, it is obvious that the question of how to redefine her national community will be fairly high on the agenda of public debate. Such a discussion will need to be informed by a concern to build a humane national community to which all groups can feel that they legitimately contribute and therefore belong. As I have suggested throughout this discussion, it can hardly be said that there is at present a broadly based or broadly defined national community which envelops all. There are, in other words, more people living in, and contributing to, Britain than there are people recognized to be part of the British national community. A starting point in the rectification of this situation must be for the state to *resume* its historical responsibilities. After all, much of these responsibilities have been denied or abandoned over the past several decades, but particularly during the 1980s. Additionally, as a minimum all groups need to take the following factors into account.

First, there is need for political space for the question of the status of non-whites to be resolved without injustice being committed against either the majority or the minority populations. Each group needs to feel that it is secure. In this respect the majority population is already secure in its certainty of demographic, economic, social and political power. It must, however, feel confident that its own cherished traditions and culture are not seriously threatened. Only where aspects of these threaten the well-being of all – for example, racial attitudes, abuse and discrimination – should public policy be expected to prescribe change and prohibit certain kinds of behaviour. These must, of course, apply not only to the majority indigenous population, but also to individuals and groups from minorities.

Second, we have to be willing to admit that we are none of us immune to negative racial attitudes which may influence our behaviour. This is rarely admitted in Britain because racial injustice has been perceived almost entirely in terms of majority/minorities relationships and a convenient simplicity that only whites practice racism has become commonplace. The concentration on the relationship between majority and minority is perfectly understandable because of the power relationship involved in most encounters between these groups. Moreover, the behaviour of the majority population in a democracy is bound to have profound effects on all. What the majority does or does not do may affect, adversely or favourably, the minorities. But there are also majority/minority relationships which may be informed by negative racial attitudes and discriminatory behaviour. They perhaps do not yet affect significantly the life chances of individuals in the minority populations. But it must be remembered that Britain's non-white minorities have met before. And the earlier meetings were in situations in which *differences* were frequently exploited by those who controlled socio-economic and political power over both groups. One of the challenges for the immediate future is whether the minorities themselves can overcome their differences so that these are used to enrich a life in Britain rather than to gain relative advantages, based on cultural and racial differences, over each other.

Third, in this regard the majority white population still has the opportunity to play an important *conduit* role vis-à-vis the minorities. In addition to historical factors, this opportunity places a new responsibility on the majority population. As the demographic, cultural and social majority, it has not discharged its responsibility particularly well, not so much because of the actions of the majority white population as such, but because of the attitudes and inactivity of political and social leaders. For example, the ignorance cultivated during the imperial age in the mass of the British population needs to be corrected and this should be a task addressed by a variety of institutions, such as schools, churches and political parties, not simply ineffectual adjunct committees in Town Halls. With respect to schooling the two very important opportunities were missed in the 1980s by the *Swann Report* and the Education Reform Act. The former compounded, and the latter simply ignored, the question of how a new national community may be encouraged.

The moral authority which should have been derived from the commendable prosecution of this responsibility has been partly lost by the majority. It is, therefore, understandable why specific visible minorities have found it necessary to put much of their energy into supporting struggles taking place in their past homelands instead of engaging themselves fully in the effort to build a better Britain. A curious situation may develop whereby groups of people engage themselves in the economic or *market* life of the country but their main political, moral and spiritual sustenance and involvement remain with the past homeland. This is a loss for all in Britain. A responsibility, therefore, is placed upon minorities themselves to ensure that this scenario does not become the norm. Too complete a commitment to the politics of the past homeland may seriously limit the extent to which a minority group can contribute to the future development of its new home.

The encouragement being given by the new pluralism to non-white minority groups to adopt the *communal option* may therefore be seen, first, as the preliminary step in a new strategy of 'divide and rule' on the part of the state and, second, as a kind of self-imposed system of apartheid by members within the minority groups who accept this option. Both these methods of rule are today responsible for many of the tragic conflicts between peoples in post-colonial societies. Fortunately, this course of development for mainland Britain can still be reversed.

This can be done through a variety of ways. First, every encouragement ought to be given to those in the majority white population who have demonstrated a willingness to adopt a non-communal approach to public affairs. For example, the election of four non-white MPs – Diane Abbot, Paul Boateng, Bernie Grant and Keith Vaz – on a party ticket, rather than simply according to the colour of the candidates' skin, is a demonstration of a desire on the part of a significant number in the majority white electorate to steer clear of the communal option. A serious attempt to pursue this course would, however, entail redefining, for example, the freedom of the irresponsible elements of the media, particularly the unrepresentative press, from exploiting racial *differences* for commercial gain. It is already well established, of course, that non-white voters do not vote according to the colour of candidates but according to parties. Long before there were non-white candidates voters from these communities have been supporting parties of their choice. Another example would be this: where in specific cases it may be necessary to give preference to non-whites, such treatment should be of a temporary nature and should have the specific objective of correcting immediate past and/or prevailing injustices. A fact that is lost in race relations discussions in Britain is that many individuals from minority groups, as well as some groups, wish to see an end to racial injustices, not the setting up of new peculiar institutions which may lead to the entrenchment of injustices of one kind or another.

Finally, both the majority white population and ethnic minorities must be willing to shed aspects of cultural practices which may be unacceptable to most reasonable men and women. Of course, this is highly problematic. For example, as soon as one group hears an outsider describing any of the group's unacceptable practices as undesirable, the group will wish to defend it as a vital part of its culture. Additionally, it is an open question as to what may be described as 'reasonable'. In the past, theorists and societies have grappled towards making a distinction between the *public* and *private* aspects of social life (M. G. Smith, 1974; Rex, 1986), but this is not possible in an increasingly mixed and complex society as Britain. Rooted within a broad Judaeo-Christian heritage British culture is now largely secular. Public concerns such as law and order in a secular society may interfere with a religious practice such as the Sikh's carrying of the *kirpan*, or the Rastafarian insistence that the use of marijuana is part of his religious devotion, or the Moslem's feeling that the burning of a book which is offensive to his faith is justified. The Moslem and Jewish method of killing animals may offend many who have come to see the care of animals as being part of a broadly defined humanism. The subjugation of women in some cultures (notably in Islam) may offend many men and women who have emerged from the Pauline Christian intolerance to embrace the humane equality of the sexes.

Clearly, however, a society cannot simultaneously embrace all these fundamentally antagonistic approaches without there being some major convulsions and disruptions. And, similarly, there can be no lasting imposed solution. What is obviously required is a *will*, a *disposition*, on the part of most, if not all groups to participate – not as groups but as individuals – in the construction of a common national community which will be able to accommodate, or tolerate, what is considered desirable and good, and abandon what may be dangerous and unwholesome, from both the majority and the minority populations in contemporary Britain. But whilst such a resolution necessitates political initiative and eventually political decision, the necessary work linking initiative and outcome is largely of a moral and broadly social nature.

Such work necessitates the vision of a Britain which is able to reject the communal option. Fortunately, much of the social cornerstones necessary to build the steps or the pillars of a truly all-embracing national community are already in evidence. The encouraging economic performance of some Asian businesses, the distinctive cuisine, music, dress, religious fervour, increasingly critical literary output and so forth are so many important factors which point to a willingness to contribute to a greater whole by groups and individuals with an Asian past who have made Britain their home. The communalism and exclusivism of both minority and majority groups will distort, if not arrest, these developments. The contributions of people from the West Indies/ Caribbean in the varied areas of music, literature, sports and so on point even more directly in the same direction, due to the closer proximity of their culture to that of the majority indigenous population. The existence of country-wide institutions, such as schools and higher institutions of learning, hospitals, social clubs, political parties, unions and so forth, organized ostensibly along non-racial lines means that some of the essential zones of confluence for individuals from all backgrounds exist. It is not, of course, enough that these exist.

They have to be galvanized into becoming active agencies for the construction of a new kind of national community. Herein lies the space for the kind of contribution the indigenous population will need to make to the construction of a new national community. The contribution of the majority indigenous population will, necessarily, be of greater significance than those of others. After all, the traveller or recent settler should be much more able to shed aspects of his or her culture than the indigenous population. Inherent within the experience of travel and new settlement is normally a willingness to change. Whilst the challenge for the social synergism of which I am speaking here is likely to come from non-white minorities, it will be largely the willingness within the majority population to abandon its own communal response to new settlers which will determine success or failure. A national project of this kind would direct our attention and energy towards the construction of an appropriate post-imperial Britishness in which difference is merely *secondary*.

Conclusion

If leadership to this end is not forthcoming, then it will be understandable if various groups continue to push themselves and each other towards that point beyond which there is no common ground for understanding. The West Indian might succumb to the lore of the communal option with its promise of immediate payoffs. Equally, it is perfectly understandable if Asians believe that their long-term security lies in their community's traditional ability to reproduce its culture, which was a necessity for survival under the extreme conditions of colonialism. Well-intentioned individuals and groups within the majority white community may also believe that they act in good faith when they do their level best to encourage ethnicity as the primary basis of social and political action. These trends, however, amount to a kind of benign practice of what used to be called 'separate but equal development'. This is a *retrogressive*, not a *progressive* step. Such development can only bode ill for all, because the conditions will then have been fully laid for Enoch Powell's prophecies of doom to be fulfilled. This is the most likely result of the *communal option* proffered by both cultural-conservatism and the new pluralists, if we accept it as the guiding principle in the effort to create a new identity for post-imperial Britain. If we share nothing else, we most certainly all share a common responsibility to minimize pain and widespread disaster.

If we can agree on this basic utilitarian principle, then we also share a common responsibility to avoid the precipice of communalism towards which we are nearly all too confidently marching with bright banners proclaiming our cultural differences as if these are indeed the immutable essence of being.

Notes

1 Introduction

1 Consider, for example, the debate over schooling and multi-culturalism which followed the publication in May 1988 of the Macdonald Report on racism in schools in Manchester. The enquiry was occasioned by the killing of a thirteen year old Asian boy by a white pupil at Burnage High School, but the debate in the media turned on the value of anti-racist education in British schools. This was perhaps the fitting moment for a critical and sober assessment of the philosophy and practice of multi-culturalism and anti-racist strategies but instead the public's attention was directed towards seeing these in terms of clear-cut good and bad policies – more frequently the latter (see, for an exception to this treatment of the issues, *The Independent*, 19 May 1988, p. 23).

2 It is increasingly difficult to speak about these groups in Britain – groups from Afro-Caribbean or Asian backgrounds – as black people (see, for example, Goulbourne, 1990).

3 Indeed, when in early 1986 I first expressed these concerns I could not help feeling that I was raising irrelevant questions and that I ought really to be tackling issues such as class. Events of the last years of the 1980s and the opening years of the 1990s, however, have made questions of race and nationalism in Britain something of a current vogue amongst hitherto sceptical academics.

4 This has been true, to one degree or another, of other European states such as France, the Netherlands and Belgium, which had colonial territories outside Europe (see, for example, Cross and Entzinger, 1988).

5 Of course, this is not unique to Britain; for example, in Japan, this ethnic definition of nationhood is even more narrowly drawn. The native population, the Ainus, and people of Korean descent in the country, are not generally regarded as members of the Japanese national community.

6 Originally I had hoped to include the Scottish Nationalist Party and Plaid Cymru in this analysis of nationalism in Britain. I am still interested in knowing how these organizations, which represent minorities with historic homelands in Britain, treat the question of non-white minorities that have settled in Scotland and Wales. I also wanted to compare the similarities and dissimilarities of the nationalism of groups with homelands in Britain and groups that have homelands in the former empire. But these aspects of the general question are not pursued in this discussion due to constraints of time and space.

2 The general problem

1 The geographer too has a role to play in elucidating the phenomena of nationalism and ethnicity, as Harold Carter argued in his Inaugural Presidential Lecture to the Geographical Society, in January 1988 (*The Independent*, 7 January 1988, p. 6). It is interesting to note also that the demand for the defence of liberalism and rationality which the Rushdie Affair of early 1989 introduced was responded to mainly by literary, rather than by academic, writers.

2 There are, of course, several detailed accounts of bastard feudalism, but one of the most interesting and stimulating treatments of the subject is to be found in Perry Anderson's work (Anderson, 1974).

3 Rex's description of what he calls a 'race relations situation' is one attempt to deal with race relations as a continuing socio-political fact despite the biologists' dismissal of the concept (Rex, 1986, chapter 2).

4 Useful discussions of the problem of definition are contained, for example, in M. Elaine Burgess (1978) as well as Rex (1986 and forthcoming).

5 The definition up to this point owes much to that suggested by C. F. Ware (1953).

6 To 'understand' the causes of Powell's anguish does not mean that one must necessarily sympathize with him or accept what he sees as the remedy.

7 There are, of course, plenty of examples of this drawn from almost every quarter of the Third World, and the work of groups such as Oxfam and other established and spontaneous charities such as those mounted by musicians and comedians in Europe and North America, are doing much to highlight the plight of ordinary men, women and children in the poverty-ridden Third World.

3 The communal option

1 The notion of 'continuous crisis' is, of course, somewhat contradictory because it is not convincing to speak of permanent crisis. The sense I wish to convey by the use of the phrase, however, is that modern men and women appear to be uncertain about the basic principles that should inform contemporary communities.

2 Some of the issues Smith raised in this study are taken up in his more appropriately named work, *The Ethnic Origins of Nations* (1986). I find the earlier of these works to be intellectually more refreshing and stimulating than the later one, although the latter is no doubt meant to be a development of the former. What I have to say, therefore, about Smith's position is based on his earlier attempt to state the ethnic case.

3 Apart from the highly suggestive thesis contained in the very imagery of the title, Anderson's work is unusual insofar as it draws upon both European and non-European experiences to make its case.

4 For example, the love Michael Heseltine expressed for the land of England in his contribution to 'Fanfare on being British' is utterly different from the ethnic nationalism expressed by Norman Tebbit in the name of patriotism in his contribution (Tebbit *et al.*, 1990).

5 Of course, it must be obvious that I do not accept the now proverbial Johnsonian understanding of patriotism: the notion that patriotism is the last refuge of the scoundrel would seem to refer not to patriotism proper but to nationalism.

6 The Afro-Caribbean, African and Asian Labour politicians elected to the House of Commons in 1986 appeared soon after their victories to believe that they represented not only their constituents but also their ethnic groups. In any event there is the expectation that they will each respond to a larger constituency than their electoral one.

7 For much of 1987 a number of Sri Lankans seeking asylum or refugee status in the United Kingdom were kept in this way until fate intervened in the form of a historic gale force wind in October of the same year and they were returned to land after much protest (see Cohen, 1987a).
8 This point is admitted by most commentators and quite forcibly by Kedourie (1985), the most anti-Romantic commentator of all.

4 Traditional and ethnic nationalism

1 Sivanandan's statement (speaking of the use of the word black to describe the struggles of both Caribbean and Asian people in Britain), that ' . . . *black* was a political colour' (Sivanandan, 1983, p. 3, emphasis added) tersely expresses this view.
2 The point has been made by several researchers into Moslem life in Britain that this is a misnomer because Moslem radicals or militants are not concerned essentially with asserting the fundamental correctness of holy writ as are Christian 'fundamentalists'. Rather, Moslem radicals or militants are concerned to assert the relevance of Islam to modern life.

5 From *imperial* British to *national* British

1 Taking the benign view of Powell, he could very well appear as the antiquarian figure, 'false Festus', who is in opposition to the heroes of the new social and political order Macaulay so dramatically portrays in his classic narrative poem, 'Horatio at the Bridge'.
2 Much has already been written about these provisions, particularly by lawyers and groups concerned about the rights of affected individuals and groups (see, for example, Evans, 1983; also Macdonald, 1983).
3 A week later the paper carried a sharp response from the Citizens Advice Bureau to Dr O'Grady's allegation (*The Coventry Citizen*, 7 January 1988, p. 7).
4 The Statute of Westminster never affected Newfoundland. For details of the measure, see O. Hood Phillips (1973), ch. 35.
5 A number of scholars have become interested in this question and are finding rich evidence in the recently released cabinet papers at the Public Records Office, London.
6 This document was prepared by Hinden, Arthur Creech-Jones and Fenner Brockway, with assistance from John Hatch (The Labour Party, *National Executive Committee, 1946–84* (1956), p. 155).
7 And, of course, the central element of this civilization as far as the vast majority of non-Europeans were concerned was British.
8 The *nation* in this context would appear to refer not to all those groups which consider themselves to be British, but only to the indigenous and/or white majority population.
9 Another interpretation may be that it is surprising, as one colleague remarked to me, that it was the Conservatives, and not Labour, who seized on the notion of equality expressed by the caption.
10 Twenty-five years later, Terry Dicks, Tory MP for the constituency went on the warpath describing West Indians as 'bone idle and lazy' as well as 'good-for-nothings who had come across here to sponge and to bring their way of life in the Caribbean to this country' (*The Guardian*, 2 September 1986).

11 This was borne out in a BBC Television special programme on the question in mid June in which the Foreign Secretary, along with an audience deemed typical of the British public and concerned individuals in Hong Kong participated in a discussion of the crisis. Asked whether people from the colony should be allowed into Britain, the audience voted overwhelmingly in favour.

6 Diasporic politics: Sikhs and the demand for Khalistan

1 The authors of this booklet were prominent public men who were attracted to the Sikh cause at the time leadership was passing from Sant Longowal, leader of the Akali Dal, the main Sikh party, to the more militant Sant Jarnail Bhindranwale, in the early 1980s. Bhullar was a retired major-general with experience on the India/China and India/Pakistan borders in the 1960s and 1970s. Gurmej Brar retired from the Indian Administrative Service to join Bhindranwale in 1983. M. S. Sidhu was a university academic.

2 This is an old unit used in India; one crore is equivalent to ten million.

3 Patriotism and nationalism here presumably refer to people's attitudes with respect to the central Indian union, not the state of Punjab.

4 However, it is said that many Hindus answered the census questions in Punjabi because they did not know Hindi at all.

5 A *morcha* is a peaceful mass agitation over public grievances.

6 The carrying of kirpans on international flights is a problem for baptized Sikhs because they are under an injunction to carry these by the Tenth Guru, the saint-warrior, Gorbind Singh. It would appear that the general understanding reached with many international airlines is that a baptized Sikh hands in his kirpan at the point of departure and collects it at the port of destination. Whilst Sikh leaders seem content with this they appear less happy for such a situation to obtain in India because, it is sometimes argued, they are travelling within their own country and should be allowed to practise their religion freely there.

7 Additionally, Sikhs claim that the Hindu Marriage Act of 1955, the Hindu Minority and Guardianship Act, the Hindu Adoption and Maintenance Act and the Hindu Succession Act of 1956, abolished many Sikh practices and replaced them with Hindu ones (Bhullar *et al.*, 1985, p. 8).

8 This view of India is, of course, not borne out by the facts. For a stimulating discussion of this view, see Manor (1988).

9 There is a belief that these men did not in fact kill Mrs Gandhi because there were more bullets found in her body than fired from their guns. One belief is that the bullets from their guns were aimed at her actual assassins, who escaped. Tully and Jacob (1985, p. 10) also point to other inconsistencies in the accounts of the assassination, such as shots found in Mrs Gandhi's back when her alleged assassins shot at her from the front.

10 There was also a great deal of anger expressed both in India and abroad over the refusal of the Indian president to grant a reprieve to those Sikhs found guilty of killing Mrs Gandhi. These men were finally executed in January 1989.

11 The Commonwealth Caribbean may be the notable exception to this. This and related points are, however, discussed in the next chapter.

12 There is a minority Sikh view which holds that the British are still responsible for the Punjab which she annexed in 1849, because at independence in 1947 there was no referendum to secure the consent of the Sikhs over their destiny.

13 The Maharaja's territories extended as far south as Delhi and included much of what

is now the states of Rajasthan, Haryana, Himachal Pradesh and the eastern part of Pakistan. The memory, however, of this period remains a glorious one for the Sikhs.

14 One prominent Sikh leader explained to me that herein lay the paradox of the British legacy in India. Whilst the British tended to leave alone the religion, language and customs of conquered peoples on the sub-continent, they tried to impress on all that they were Indians.

15 The various publications of the Sikh Missionary Society in the United Kingdom, based in Kent, certainly place great stress on this interpretation of the development of Sikhism.

16 *Keshadhari* Sikhs are those who adhere to the Five Ks of the faith. These are *Kesh* (the uncut hair, rather like the Nazarites within ancient Judaism), *Kangha* (a comb), *Kirpan* (a sword/knife), *Kachha* (a pair of shorts) and *Kara* (a steel bangle). *Sahajdhari* Sikhs are those who referred to themselves as the 'slow adopters' because they do not adhere to the Five Ks.

17 Some Sikhs believe that the class interests of Sikh leaders at the time were more important to them than the long-term well-being of the Sikh nation. Many of them had properties throughout India and stood to lose much if they asked for an independent Punjab/Sikhistan.

18 Estimates of Sikhs in Britain vary enormously and a figure as large as 400,000 has been mentioned. It is important to note, however, that ethnic minorities in Britain are enumerated, like the majority population, according to place of birth, and religion does not feature prominently in nation-wide estimates (see, for example, Population Statistics Division, *Population Trends 46*, OPCS, 1986). Regional population studies, however, sometimes include breakdowns according to religion. For example, for the five groups with Asian languages/religions in the city of Leicester (the site of major settlement by East African Asians), the estimated breakdowns in 1983 were as follows: Gujerati-speaking Hindus, 36,100; Punjabi-speaking Sikhs, 9,600; Gujerati-speaking Moslems, 2,900; Urdu-speaking Moslems, 1,200 (Leicester City Council, *Survey of Leicester, 1983: Initial Report of Survey*, 1984). The actual size of the Sikh population in the UK is not, however, of major importance to my argument. It is enough to note that their presence in Britain constitutes one of the largest, if not the largest, community of Sikhs outside India.

19 These were some of the questions asked in a general questionnaire answered by individual devout Sikhs as well as leaders interviewed in 1987.

20 A brotherhood of equal men and women, the *Khalsa* is a band of saint-soldiers, like Guru Gorbind Singh himself, dedicated to peace and the brotherhood of humanity. Initiation into this brotherhood signifies a rejection of the caste system.

21 The government's decision in early 1988 to make this Act a permanent one on the statute books is cause for concern for minorities from South Asia because ministers have sought to defend this move in parliament by reference to acts of terrorism in that region.

22 And part of the evidence against him in an earlier crime was that a 'sliver of glass' was found in his turban similar to pieces found at the shop of Sohan Singh Liddar where he was shot and injured for supporting the government of Rajiv Gandhi (*The Guardian*, 9 May 1987, p. 2). Concerned Sikhs have expressed to me that this was a case in which the police acted upon assumptions about Sikhs which are contrary to Sikh practice: a Sikh, for example, always undoes his turban at the end of the day and shakes it out – cleanliness is a virtue not likely to be overlooked by a practising Sikh. The possibility, therefore, of a sliver of glass being found in a turban some time after the event seemed rather far-fetched in the view of some Sikhs. It was

perhaps for this reason that the Director of Public Prosecutions 'decided not to proceed' in this earlier case against Surai (*The Guardian*, 9 May 1987).

23 A number of writers and researchers are now interested in the background of the treatment given, historically as well as presently, by the authorities to groups in Britain which support militant causes abroad (see Cohen, 1987a).

24 These were the Khalistan Council led, until late 1988, by Dr J. S. Chohan (sometimes spelt Chauhan) and another group led by Dr H. S. Dilgir (sometimes spelt Dilgeer) who, in 1979, had been one of the leaders of the 'revolutionary' Akali Dal.

25 This is the same J. S. Bhullar who wrote with G. S. Singh Brar and M. S. Sidhu, *The Betrayal of the Sikhs* (1985), a text on which I have relied greatly with respect to the grievances of the Sikhs.

26 Throughout his political career Master Tara Singh, a convert from Hinduism to Sikhism, operated within the framework of the union of India of which the Punjab and the Sikhs were permanent and important parts. He was, however, the Sikh leader most aware of the threat of Hinduism to Sikhism during the decades of the 1940s–60s. It is therefore not surprising that Parmar and Chohan make this claim of some kind of connection with the reputedly tough old Master.

27 He is the fourth generation of a family of medical doctors. He received his training at the Punjab University but came to London in 1966 to take a course in preventive medicine at London University.

28 It was said in 1987 by some supporters of Khalistan that the Akali Dal in the United Kingdom refers to itself as the Akali Khalistan in order to indicate its support for the demand for a free Khalistan.

29 The meeting was very open and democratic. Even I, a researcher, was invited to contribute to the questions delegates were discussing or to any related matter.

30 This ceased publication in late 1988 but reappeared in June/July 1989.

31 This statement is to be found in most texts written by militant Sikhs on the Punjab problem.

32 There is, however, a draft 'Constitution of Khalistan', prepared by Dr H. S. Dilgir, the Preamble of which reads:

> Khalistan shall be a nation based upon the ideals of the Sikh Gurus. It shall be a state-less zone of the humanity where everyone shall be sovereign. Everything that is profane shall be alien to this land.
>
> (Constitution of Khalistan, n.d.).

7 Diasporic politics: the demand for democracy in Guyana

1 The term *West Indies* is, of course, a misnomer formulated by Christopher Columbus. During his search for the western route to India he arrived in the Caribbean but mistakenly thought he was in the western part of India. His ignorance is sometimes used to make a useful and necessary point, however, about the continuing widespread ignorance of the region in Britain (*Times Higher Education Supplement*, 18 March 1988, p. 13).

2 Richard Hart, the veteran Jamaican politician, activist and writer, expressed the view that one of the failures of the British in the region was not to have brought the islands of the Eastern Caribbean together when it would have had a chance of succeeding (Interview with Richard Hart, 25 March 1988).

3 Between Jamaica's and Trinidad and Tobago's political independence in 1962 and that of St Kitts-Nevis in 1983, eleven others also became independent from the

United Kingdom. These included Barbados and Guyana in 1966, Bahamas in 1966, Grenada in 1974, Dominica in 1978, St Lucia and St Vincent in 1979, Antigua, and Belize and Bermuda in 1981. There are, of course, also the Turks and Caicos islands which enjoy internal autonomy but whose foreign and defence needs are seen to by Britain.

4 This is well illustrated by the national motto of Trinidad and Tobago – *Together We Aspire, Together We Achieve*, or that of Jamaica – *Out of Many, One People*.

5 Creole society in the Caribbean may be a crude glimpse or pointer to what a higher humanity may be like. This must seem like a very large claim for societies which today appear to be remote and almost irrelevant to the main thrust or direction of British society. But a society is not composed exclusively of the artifacts of the present, of the impatient men and women of the moment demanding answers to the problems of the here and now. There can be few societies today which should be able to appreciate this more than British society due to the tremendous responsibility she bears for much of both the good and the bad in the heritage she bequeathed societies which are today preoccupied with the overwhelming non-Prufrockian question of what course of social development to follow.

6 A valuable collection marred by a deplorable Introduction by the editor.

7 The following account of the situation was related to me by a person who was a senior officer of the University of Dar es Salaam at the time of Rodney's return to Tanzania, after his banishment from Jamaica. When Rodney arrived at the Dar es Salaam airport, he was barred from entry into the country. The immigration officers could not explain why this was necessary. But they allowed Rodney to make a telephone call to the University where he had previously taught and where his family was already in residence. Fortunately, the university official, a Pan-Africanist of the old school, was available and was able to convince senior government officers that Rodney was a 'true son of Africa' who, through his writings, was helping to enlighten the African people.

8 This was one of the main points in Thomas' brilliant *Walter Rodney Memorial Lecture*, 9 May 1988, University of Warwick.

9 The power relations of the world had changed and Britain recognized this. But faithful colonial enclave as the Anglophone Caribbean was, it did not quite understand this. Thus, as Munroe argues, Jamaican nationalists were slow in formulating a policy for British withdrawal and were divided over the desirability of such a withdrawal (Munroe, 1972, chs. 2 and 3).

10 For example, homes without baths or indoor toilets, many families sharing the same house, working men and women renting rather than owning their homes and so on.

11 The interest of the Metropolitan Police in what they called, in 1988, the *yardies* in parts of the London Jamaican community, may be a case in point (see, for example, *The Independent*, 7 January 1988, p. 5).

12 As one prominent and active Grenadian explained to me in 1985, after the 1979 New Jewel Revolution the dissidents who found Grenada unacceptable went to the USA; after the US invasion of the island in 1983, some who felt completely opposed to the American-supported regime came to the United Kingdom.

13 The information section of the High Commission issued a January–April 1988 issue, in May 1988. It is a useful bulletin of news items from 'back home' as well as of events taking place in the UK.

14 In 1987 this was Calvin Trotman whom it has proved difficult to contact for an interview.

15 *Guyana Voice* is the 'Journal of the People's Progressive party (United Kingdom

Branch)'; some issues, like this one, carry only the volume and number. It is generally easy to tell the year, however, from the entries. I therefore presume that the year of this issue was 1984.

16 Indeed, in the early 1980s the PNC government alerted Guyanese to a possible plot to invade the country by a group of Guyanese living in the USA.

17 Someone has quipped that Guyana has had the unfortunate history of always having been *BG* (what it used to be called before independence): *British Guiana*, *Bookers' Guiana* (after the well-known British company which owned much of the country before nationalization of sugar) and during the past decades, *Burnham's Guyana*.

18 The WPA internal discussion paper from which this quotation is taken does not have a date or an author. From its contents, however, it would appear to be a paper written sometime in 1984/5.

19 For example, parties such as the WPA and the PNP are members of the Socialist International (SI) based in Europe, whilst right-wing leaders such as the Jamaica Labour Party's Edward Seaga and Eugenia Charles of Dominica are closer to the USA's Republican Party. The PPP, and other communist parties of the region such as the Workers' Party of Jamaica (WPJ) of Dr Trevor Munroe, are close to the communist parties in both Europe and the USA. Whereas, however, the communist parties in Europe are important political forces – although far from the Caribbean – the Communist Party of the USA is merely a *fringe* party.

20 For example, to the right of the PPP and the PNC on the political spectrum, the United Force, and to the centre-right of either, the Vanguard for Liberation and Democracy led from its formation out of three smaller groups in 1979 for much of the 1980s by Dr Ganraj Kumar.

21 John Stuart Mill, for example, lost his Westminster seat in the mid 1860s because he championed the cause of those who rebelled at Morant Bay in Jamaica in 1865.

22 This decision by a government headed by the outstanding academic who had written the seminal *Capitalism and Slavery*, must have surprised Jagan more than he lets on here because if Jagan and Guyana were the examples of radicalism in the region, Williams' public persona in Trinidad was the region's example of the intellectual in politics.

23 This is the title of Burnham's book (Burnham, 1970).

24 This, of course, is the problem of the Fijian indigenous folks today. And it is this contradiction between majoritarian-type democracy and ethnic/minority rights which led them to seize state power and thereby 'offend' the British crown which they so deeply respect.

25 One of the prominent men who resigned during this period was Lionel Jeffrey who has since settled in London.

26 Dr Shahabbuddeen was elected to a seat at the World Court of Justice at the Hague in mid 1988.

8 Nationalism and the new pluralism in Britain

1 This is if we take the English and American Revolutions rather than the more dramatic French Revolution as the starting points of nationalist revolutions.

2 The Labour party's policies in the late 1980s and the beginning of the 1990s to establish a number of regional assemblies in England and Wales and to increase Scotland's autonomy do not amount to independence but, if implemented, will extend democratic participation in the country.

3 It is also a commonplace today for many radicals to assert that every social activity
   and forms of personal behaviour are politics. This perception of politics robs it of
   any meaning and is therefore quite incomprehensible.
4 The relationship between academic and intellectual labour and the primary world of
   social and political action could be illuminated by a close study of how this
   vocabulary has come to be part of what may be termed *popular* political and sociological discourses.

Bibliography

Acton, Lord, (1862) 1907. 'Nationality', *History and Freedom and Other Essays*, J. M. Figgis and R. V. Laurence (eds), London: Macmillan & Co. Ltd.

Agassi, J. 1984. 'Nationalism and the Philosophy of Zionism', *Inquiry*, 27.

Ali, Ahmed, 1982. 'Fiji: The Politics of a Plural Society', Crocombe, R. and Ali, Ahmed (eds), *Politics in Melanesia*, Institute of Pacific Studies of the University of the South Pacific.

Ali, Arif (ed.), 1988. *Third World Impact, Eighth Edition*, London: Hansib Publications.

Ali, Yasmin, 1989. 'Why I'm Outraged', *New Statesman and Society*, 17 March, pp. 16–17.

Alibhai, Yasmin, 1989. 'Satanic Betrayals', *New Statesman and Society*, 24 February, p. 12.

Almond, G. C. and Coleman, J. S. (eds), 1960. *The Politics of the Developing Areas*, Princeton University Press.

Almond G. C. and Powell, G. B. 1966. *Comparative Politics. A Developmental Approach*, Boston and Toronto: Little, Brown & Co. Ltd.

Alpers, E. A. and Fontaine, P.-M. (eds), 1982. *Walter Rodney Revolutionary and Scholar: A Tribute*, Los Angeles: Center for Afro-American Studies and African Studies Center, University of California.

Althusser, Louis, 1971. *Lenin and Philosophy and Other Essays*, London: New Left Review Editions.

Amin, Samir, 1976. *Unequal Development: An Essay on the Social Formations of Peripheral Capitalism*, translated by Brian Pearce, Sussex: The Harvester Press.

Anderson, B. 1983. *Imagined Communities: Reflections on the Origins and Spread of Nationalism*, London: Verso and New Left Books.

Anderson, Perry, 1974. *Lineages of the Absolutist State*, London: New Left Books.

Anwar, M. 1979. *The Myth of Return*, London: Heinemann.

Anwar, M. 1986. *Race and Politics: Ethnic Minorities and the British Political System*, London: Tavistock Publications.

Anwar, M. 1990. 'Some Recent Trends in the Voting Behaviour of Britain's Black Electorate', in H. Goulbourne (ed.), *Black Politics in Britain*, Aldershot: Gower Publishing Company.

Appignanesi, Lisa and Maitland, Sara (eds), 1989. *The Rushdie File*, London: Fourth Estate Ltd.

Atkins, F. 1986. 'Thatcherism, Populist Authoritarianism and the Search for a New Left Political Strategy', *Capital and Class*, no. 28.

Baber, C. and Jeffrey, H. B. 1986. *Guyana: Politics, Economics and Society*, London: Frances Pinter (Publishers).

Bacchus, M. K. 1969. 'Patterns of Educational Expenditure in an Emergent Nation: A Study of Guiana 1945–65', *Social and Economic Studies*, vol. 17, no. 3.

Bachrach, Peter and Baratz, Morton S. 1962. 'The Two Faces of Power', *American Political Science Review*, 56, pp. 947–52.

Bachrach, Peter and Baratz, Morton S. 1963. 'Decisions and Nondecisions: An Analytical Framework', *American Political Science Review*, 57, pp. 641–51.

Barbalet, J. M. 1988. *Citizenship*, Open University Press.

Beckford, George, 1972. *Persistent Poverty: Underdevelopment in Plantation Economies in the Third World*, New York: Oxford University Press.

Beckford, George and Witter, Mike, 1982. *Small Garden . . . Bitter Weed: The Political Economy of Struggle and Change in Jamaica*, Morant Bay and London: Maroon Publishing House/Zed Press.

Bennett, N. *et al.* 1989. *Europe: Onwards from Bruges by the 'No Turning Back' Group of Conservative MPs*, Conservative Political Centre.

Bentley, Arthur, (1908) 1967. *The Process of Government*, Harvard University Press.

Best, Lloyd, 1968. 'A Model of Pure Plantation Economy', *Social and Economic Studies*, September.

Billington, R. A. (ed.), 1966. *The Frontier Thesis: Valid Interpretation of American History?*, London and New York: Holt, Rhinehart & Winston.

Blaut, J. M. 1982. 'Nationalism as an Autonomous Force', *Science and Society*, vol. 46, no. 3.

Booth, H. 1985. 'Which "Ethnic Question"? The Development of Questions Identifying Ethnic Origin in Official Statistics', *Sociological Review*, vol. 33, no. 2.

Braithwaite, Lloyd, 1953. 'Social Stratification in Trinidad: A Preliminary Analysis', *Social and Economic Studies*, vol. ii, no. ii, pp. 5–175.

Brathwaite, E. (1971) 1978. *The Development of Creole Society in Jamaica 1770–1820*, Oxford: Clarendon Press.

Brereton, B. 1981. *A History of Modern Trinidad 1783–1962*, Kingston and London: Heinemann.

Brotz, Howard, 1988. 'Review of Geoff Dench, Minorities in the Open Society: Prisoners of Ambivalence', *New Community*, vol. 15, no. 1, October.

Brueilly, J. 1985. 'Reflections on Nationalism', *Philosophy of the Social Sciences*, 15.

Brutents, K. N. 1977. *National Liberation Revolutions Today*, Moscow: Progress Publishers, 2 vols.

Bukharin, N. 1972. *Imperialism and World Economy*, London: The Merlin Press.

Burgess, M. E. 1978. 'The Resurgence of Ethnicity: Myth or Reality?', *Ethnic and Racial Studies*, vol. 1, no. 3.

Burnham, Forbes, 1970. *A Destiny to Mould*, London: Caribbean Longman.

Butani, D. H. 1986. *The Third Sikh War? Towards or Away from Khalistan?*, New Delhi: Promilla & Co., Publishers.

Carter, T. 1986. *Shattering Illusions: West Indians in British Politics*, London: Lawrence & Wishart.

Chernick, S. E. 1978. *The Commonwealth Caribbean: The Integration Experience*, Report of a mission sent to the Commonwealth Caribbean by the World Bank, Baltimore and London: The World Bank/The Johns Hopkins University Press.

Cohen, Robin, 1987a. 'The Detention of Asylum Seekers in the UK', paper presented at a conference on Refugees in Europe at the Centre for Research in Ethnic Relations, University of Warwick, 24–5 October.

Cohen, Robin, 1987b. *The New Helots: Migrants in the International Division of Labour*, Aldershot/Vermont: Gower Publishing Co.

Cohen, Robin, forthcoming. 'An Academic Perspective', in C. Clarke and T. Payne (eds), *Politics, Security and Development in Small States*, London: Allen & Unwin.

Crenson, M. A. 1971. *The Un-Politics of Air Pollution: A Study of Non-Decisionmaking in the Cities*, Baltimore and London: The Johns Hopkins Press.

Cross, Malcolm, (1972) 1980. *The East Indians of Guyana and Trinidad*, London: Minority Rights Group, Report no. 13.

Cross, Malcolm and Entzinger, Han (eds), 1988. *Lost Illusions: Caribbean Minorities in Britain and the Netherlands*, London: Routledge.

Cummins, I. 1980. *Marx, Engels and National Movements*, London: Croom Helm.

Dabydeen, D. and Samaroo, B. (eds), 1987. *India in the Caribbean*, London: Hansib/ Centre for Caribbean Studies, University of Warwick.

Dahl, Robert A. 1961. *Who Governs?: Democracy and Power in an American City*, New Haven and London: Yale University Press.

Daly, M. and Troup, C. 1989. 'Oxford no' come back again', *Times Higher Education Supplement*, 6 January.

Dench, G. 1986. *Minorities in the Open Society: Prisoners of Ambivalence*, London: Routledge & Kegan Paul.

Deutsch, K. 1968. *The Nerves of Government*, New York: The Free Press.

Dharam, S. S. 1986. *Internal and External Threats to Sikhism*, Illinois: Gurmat Publishers.

Dixon, D. 1983. 'Thatcher's People: The British Nationality Act 1981', *Journal of Law and Society*, vol. 10, no. 2.

Dubnow, S. (1958) 1970. *Nationalism and History*, New York: Atheneum.

Dummett, Ann, 1976. *Citizenship and Nationality*, London: The Runnymede Trust.

Dummett, Ann, 1984. *A Portrait of English Racism*, London: CARAF Publications.

Dummett, Ann with Ian Martin, 1982. *British Nationalism: The AGIN Guide to the New Law*, London: Action Group on Immigration and Nationality/National Council for Civil Liberties.

Emmanuel, A. 1972. *Unequal Exchange: A Study of the Imperialism of Trade*, London: New Left Books/Monthly Review Press.

Evans, J. M. 1983. *Immigration Law*, London: Sweet and Maxwell.

Fanon, Franz, (1963), 1967. *The Wretched of the Earth*, Penguin Books.

Figueroa, M. 1985. 'An Assessment of Overvoting in Jamaican Elections', *Social and Economic Studies*, vol. 34, no. 3, pp. 71–106.

Flew, Anthony, 1986. 'Three Concepts of Racism', *The Salisbury Review*, October, pp. 2ff.

Foot, P. 1969. *The Rise of Enoch Powell*, Harmondsworth: Penguin.

Frank, A. G. 1969. *Capitalism and Underdevelopment in Latin America*, New York: Monthly Review Press.

Furnivall, J. S. 1948. *Colonial Policy and Practice*, Cambridge University Press.

Fusaro, A. 1979. 'Two Faces of British Nationalism: The Scottish National Party and Plaid Cymru Compared', *Polity*, vol. xi, no. 3.

Gellner, Ernest, 1983. *Nations and Nationalism*, Oxford: Basil Blackwell Publisher Limited.

Ghai, Y. P. and McAuslan, J. P. W. B. 1970. *Public Law and Political Change in*

Kenya: A Study of the Legal Framework of Government from Colonial Times to the Present, Nairobi: Oxford University Press.

Gilkes, Michael, 1986. *Creative Schizophrenia: The Caribbean Cultural Challenge*, Third Walter Rodney Memorial Lecture, Coventry: Centre for Caribbean Studies, University of Warwick.

Gilroy, P. 1987. *There Ain't No Black in the Union Jack: The Cultural Politics of Race and Nation*, London: Hutchinson.

Gordon, Derek, 1987. *Class, Status and Social Mobility in Jamaica*, Kingston: Institute of Social and Economic Research, University of the West Indies.

Goulbourne, H. D. (ed.), 1979. *Politics and State in the Third World*, London: Macmillan.

Goulbourne, H. D. 1984. 'On Explanations of Violence and Public Order in Jamaica', *Social and Economic Studies*, vol. 33, no. 4, pp. 151–69.

Goulbourne, H. D. 1985. *The State, Politics and Violence in the Anglophone Caribbean*, The First Walter Rodney Memorial Lecture, Coventry: Centre for Caribbean Studies, University of Warwick.

Goulbourne, H. D. 1987. 'The State, Development and the Need for Participatory Democracy in Africa', in Peter Anyang' Nyong'o (ed.), *Popular Struggles for Democracy in Africa*, London and New Jersey: Zed Books Ltd and United Nations University.

Goulbourne, H. D. 1988a. *Teachers, Education and Politics in Jamaica, 1892–1972*, London: Macmillan.

Goulbourne, H. D. 1988b. *West Indian Political Leadership in Britain*, The Byfield Memorial Lecture 1987, Occasional Papers in Ethnic Relations, University of Warwick.

Goulbourne, H. D. 1988c. 'The Contributions of Caribbean People to British Society', in Arif Ali (ed.), *Third World Impact, Eighth Edition*, London: Hansib Publications.

Goulbourne, H. D. (ed.), 1990. *Black Politics in Britain*, Aldershot: Gower Publishing Company.

Goulbourne, S. M. 1985. *Minority Entry to the Legal Profession: A Discussion Paper*, Policy Paper in Ethnic Relations, Coventry: Centre for Research in Ethnic Relations, University of Warwick.

Goulbourne, S. M. 1986. 'European Immigration and Nationality Law', unpublished MS, Coventry: Centre for Research in Race and Ethnic Relations, University of Warwick.

Greene, J. E. 1974. *Race vs Politics in Guyana: Political Cleavages and Political Mobilization in the 1968 General Election*, Kingston: Institute of Social and Economic Research, University of the West Indies.

Griffith, J. A. G. *et al.* 1960. *Coloured Immigrants in Britain*, Institute of Race Relations/Oxford University Press.

Hamilton, A., Madison, J. and Jay, J. 1961. *The Federalist Papers*, Introduction by Clinton Rossiter, The New American Library.

Hanham, H. J. 1969a. *Scottish Nationalism*, London: Faber & Faber.

Hanham, H. J. 1969b. 'The Development of the Scottish Office', in J. N. Wolfe (ed.), *Government and Nationalism in Scotland: An Enquiry by Members of the University of Edinburgh*, Edinburgh University Press.

Hawkins, F. 1986. 'The Experience of Non-European Receiving Countries', paper presented at a conference on the Future of Migration, 13–16 May.

Hayes, C. J. H. 1931. *The Historical Evolution of Modern Nationalism*, New York: The Macmillan Co.

Herskovits, M. (1941) 1970. *The Myth of the Negro Past*, Massachusetts: Peter Smith.
Hinden, R. 1946. *The Labour Party and the Colonies*, Labour Discussion Series, No. 8, London: The Labour Party.
Hintzen, Percy, 1985. 'Ethnicity, Class and Internal Capitalist Penetration in Guyana and Trinidad', *Social and Economic Studies*, vol. 34, no. 3, pp. 107–64.
Hiro, Dilip, 1971. *Black British White British*, London: Eyre & Spottiswoode.
Hock, P. 1984. 'The Eminent Emigrants', *The Times Higher Education Supplement*, 14 September.
Hock, P. 1986. 'Emigres in Science and Technology Transfer', *Physical Technology*, 17.
Hoetink, H. 1967. *Caribbean Race Relations*, Oxford University Press.
Honeyford, R. 1988. *Integration or Disintegration?: Towards a Non-Racist Society*, London and Lexington: The Claridge Press.
Hosking, G. 1988. 'The Flamed Melting Pot', The 1988 Reith Lectures, *The Listener*, 1 December, pp. 13–16.
Humphry, D. and Ward, M. 1974. *Passports and Politics*, Penguin Books.
Jagan, Cheddi, (1966) 1971. *The West on Trial: The Fight for Guyana's Freedom*, New York: International Publishers.
Jagan, Cheddi, 1979. *The Caribbean Revolution*, Prague: Orbis Press Agency.
Kapur, R. A. 1986. *Sikh Separatism: The Politics of Faith*, London: Allen & Unwin.
Kariel, H. 1961. *The Decline of American Pluralism*, Stanford University Press.
Kay, G. 1975. *Development and Underdevelopment: A Marxist Analysis*, London: Macmillan.
Kedourie, Elie (ed.), 1970. *Nationalism in Asia and Africa*, London: Frank Cass.
Kedourie, Elie, (1960) 1985. *Nationalism*, London: Hutchinson
Keegan, W. 1986. 'New Right Theories and the Politicians', in Nicholas Deakin (ed.), *The New Right: Image and Reality*, London: The Runnymede Press.
Kemp, T. 1967. *Theories of Imperialism*, London: Dobson Books.
Kidron, M. and Segal, R. 1987. *The State of the World Atlas*, London: Pluto Projects/ Pan Books.
Kofman, M. 1968. 'The Reaction of Two Anarchists to Nationalism: Proudhon and Bakunin on the Polish Question', *Labour History*, no. 14.
Kohn, Hans, (1944) 1961. *The Idea of Nationalism: A Study in its Origins and Background*, New York: The Macmillan Company.
Kohn, Hans, 1968. 'Nationalism', *Encyclopaedia of the Social Sciences*, New York: The Macmillan Co. Ltd. & The Free Press, vol. 11.
Kumar, Pramod *et al.* 1984. *Punjab Crisis: Context and Trends*, Chandigarh: Centre for Research in Rural and Industrial Development.
Kuper, L. and Smith, M. G. (eds), 1969. *Pluralism in Africa*, Berkeley and Los Angeles: University of California.
Lacey, R. 1977. *Violence and Politics in Jamaica, 1960–70: Internal Security in a Developing Country*, Manchester University Press.
Laclau, Ernesto, 1977. *Politics and Ideology in Marxist Theory: Capitalism, Fascism, Populism*, London: New Left Books.
Laski, Harold, 1919. *Authority in the Modern State*, Yale University Press.
Laski, Harold, 1921. *The Foundations of Sovereignty and Other Essays*, London: George Allen & Unwin Ltd.
Lasswell, Harold D. (1936) 1958. *Politics: Who Gets What, When, How*, with Postscript, Cleveland/New York: Meridian Books.
Latham, E. 1964. 'The Group Basis of Politics: Notes for a Theory', in Munger, F. J.

and Price, D. (eds), *Political Parties and Pressure Groups*, New York: Thomas Crowell & Co.

Layton-Henry, Zig, 1984. *The Politics of Race in Britain*, London: Allen & Unwin.

Layton-Henry, Z. and Rich, P. (eds), 1986. *Race, Government and Politics in Britain*, London: Macmillan.

Lewis, Rupert, 1987. *Marcus Garvey Anti-Colonial Champion*, London: Karia Press.

Lukes, S. (1974) 1976. *Power: A Radical View*, London: Macmillan.

Macdonald, Ian, 1983. *Immigration Law and Practice*, London: Butterworth.

Maclean, C. (ed.), 1979. *The Crown and the Thistle: The Nature of Nationhood*, Edinburgh: Scottish Academic Press.

Mamdani, Mahmood, 1973. *From Citizen to Refugee: Uganda Asians Come to Britain*, London: Frances Pinter (Publishers) Ltd.

Manley, Michael, 1982. *Jamaica: Struggle in the Periphery*, London: Third World Media Limited.

Manley, Michael and Brandt, Willy, 1985. *Global Challenge – From Crisis to Cooperation: Breaking the North-South Stalemate*, Report of the Socialist International Committee on Economic Policy, London: Pan Books Ltd.

Manor, J. 1988. 'Conflict and Collective Violence in India', paper presented at the Political Studies Conference, Plymouth Polytechnic, April 1988.

Marshall, P. J. 1985. 'The Moral Swing to the East: British Humanitarianism, India and the West Indies', in C. Abel and M. Twaddle (eds.), *Collected Seminar Papers on Caribbean Societies*, mimeo, Institute of Commonwealth Studies, University of London.

Marx, Karl, (1859) 1969. 'Preface to A Contribution to the Critique of Political Economy', in K. Marx and F. Engels, *Selected Works*, Moscow: Progress Publishers.

Marx, Karl, (1867) 1974. *Capital: A Critical Analysis of Capitalist Production*, vol. 1, Moscow: Progress Publishers.

May, R. and Cohen, R. 1975. 'The Interaction between Race and Colonialism: A Case Study of the Liverpool Race Riots of 1919', *Race & Class*, vol. 16, no. 2.

Mboya, Tom, 1970. *The Challenge of Nationhood: A Collection of Speeches and Writings*, Nairobi: Heinemann Educational Books.

Mckenzie, R. T. 1967. 'Parties, Pressure Groups and the British Political Process', in R. Rose (ed.), *Studies in British Politics*, New York: Macmillan & St Martin's Press.

Miles, R. and Phizacklea, A. 1979. *Racism and Political Action*, London: Routledge & Kegan Paul.

Miliband, Ralph, (1969) 1973. *The State in Capitalist Society: The Analysis of the Western System of Power*, London: Quarter Books.

Miliband, Ralph, 1977. *Marxism and Politics*, Oxford University Press.

Mill, J. S. 1861. *Considerations on Representative Government*, London: Longman, Green, Longman, Roberts & Green.

Minogue, K. R. 1967. *Nationalism*, London: B. T. Batsford.

Mishan, E. J. 1988. 'What Future for a Multi-Racial Britain? Part I and Part II', *The Salisbury Review*, June, pp. 18ff., and September, pp. 4ff., respectively.

Modood, T. 1988. '"Black", Racial Equality and Asian Identity', *New Community*, vol. xiv, no. 3.

Munroe, Trevor, 1972. *The Politics of Constitutional Decolonization: Jamaica 1944–62*, Kingston: Institute of Social and Economic Research.

Nairn, T. 1981. *The Break-Up of Britain*, London: Verso.

Nayar, Baldev R. 1966. *Minority Politics in the Punjab*, Princeton University Press.

Nayar, Kuldip and Singh, Khushwant, 1984. *Tragedy of Punjab: Operation Bluestar and After*, New Delhi: Vision Books.

Nellis, J. 1972. *A Theory of Ideology: The Tanzanian Example*, Nairobi: Oxford University Press.

Nesbitt, E. 1985. 'The Nanaksar Movement', *Religion*, 15.

Nettleford, Rex, 1971. *Norman Washington Manley and the New Jamaica: Selected Speeches and Writings 1938–68*, London: Longman Caribbean.

Nettleford, Rex, 1972. *Identity, Race and Protest in Jamaica*, New York: William Morrow & Company, Inc.

Nicholls, D. 1974. *Three Varieties of Pluralism*, London: Macmillan.

Nielsson, Gunnar P. 1985. 'States and "Nation-Groups": A Global Taxonomy', in E. A. Tiryakian and R. Rugowski (eds), *New Nationalisms of the Developed West: Toward Explanations*, London: Allen & Unwin.

Nyerere, J. K. 1966. *Freedom and Unity/Uhuru na Umoja: A Selection from Writings and Speeches, 1952–65*, Dar es Salaam: Oxford University Press.

Omi, M. and Winant, H. 1986. *Racial Formation in the United States from the 1960s to the 1980s*, New York and London: Routledge & Kegan Paul.

O'Shaughnessy, Hugh, 1984. *Grenada: Revolution, Invasion and Aftermath*, London: Sphere Books/The Observer.

Owen, R. and Sutcliffe, B. (eds), 1972. *Studies in the Theory of Imperialism*, London: Longman.

Parekh, Bhikhu, (ed.), 1973. *Bentham's Political Thought*, London: Croom Helm.

Parekh, Bhikhu, 1986. 'The "New Right" and the Politics of Nationhood', in Nicholas Deakin (ed.), *The New Right: Image and Reality*, London: The Runnymede Trust.

Parekh, Bhikhu, 1989. 'The Hermeneutics of the Swann Report', in G. K. Verma (ed.), *Education for All: A Landmark in Pluralism*, London: The Falmer Press.

Patterson, Orlando, 1977. *Ethnic Chauvinism: The Reactionary Impulse*, New York: Stein & Day.

Peach, Ceri, 1982. 'The Growth and Distribution of the Black Population in Britain 1945–1980', in D. A. Coleman (ed.), *Demography of Immigrants and Minority Groups in the United Kingdom*, Academic Press.

Petrus, J. A. 1971. 'Marx and Engels on the National Question', *The Journal of Politics*, vol. 33.

Phillips, Mike, 1974. 'Landfall', *The Listener*, 21 November, pp. 600–1.

Phillips, O. Hood, 1973. *Constitutional and Administrative Law*, London: Sweet & Maxwell.

Population Statistics Division, OPCS, 1986. *Population Trends 44*, London: HMSO.

Post, Ken, 1978. *Arise Ye Starvellings: The Jamaican Labour Rebellion of 1938 and its Aftermath*, The Hague: Martinus Nijhoff.

Poulantzas, Nicos, 1973. *Political Power and Social Classes*, London: New Left Books.

Powell, J. Enoch, 1988a. 'The UK and Immigration', *The Salisbury Review*, December, pp. 40ff.

Powell, J. Enoch, 1988b. 'By Our Consent', *The Salisbury Review*, March, pp. 22ff.

Rex, John, 1979. 'Black Militancy and Class Conflict', in R. Miles and A. Phizacklea (eds), *Racism and Political Action*, London: Routledge & Kegan Paul.

Rex, John, 1986. *Race and Ethnicity*, Open University Press.

Rex, John, (forthcoming). 'Race and Ethnicity', *Blackwell Dictionary of Twentieth Century Social Thought*, Oxford: Blackwell.

Rex, John and Tomlinson, Sally, 1979. *Colonial Immigrants in a British City: A Class Analysis*, London: Routledge & Kegan Paul.

Rhodes, R. I. (ed.), 1970. *Imperialism and Underdevelopment: A Reader*, London and New York: Monthly Review Press.

Rich, P. 1986. *Race and Empire in British Politics*, Cambridge University Press/Centre for Research in Ethnic Relations, University of Warwick Series.

Richardson, B. C. 1983. *Caribbean Migrants: Environment and Human Survival on St Kitts and Nevis*, Knoxville: University of Tennessee Press.

Rodney, Walter, 1969. *The Groundings With My Brothers*, London: Bogle L'Ouverture Publications.

Rodney, Walter, 1981. *A History of the Guyanese Working People, 1881–1905*, London: Heinemann Educational Books.

Rousseau, Jean-Jacques, (1781) 1954. *The Confessions*, translated by J. M. Cohen, London: Penguin Books.

Rushdie, Salman, 1988. 'Colour Guard' (review of R. L. Lewis, *Anti-Racism: A Mania Exposed, with an Introduction by Enoch Powell*), *Observer*, Sunday 24 July, p. 42.

Rushdie, Salman, 1990. 'In Good Faith', *The Independent on Sunday*, 4 February.

Rustow, A. R. 1968. 'Nation', *Encyclopaedia of the Social Sciences*, New York: The Macmillan Co. & The Free Press, vol. 11.

Rustow, D. 1967. *A World of Nations: Problems of Political Modernization*, Washington: The Brookings Institution.

Ryan, S. D. 1972. *Race and Nationalism in Trinidad and Tobago: A Study of Decolonization in a Multi-Racial Society*, University of Toronto Press.

Sadler, E. M. 1901. *Great Britain: Board of Education Special Reports on Educational Subjects*, vol. iv, Cd. 416, London: HMSO.

Saha, P. 1970. *Immigration of Indian Labour 1834–1900*, Delhi: People's Publishing House.

Sarre, P., Phillips, D. and Skellington, R. 1990. *Ethnic Minority Housing: Explanations and Policies*, Aldershot: Gower Publishing.

Segal, Ronald, 1967. *The Race War: The World-Wide Conflict of Races*, London: Penguin Books.

Shackle, C. 1984. *The Sikhs*, London: Minority Rights Group Report No. 65.

Sheehy, A. and Nahaylo, B. (1971) 1980. *The Crimean Tatars, Volga Germans and Meskhetians: Soviet Treatment of Some National Minorities*, London: Minority Rights Group, Report No. 6.

Sherlock, Phillip, 1980. *Norman Manley*, London: Macmillan.

Shukra, Kalbir, 1990. 'Black Sections and the Labour Party', in H. D. Goulbourne (ed.), *Black Politics in Britain*.

Singh, Paul, 1983. 'Constitutional Change and Political Culture: Authoritarian Dynamics in the Making of the New (1980) Guyana Constitution', *Transition*, 7, pp. 1–13.

Sinha, Sachchidanand *et al.* 1984. *Army Action in Punjab: Prelude and Aftermath*, New Delhi: Samata Era Publication.

Sivanandan, A. 1983. 'Challenging Racism: Strategies for the '80s', *Race and Class*, vol. xxv, no. 2.

Sked, Alan, 1987. *Britain's Decline: Problems and Perspectives*, Oxford: Basil Blackwell Ltd.

Smith, A. D. 1981. *The Ethnic Revival*, Cambridge University Press.

Smith, A. D. 1986. *The Ethnic Origins of Nations*, Oxford: Basil Blackwell, Inc.

Smith, M. G. 1965. *The Plural Society in the British West Indies*, University of California Press.

Smith, M. G. 1974. *Corporations and Society*, London: Duckworth.

Smith, M. G. 1984. *Culture, Race and Class in the Commonwealth Caribbean*, Kingston: Department of Extra-Mural Studies, University of the West Indies.

Snyder, Louis L. 1954. *The Meaning of Nationalism*, Rutgers University Press.

St John-Brooks, C. 1986. 'Light on Blacks', *New Society*, 27 June, p. 7.

Stalin, Joseph, 1913. *Marxism and the National and Colonial Question*, London: Martin Lawrence Ltd.

Stephens, E. H. and Stephens, J. D. 1986. *Democratic Socialism in Jamaica: The Political Movement and Social Transformation in Dependent Capitalism*, London: Macmillan.

Stone, Carl, 1983. *Democracy and Clientism in Jamaica*, New Jersey: Transaction Books.

Stone, Carl, 1985. *Class, State and Democracy in Jamaica*, Kingston: Blackett Publishers.

Stone, Carl, 1989. 'Racism in Jamaica', *Caribbean Contact*, May, vol. 16, no. 12.

Sundberg-Weitman, B. 1977. *Discrimination on Grounds of Nationality: Free Movement of Labour and Freedom of Establishment under the EEC Treaty*, Amsterdam: North-Holland Publishing Co.

Sutton, Paul (ed.), 1981. *Forged from the Love of Liberty: Selected Speeches of Dr Eric Williams*, n.p. but presumably Port of Spain: Longman Caribbean.

Tandon, Yashpal, 1973. *The New Position of East Africa's Asians: Problems of a Displaced Minority*, London: Minority Rights Group, Report No. 16 (revised ed.).

Tebbit, Norman *et al.* 1990. 'Fanfare of Being British', *The Field*, May.

Thomas, C. Y. 1974. *Dependence and Transformation: The Economics of the Transition to Socialism*, New York: Monthly Review Press.

Thomas, C. Y. 1978. 'Class Struggle, Social Development and the Theory of the Non-Capitalist Path', in Mai Palmberg (ed.), *Problems of Socialist Orientation in Africa*, Uppsala: The Scandinavian Institute of African Studies.

Thomas, C. Y. 1984. *Plantations, Peasants and State: A Study of the Mode of Sugar Production in Guyana*, California and Kingston: Center for Afro-American Studies, UCLA & Institute for Social and Economic Research, University of the West Indies.

Tinker, Hugh, 1974. *A New System of Slavery: The Export of Indian Labour Overseas, 1830–1920*, Oxford University Press/Institute of Race Relations.

Tinker, Hugh, 1977. *Race, Conflict and the International Order: From Empire to United Nations*, London: Macmillan.

Tocqueville, Alexis de, (1856) 1955. *The Old Regime and the French Revolution*, New York: Doubleday.

Tomlinson, Sally, 1987. 'Towards A.D. 2000: The Political Contexts of Multi-Cultural Education', *New Community*, vol. xiv, nos. 1/2, Autumn.

Tomlinson, Sally, forthcoming. *Multicultural Education in White Schools*.

Tully, Mark and Jacob, Satish, 1985. *Amritsar: Mrs Gandhi's Last Battle*, London: Pan Books Ltd/Rupa & Co.

Turner, F. J. (1920) 1962. *The Frontier in American History*, with a Foreword by R. A. Billington, New York: Holt, Rhinehart & Winston.

Verma, G. K. (ed.), 1989. *Education for All: A Landmark in Pluralism*, London: The Falmer Press.

Ward, R. and Jenkins, R. (eds), 1984. *Ethnic Communities in Business: Strategies for Economic Survival*, Cambridge University Press.

Ware, C. F. 1953. 'Ethnic Groups', *Encyclopedia of the Social Sciences*, New York: The Macmillan Press, vol. 5.

Warren, Bill, 1980. *Imperialism: The Pioneer of Capitalism*, London: Verso.
Watson, Hilbourne, 1989. 'Racism in Barbados', *Caribbean Contact*, May, vol. 16, no. 12.
Webb, K. 1977. *The Growth of Nationalism in Scotland*, Glasgow: The Molendinar Press.
Weber, Max, 1947. *The Theory of Social and Economic Organization*, translated by A. M. Henderson and Talcott Parsons, ed. by Talcott Parsons, New York and London: The Free Press/Collier Macmillan Publishers.
Weir, S. 1989. 'The Sound of Silence', *New Statesman and Society*, 24 February, pp. 10–11.
Williams, C. H. 1982. *National Separatism*, Cardiff: University of Wales Press.
Williams, Eric, (1962) 1964. *History of the People of Trinidad and Tobago*, London: Andre Deutsch.
Wolf, Ken, 1979. 'Kohn, Hans', *Encyclopedia of the Social Sciences: Biographical Supplement*, vol. 18, D. I. Sills (ed.), New York/London: The Free Press.
Wolff, R. P. 1968. *The Poverty of Liberalism*, Boston: Beacon Press.
Yuval-Davies, N. 1986. 'Ethnic/Racial Divisons and the Nation in Britain and Australia', *Capital and Class*, no. 28.
Zwick, P. 1983. *National Communism*, Boulder: Westview Press.

Official Reports, Pamphlets, Newspapers, Popular Journals, Manifestoes, etc.

Amnesty International, 1983. *Political Killings by Governments*, London: Amnesty International Publications.
Bhullar, J. S., Brar, G. S. and Sidhu, M. S. 1985. *The Betrayal of the Sikhs*, London: International Sikh Youth Federation.
Bidwell, Sydney, 1987. *The Turban Victory*, Southall: The Sikh Missionary Society.
Birmingham Community Relations Council, 1985. *Ethnic Minorities in Birmingham*, Birmingham: Community Relations Council.
British Nationality Acts, 1914, 1918, 1948, 1981.
Cabinet Papers (C.P.) 1946–1952 at the Public Record Office, Kew Gardens.
Caribbean Contact (Barbados) 1980–88 *passim*.
Caribbean Labour Solidarity 1986–88. *Circulars*.
Caribbean Labour Solidarity 1986–88. *Press Releases*.
Chauhan, M. S. 1984. *The Genocide of Sikhs in Punjab: Where Do You Stand?*, Southall: Sikh Missionary Society.
Commerce Weekly (Bombay) 1987, *passim*.
Commission for Racial Equality, 1990. *Britain: A Plural Society, Report of a Seminar*, Discussion Papers 3, London: Commission for Racial Equality.
Commission for Racial Equality, 1990. *Law, Blasphemy and the Multi-Faith Society, Report of a Seminar*, Discussion Papers 1, London: Commission for Racial Equality.
Committee for Human Rights in Grenada (UK) 1987–88. *Newsletter*.
Cutlass: Bulletin of Caribbean Labour Solidarity (London) 1986–88, *passim*.
Dalit Sahitya Akademy, n.d., but presumably 1985/6. *The Birth Pangs of Khalistan*, Southall: International Centre for Sikh Studies.
Delors, Jacques, n.d., but presumably 1988. *Europe 1992: The Social Dimension, Address by Jacques Delors, President of the Commission of the European Communities, to the Trades Union Congress, Bournemouth, 8 September 1988*, London: Commission of the European Communities Offices for the United Kingdom.

Dilgi, H. S. n.d. *Constitution of Khalistan*, n.p. *Economic and Political Weekly*, (Bombay) 1987, *passim*.
Education Reform Act 1988, London: HMSO, 1988.
Frontline, vol. 1, no. 4, 1985.
Goa Today, (Goa) August 1986.
Grewal, B. S. *et al.* n.d. *Glimpses of Sikhism*, Southall: The Sikh Missionary Society.
Guyana Human Rights Association 1987–88, *passim, Press Releases*.
Guyana News, (Guyana High Commission, London) 1988.
Guyana Update (London) 1983–85.
Hansard, Session 1947–8. *Parliamentary Debates, Commons*, vols. 443, 453, 454 [5th Series].
Hansard, Session 1980–81. *Parliamentary Debates, Commons*, vol. 995, [5th Series], col. 298.
Hansard, 11 November 1988. *Parliamentary Debates, House of Commons Official Report*, vol. 140, no. 216, London: HMSO.
Hart, Richard, 1987. *Imperialist Control of the Caribbean Area: The Transition from European to US Domination*, London: Caribbean Labour Solidarity.
Home Office, 1977. *British Nationality Law: Discussion of Possible Changes*, Cmnd. 6795, London: HMSO.
House of Commons, 1978. *First Report from the Select Committee on Race Relations and Immigration, Session 1977–78: Immigration, vol. 1*, London: HMSO.
India Today, (International Edition) 1987–88 *passim*.
Jagan, Cheddi, n.d., but presumably 1988. 'Race, Class and Nationhood', mimeo.
Jamaica Workers Support Group (London) 1988.
Kapoor, S. S. 1984. *The Invasion of the Golden Temple*, Middlesex: The World Sikh Organization.
Khalistan News: Newsletter from Khalistan Council, (London) 1987–88/89.
Khalistan News Service, (London) 1987–88.
Lalvani, D. T. 1979. *Nanak the Indian Mystic*, Edgware: Guru Nanak Foundation.
Latin American Bureau, 1984a. *Guyana: Fraudulent Revolution*, London: Latin American Bureau (Research and Action) Ltd.
Latin American Bureau, 1984b. *Grenada: Whose Freedom?*, London: Latin American Bureau (Research and Action) Ltd.
Leicester City Council, n.d., but presumably 1984. *Survey of Leicester, 1983: Initial Report of Survey*, Leicester: Leicester City Council.
Lord Mayor's Committee for Racial Harmony, 1982. *Coventry: A Multi-Cultural City*, Coventry: Council House.
McCormack, M. K. n.d. *Brief Outline of the Sikh Faith*, Edgware: The Sikh Courier.
Nanak Dham, vol. 1, no. 9, November 1987.
New Life, 1987–9 *passim*.
Open Word (Georgetown), 1982–87 *passim*.
Owen, Geoffrey *et al.* 1987. *The Thatcher Years: The Policies and the Prospects*, London: The Financial Times.
People's Progressive Party, 1984–87, *passim. Guyana Voice: Journal of the People's Progressive Party (U.K. Branch)*.
People's Progressive Party, 1986–8, *passim. Guyana Information Bulletin*.
People's Progressive Party, 1987–8, *passim. Thunder*.
Pettigrew, J. 1985. *Take Not Arms Against Thy Sovereign: The Present Punjab Crisis and the Storming of the Golden Temple*, Birmingham: Sikh Youth Federation.
Punjab Research Group Discussion Papers Series, (Coventry), 1984– *passim*.

Qureshi, S. and Khan, J. 1989. *The Politics of Satanic Verses, Unmasking Western Attitudes*, Muslim Community Surveys Occasional Paper No. 3, Leicester: Muslim Community Studies Institute.

Rampton, Anthony, 1981. *West Indian Children in Our Schools Interim Report of the Committee of Inquiry into the Education of Children from Ethnic Groups*, Cmnd. 8273, London: HMSO.

Rhode, S. S. and Rhode, R. K. 1980. *Guru Nanak: Founder of Sikh Faith*, Surrey: Rhodes Publishing Company.

Sandhu, P. S. 1985. *Genocide/Sikh Victims: An Appeal to the World Conscience*, London: Khalistan Publication. This is a UK publication of the Report of a joint Inquiry into the Causes and Impact of the Riots in Delhi from 31 October to 10 November by the People's Union for Democratic Rights and the People's Union for Civil Liberties.

Scarman, The Lord, 1982. *The Brixton Disorders 10–12 April 1981*, Cmnd. 8427. London: HMSO.

SDP/Liberal Alliance, 1987. *Britain United: The Time Has Come*, London: SDP.

Siddiqui, K. 1989. 'The Implications of the Rushdie Affair for Muslims in Britain', London: The Muslim Institute.

Sidhu, G. S. 1973. *A Brief Introduction to Sikhism*, Southall: The Sikh Missionary Society.

Sidhu, G. S. 1977. *The Sikh Woman*, Southall: The Sikh Missionary Society.

Sidhu, G. S. et al. 1974. *The Saint-Soldier: Guru Gorbind Singh*, Gravesend: The Sikh Missionary Society.

Sikh Bulletin, 1984– passim.

Sikh Community in Calgary, 1986. *Sikhs in the Canadian Mosaic*, Calgary: Sikh Community.

Sikh Youth International, 1984. *Why Khalistan?*, Warley: Guru Nanak Gurwara 130 High St. Smethwick.

Sikh Youth International, 1984– passim.

Sikri, S. M. 1985. *Massacre of the Sikhs in India: Report of the Citizens' Commission, Delhi, 31 October to 4 November 1984*, Delhi: Citizens' Commission.

Singh, Dervinderjit, 1986. *Sikhs, Arms and Terrorism*, Cambridge University Sikh Society.

Singh, G, and Kaur, A. 1986. *Rehat Maryada/The Sikh Code of Discipline*, n.p., but printed in the UK.

Singh, Kirpal, 1971. *The Sikh Symbols*, Southall: The Sikh Missionary Society.

Singh, S. K. n.d., but presumably sometime after 1984. *Khalsa Shall Rule*, Birmingham: Babbar Khalsa International.

Singh, Trilochan, 1977. *The Turban and the Sword of the Sikhs*, Gravesend: The Sikh Missionary Society.

Swann, The Lord, 1985. *Education For All: The Report of the Committee of Inquiry into the Education of Children from Ethnic Minority Groups*, Cmnd. 9453, London: HMSO.

Thatcher, Margaret, 1988. *Britain and Europe: Text of the Speech Delivered in Bruges by the Prime Minister on 20 September 1988*, Conservative Political Centre.

The Conservative Party (National Union of Conservative and Unionist Associations), 1960–1977. *Annual Conference*, London: The Conservative Party.

The Conservative Party (National Union of Conservative and Unionist Associations), 1984. *The Monday Club, the Law, Order and Race Relations, Policy Paper No. I.R.3.*

The Conservative Party (National Union of Conservative and Unionist Associations), 1986–9 *passim, Politics Today.*

The Economist Intelligence Unit, 1986. *India to 1990: How Far Will Reform Go?*, Special Report No. 1054, London: The Economist Publications Ltd.

The Government of India, n.d., but presumably 1984/5. *The Sikhs in Their Homeland India*, n.p. but presumably Delhi: NHPL/Thompson Press.

The Government of India, n.d., but presumably 1987. *Text of Indo-Sri Lanka Agreement.*

The Guardian, 1986–89, *passim.*

The Independent, 1987–89, *passim.*

The Jamaican Historical Society, 1986. 'Minorities in Jamaican History', *The Jamaican Historical Review,* vol. xv.

The Khalsa: The Sikh Fortnightly, passim.

The Labour Party, 1946–84. *National Executive Committee Report.*

The Labour Party, 1956. *Labour's Colonial Policy: The Plural Society.*

The Labour Party, 1961, *passim, Talking Point.*

The Labour Party, 1962. *The Integration of Immigrants: A Guide.*

The Labour Party, 1964, 1966, 1987. *Manifesto.*

The Labour Party, 1980. *Citizenship and Immigration.*

The Labour Party, 1981. *British Nationality Law – Our Alternative to Tory Legislation.*

The Labour Party, 1982. *Immigration: Labour's Approach.*

The Labour Party, n.d., but presumably 1988. *Social Justice and Economic Efficiency: First Report of Labour's Policy Review for the 1990s.*

The Scottish National Party, 1984. *SNP – Scotland's Voice in Europe: Manifesto of the Scottish National Party for the 1984 Elections to the European Parliament,* Edinburgh: The Scottish National Party.

The Scottish National Party, 1987. *Play the Scottish Card: SNP General Election Manifesto 1987.*

The Scottish National Party, 1987. *The Scottish National Party's Vision for a New Scotland,* Edinburgh: The Scottish National Party.

The Sikh Cultural Centre and All India Sikh Forum, 1984. *Truth About the Punjab Tragedy: A Chronological Account of the Great Betrayal of Sikhs,* Calcutta: The Sikh Cultural Centre and All India Sikh Forum.

The Sikh Herald, vol. 1, no. 4.

The Times, 1986–89, *passim.*

UK Action Committee on Islamic Affairs (UKACIA), 1989. *The British Muslim Response to Mr Patten,* London: UKACIA.

UK Parliamentary Human Rights Group, 1981. *Something to Remember Guyana 1980 Elections,* London.

West Indian Digest, 1980–88, *passim.*

West Indian Standing Conference, 1986–88, *passim. Team Work: Journal of the West Indian Standing Conference.*

Working People's Alliance, 1982–87. *Support Group (UK) Press Statements.*

Working People's Alliance, 1984–88, *passim. Press Releases.*

Working People's Alliance, 1984–88. *Circulars.*

Working People's Alliance, n.d., but presumably 1978. *Toward a Revolutionary Socialist Guyana: Principles and Programme of the Working People's Alliance,* London: Reprinted by the WPA Support Group (UK).

Index

(Compiled by Lyn Greenwood)

Printed in Great Britain
by Amazon

37265669R00225